Rule and Rupture

Development and Change Book Series

As a journal, *Development and Change* distinguishes itself by its multidisciplinary approach and its breadth of coverage, publishing articles on a wide spectrum of development issues. Accommodating a deeper analysis and a more concentrated focus, it also publishes regular special issues on selected themes. *Development and Change* and Wiley Blackwell collaborate to produce these themed issues as a series of books, with the aim of bringing these pertinent resources to a wider audience.

Titles in the series include:

Rule and Rupture: State Formation through the Production of Property and Citizenship
Edited by Christian Lund and Michael Eilenberg

Transition and Justice: Negotiating the Terms of New Beginnings in Africa
Edited by Gerhard Anders and Olaf Zenker

Governing Global Land Deals: The Role of the State in the Rush for Land
Edited by Wendy Wolford, Saturnino M. Borras, Jr., Ruth Hall, Ian Scoones and Ben White

Seen, Heard and Counted: Rethinking Care in a Development Context
Edited by Shahra Razavi

Negotiating Statehood: Dynamics of Power and Domination in Africa
Edited by Tobias Hagmann and Didier Péclard

The Politics of Possession: Property, Authority, and Access to Natural Resources
Edited by Thomas Sikor and Christian Lund

Gender Myths and Feminist Fables: The Struggle for Interpretive Power in Gender and Development
Edited by Andrea Cornwall, Elizabeth Harrison and Ann Whitehead

Twilight Institutions: Public Authority and Local Politics in Africa
Edited by Christian Lund

China's Limits to Growth: Greening State and Society
Edited by Peter Ho and Eduard B. Vermeer

Catalysing Development? A Debate on Aid
Jan Pronk et al.

State Failure, Collapse and Reconstruction
Edited by Jennifer Milliken

Forests: Nature, People, Power
Edited by Martin Doornbos, Ashwani Saith and Ben White

Gendered Poverty and Well-being
Edited by Shahra Razavi

Globalization and Identity
Edited by Birgit Meyer and Peter Geschiere

Social Futures, Global Visions
Edited by Cynthia Hewitt de Alcantara

Rule and Rupture: State Formation through the Production of Property and Citizenship

Edited by

Christian Lund and Michael Eilenberg

WILEY Blackwell

This edition first published 2017
Originally published as Volume 47, Issue 6 of *Development and Change*
Chapters © 2017 by International Institute of Social Studies
Book Compilation © Blackwell Publishing Ltd.

Blackwell Publishing was acquired by John Wiley & Sons in February 2007. Blackwell's publishing program has been merged with Wiley's global Scientific, Technical, and Medical business to form Wiley-Blackwell.

Registered Office
John Wiley & Sons Ltd, The Atrium, Southern Gate, Chichester, West Sussex, PO19 8SQ, United Kingdom

Editorial Offices
350 Main Street, Malden, MA 02148-5020, USA
9600 Garsington Road, Oxford, OX4 2DQ, UK
The Atrium, Southern Gate, Chichester, West Sussex, PO19 8SQ, UK

For details of our global editorial offices, for customer services, and for information about how to apply for permission to reuse the copyright material in this book please see our website at www.wiley.com/wiley-blackwell.

The rights of Christian Lund and Michael Eilenberg to be identified as the authors of the editorial material in this work has been asserted in accordance with the UK Copyright, Designs and Patents Act 1988.

Library of Congress Cataloging-in-Publication Data applied for.

9781119384731 (Paperback)

A catalogue record for this book is available from the British Library.

Front cover image: Dirt road through oil palm plantation in West Kalimantan, Indonesia © Michael Eilenberg
Cover design by Wiley

This book is published in the following electronic formats: ePDFs 9781119384793; Wiley Online Library 9781119384816; ePub 9781119384809.

Set in 10.75/12pt Times New Roman by Aptara Inc., New Delhi, India

Printed in Singapore by C.O.S. Printers Pte Ltd

10 9 8 7 6 5 4 3 2 1

Contents

Notes on Contributors

An Ansoms (e-mail: an.ansoms@uclouvain.be) is assistant professor in Development Studies at the Université Catholique de Louvain, Belgium. She is involved in research on rural development in land-scarce (post-)conflict environments, and particularly focuses on the Great Lakes Region in Africa. She has co-edited two books, *Natural Resources and Local Livelihoods in the Great Lakes Region: A Political Economy Perspective* (Palgrave, 2011) and *Emotional and Ethical Challenges for Field Research in Africa: The Story Behind the Findings* (Palgrave, 2013).

Adam Baczko (e-mail: adam.baczko@gmail.com) is a PhD student in political science at the Ecole des Hautes Etudes en Sciences Sociales (EHESS) and a Junior Research Fellow at the ERC-funded programme 'Social Dynamics of Civil War' at Panthéon-Sorbonne University, Paris, France. His research focuses on the Taliban system of justice since 2001. With Arthur Quesnay and Gilles Dorronsoro, he co-authored *Syrie, Anatomie d'une guerre civile* (CNRS Editions, 2016).

Sarah Byrne (corresponding author; e-mail: sarah.byrne@geo.uzh.ch) is Associate Researcher in Political Geography at the University of Zurich, Switzerland. This article stems from her recently completed PhD thesis entitled 'Becoming a Contender: Legitimacy, Authority and the Power of Making Do in Nepal's Permanent Transition'. She is currently working as a Governance Advisor with Helvetas Swiss Intercooperation.

Verónica Calvo (e-mail: veronica.calvovalenzuela@sciencespo.fr) is a PhD candidate in political science at CERI, Paris, France. Her areas of specialization are comparative political sociology and political anthropology. Her research field concerns forms of subjectivation related to the adoption of new indigenous rights in contemporary Bolivia.

Giuseppe Cioffo (corresponding author; e-mail: giuseppe.cioffo@gmail.com) is a PhD candidate at the Université Catholique de Louvain (Belgium) where he studies processes of agrarian modernization in Rwanda. He is interested in the social and environmental dynamics linked to Green Revolution models, as well as small family farming and agrarian change in developing countries.

Erin Collins (e-mail: ecollins@american.edu) is Assistant Professor of Global Urban Studies in the School of International Service at American University, Washington DC, USA. Her research interests include the political economy and cultural politics of Southeast Asian cities and their manifold transformations.

Michael Eilenberg (e-mail: etnome@cas.au.dk) is Associate Professor in Anthropology at Aarhus University, Denmark. His work on state formation, sovereignty, autonomy and agrarian expansion in frontier regions of Southeast Asia has appeared in various book chapters and journals such as *Journal of Peasant Studies, Modern Asian Studies* and *Identities: Global Studies in Culture and Society*. His book *At the Edges of States* (KITLV Press and Brill Academic Publishers, 2012) deals with the dynamics of state formation in the borderlands of Indonesia and Malaysia.

Jacobo Grajales (e-mail: jacobo.grajaleslopez@univ-lille2.fr) is Associate Professor of political science at the Centre for European Research on Administration, Politics and Society, University of Lille, France. He is the author of *Gouverner dans la violence: le paramilitarisme en Colombie* [*Governing in the Midst of Violence: Paramilitary Politics in Colombia*] (Karthala, 2016), as well as several articles on the agrarian dimension of the Colombian conflict published by *Development and Change* and *The Journal of Peasant Studies*. His current research, focused on the link between post-conflict situations and the political economy of rural land, has led him to undertake comparative field research in Colombia and Côte d'Ivoire.

Markus Virgil Hoehne (e-mail: markus.hoehne@uni-leipzig.de) is Lecturer at the Institute of Social Anthropology at the University of Leipzig, Germany. He works on conflict, identity, state formation, borderlands, transitional justice and forensic anthropology in Somalia. Currently he is preparing for new research in Peru.

Kasper Hoffmann (corresponding author; e-mail: kh@ifro.ku.dk) is a postdoctoral researcher at the Department of Food and Resource Economics (IFRO) at Copenhagen University, Denmark. He is also affiliated with the Conflict Research Group (CRG) at Ghent University, Belgium. His research focuses on the constitution of political and legal identities, rebel governance, the production of political space, and land conflicts and governance, in eastern Democratic Republic of Congo.

Benedikt Korf is Associate Professor in Political Geography at the University of Zurich, Switzerland. His most recent book is *Checkpoint, Temple, Church and Mosque: A Collaborative Ethnography of War and Peace*, co-authored with Jonathan Spencer, Jonathan Goodhand, Shahul Hasbullah, Bart Klem and Tudor Silva (Polity, 2015).

Christian Lund is Professor at the Department of Food and Resource Economics, University of Copenhagen (clund@ifro.ku.dk). He is the author of *Law, Power and Politics in Niger. Land Struggles and the Rural Code* (Lit Verlag/Transaction Publishers) and *Local Politics and the Dynamics of*

Property in Africa (Cambridge University Press). He currently works on local politics, property and citizenship in Indonesia.

Gauthier Marchais is a Research Fellow in the Conflict and Violence Research Cluster at the Institute for Development Studies (IDS), University of Sussex, Brighton, UK. He recently completed a PhD at the London School of Economics and Political Science on the dynamics of participation in armed groups in eastern Democratic Republic of Congo, and has been involved in several research projects focused on the region.

Andrea J. Nightingale is Chair of Rural Development in the Global South at the Swedish University of Agricultural Sciences (SLU). Her research looks at political violence in climate change adaptation programmes. Her forthcoming textbook is entitled *Environment and Sustainability in a Globalizing World* (Routledge, 2017).

Noer Fauzi Rachman (e-mail: noerfauziberkeley@gmail.com) is Senior Researcher at Sajogyo Institute, the Indonesian Center for Agrarian and Rural Studies, Bogor, Indonesia. His latest book in Bahasa Indonesia is *Land Reform dan Gerakan Agraria Indonesia* (Insist Press, 2016), which is a translation of his dissertation at the University of California, Berkeley, 'The Resurgence of Land Reform Policy and Agrarian Movements in Indonesia'. He currently works on agrarian reform policy processes at the national level in Indonesia.

Koen Vlassenroot is Professor of Political Sciences and the director of the Conflict Research Group (CRG) at Ghent University, Belgium. He conducts research on armed groups, conflict and governance in Central Africa, with a particular focus on eastern Congo. He is currently one of the research directors of the DfID-funded Justice and Security Research Programme.

Rule and Rupture: State Formation through the Production of Property and Citizenship

Christian Lund

INTRODUCTION

Weak, fragile and failed. Mainstream work on states in post-colonial societies has often used these adjectives to describe dysfunctional public administrations. Kaplan's seminal article, 'The Coming Anarchy', which sketched out imminent lawlessness and state disintegration, was the forerunner of huge scholarly interest in state formation in poor countries (Kaplan, 1994). The first generation of the fragile states literature, with its somewhat skewed focus on how *real* government structures fall short of an *ideal* Weberian index of a rational state was essentialist, ahistorical and teleological. In a recent literature review on failed states, Hoffmann and Kirk (2013) map out how subsequent research has emerged. While this newer body of scholarship is varied, a few features seem generally shared. These include an interest in how public authority actually works, a focus on competition, contestation and conflict as enduring parts of public authority, and, not least, the acknowledgement that public authority is always *in the making*. Some particularly interesting contributions have analysed how a broad range of institutions compete over territorial governance, over different forms of rent from resources, and over the grand narrative of history.[1] These perspectives are shared in this Introductory essay, as well as the special issue which follows. However, the present ambition is to elaborate an approach that does not only take the competing institutions as given entities exercising governance with greater, or lesser, effect, ceremony and gusto: by reorienting the enquiry a little, I want to also capture how governance of vital resources *creates* statehood, or state quality, in these institutions.

In what follows, I therefore present a series of propositions about the interconnectedness of authority and rights. I suggest that property and citizenship, on the one hand, and authority, on the other, are mutually constitutive and represent social contracts of recognition. I then discuss various dynamics of recognition, such as how state quality emerges out of contracts of recognition,

---

1. For example, Hagmann and Péclard (2010); see also Aspinall and van Klinken (2011); Bierschenk and Olivier de Sardan (2014); Blundo and Le Meur (2009); Das and Poole (2004); Geiger (2008); Grimm et al. (2014); Hansen and Stepputat (2001); Lund (2006a, 2010); Sikor and Lund (2009).

and how this ought to be the centre of analysis of the formation of political
authority. Finally, I provide two concise examples from Ghana and Indonesia.

THE ARGUMENT

Dynamics of State Formation and Institutional Pluralism

Treating the 'state' as a finished product gets in the way of understanding
it. The state is always in the making. Political authority is (re-)produced
through its successful exercise over an important issue in relation to the
social actors concerned.[2] To move beyond the mere incantation of this claim,
this Introduction investigates and specifies contracts of recognition as the
key dynamic of the constitution of authority, and the chapters which follow
describe and demonstrate it.

The argument I pursue is that the ability to entitle and disenfranchise
people with regard to property, to establish the conditions under which they
hold that property — together with the ability to define who belongs and who
does not, and to establish and uphold rank, privilege and social servitude in
its many forms — is constitutive of state power. Claims to rights prompt the
exercise of authority. Struggles over property and citizenship are therefore as
much about the scope and constitution of political authority as they are about
access to resources and membership of polities. Hence, investigating the
social production of property and citizenship enables concrete understanding
of the dynamics of authority or state formation.

Granted, there are many problematics of government (Rose and Miller,
1992), and not all questions of state formation can be reduced to property
and citizenship. Government — or authority — forms around the control
over central resources, and in some historical periods, and in some places,
key resources may be trading points and routes; they may be 'knowledge'
or 'security', or even more abstract sources of wealth. It seems prudent to
remain open to different kinds of combinations at all times. Yet, property
(especially in land) and citizenship *are* increasingly such central resources
in most societies, and engaging with these two fundamental and substantive
questions in terms of their production allows us to traverse a broad series
of dynamic questions of how property and citizenship are made.[3] This takes

---

2. I use *public* and *political* authority interchangeably. *Public* points to the 'not private and not
   secret' aspect of exercised authority. *Political*, on the other hand, points to its contentious
   element. In most cases, both features apply.
3. I draw on a broad literature on state and political authority, property and citizenship, including:
   Abrams (1988); Arendt (1948/1979); Asad (2004); Bailey (1968); Baitenman (2005); Barkey
   (1994); von Benda-Beckmann (1993); Berry (1993, 2002); Boone (2003, 2014); Bourdieu
   (1994, 2012); Comaroff (2002); Corrigan (1994); Corrigan and Sayer (1985); Das and Poole
   (2004); Derrida (1986, 2002); Elias (1939/1994); Engeman and Metzer (2004); Foucault
   (2003); Geschiere (2009); Gramsci (1971); Hansen and Stepputat (2001); Hibou (2004);

us through questions of how notions of ownership are conceptualized, how political identities are constructed, how taxes are recovered, how conflicts are adjudicated, how violence and other sanctions are exercised and legitimated, and so on. There are therefore good reasons to investigate the rights–authority relations from a process perspective.

The mutual constitution of rights and authority takes place in many institutional settings. Thus, no single institution defines and enforces rights and exercises public authority as such. Governance is not reserved for statutory institutions alone. The ability to govern can reside in institutions other than formal government. Statutory institutions (legislative, judiciary and executive) may effectively govern, but it is more appropriate to treat this as an empirical question than a pre-established fact, and more productive to identify the actual authorities in semi-autonomous social fields of property and citizenship (S.F. Moore, 1978). In other words, government institutions are not the only source of state effects. Claims to rights are therefore ways to invoke public authority and governing capacity in different institutions, be they statutory or not. And, conversely, a claim to authority through the categorization of property and citizenship is a way to acquire and exercise state quality. In a nutshell, it is a claim to 'state'.

To grasp the dialectics of rights and authority, we need to dispense with simple assumptions that political authority exists prior to rights of property and citizenship. Rights and political authority are contemporaneous, and the control exercised by institutions over resources and political subjectivities does not *represent* a pre-existing authority. It *produces* authority. Conversely, effective rights do not represent pre-existing natural rights. They are political constructions and achievements. Yet, the idea of the 'state' as something established is very powerful and can easily divert our attention from its constant reproductive and relational character. Hence, if we investigate societies with relative stability, there is a risk that we will see 'rights' (changing and new) as *flowing from* a set of governing institutions. To avoid that, the present collection investigates processes of state formation through the production of property and citizenship from the particular angle of 'rupture'.

Jacob and Le Meur (2010); Jessop (1990); Joseph and Nugent (1994); Krupa and Nugent (2015); Li (2000); Lund (2006a, 2006b, 2008, 2011); Mann (1993); Mbembe (2001); Metzer and Engerman (2004); Migdal (2001); T. Mitchell (1991); B. Moore (1966); S.F. Moore (1978, 1986); North and Thomas (1973); Nugent (2010); Pottage (2004); Roitman (2005); Rose and Miller (1992); Roseberry (1994, 2002); Spencer (2007); Strathern (1999); Tilly (1985, 2005); Weber (1922/1968); Winichakul (1994); Wolf (1999). The ambition of this Introduction and the collection is not to make a comparative analysis between different theoretical approaches, but rather to come up with an analytical approach drawing on others in a productive combination. This is a deliberately broad theoretical sweep for a complex issue: it is materialist (people struggle over real things such as property and wealth); they produce political identity but not in isolation (discourses of who and what people are and what they are entitled to are contentious); this has institutional consequences; and when we look at these consequences in the post-colonial world in particular, institutional and legal pluralism is a predominant phenomenon.

Rupture and the Example of Colonialism

Ruptures are 'open moments' when opportunities and risks multiply, when the scope of outcomes widens, and when new structural scaffolding is erected. These are particularly propitious moments for observing and analysing how authority is as much at stake and as much under construction as the very rights produced through its exercise. This perspective draws inspiration from different quarters. A 'revelatory crisis' as developed by Sahlins (1972) and further elaborated by Solway (1994) makes central contradictions visible. Structures, interests and powers are mobilized and activated for the observer to see. 'Trouble cases', 'situational analyses', or 'diagnostic events' emanating from the Manchester School also take their point of departure in particular events in order to say something more general about structural features in society (Holleman, 1973; Lund, 2014; J.C. Mitchell, 1983; S.F. Moore, 1987; van Velsen, 1967). By looking at ruptures, however, we do more than simply account for the structural *pre*-conditions; we can inspect the very construction of new contracts of recognition. When we focus on moments of rupture in this issue, it is therefore not because they are inherently more important forms of change than any incremental transformations. Both forms of change can give rise to profound reconfigurations of polities, institutions, norms and the prevailing social contract. Above all, the choice of rupture is epistemological.[4]

'Colonization' describes the most dramatic and violent rupture and re-ordering of property and political subjectivity in human history. Colonial agents — governments and private companies in various combinations — dispossessed colonial subjects and established new property regimes. By the same token, they established new subject categories and various degrees of (dis-)enfranchisement of people in their new dominions. New identities and new categories of property were produced through the colonial administration's everyday power to categorize, regulate and exclude. The capacity to form and reproduce categorical distinctions as principles for recognizing or dismissing claims — for granting or denying rights to property and political participation for entire groups — was key in the colonial enterprise, as it is in state formation more generally.[5] To take an old example, the Norman conquest of England in 1066, and the compilation of the Domesday Book

---

4. The contributions in this issue focus on ruptures of national scale. In principle, however, ruptures can happen at smaller scales as well. Land grabbing (with all its conceptual warts) often occurs in areas where economic prospects have attracted particular interest, disrupting the ability of specific local authorities to define property rights.
5. The literature in this field abounds. Some of the most striking works include von Benda-Beckmann and von Benda-Beckman (2014); Benton (2002); Breman (1983, 2015); Chanock (1998); Colombijn (2013); Comaroff and Comaroff (2006, 2009); Guha (1997); Holston (2008); James (1963); Mamdani (1996); Mbembe (2001); T. Mitchell (1988); S.F. Moore (1986); Peluso (1992); Said (1978); Stoler (1995); Wolf (1971).

in 1086, was a dramatic rupture and reordering of the state of England. The Book recorded the new situation after the conquest, listing the new propertied classes in England and what they owned (Clanchy, 2013; Corrigan and Sayer, 1985). But recording identity and property did more than that; it also established, with bureaucratic and regal ceremony, that the propertied classes were beholden to the new king, William the Conqueror, for their rights. The Domesday Book established the sovereign as much as it established rights.

Colonial power worked through 'difference' and the reproduction of the 'self' and the 'other' (Mamdani, 2012; T. Mitchell, 1988; Said, 1978). Yet, processes of 'othering' continue to be fundamental to modern society (Chari and Verdery, 2009: 25). The ends of conflicts, of colonialism, of socialism, of liberalism and of authoritarianism have marked ruptures and 'new beginnings' in many places — just as their advents had marked earlier ruptures. Property structures that had been reworked as colonial possessions were challenged, socialized property was undone in different ways, and land concentrations amassed during authoritarian rule were called into question. Likewise, racialized categories of colonial citizenship and different categories of 'patriots' and 'enemies of the state' have been reshuffled in moments of rupture (like the fall of Khmer Rouge in Cambodia, the genocide in Rwanda, the end of authoritarian rule in Indonesia, the war in Afghanistan and so on, as the following chapters demonstrate). However, while property and political subjectivities have been seriously upset, old interests, categorical inequalities, and discourses die hard; and the emerging, recombinant configurations of property and citizenship tell complex stories of how states form through their production. Hence, when we use words like post-colonial, post-liberal, post-socialist, or post-authoritarian, it is to suggest a dramatic break from a previous social organization, without implying that all colonial features have disappeared, all liberal freedoms have been curbed, all socialist property forms are extinct, or all authoritarian edicts have been superseded. Likewise, post-conflict is hardly the definitive end of violence. 'Post' is not necessarily 'past' (Salemink and Rasmussen, 2016). Although such changes are dramatic, most new orders combine with the institutional debris of the past. Thus, while independence — like other ruptures — held promise of fundamental change, the production of categorical distinctions for inclusion and exclusion often continued. Indeed, post-colonial governments have in many instances preserved — sometimes even furthered — colonial patterns of exclusionary property and subject formation.

CONCEPTS: PROPERTY, CITIZENSHIP AND RECOGNITION

Before I develop an analytical approach for engaging social dynamics of the production of authority through property and citizenship, it is necessary to specify more precisely what is meant by these concepts, and by their shared characteristic: recognition.

Property and Citizenship

By property we have to understand more than 'private property'. Property is often — quite perfunctorily — equated with absolute, unfettered ownership. However, the idea of ownership as 'total exclusion of the right of any other individual in the Universe' is indeed an *idea* (Rose, 1998: 601). Ownership is always circumscribed by others' rights, which limit the exercise of an abstract total right to property. I therefore understand property as a legitimized claim to something of value sanctioned by some form of political authority (Godelier, 1986; Le Roy et al., 1996; MacPherson, 1978; Rose, 1994; Sikor and Lund, 2009). Struggles over property — very often in the form of land — can therefore be seen as struggles for the recognition of a wide variety of rights to access resources in various ways. These range from rights to reside and settle, through rights to use and extract, and extend to the right to transact those rights. Land conflicts are sometimes about more than property, however. Conflicts over spatial control have different dimensions that intertwine. What belongs to whom, and who belongs where, connect the legal control over spatial property and the political control over territory. Whether space is seen as property or territory engages a particularly productive tension between spatial control as ownership or rule (Lund, 2013). Territorialization and the spatial ordering of people combine different political and legal techniques of classification, registration and mapping. The processes do not merely structure physical space; they also organize the social and political perception of it (Rasmussen and Lund, forthcoming; Vandergeest and Peluso, 1995). Territorializing strategies allow and disallow certain forms of land use and access; they regulate certain forms of mobility and transactions; and, by differentiating rights to natural resources, territorialization contributes to the structuring of citizenship.

Citizenship can be defined as meaningful membership of an organized political body. Struggles for citizenship are, generally, struggles for the recognition of the very right to have rights in a body politic (Arendt, 1948/1979; Lund, 2011; Somers, 2008). Formal national citizenship is just one of several configurations of socially constructed collective subjectivities. For most people, several political bodies are relevant for different aspects of life (von Benda-Beckmann, 1997). Citizenship is therefore shorthand for people's agency and recognized political subjectivity. It makes up their political 'visibility' and denotes the political institution through which a person derives rights of membership to a community. In many places, land is a resource to which access is ensured not merely through the market or by membership of a national community: local citizenship and status are often just as important.

Projects of rule, taxation, conscription, confiscation, eviction and so on have made people very suspicious of public authority, with good reason (Scott, 2009). However, for many people, the grim reality is — to paraphrase Oscar Wilde — that there is only one thing worse than being seen by political authority, and that is not being seen. To be recognized — and reckoned with — by society and its institutions of authority renders citizenship, at its most basic, a mechanism for inclusion and exclusion, and signifies the right to have rights (Arendt, 1948/1979: 296; Somers, 2008: 21). Not to be seen as a rights-bearing subject delegitimizes all claims.

Property and citizenship are thus intimately related in their constitution. The core element of both rights is recognition. The processes of recognition of claims to land and other resources as property, and of political identity as citizenship with entitlements, simultaneously invest the institution that provides such recognition with recognition of its authority to do so. That is to say, the act of authorizing recursively authorizes the authorizer.

Recognition

Recognition has been the subject of much sophisticated theorization. A broad Hegelian tradition takes recognition as a fundamental human expression of acknowledgement of the 'other' (Fraser, 2001; Taylor, 1989, 1994). Honneth's work on the grammar of recognition is evocative.[6] For our purposes, so-called 'simple legal recognition' is central (Honneth, 1995: 109). It may be recognition of rights to property, and it may be rights to belonging and political subjectivity. It is important not to employ a legalistic understanding of 'legal' in this connection. Rather, I am looking for an effective recognition of rights by an institution and a reciprocal recognition of its authority by their subjects. By 'effective', I mean sufficient to define and enforce the claims as rights. This connects to the key element in this understanding of recognition, namely that it is reciprocal. The effective recognition of claims as rights produces state quality in recognizing institutions.

The mutual recognition constitutes a contract, one might say (*pace* Rousseau), that links property and citizenship to political authority in society. In exchange for recognized valuable property rights in land and other entitlements, people recognize the political power of the institution by payment of tax in the form of money, tribute, labour, allegiance, or other resources (see Martin et al., 2009). I use the word 'contract' loosely, because such contracts are not exactly voluntary, not always consensual, often contentious, and always under renegotiation.[7] Thus, they do not necessarily imply continuous or stable recognition of the *legitimacy* of the contractual terms. What actors have and who they are is made up, therefore, not of individual features but

6. Honneth operates with three dimensions of intersubjective recognition: recognition of the other as an individual with 'universal rights', an 'intimate other', and a 'legal subject'. Thus, it involves existential, emotive and institutional dimensions (Honneth, 1995: 92–139). Honneth focuses on what he calls 'post-traditional societies'. I find this category somewhat opaque, but see the dimensions as generally useful.

7. Distilling relations of mutual recognition as fundamental does not mean that they are the only ones that matter. Durkheim (1893/2014) argues that rational contracts require a so-called 'non-contractual' element — in other words, a shared understanding of the relationship by the parties involved. This reminder is useful for considering how these social relations (or 'contracts') are embedded and imbricated in other relations, meanings and histories.

of relational — political — attributes. As rights and public authority are co-produced, the erosion of one also means the dissipation of the other. Ruptures may break the contract, and rights held under one regime may evaporate under the next.

Rights entailed through recognition as a political subject may be limited or extensive. In fact, the recognition may entail no rights at all, as the capacity to recognize rights is also the capacity to deny and expunge them.[8] The relative strength between the political institution and the political subjects can vary tremendously between contexts. The relationship can range from the comprehensive subjugation of subjects by despotic institutions that tax heavily, to citizens holding governing bodies accountable (Fox, 1994). Obviously, the relations are always up for negotiation, where people dispute categorical disadvantageous positions, derived from gender, race and caste, as well as class, creed and conviction. But during open moments more radical reconfigurations of the social contract are possible.

DYNAMICS OF RECOGNITION

I have now established that political authority and rights are mutually constitutive. Moreover, I have argued that property and citizenship are recognized claims and that recognition should be the fulcrum of analysis. It is, therefore, time to explore some of the different dynamics of recognition that play out and interlace in contexts of institutional and legal pluralism, post-rupture. In some situations, firm hegemonic constellations emerge, or particular institutions acquire and consolidate a high degree of sovereignty where they are (practically) not beholden to other political authorities. In this issue, the contributions from Collins, Ansoms and Cioffo, Byrne, Korf and Nightingale, and Grajales analyse such moments of sovereignty.[9] However, few property and citizenship issues are unambiguously situated with particular institutions, especially if we look at land struggles and view them over time. Many issues appear in multiple institutional realms at any particular moment in time. Which institution supports what claims as rights, and, especially, *how* — all combine to constitute a significant point of struggle. This becomes complicated when several competing normative and legal orders

---

8. This may, at first sight, resemble Agamben's description of the state of exception (2005). However, I focus on power exercised through a relationship of mutual recognition rather than power exercised without any dependence on its subjects.

9. Sovereignty is conventionally understood as unlimited and indivisible rule by a state over a territory; governments generally claim legal sovereignty over a territory and a population in the name of the state. This perspective is generally used for addressing international concerns. In contrast, I focus on internal issues of state formation. I focus on *de facto*, effective, or 'positive' sovereignty as the power to determine the issues of property and citizenship, as opposed to a formal 'negative' *de jure* concept of sovereignty reflecting a law-centred ideology (see Hansen and Stepputat, 2006: 296).

legitimize competing claims, and several groups and institutions compete over jurisdiction to settle disputes and set norms by precedent. In many such situations, therefore, public authority is challenged or completely fragmented by uneven interdependence, antagonistic collaboration and fickle alliances between institutions. Such a spectrum of cases is studied here by Lund and Rachman, Eilenberg, Calvo, Hoehne, Baczko, and Hoffmann, Vlassenroot and Marchais. In this Introduction I therefore first discuss the contracts of recognition between claimants of rights and institutions of authority, and then examine dynamics of categorization and competition over jurisdictions.

Contracts of Rights and Authority

Rights originate in claims. Sometimes they are hard-fought and not all claims result in rights. Rights are not simply there, bestowed on people by a benevolent higher body; they are wrested from power. But as the repertoires of claims are wide, there is also a broad array of processes in which people engage in order to pursue their interests, ranging from informal everyday negotiations to full-scale political and legal conflicts. Claims are recognized to a certain degree by significant political institutions; as rights they become more or less solidified and entrenched to the extent that they are successfully vindicated. Sometimes rights and privileges emerge from norms and practices, which are generally accepted as 'good' and 'proper' in society. It may be difficult to identify precise links to institutions in times of tacit consensus or consolidated hegemony. Such rights seem simply to 'exist'. However, sometimes the naturalness of such rights is contested — be it men's rights to control the land of women, nobles' rights to control the labour of slaves, first settlers' rights to control the settlement of latecomers, or governments' rights to evict squatters. In such moments of tension, it becomes more readily visible to whom people are beholden for their rights and, by implication, what institutions validate or ignore the plight of the disadvantaged (women, slaves, latecomers, squatters). Some institutions emerge to reproduce and protect entrenched rights, while other institutions undermine them by being responsive to claims challenging established contracts. Hence, political subjectivity does not only concern relations to formal governments or singular institutions. It concerns relations to any institutional actor that recognizes claims by political subjects as valid, and protects them as rights. This is where the dynamics of property and citizenship intertwine.

An individual is beholden to different institutions for different rights. In turn, different institutions are validated through these relationships. In societies with multiple competing institutions, multiple relationships are therefore established, reproduced and undermined between people and a range of institutions simultaneously, and the authority of one institution may challenge or support that of another. New claims to rights will emerge while others fade, just as institutions' claims to authority evolve. In this process

claimants and authorities look for mutual visibility. There are many examples
of how ordinary people attempt to become visible to the relevant authorities
to which they would otherwise be invisible. Agrawal's work on community forestry in India (2001, 2005) demonstrates how organization in village
committees rendered communities visible to government and 'compatible'
with its policies. In the Amazon, Campbell (2015) shows that people act in
anticipation of government regulation long before any is adopted. This way,
property and its regulation are conjured up by popular state practices in a
supposedly ungoverned frontier region. Similarly, Körling (2011), Nielsen
(2011) and Winayanti (2010) show how residents of informal urban settlements in Niamey, Maputo and Jakarta have organized their settlements in
conformity with the formal technical norms (such as street width or the num-
bering of houses). By forming 'societies' or 'associations' with *présidents
de secteurs*, people may resist and avert eviction and ensure access to public
utilities; established presence may enable people to acquire identity cards (or
proxies such as voting cards, or membership cards of political or cultural associations); paying for utilities provides customers with receipts documenting and legitimizing residence; and people's possession of land — along
with the fact that government institutions ignore or tolerate a land market —
allows for the gradual build-up of expectations of recognition. Likewise, by
forming health committees, market guilds, or parent–teacher associations
before there is a clinic, a marketplace or a school, citizens enter the orbit of
certain governing institutions and conjure up the exercise of authority and
recognition by anticipating the 'contract'. In order to establish a 'contract'
of mutual recognition, the inhabitants may be able to act and organize as
they anticipate the municipality would expect proper citizens to act. Certain
land claimant groups in South Africa, for example, were not yet formally
registered as Communal Property Associations (CPAs) — a legal step necessary for land to be transferred to them through the restitution programme.
However, they acted as if they *were* registered CPAs, fulfilling the criteria of
a certain number of meetings, holding elections and having a constitution,
in the hope that the government would be more likely to recognize them as
serious and legitimate claimants when it came to the registration and transfer
of land.[10]

In her work on public rural water supply in Senegal, Gomez-Temesio
(2014) shows how the local population was beholden to the government
agencies for the water supply, and the government agents were beholden to
local villagers for facilitating their task. The actual face-to-face encounters
between them became an exchange in which the agents delivered services,
and the population facilitated the development of practical (technically non-
legal) norms without which the administration could not function and service

10. Personal communication with Tara Weinberg, Centre for Law and Society, University of
    Cape Town.

could not be delivered. The work of Bierschenk, De Herdt and Olivier de Sardan is interesting in this respect (see Bierschenk and Olivier de Sardan, 2014; De Herdt and Olivier de Sardan, 2015). They show how official norms, rules and laws exist for bureaucrats and citizens as socio-legal markers. Yet, actual conditions often prohibit the observance of official norms and rules, and new practical norms develop. Thus, parallel, practical contracts of recognition emerge where authority and rights are functional and effective but have only faint connections to official norms and law.[11] People have rights, but they do not have exclusively rightful means of exercising them. This is why they revert to informal arrangements — not to act in illegality, but, on the contrary, to access what they believe is legally theirs. This instrumentalization of practical norms, then, does not undermine the ideas of the state, law and rights. It underpins them.

Consolidating rights is hard work. Strategies of visibility and obscurity depend on the context, on the authorities' ambitions and resources, and on people's available options. While being careful to avoid certain governing agencies, people simultaneously exert great effort, imagination and flexibility in order to be seen by others. Very often, people consolidate their visibility by engaging with several institutions — statutory or not. Rights are then often established by increments of vindicated 'smaller' claims and the gradual recognition by different, often competing, governing bodies such as legal courts, health authorities, land administrations, school administrations, public utility services, tax authorities, *État civil*, NGOs, chiefs, neighbourhood tribunals, militias, 'area boys', and others. Participation in ceremonies (in the widest sense), payment of tribute, and various forms of allegiance — as much as payment of property tax, registration in a census, payment of utilities, organization in neighbourhood committees that can address government institutions for infrastructure, health and school services — all work to undergird the claims people make to property, to residence and to rights of membership. By the same token, people breathe life into the institutions' claims to authority.

However, there are also many instances in which such pursuits can be obstructed, and established rights dismantled. They may easily be eroded if the institution securing them is weakened. If someone holds land thanks to custom, rights may become weaker if a particular customary authority is marginalized. And if a landholder has a plot on the basis of municipal allotments, such rights may be vacuous if there is no enforcement. In Paraguay, Hetherington (2011) explains, *campesinos* held rights to land thanks to 'improvements' backed by the land reform, whereas large-scale soy farmers claimed the same space backed by the Civil Code. Which right actually

---

11. See also Akinyele (2009); Berry (2009); Das (2011); De Boeck (2011); Hetherington (2011); Jacob and Le Meur (2010); Joiremann (2011); Lentz (2013); Nurman and Lund (2016); Onoma (2010); Roitman (2005); Stacey and Lund (forthcoming, 2016); Ubink (2008); Winayanti and Lang (2004).

prevailed was as much a political as a legal question. The scope for opportunity as well as the risk of marginalization widens with the complex intersectionality of societies characterized by institutional pluralism. This takes us to the question of categorization and the power to categorize.

Dynamics of Categorization and Competition over Jurisdictions

The production, reproduction and erosion of categories are central political processes. Claimants are categorized and institutions' effective jurisdictions are established as rights and authority are claimed in mutually constitutive processes. Let us first focus on how claimants are categorized by themselves and others, and then on how institutions jockey to obtain authority and jurisdiction.

Who can acquire, hold and transact property? This involves questions of identity, since engagement with institutions is very often differentiated along ethnic, gender, occupational and age lines, as well as by class and wealth. Categories such as men/women, old/young, insiders/outsiders, noble/commoner, true believer/infidel, ethnic-this/ethnic-that have proved to be important when people struggle to legitimize land claims. Individuals and groups work to create, maintain, downplay, or unmake their own membership categories — but not under conditions of their own choosing. Often, actors stronger than those whose identities are at stake manipulate the available terms of recognition.

Formal national citizenship with the promise of universal rights is often conjugated with governments' and other authorities' actual practice of objectifying and instrumentalizing identities to differentiate between groups of people and their land rights. Gender, race and caste are sometimes (re-) produced through customary or statutory law. Even when statutory law has formally eliminated such distinctions, they may reproduce through a range of administrative, political and social practices (Sundar, 2011). Sometimes, certain communities are seen, *en bloc*, as belonging to one or another group, and entire communities — often defined in terms of ethnicity — can therefore be seen as either worthy of recognition of rights, or as requiring control and exclusion. The concept of Bantustans in apartheid South Africa is a particularly poignant example. Here, the reproduction of race as a key category consolidated the authority of chiefs by implication (Oomen, 2005). In other circumstances, categories such as landless people, peasants, autochthones, or *comuneros* may be produced by politically effective agents. Rivalry and competition over land easily take a communal form, and violence often follows such a pattern (Jega, 2000; Jensen, 2008; Locatelli and Nugent, 2009; Vlassenroot and Raeymaekers, 2009). Yet communal violence is rarely a simple result of difference in entitlement or political identity; it is stoked and structured by the institutions that feed on categorical inequality.

Collective action often starts from a specific grievance and an issue (access to land, to political participation, to public service, to justice). The Mijikenda in Mombasa, for example, was the creative result of local groups defying colonial categories. On the basis of mutual economic interest they self-identified and assimilated into a single new group with a common culture, language and religion (Willis, 1993). Sometimes, groups are also edited out of history. The Nawuri, for example, aspired to become a recognized ethnic group in colonial Ghana. They failed to become institutionally visible and have disappeared from Ghana's administrative system (Stacey, 2014). Ideologies and legalities structure the categories through which legitimate claims to land and other valuable resources can be put forward. 'Durable inequality among categories arises', Tilly argues, 'because people who control access to value-producing resources solve pressing organizational problems by means of categorical distinctions. Inadvertently, or otherwise, those people set up systems of social closure, exclusion, and control. Multiple parties — not all of them powerful, some of them even victims of exploitation — then acquire stakes in those solutions' (Tilly, 1998: 7–8). Not all distinctions have single or easily identifiable authors (such as government) or formal policies. And distinct authorship may dim over time. Some distinctions will be ephemeral and short-lived, be undermined, and rapidly rendered irrelevant — to be conjured up later, perhaps. Others, however, will reproduce effectively, harden and institutionalize, and be propped up by statutory law, regulation, force and other practices. They may become habitual and sometimes even essential to all involved. Obviously, these categorizations are the result of complex historical processes. Some categorizations (such as seniority, gender, caste and the like) date back to pre-colonial times, and others are more recent. Some were brought about in colonial times when governments established courts with jurisdictions over certain categories of people based on religion or race. Spatial segregation of people along criteria such as race, 'stage of civilization', ethnicity, trade and religion, was a work of Sisyphus for colonial governments (Benton, 2002; Chanock, 1991; Comaroff, 2002; Fourchard, 2009; Guha, 1997; Hoffmann, 2014; Mamdani, 1996, 2012; T. Mitchell, 2002; Sundar, 2009, 2011). Absolute categories are probably impossible in reality, yet categorization can have enduring institutional effects.

Institutions compete to control categorical distinctions. This allows them to become institutional references — the institutions that people address when they have claims to vindicate. The categories they control are used to group people who, in turn, validate the institution. So, just as people render themselves visible in different ways, potential political authorities must also display the capacity to recognize claims. That is, institutions shop for clients, members and followers (K. von Benda-Beckmann, 1981). However, just as institutions compete over jurisdiction, they also, sometimes, depend on each other's recognition and endorsement of their respective authorities.

Not only statutory law, but also political power and practice shape the actual definition and enforcement of claims as rights, and work to define effective jurisdictions and authority. Institutions — like city councils, may-ors, ministries of the interior, neighbourhood associations, chieftaincies — are often organized in formal, functional and structured hierarchies of power, and jurisdictions with accountabilities enshrined in a constitution or other legislation. However, while relations and powers are formally scripted, the actual practice very often abandons the script and establishes the real, effec-tive, relations of collaboration and competition, of coordination and assertion of jurisdictions. Non-statutory institutions also participate in this dynamic. We can think of jurisdictions as overlapping and interfering fields of author-ity in the making, rather than discrete realms of defined legal scope. They may be thought of in terms of spatial or territorial jurisdiction, in terms of functional jurisdiction, and as jurisdiction over persons, depending on what issue is at stake. Such jurisdictional claims are not mutually exclusive: they can be compounding, as well as bases for competition (Lund and Boone, 2013; S.F. Moore, 1978).

Territorial jurisdictions can vary in terms of how unambiguously they are delimited, how they nest into administrative hierarchies of government, and the extent to which the institutions are recognized by key actors as setting the boundaries of (enclosing) legitimate and rightful territorial domains and social groupings. In his work on the political economy of oil in Nigeria, Watts (2004) identifies different forms of governable spaces, only partially imbricated in one another, in which different cultural, political and legal repertoires are backed by different power resources. By design or default, spatial jurisdictions are sometimes carved out from the national territory. These can range from small-scale segments where certain neighbourhoods are 'black spots' in which local big men or gangs govern over spaces that have been occupied by movements or militias, to *de facto* secession of territory. Sometimes this process is even orchestrated by government itself (Hagmann and Hoehne, 2009; Ng'weno, 2007; Pratten and Sen, 2007; Taussig, 2005; I. Wilson, 2010; L. Wilson, 2011; Wolford, 2010; in this issue, see Lund and Rachman, and Hoffmann, Vlassenroot and Marchais). The same space, thus, can comprise various *functional jurisdictions* exercised by different authorities. These functional divisions can be well specified, or ambiguously delineated and contested. Not infrequently, institutions compete to establish functional jurisdiction over a particular field: what institution allocates land and adjudicates conflicts, for example, or what institution adjudicates in inheritance disputes? Is it statutory institutions, neo-traditional ones, or is it a syncretistic negotiation between government bureaucrats, companies and local leaders? Neighbourhood associations, religious institutions, political parties, local strongmen, vigilantes and militias all compete to be able to define and enforce identity and property claims as rights. The actual relations between institutions are thus 'in the making'.

Finally, within a given territorial jurisdiction, *jurisdiction over persons* can be fractured between and within different authorities. In British India, the East India Company represented the Crown. In civil cases, courts in a given territorial jurisdiction were to apply Islamic and Hindu laws to Muslims and Hindus, respectively. For criminal cases, jurisdictions configured differently. This 'jumble' animated disputes over jurisdictions (both in terms of legal subjects and subject matter). Competing principles of what was considered British, Muslim and Hindu law were instrumentalized, and forum shopping was widespread (Benton, 2002: 129–40). This does not mean that there is no hierarchy, no delimitation of jurisdiction, or mutual recognition of powers. The world is not flat. It simply means that we should see this as a constant dynamic. Two cases illustrate the issues at stake.

TWO CASES: GHANA AND INDONESIA

Let us first look at the example of chieftaincy in southern Ghana.[12] In Ghana, as in most British colonies, a system of indirect rule developed. The colonial administration would rule through native chiefs. For the colonizer, the system had an appealing simplicity: it built on local customs and institutions, and it was cheap. Yet, what was meant to look like a continuation of chiefly power was, in fact, a rupture. For the chiefs, propped up by colonial power, indirect rule meant a unique opportunity to edit and create customs and justify convenient practice as 'tradition' by the mere status of chieftaincy. Chieftaincies managed to consolidate and reinvent their authority to become rulers of territory, owners of land and resources, and gatekeepers for migrants into society. But statutory government and chieftaincy have competed for authority over land throughout Ghana's modern history (Amanor, 2009; Berry, 2009; Lentz, 2013).

Cocoa production became very important in southern Ghana in the early twentieth century. Migrants from the north headed south to farm cocoa; from the early days, chiefs had the authority to settle migrants and allocate land to them. The colonial government had an interest in cocoa production and consequently in the massive migration of labour, and it had an interest in keeping production costs down. By considering that land belonged to the realm of 'tradition', and that markets were 'non-traditional', land could remain non-commoditized and cheap. Consequently, the government consolidated the chiefs' authority to accept and 'naturalize' strangers, to control land allocation, and to gain land rent as revenue. Aside from this, chiefs' jurisdictions were not subject to interference.

From the late 1940s and in the decades that followed, however, central government tried to recapture some control over land by a series of measures aimed at curbing chiefs' jurisdictions. Government assumed the authority

---

12. This example draws on Amanor (2009); Berry (2009); Boni (2006, 2008); Lentz (2013); Ubink (2008); Ubink and Amanor (2009).

to expropriate land for major infrastructure projects. In fact, Amanor argues:

> [An] accommodation was reached between the state and customary authorities. The state recognized the rights of the chiefs to control land and revenue, and the chiefs consented to the state gaining a share of these revenues and actively participating in the management of stool revenues. The chiefs also complied with facilitating the expropriation of land for the 'national interest' and for commercial sectors and investors supported by the state. This arrangement has served to undermine the rights in land of farmers and other land users. The most farmers could gain was compensation for the crops they had planted on the land. (Amanor, 2009: 109)

Government did not nationalize the land but took it 'in trust' whenever needed, with the help of the chiefs. While these policies restricted chiefs' land authority, at least on paper, chiefs would continue to control land allocation locally. Furthermore, chiefs regained a formal position through a number of constitutional amendments from 1979 to 1992. At the beginning of the twenty-first century, a Customary Land Secretariat was established which was intended to allow communities to have a say in management of land held under customary tenure. Effectively, however, the Secretariat was placed under the authority of the chiefs, strengthening their authority in the matter. This secured the Chiefs' competencies to allocate land and to define and enforce property.

As land had gradually become scarce in the 1990s, the power of chiefs to accept 'strangers' in local communities had come to be challenged from within. Local youth, worried that what they considered their birth-right was being squandered on strangers, often put pressure on their chiefs to tighten and narrow the access to land, to privilege the autochthonous population, and to weaken the property rights of 'strangers' and their descendants — also retroactively. Charging a higher rent for land held on weaker terms by 'strangers' also worked in the interest of chiefs. This ability to define and enforce local citizenship rights — producing first- and second-class citizens among people who, in principle, all enjoy Ghanaian citizenship — demonstrates the power of chiefly jurisdiction.

This example of the rupture of colonization demonstrates that competition over jurisdiction is not simply a question of crass confrontation but equally one of clever collusion to reduce land users' rights. While statutory institutions could trump an individual chief and acquire a particular piece of land, chiefs would manage most of the land most of the time. Moreover, with the support of statutory institutions, chiefs managed to rework the terms of the social contract of property with the land users to their advantage. Finally, their capacity to define citizenship and its ensuing rights was strengthened as it combined with increasing scarcity of land. This meant that jurisdiction over persons, at least locally, also tipped in favour of the chiefs. As long as the general discourse favoured 'tradition', 'the past', 'history' and 'culture', more egalitarian republican values of civic equality and the

institutions associated with them would seem to yield. Discourse and terminology are therefore central fields of political struggle.

Another example comes from Indonesia.[13] The country has a very turbulent history characterized by a series of ruptures, and violent entrepreneurs
play a significant role in it. The Indonesian government and especially the
army and police have regularly made use of groups of violent entrepreneurs
as part of a network of sub-contracted enforcers.

In pre-colonial times, the 'social landscape was peppered with an assortment of bandits, warriors, mercenaries, mystics, warlords, princes and
a host of strongmen and violence wielding groups' (I. Wilson, 2015: 11).
Gradually, some became incorporated into the Dutch indirect rule while
others remained 'outlaws'. The latter were even sometimes referred to as
'republics' (ibid.: 13). Later, during the early twentieth century, many such
groups (notably on Java) were recruited or developed into anti-colonial political movements, and the revolution and war of independence (1945–9) were
fought by a multitude of different armed groups. Often, they delivered more
organized resistance than the new official republican army. The republican
leaders, Sukarno and Hatta, made efforts to incorporate these many militias
into the Indonesian army. Many were integrated but, as Bakker (2015) has
shown:

> [the revolutionary concept of] 'total people's defence and security', which declared citi-
> zens to bear responsibility for the defence of the nation, legitimized the continued existence
> of paramilitary groups within the independent state. Notably during the New Order era,
> the border between paramilitaries and private muscle ... groups [was] vague as military-
> trained paramilitary groups were used by the regime to carry out illegal violent and repres-
> sive actions against the civilian population. In exchange for their allegiance, these groups
> were allowed to engage in criminal activities and usually confirmed their loyalty by pay-
> ing part of the profits they generated through violence, extortion, and other crimes to their
> patrons. Such ... violence and criminality were normalized as practices affiliated with
> the regime and maintained through patrimonial alliances to the ruling elite. (Bakker, 2015:
> 80–81)

These groups are not revolutionary or antithetical to the Indonesian government. Generally, they are recognized as mass organizations (*ormas —
organisasi kemasyarakatan*). This is a particular legal category for a range
of non-government community, religious, ethnic, environmental and welfare
organizations engaged in social activities. This label gives even the violent
organizations legal visibility and, in principle, subjects them to government
control. So, formally, government recognizes these *ormas* as legal and legitimate provided they comply with the legal requirements for reporting,
registering, etc. Many do not comply, and hence are essentially operating

---

13. This example draws on Aspinall and van Klinken (2011); Bakker (2009, 2015); Barker
(2007); van Klinken (2007); Onghokham (2003); I. Wilson (2010, 2015); L. Wilson (2011).
See also Volkov (2002).

illegally, but are nevertheless often on good terms with local government. In practice, the relationship between municipalities, police and army, and the *ormas* of the violent entrepreneur type, makes up a 'patchwork of jurisdictions' (Barker, 2007), which is both collaborative and competitive.

This relationship varies over time. Broad historical brush strokes would show that the colonial government, the Sukarno regime after independence, and Suharto's New Order from 1965 all attempted to domesticate these groups and succeeded to some extent. Yet these *ormas* do not simply derive their power from government recognition. In some periods — notably in the rupture after the New Order regime and Suharto's fall in 1998 — democratization and decentralization in Indonesia changed the context, and centralized control over these groups by the military and police was relaxed. Democracy and decentralization led to the emergence of new political entrepreneurs in a much more fragmented landscape. During the New Order, loyalties had to be with Suharto, the military and the state party, Golkar, as a unitary image of the Indonesian state, but the post-New Order changed that. The groups of violent entrepreneurs did not disappear; instead, they developed more autonomous profiles.

The weakening and fragmentation of the central political authority led to a proliferation of violent entrepreneurs searching for new social contracts. In addition to their conventional racketeering, territorial control over urban informal settlements and violent acquisition of land for different developments at the urban fringe became important in cities like Medan. Democracy meant that the capacity of the *ormas* to mobilize an electorate became very valuable for politicians. The ability to garner votes and wide-scale support depended on the *ormas*' ability to deliver protection — for housing, businesses, amenities, services and other elements of everyday social infrastructure — and some form of representation. Thus, rather than being the regime's sub-contracted muscle, some of the *ormas* of the violent entrepreneur type began to define and protect rights to land and livelihood in poor urban areas, thus emerging as authorities able to negotiate concessions, privilege and impunity with institutional actors that needed their support. These violent entrepreneurs were often affiliated with social and religious organizations, and the local, communal ideology of the latter began to colour the repertoires of legitimation and replace the once enthusiastic support of the 'nation'. This resonates with the idea of bandit republics in the colonial era.

The Indonesian example shows that the ability to control and protect central resources, to define membership, and to exercise a modicum of political representation, enabled some of the violent entrepreneurs in contemporary Indonesia to establish themselves as authorities — at least for a while. They were not alone in the field. They picked their fights and chose their alliances with other *ormas*, with municipalities and police, with politicians and their parties, and with businessmen of all shades, all of whom thus claimed a stake in the politics of land and belonging.

STATE FORMATION THROUGH THE PRODUCTION OF PROPERTY AND CITIZENSHIP

Claims to rights invoke political authority and the governing capacity of institutions, and the categorization of property and citizens is a way for institutions to claim authority and acquire and exercise state quality. Different combinations of property and citizenship are constantly produced and reproduced in this dynamic, and new institutional alliances with the capacity to define and enforce rules of property and citizenship frequently emerge. This requires a specific research endeavour of grounded, empirical research allowing us to go beyond state theories modelled after ahistorical ideal types. The concern of this special issue, therefore, is to identify and map out political, social and legal dynamics and techniques, which establish relations of authority through the production of property and of citizenship, as well as the dynamics that challenge and undermine calls for rights and claims to authority.

The fragmented nature of authority over land, and the multiple options for political identity have a significant impact on struggles between rights claimants. In concert, they fuel struggles over rights, over identities and categories, and involve strategies of visibility, of legitimation and, sometimes, of violence. The multiplicity of relationships not only creates heterogeneity and difference; it also creates and consolidates complex inequality. When different relationships re-confirm each other, recursive dynamics are in play. Examples include being a landowner or a landlord, and a member of the powerful political factions; being an ethnic group with clout, associated with a strong guild; or, in contrast, being a squatter, a day labourer, of low status, and a migrant. Obviously, a vast range of combinations is possible. We must therefore investigate the configuration of recognition that arises when competing institutions structure interaction according to cultural and legal norms. We need to pay particular attention to dynamics that impede parity of participation and exclude certain groups, as well as dynamics that enable others to compound different institutional sources of recognition of claims to status and wealth.

The Contributions

The contributions to this issue investigate how new forms of property and political subjectivities are produced; how old ones are challenged and sometimes reproduced; and, most significantly, how political authorities have emerged through ruptures by their ability to create, bestow and protect rights of property and citizenship. The contributions are all the result of extensive fieldwork following different ruptures. They share a keen attention to historical empirical detail. Hence, simple labels — 'weak', 'fragile', 'failed' — are shown to be facile and inadequate. The chapters are grouped according to the outcome of the rupture and the ways in which the production and rearrangement of property and citizenship have consolidated, challenged, or fragmented political authority. First, we engage places where political power has been *reconstituted and consolidated* through successful control over the production of property rights and the construction of political identity as determinants of inclusion and exclusion. Second, a group of contributions deal with places where government authority has been *challenged* in certain spaces. Alternative forms of authority not only destabilize government; they also manage to consolidate through their capacity to carve out space, territorialize it, and establish reciprocal relations of recognition with political members or subjects. Finally, a third group of chapters investigate spaces where competition for authority is intense and no unequivocal political domination can be identified. Instead, political power is *fragmented* and any consolidation short-lived.

Erin Collins analyses the situation in Cambodia after the demise of the Khmer Rouge. She shows how the refugees and the humanitarian intervention provided a moment for establishing new political authority. Through the active, deliberate definition of certain refugees as citizens with legitimate claims to property, and others as the nation's strangers, political power firmed up in the hands of government. The creation of 'strangers' and their exclusion was as important for political power as the creation of 'citizens' with rights. Another post-genocide moment — in Rwanda — is analysed by An Ansoms and Giuseppe Cioffo. The Rwandan government set out to define the 'exemplary citizen' as non-ethnic subjects who insert themselves into a government-engineered project of development and modernity. Through rural development policies, the government re-territorialized the country and established detailed directives on how people should farm and what to cultivate. This was met with both subtle and more open forms of resistance. The case illustrates how, time and again, property and citizenship are central issues around which the social contract is hammered out. In Nepal, repeated ruptures and continuous 'transitions' in the relationship between authority and territory intersperse a turbulent context of civil war (1996–2006) and ongoing state (trans-)formation. Sarah Byrne, Benedikt Korf and Andrea Nightingale analyse the case of a contested forest in Nepal's mid-Western hills, focusing on the claims for recognition of political and resource use rights that emerge in counterpoint to the territorial dimensions of these reconstitutions of political power. These claims take a number of practical and discursive forms, including forming an independent forest users' group, encroaching on forestland, and repeatedly referencing conservation. The authors show that territorialization operates simultaneously at different scales and trace how practices of territorial claims making often remain strikingly consistent throughout different struggles over political authority. The ability to become the political authority to which communities are beholden for forest rights at local scale, for example, is as crucial to government as larger-scale claims to territorial sovereignty. Jacobo Grajales analyses the reconstitution of political authority in the wake of demobilization of paramilitary groups in Colombia around the turn of the century. The paramilitary groups played an important part in plantation companies' violent acquisition of smallholder land. Smallholders had benefited from land reform, and the land grab challenged government land agencies. While the paramilitary groups persisted with different forms of trafficking, protection rackets and violent intimidations, the government managed to address the land grabs and thereby reassert itself as the key political authority over land. Whether this will actually lead to the restitution of land to dispossessed smallholders remains uncertain.

In some cases, government control over property and citizenship is effectively suspended. Christian Lund and Noer Fauzi Rachman analyse how land occupations in Indonesia in the post-Suharto era effectively created new social contracts of property, citizenship and public authority between members and leadership of peasant movements. Land allocation, registration and taxation took place outside of government control. However, the authors equally demonstrate the tenuousness of such social contracts when smallholders attempt to become politically and fiscally visible to government. The post-authoritarian moment following Suharto's fall also created particular opportunities in the periphery of Indonesia. Michael Eilenberg analyses how decentralization allowed local political forces in West Kalimantan to work for the creation of new districts with resource control. Such claims combined ideas of customary territory and community with the state rhetoric of citizenship and development. Thus, on the basis of a particular local citizenry and a claim to resources through customary spatial orders, new local polities with semi-autonomous aspirations emerged as contenders for political power. In Bolivia, Verónica Calvo Valenzuela analyses the competition for public authority between peasant unions, indigenous people's movements and neighbourhood associations in a municipality. Each of these political organizations has spatial claims and each represents very particular rights subjects: peasants, indigenes and neighbours. Different political identities and social contracts entitle people to property differently. Thus the recent adoption of the Peasant-Native-Indigenous Autonomy law has opened a hornets' nest of competing claims to property and citizenship.

The third group of chapters is introduced by Markus Hoehne's contribution on a tension in Somalia's recent history between network logics of social organization and territorial logics of spatial control. Historically, political power was predominantly derived from control over people. Membership of groups defined the political structure, whereas fixed spatial borders and contiguity of spatial domains were of lesser concern. More recently, however, territorialization and spatial control have emerged as the challenging logic for political organization. Non-territorial citizenship logics and spatial logics akin to property thus compete to be the most effective conduit for political power. Different logics are equally confronted in Adam Baczko's chapter on tribes, the Taliban and the US Army in Afghanistan. While all three authorities engaged with the population in attempts to build social contracts around property to define the rights of citizens, they did so in very different ways. While tribal leaders would regulate conflicts through negotiation and sometimes arbitration by elders from different groups, much of this system collapsed during the Soviet occupation. The US Army, by contrast, attempted to consolidate territorial control through very personalized networks of favoured friends. Their image of the 'tribal Afghan' effectively undermined the idea of a non-ethnic, de-personalized Afghan state that the invasion was intended to support. Somewhat ironically, the territorial judicial organization promoted by the Taliban was deliberately non-ethnic and formalized with reference to Islamic law. Finally, Kasper Hoffmann, Koen Vlassenroot and Gauthier Marchais analyse the role of taxation for the constitution of authority in the Democratic Republic of the Congo. Taxation ranges from simple plunder, through protection rackets, to the material reciprocation of the recognition of rights. The long series of wars and political ruptures in Congo has routinely thwarted attempts at consolidation of political power in the country. Yet, while the political structure is fragmented and competition over power seems endless and chaotic, there is also a strong thread of continuity in mutually constitutive patterns of territorialization on the basis of an actively cultivated imaginary of ethnically organized space and extractive, indirect and coercive practices of taxation.

Individually and collectively, the contributions clearly show that the ability to establish political power runs through the capacity to determine who can be a rights subject, and what rights can be enjoyed. Indeed, the capacity to institute membership, or citizenship, in a body politic, and the power to establish and defend rights, especially to property, is the essence of public authority; the essence of state.

Acknowledgements

Comments and questions from many people have helped me to structure and develop the argument in this Introduction. In particular, inputs from Adam Baczko, Alice Kelly, An Ansoms, Andrea Nightingale, Ari Nurman, Benedikt Korf, Bruno Braak, Catherine Boone, Duncan McDuie-Ra, Eric Hahonou, Erin Collins, Gauthier Marchais, Giuseppe Cioffo, Jacobo Grajales, Jesse Ribot, Kasper Hoffmann, Koen Vlassenroot, Laurens Bakker, Markus Höhne, Mattias Borg Rasmussen, Michael Eilenberg, Nancy Peluso, Noer Fauzi Rachman, Paul Stacey, Tara Weinberg, Tobias Udsholt, Sarah Byrne, Siddharth Sareen, Verónica Calvo Valenzuela, Veronica Gomez-Temesio and Willem van der Muur have improved the text. I also owe a debt of gratitude to Jan Michiel Otto and Adriaan Bedner for hosting me at the Van Vollenhoven Institute and discussing my work. Thanks are also due to the reviewers for illuminating and instructive comments and suggestions.

Finally, credit goes to Mike Kirkwood who language edited this and most of the other texts in the collection. The remaining errors and infelicities are mine. A note on self-plagiarism: the chapter builds on and develops a question I have worked on for many years. There are therefore a few sentences (and many words) that have flitted across my screen before.

REFERENCES

Abrams, P. (1988) 'Notes on the Difficulty of Studying the State', *Journal of Historical Sociology* 1(1): 58–89.

Agamben, G. (2005) *State of Exception*. Stanford, CA: Stanford University Press.

Agrawal, A. (2001) 'State Formation in Community Spaces? Decentralization of Control over Forests in the Kumaon Himalaya, India', *Journal of Asian Studies* 60(1): 9–40.

Agrawal, A. (2005) *Environmentality. Technologies of Government and the Making of Subjects.* Durham, NC and London: Duke University Press.

Akinyele, R.T. (2009) 'Contesting for Space in an Urban Centre. The Omo Onile Syndrome in Lagos', in F. Locatelli and P. Nugent (eds) *African Cities. Competing Claims on Urban Spaces*, pp. 187–217. Leiden: Brill.

Amanor, K. (2009) 'Securing Land Rights in Ghana', in J. Ubink, A. Hoekema and W. Assies (eds) *Legalizing Land Rights, Local Practices, State Responses and Tenure Security in Africa, Asia and Latin America*, pp. 97–131. Leiden: Leiden University Press.

Arendt, H. (1948/1979) *The Origins of Totalitarianism*. New York: Harvest.

Asad, T. (2004) 'Where Are the Margins of the State?', in V. Das and D. Poole (eds) *Anthropology in the Margins of the State*, pp. 279–88. Santa Fe, NM: School of American Research Press; Oxford: James Currey.

Aspinall, E. and G. van Klinken (eds) (2011) *The State and Illegality in Indonesia*. Leiden: KITLV Press.

Bailey, F.G. (1968) 'Parapolitical Systems', in M.J. Swartz (ed.) *Local-Level Politics. Social and Cultural Perspectives*, pp. 281–94. London: University of London Press.

Baitenmann, H. (2005) 'Counting on State Subjects. State Formation and Citizenship in Twentieth-century Mexico', in C. Krohn-Hansen and G. Nustad (eds) *State Formation. Anthropological Perspectives*, pp. 171–94. London: Pluto Press.

Bakker, L. (2009) 'Who Owns the Land? Looking for Law and Power in Reformasi East Kalimantan'. PhD Thesis, University of Nijmegen.

Bakker, L. (2015) 'Illegality for the General Good? Vigilantism and Social Responsibility in Contemporary Indonesia', *Critique of Anthropology* 35(1): 78–93.

Bakker, L. and S. Moniaga (2010) 'The Space Between: Land Claims and the Law in Indonesia', *Asian Journal of Social Science* 38: 187–201.

Barker, J. (2007) 'Vigilantes and the State', in T. Day (ed.) *Identifying with Freedom: Indonesia after Suharto*, pp. 87–94. New York: Berghahn Books.

Barkey, K. (1994) *Bandits and Bureaucrats. The Ottoman Route to State Centralization*. Ithaca, NY: Cornell University Press.

von Benda-Beckmann, F. (1993) 'Le monopole d'État de la violence dans la perspective de l'anthropologie juridique' ['The State's Monopoly of Violence in a Legal Anthropological Perspective'], in E. Le Roy and T. von Trotha (eds) *La violence et l'État. Formes et évolution d'un monopole* [*State Violence. Forms and Evolution of a Monopoly*], pp. 35–57. Paris: l'Harmattan.

von Benda-Beckmann, F. (1997) 'Citizens, Strangers and Indigenous Peoples. Conceptual Politics and Legal Pluralism', in F. von Benda Beckman et al. (eds) *Natural Resources, Environment and Legal Pluralism, Law and Anthropology Yearbook 9*, pp. 1–42. Berlin: Springer Verlag.

von Benda-Beckmann, F. and K. von Benda-Beckmann (2014) *Political and Legal Transformations of an Indonesian Polity. The Nagari from Colonialism to Decentralisation*. Cambridge: Cambridge University Press.

von Benda-Beckmann, K. (1981) 'Forum Shopping and Shopping Forums: Dispute Processing in a Minangkabau Village in West Sumatra', *Journal of Legal Pluralism* 13(19): 117–62.

Benton, L. (2002) *Law and Colonial Cultures. Legal Regimes in World History, 1400–1900*. Cambridge: Cambridge University Press.

Berry, S. (1993) *No Condition is Permanent: The Social Dynamics of Agrarian Change in Sub-Saharan Africa*. Madison, WI: University of Wisconsin Press.

Berry, S. (2002) 'Debating the Land Questions', *Comparative Studies in Society and History* 44(4): 638–68.

Berry, S. (2009) 'Property, Authority and Citizenship. Land Claims, Politics and the Dynamics of Social Division in West Africa, in T. Sikor and C. Lund (eds) *Politics of Possession*, pp. 23–45. Chichester and Oxford: Wiley-Blackwell.

Bierschenk, T. and J.-P. Olivier de Sardan (eds) (2014) *States at Work*. Leiden: Brill.

Blundo, G. and P.-Y. Le Meur (eds) (2009) *The Governance of Daily Life in Africa. Ethnographic Explorations of Public and Collective Services*. Leiden: Brill.

Boni, S. (2006) 'Indigenous Blood and Foreign Labor: The "Ancesteralization" of Land Rights in Sefwi (Ghana)', in R. Kuba and C. Lentz (eds) *Land and the Politics of Belonging in West Africa*, pp. 161–85. Leiden: Brill.

Boni, S. (2008) 'Traditional Ambiguities and Authoritarian Interpretations in Safwi Land Disputes', in J. Ubink and K. Amanor (eds) *Contesting Land and Custom in Ghana: State, Chief and the Citizen*, pp. 81–109. Leiden: Leiden University Press.

Boone, C. (2003) *Political Topographies of the African State. Territorial Authority and Institutional Choice*. Cambridge: Cambridge University Press.

Boone, C. (2014) *Property and Political Order in Africa, Land Rights and the Structure of Politics*. Cambridge: Cambridge University Press.

Bourdieu, P. (1994) 'Re-thinking the State. Genesis and Structure of the Bureaucratic Field', *Sociological Theory* 12(1): 1–18.

Bourdieu, P. (2012) *Sur l'État. Cours au college de France 1989–1992 [On the State. Courses at College de France 1989–1992]*. Paris: Seuil.

Breman, J. (1983) *Control of Land and Labour in Colonial Java*. Leiden: Foris.

Breman, J. (2015) *Mobilizing Labour for the Global Coffee Market: Profits from an Unfree Work Regime in Colonial Java*. Amsterdam: Amsterdam University Press.

Campbell, J.M. (2015) *Conjuring Property: Speculation and Environmental Futures in the Brazilian Amazon*. Seattle, WA: University of Washington Press.

Chanock, M. (1991) 'A Peculiar Sharpness: An Essay on Property in the History of Customary Law in Colonial Africa', *Journal of African History* 32(1): 65–88.

Chanock, M. (1998) *Law, Custom and Social Order. The Colonial Experience in Malawi and Zambia*. Portsmouth, NH: Heinemann.

Chari, S. and K. Verdery (2009) 'Thinking between the Posts: Postcolonialism, Postsocialism, and Ethnography after the Cold War', *Comparative Studies in Society and History* 51(1): 6–34.

Clanchy, M.T. (2013) *From Memory to Written Record. England 1066–1307* (3rd edn). Chichester and Oxford: Wiley-Blackwell.

Colombijn, F. (2013) *Under Construction: The Politics of Urban Space and Housing during the Decolonization of Indonesia, 1930–1960*. Leiden: KITLV Press.

Comaroff, J. (2002) 'Governmentality, Materiality, Legality, Modernity. On the Colonial State in Africa', in J.-G. Deutsch, P. Probst and H. Schmidt (eds) *African Modernities: Entangled Meanings in Current Debate*, pp. 107–34. Portsmouth, NH: Heinemann.

Comaroff, J. and J. Comaroff (eds) (2006) *Law and Order in the Postcolony*. Chicago, IL: University of Chicago Press.

Comaroff, J. and J. Comaroff (2009) 'Reflexions on the Anthropology of Law, Governance and Sovereignty', in F. von Benda-Beckmann et al. (eds) *Rules of Law and Laws of Ruling*, pp. 31–60. London: Ashgate.

Corrigan, P. (1994) 'State Formation', in G. Joseph and D. Nugent (eds) *Everyday Forms of State Formation. Revolution and the Negotiation of Rule in Modern Mexico*, pp. xvii–xix. Durham, NC: Duke University Press.

Corrigan, P. and D. Sayer (1985) *The Great Arch. English State Formation as Cultural Revolution.* Oxford: Blackwell.

Das, V. (2011) 'State, Citizenship, and the Urban Poor', *Citizenship Studies* 15(3–4): 319–33.

Das, V. and D. Poole (eds) (2004) *Anthropology in the Margins of the State.* Santa Fe, NM: School of American Research Press; Oxford: James Currey.

De Boeck, F. (2011) 'Inhabiting the Ocular Ground. Kinshasa's Future in the Light of Congo's Spectral Urban Politics', *Cultural Anthropology* 26(2): 266–86.

De Herdt, T. and J.-P. Olivier de Sardan (eds) (2015) *Real Governance and Practical Norms in Sub-Saharan Africa.* London: Routledge.

Derrida, J. (1986) 'Declarations of Independence', *New Political Science* 7(1): 7–15.

Derrida, J. (2002) 'Force of Law. The "Mystical Foundation of Authority"', in J. Derrida *Acts of Religion*, pp. 230–98. London: Routledge.

Durkheim, É. (1893/2014) *The Division of Labour in Society.* London: Free Press.

Elias, N. (1939/1994) *The Civilizing Process.* Oxford: Blackwell.

Engeman, S.L. and J. Metzer (eds) (2004) *Land Rights, Ethno-Nationality, and Sovereignty in History.* London: Routledge.

Foucault, M. (2003) *Society Must Be Defended. Lectures at the Collège de France, 1975–76.* London: Picador.

Fourchard, L. (2009) 'Dealing with "Strangers". Allocating Urban Space to Migrants in Nigeria and French West Africa, End of the Nineteenth Century to 1960', in F. Locatelli and P. Nugent (eds) *African Cities. Competing Claims on Urban Spaces*, pp. 187–217. Leiden: Brill.

Fox, J. (1994) 'The Difficult Transition from Clientelism to Citizenship. Lessons from Mexico', *World Politics* 46(2): 151–84.

Fraser, N. (2001) 'Recognition without Ethics?', *Theory, Culture and Society* 18(2–3): 21–42.

Geiger, D. (2008) 'Turner in the Tropics. The "Frontier" Concept Revisited', in D. Geiger (ed.) *Frontier Encounters. Indigenous Communities and Settlers in Asia and Latin America*, pp. 75–215. Copenhagen: IWGIA.

Geschiere, P. (2009) *The Perils of Belonging. Autochthony, Citizenship, and Exclusion in Africa and Europe.* Chicago, IL: University of Chicago Press.

Godelier, M. (1986) *The Mental and the Material.* London: Verso.

Gomez-Temesio, V. (2014) 'L'État sourcier. Anthropologie politique de l'hydraulique rurale au Sénégal' ['Sources of State. A Political Anthropology of Rural Water Supply in Senegal']. PhD thesis, EHESS, Marseille.

Gramsci, A. (1971) *Selections from the Prison Notebooks.* London: Lawrence and Wishart.

Grimm, S., N. Lemay-Hébert and O. Nay (2014) '"Fragile States": Introducing a Political Concept', *Third World Quarterly* 35(2): 197–209.

Guha, R. (1997) *Dominance without Hegemony. History and Power in Colonial India.* Cambridge, MA: Harvard University Press.

Hagmann, T. and M. Hoehne (2009) 'Failures of the State Failure Debate: Evidence from the Somali Territories', *Journal of International Development* 21(1): 42–57.

Hagmann, T. and D. Péclard (2010) 'Negotiating Statehood: Dynamics of Power and Domination in Africa', *Development and Change* 41(4): 539–62.

Hansen, T.B. and F. Stepputat (eds) (2001) *States of Imagination. Ethnographic Explorations of the Postcolonial State.* Durham, NC: Duke University Press.

Hansen, T.B. and F. Stepputat (2006) 'Sovereignty Revisited', *Annual Review of Anthropology* 35: 295–315.

26 *Christian Lund*

Hetherington, K. (2011) *Guerrilla Auditors. The Politics of Transparency in Neoliberal Paraguay.* Durham, NC: Duke University Press.
Hibou, B. (ed.) (2004) *Privatizing the State.* New York: University of Columbia Press.
Hoffmann, K. (2014) 'Ethnogovernmentality. The Making of Ethnic Territories and Subjects in Eastern Congo'. PhD Dissertation. Roskilde University.
Hoffmann, K. and T. Kirk (2013) 'Public Authority and the Provision of Public Goods in Conflict-Affected and Transitioning Regions'. JRSP Paper No. 7. London: LSE Justice and Security Research Programme.
Holleman, J.F. (1973) 'Trouble-cases and Trouble-less Cases in the Study of Customary Law and Legal Reform', *Law & Society Review* 7(4): 585–609.
Holston, J. (2008) *Insurgent Citizenship. Disjunctions of Democracy and Modernity in Brazil.* Princeton, NJ: Princeton University Press.
Honneth, A. (1995) *The Struggle for Recognition. The Moral Grammar of Social Conflicts.* Cambridge: Polity Press.
Jacob, J.-P. and P.-Y. Le Meur (eds) (2010) *Politique de la terre et de l'appartenance. Droits fonciers et citoyenneté locale dans les sociétés du Sud* [*Politics of Land and Belonging. Land Rights and Local Citizenship in the Global South*]. Paris: Karthala.
James, C.L.R. (1963) *The Black Jacobins. Toussaint L'Ouverture and the San Domingo Revolution.* New York: Vintage Books.
Jega, A. (ed.) (2000) *Identity Transformation and Identity Politics under Structural Adjustment in Nigeria.* Uppsala: Nordic Africa Institute.
Jensen, S. (2008) *Gangs, Politics and Dignity in Cape Town.* Oxford: James Currey.
Jessop, B. (1990) *State Theory. Putting Capitalist States in their Place.* Oxford: Polity Press.
Joireman, S. (2011) *Where There Is No Government. Enforcing Property Rights in Common Law Africa.* Oxford: Oxford University Press.
Joseph, G. and D. Nugent (eds) (1994) *Everyday Forms of State Formation. Revolution and the Negotiation of Rule in Modern Mexico.* Durham, NC: Duke University Press.
Kaplan, R. (1994) 'The Coming Anarchy', *Atlantic Monthly* February. http://www.theatlantic.com/magazine/archive/1994/02/the-coming-anarchy/304670/
van Klinken, G. (2007) *Communal Violence and Democratization in Indonesia. Small Town Wars.* London: Routledge.
Körling, G. (2011) *In the Search of the State. An Ethnography of Public Service Provision in Urban Niger.* Uppsala: Uppsala University.
Krupa, C. and D. Nugent (2015) 'Off-centered States. Rethinking State Theory through an Andean Lens', in C. Krupa and D. Nugent (eds) *State Theory and Andean Politics. New Approaches to the Study of Rule*, pp. 1–31. Philadelphia, PA: University of Pennsylvania Press.
Le Roy, É., A. Karsenty and A. Bertrand (1996) *La sécurisation foncière en Afrique* [*Securing Land Tenure in Africa*]. Paris: Karthala.
Lentz, C. (2013) *Land, Mobility, and Belonging in West Africa.* Bloomington, IN: Indiana University Press.
Li, T.M. (2000) 'Articulating Indigenous Identity in Indonesia. Resource Politics and the Tribal Slot', *Comparative Studies in Society and History* 4(1): 149–79.
Locatelli, F. and P. Nugent (eds) (2009) *African Cities. Competing Claims on Urban Spaces.* Leiden: Brill.
Lund, C. (ed.) (2006a) *Twilight Institutions. Public Authority and Local Politics in Africa.* Special issue, *Development and Change* 37(4).
Lund, C. (2006b) 'Twilight Institutions. Public Authority and Local Politics in Africa', *Development and Change* 37(4): 685–705.
Lund, C. (2008) *Local Politics and the Dynamics of Property in Africa.* Cambridge: Cambridge University Press.
Lund, C. (2010) 'Approaching Development: An Opinionated Review', *Progress in Development Studies* 10(1): 19–34.

Lund, C. (2011) 'Property and Citizenship. Conceptually Connecting Land Rights and Belonging in Africa', *Africa Spectrum* 46(3): 71–5.

Lund, C. (2013) 'The Past and Space. On Arguments in African Land Control', *Africa* 83(1): 14–35.

Lund, C. (2014) 'Of What Is This a Case? Analytical Movements in Qualitative Social Science Research', *Human Organization* 73(3): 224–34.

Lund, C. and C. Boone (2013) 'Land Politics in Africa. Constituting Authority over Territory, Property, and Persons', *Africa* 83(1): 1–13.

MacPherson, C.B. (1978) *Property: Mainstream and Critical Positions*. Oxford: Basil Blackwell.

Mamdani, M. (1996) *Citizen and Subject. Contemporary Africa and the Legacy of Late Colonialism*. London: James Currey.

Mamdani, M. (2012) *Define and Rule. Native as Political Identity*. Cambridge, MA: Harvard University Press.

Mann, M. (1993) *The Sources of Social Power*. New York: Cambridge University Press.

Martin, I.W., A.K. Mehrotra and M. Prasad (2009) 'The Thunder of History. The Origins and Development of the New Fiscal Sociology', in I.W. Martin et al. (eds) *The New Fiscal Sociology. Taxation in Comparative and Historical Perspective*, pp. 1–27. Cambridge: Cambridge University Press.

Mbembe, A. (2001) *On the Postcolony*. Berkeley, CA: University of California Press.

Metzer, J. and S.L. Engerman (2004) 'Some Considerations of Ethno-nationality (and Other Distinctions), Property Rights in Land, and Territorial Sovereignty', in S.L. Engerman and J. Metzer (eds) *Land Rights, Ethno-Nationality, and Sovereignty in History*, pp. 7–28. London: Routledge.

Migdal, J. (2001) *State in Society. Studying How States and Societies Transform and Constitute One Another*. Cambridge: Cambridge University Press.

Mitchell, J.C. (1983) 'Case and Situation Analysis', *The Sociological Review* 31(2): 187–21.

Mitchell, T. (1988) *Colonizing Egypt*. Berkeley, CA: University of California Press.

Mitchell, T. (1991) 'The Limits of the State: Beyond Statist Approaches and their Critics', *American Political Science Review* 85(1): 77–96.

Mitchell, T. (2002) *Rule of Experts. Egypt, Techno-Politics, Modernity*. Berkeley, CA: University of California Press.

Moore, B. (1966) *Social Origins of Dictatorship and Democracy. Lord and Peasant in the Making of the Modern World*. Hammondsworth: Penguin.

Moore, S.F. (1978) *Law as Process*. London: Routledge & Kegan Paul.

Moore, S.F. (1986) *Social Facts and Fabrications: 'Customary' Law on Kilimanjaro 1880–1980*. Cambridge: Cambridge University Press.

Moore, S.F. (1987) 'Explaining the Present: Theoretical Dilemmas in Processual Ethnography', *American Ethnologist* 14(4): 727–36.

Ng'weno, B. (2007) *Turf Wars. Territory and Citizenship in the Contemporary State*. Stanford, CA: Stanford University Press.

Nielsen, M. (2011) 'Inverse Governmentality. The Paradoxical Production of Peri-urban Planning in Maputo, Mozambique', *Critique of Anthropology* 31(4): 329–58.

North, D.C. and R.P Thomas (1973) *The Rise of the Western World*. Cambridge: Cambridge University Press.

Nugent, P. (2010) 'States and Social Contracts in Africa', *New Left Review* 63: 35–68.

Nurman, A. and C. Lund (2016) 'On Track. Spontaneous Privatization of Public Land in Urban Indonesia', *South East Asia Research* 24(1): 41–60.

Onghokham (2003) *The Thugs, the Curtain Thief, and the Sugar Lord. Power, Politics and Culture in Colonial Java*. Jakarta: Metaphor Publishing.

Onoma, A.K. (2010) *The Politics of Property Rights Institutions in Africa*. Cambridge: Cambridge University Press.

Oomen, B. (2005) *Chiefs in South Africa. Law, Power and Culture in the Post-Apartheid Era*. Oxford: James Currey.

Peluso, N. (1992) *Rich Forests, Poor People. Resource Control and Resistance in Java*. Berkeley, CA: University of California Press.

Pottage, A. (2004) 'The Fabrication of Persons and Things', in A. Pottage and M. Mundy (eds) *Law, Anthropology, and the Constitution of the Social. Making Persons and Things*, pp. 1–39. Cambridge: Cambridge University Press.

Pratten, D. and A. Sen (eds) (2007) *Global Vigilantes*. London: Hurst.

Rasmussen, M.B. and C. Lund (forthcoming) 'Reconfiguring Frontier Spaces: The Territoriality of Resource Control', *World Development*.

Roitman, J. (2005) *Fiscal Disobedience. An Anthropology of Economic Regulation in Central Africa*. Princeton, NJ: Princeton University Press.

Rose, C. (1994) *Property and Persuasion. Essays on the History, Theory and Rhetoric of Ownership*. Boulder, CO: Westview Press.

Rose, C. (1998) 'Canons of Property Talk, or, Blackstone's Anxiety', *Yale Law Journal* 108(3): 601–32.

Rose, N. and P. Miller (1992) 'Political Power beyond the State: Problematics of Government', *British Journal of Sociology* 43(2): 173–205.

Roseberry, W. (1994) 'Hegemony and the Language of Contention', in G. Joseph and D. Nugent (eds) *Everyday Forms of State Formation. Revolution and the Negotiation of Rule in Modern Mexico*, pp. 355–66. Durham, NC: Duke University Press.

Roseberry, W. (2002) 'Understanding Capitalism, Historically, Structurally, Spatially', in D. Nugent (ed.) *Locating Capitalism in Time and Space*, pp. 61–79. Stanford, CA: Stanford University Press.

Sahlins, M. (1972) *Stone Age Economics*. Chicago, IL: Aldine-Atherton Inc.

Said, E. (1978) *Orientalism*. New York: Vintage Books.

Salemink, O. and M.B. Rasmussen (2016) 'After Dispossession. Ethnographic Approaches to Neoliberalism', *Focaal* 74: 3–12.

Scott, J. (2009) *The Art of Not Being Governed. An Anarchist History of Upland Southeast Asia*. New Haven, CT: Yale University Press.

Sikor, T. and C. Lund (eds) (2009) *The Politics of Possession. Property, Authority and Access to Natural Resources*. Chichester and Oxford: Wiley-Blackwell.

Solway, J. (1994) 'Drought as a "Revelatory Crisis": An Exploration of Shifting Entitlements and Hierarchies in the Kalahari, Botswana', *Development and Change* 25(3): 471–96.

Somers, M. (2008) *Genealogies of Citizenship. Markets, Statelessness, and the Right To Have Rights*. Cambridge: Cambridge University Press.

Spencer, J. (2007) *Anthropology, Politics and the State. Democracy and Violence in South Asia*. Cambridge: Cambridge University Press.

Stacey, P. (2014) '"The Chiefs, Elders, and People Have for Many Years Suffered Untold Hardships": Protests by Coalitions of the Excluded in British Northern Togoland, UN Trusteeship 1950–57,' *Journal of African History* 55(3): 423–44.

Stacey, P. and C. Lund (forthcoming, 2016) 'In a State of Slum: Governance in an Informal Urban Settlement in Ghana', *Journal of Modern African Studies* 54(4).

Stoler, A.L. (1995) *Race and the Education of Desire. Foucault's 'History of Sexuality' and the Colonial Order of Things*. Durham, NC: Duke University Press.

Strathern, M. (1999) *Property, Substance and Effect. Anthropological Essays on Persons and Things*. London: The Athlone Press.

Sundar, N. (ed.) (2009) *Legal Grounds. Natural Resources, Identity, and the Law in Jharkhand*. New Delhi: Oxford University Press.

Sundar, N. (2011) 'The Rule of Law and Citizenship in Central India. Post-colonial Dilemmas', *Citizenship Studies* 15(3–4): 419–32.

Taussig, M. (2005) *Law in a Lawless Land. Diary of a Limpieza in Colombia*. Chicago, IL: University of Chicago Press.

Taylor, C. (1989) *Sources of the Self. The Making of Modern Identity*. Cambridge: Cambridge University Press.

Taylor, C. (1994) 'The Politics of Recognition', in A. Gutmann (ed.) *Multiculturalism*, pp. 107–48. Princeton, NJ: Princeton University Press.

Tilly, C. (1985) 'War Making and State Making as Organized Crime', in P. Evans et al. (eds) *Bringing the State Back In*, pp. 161–91. Cambridge: Cambridge University Press.

Tilly, C. (1998) *Durable Inequality*. Berkeley, CA: University of California Press.

Tilly, C. (2005) *Identities, Boundaries, and Social Ties*. Boulder, Co and London: Paradigm Publishers.

Ubink, J. (2008) *In the Land of the Chiefs. Customary Law, Land Conflicts, and the Role of the State in Peri-Urban Ghana*. Leiden: Leiden University Press.

Ubink, J. and K. Amanor (eds) (2009) *Contesting Land and Custom in Ghana*. Leiden: Leiden University Press.

Vandergeest, P. and N.L. Peluso (1995) 'Territorialization and State Power in Thailand', *Theory and Society* 24(3): 385–426.

van Velsen, J. (1967) 'The Extended-case Method and Situational Analysis', in A.L. Epstein (ed.) *The Craft of Social Anthropology*, pp. 129–49. London: Tavistock Publications.

Vlassenroot, K. and T. Raeymaekers (2009) 'Kivu's Intractable Security Conundrum', *African Affairs* 108(432): 475–84.

Volkov, V. (2002) *Violent Entrepreneurs*. Ithaca, NY: Cornell University Press.

Watts, M. (2004) 'Resource Curse? Governmentality, Oil and Power in the Niger Delta, Nigeria', *Geopolitics* 9(1): 50–80.

Weber, M. (1922/1968) *Economy and Society: An Outline of Interpretive Sociology*. Berkeley, CA: University of California Press

Willis, J. (1993) *Mombassa, the Swahili, and the Making of the Mijikenda*. Oxford: Clarendon Press.

Wilson, I. (2010) 'Reconfiguring Rackets. Racket Regimes, Protection and the State in Post-New Order Jakarta', in E. Aspinall and G. van Klinken (eds) *The State and Illegality in Indonesia*, pp. 239–60. Leiden: KITLV Press.

Wilson, I. (2015) *The Politics of Protection Rackets in Post-New Order Indonesia. Coercive Capital, Authority and Street Politics*. London: Routledge.

Wilson, L. (2011) 'Beyond the Exemplary Centre: Knowledge, Power, and Sovereign Bodies in Java', *Journal of the Royal Anthropological Institute* 17(2): 301–17.

Winayanti, L. (2010) *Community Struggles for Land in Jakarta. A Case Study of Kampung Community Struggle to Obtain Security of Tenure*. Saarbrücken: Lambert Academic Publishing.

Winayanti, L. and H. Lang (2004) 'Provision of Urban Services in an Informal Settlement. A Case Study of Kampung Penas Tanggul, Jakarta', *Habitat International* 28: 41–65.

Winichakul, T. (1994) *Siam Mapped. A History of the Geo-Body of a Nation*. Honolulu, HI: University of Hawai'i Press.

Wolf, E. (1971) *Peasant Wars in the Twentieth Century*. London: Faber and Faber.

Wolf, E. (1999) *Envisioning Power. Ideologies of Dominance and Crisis*. Berkeley, CA: University of California Press.

Wolford, W. (2010) *This Land is Ours Now. Social Mobilization and the Meaning of Land in Brazil*. Durham, NC: Duke University Press.

2

Repatriation, *Refoulement*, Repair

Erin Collins

REFOULEMENT

Refoulement is a political term for forced repatriation. It means to push or force refugees back across a national border. Refoulement also names the process by which water is forced back into the channel of a river. During the dry season, Cambodia's Tonle Sap River flows into the Mekong at the juncture of the capital city of Phnom Penh. However, with the advent of the monsoon rains, the rising waters of the Mekong flow into the Tonle Sap, reversing the course of the smaller river. In a normal year this pulse pushes 38 million cubic metres of water north and west towards the Tonle Sap Lake, inundating the surrounding low-lying floodplain and covering the region in nutrient-rich silt (Molyvann, 2003: 146). The refoulement of water and sediment is often mobilized as a metaphor for the nation's troubled history of sovereignty lost and regained. Gottesman (2004: 12–13) opens his excellent political history of post-Khmer Rouge Cambodia thus:

> Cambodia's rivers tell many stories. The Mekong, the longest river in Southeast Asia, originates in the Himalayas and passes through China, Thailand, and Laos before entering Cambodia and heading toward the delta of southern Vietnam. A route for trade and immigration, it links Cambodia to the rest of the region geographically, politically, and economically. The Tonle Sap, by contrast, is a purely Cambodian river that flows from a lake of the same name in the center of the country south to Phnom Penh, where, a mere 110 kilometers from its source it joins the Mekong.

> Separately, each river represents a way to look at Cambodia — as a country swept along by regional and global trends or as a unique nation proceeding according to its own traditions. Small and vulnerable, Cambodia has been colonized, overwhelmed by foreign ideologies, torn apart by international conflict, and occupied by other countries. Faced with these incursions, Cambodians have attempted to define an uncontaminated national identity. One version of history thus inspires the other. In riparian terms, the mightier the flow of the international Mekong, the more the Tonle Sap stands as a symbol of Cambodian purity.

I want to thank Michael Eilenberg, Christian Lund and Jake Kosek for valuable discussions and advice. Four anonymous reviewers also provided very helpful suggestions and feedback. A National Science Foundation Graduate Research Fellowship and a University of California Pacific Rim Dissertation Fellowship supported this research.

Rule and Rupture: State Formation through the Production of Property and Citizenship, First Edition.
Edited by Christian Lund and Michael Eilenberg.
Chapters © 2017 by The Institute of Social Studies. Book compilation © 2017 John Wiley & Sons Ltd.

Ecological metaphors naturalize particular political paradigms. In Gottes-man's narrative, the complex ecology of the Mekong Delta region is parsed into separate elements: one ascribed a pure, national nature while the other is caricatured as a vector of foreign incursion. Yet, in Cambodia where civil war and cold war geopolitics were co-constituted, and national repair was yoked to a United Nations intervention, refoulement gathers together other histories of sovereign (re)making. Refoulement indexes Cambodia's tangled history of mass displacement, forced repatriation and racialized dispossession.

Attention to Cambodia's recent history of post-conflict reconciliation illuminates the biopolitical dimensions of sovereign power, engendered through modes of circulation and racial differentiation that overspill, as well as infuse, territorial forms of rule. While the term biopolitics is most often used to designate precisely that which is 'non-sovereign' and/or 'post-sovereign', Coleman and Grove (2009: 489–92) point out that Foucault more precisely contrasted biopolitics to a contract theory of sovereignty that 'equat[es] law with peace' and 'binds nation to state'. Where thick lines on geopolitical maps demarcate the borders of territorial sovereignty, state powers differentially claim, abandon and act on bodies as they circulate across borders.[1] Refoulement, as material process and as metaphor, links biological circulation to geopolitical violence.

In the sections that follow, I draw on diverse textual sources to analyse the rupture and reconstitution of Cambodian sovereignty through processes of circulation and differentiation. I analyse documents of the United Nations, the remnants of the Khmer Rouge[2] and the State of Cambodia apparatus, ranging from propaganda to records of meetings, to bureaucratic forms and to radio addresses.[3] These sources provide an account of the ways in which

1. Much recent scholarship has queried the conceptual coherence of sovereignty in an era of fractured polities and global flows. The ubiquity of the nation state system today obscures the geo-historical particularity of a territorially-based definition of sovereignty enshrined in the Treaty of Westphalia. As such, Agnew (2005) argues for a turn towards the more circumspect concept of 'effective sovereignty' scaled to the diversity of contemporary regimes and their extra-territorial natures. Meanwhile, Ong (2006) theorizes graduated sovereignty as the differential governance of groups and spaces in the throes of global neoliberalization. See also Berlant (2011: 98) for discussion of the affective relations of what she calls 'practical sovereignty'. Finally, Lund (2011) argues that property relations, as a forum of mutual recognition, produce fragmented sovereignty. See Coleman and Grove (2009) for an excellent discussion of the parallels between the taken for granted content of sovereignty in the twentieth century and the often taken for granted content of contemporary discussions of biopolitics.
2. The official name for the regime popularly known as the Khmer Rouge was the Communist Party of Kampuchea (CPK), which ruled between 1975 and 1979 as the regime of Democratic Kampuchea (DK).
3. Primary research was conducted by the author and two research assistants into the unsorted State of Cambodia and People's Republic of Kampuchea state papers at the National Archive (NAC) of Cambodia in Phnom Penh, the United Nations Transitional Authority in Cambodia (UNTAC) land dispute files (NAC), and the UNTAC Cambodian Election Materials, 1992–1993. For more information, see: http://www.crl.edu/areastudies/SEAM/index.htm

vying authorities conceived of, manipulated and dispatched refugee bodies in their bid for sovereign power. I attend to the watery metaphors of purity and contamination that course through the discourse of these three state bodies, conditioning claims to citizenship, property and rights. I contend that this language of rivers and flows did political work by naturalizing diverse programmes of population displacement.

I first discuss how Cambodia's refugee population became the focal point of contested national sovereignty in the 1980s and early 1990s. Control over migrant bodies was a basis of the Khmer Rouge's extra-territorial state power and international legitimacy in the border camps throughout the 1980s. Then, as cold war geopolitics thawed at the end of that decade, resolving Cambodia's refugee crisis became a matter of international urgency, and Cambodia a proving ground for an expanded United Nations mission. I next document the reincorporation of ethnic Khmer refugees and the simultaneous displacement of ethnic Vietnamese Cambodians in the course of national reconciliation from 1991 to 1993. The Khmer Rouge and the State of Cambodia regime leadership each, in their own way, deployed anti-Vietnamese racism as a means of sovereign differentiation, 'fragmenting the field of the biological that power controls' (Foucault et al., 2003: 255). The chapter concludes that it was the differential sorting of the population into racialized categories, as well as the realignment of national population and territory, that contoured Cambodia's sovereign remaking.

NATIONAL BODIES

On 17 April 1975 the Khmer Rouge overwhelmed Cambodia's capital city of Phnom Penh and inaugurated the short but devastating rule of Democratic Kampuchea. The regime quickly depopulated the capital city and other urban centres, separating families and forcibly redistributing the population among rural agricultural collectives and infrastructural work camps throughout the country. In line with the regime's paranoid and erratic style of rule most people were moved several times, engendering further dislocation. While the scale of horror wrought by Khmer Rouge cannot be reduced to a death toll, the statistics are nonetheless staggering. In a little less than four years, between a quarter and a fifth of the total population was 'let to die' or made to die (Kiernan, 2014: 458–63). Those who did survive were in general traumatized and malnourished, and had no way of knowing if their loved ones lived, or where they were.

When the mixed Khmer and Vietnamese forces crossed the Vietnamese border and overthrew the genocidal regime in December 1978, remnants of Khmer Rouge forces retreated to the Thai border. As they fled, they compelled a sizable population of between 50,000 and 80,000 people to flee with them (Evans and Rowley, 1990: 3). Meanwhile, an equal number of other survivors walked willingly to the border in search of food, aid and security.

This mixed collective arrived on Thai national soil in early 1979, and were first accommodated as refugees. As refugees, they were eligible for third country resettlement and protected against refoulement.[4] However, at the end of April 1979 the Thai government closed the border to Cambodians seeking asylum, forcing new arrivals back into Cambodian territory (Robinson, 1998/2000: 67). Having survived a genocide, Cambodians who arrived between April and October were forced back through mountainous, malarial and land-mined terrain.

The shocking images and high death toll that resulted from these acts of refoulement precipitated a United Nations Summit, at which a semantic solution was found for a political problem. Thailand agreed to again admit Cambodians into Thai territory as 'displaced persons', a nomenclature stripped of the rights of the refugee (Terry, 2013: 114). Other asylum seekers, such as Vietnamese boat people, were categorized as economic migrants or illegal migrants, designations that differentially exposed them to brutality and arbitrary outcomes (Jackson, 1987). The decade of the 1980s was punctuated by a number of policy reversals by Thailand. In January 1988, the Thai state adopted an aggressive 'pushback policy' towards refugees, whereby boats from Vietnam were forced back into the ocean (Robinson, 1998/2000: 182). A few months later they changed course again, re-extending first asylum rights to Vietnamese refugees (ibid.).

Over the course of the 1980s, border camps grew into displaced cities.[5] As stateless polities they were subject to Thai martial law and governed by whichever of Cambodia's rebel factions controlled the camp. Remnants of the Khmer Rouge leadership controlled five camps, including the two largest, while the Khmer People's National Liberation Front (KPNLF) controlled two camps, and forces loyal to the deposed Prince Sihanouk controlled one (Jackson, 1987: 6). These three factions were loosely united within the Coalition Government of Democratic Kampuchea (CGDK), an entity united only by their common opposition to the Vietnamese occupation and the Vietnamese-supported People's Republic of Kampuchea (PRK) state, ensconced in Phnom Penh (Ledgerwood and Un, 2002: 5).

The Cambodian refugee crisis refracted multi-scalar cold war geopolitics. The United States, China and the United Nations recognized the CGDK as the Cambodian state in exile, while the USSR and its allies recognized the PRK as the legitimate Cambodian state (Jordans, 1996: 138). These geopolitical entanglements left the refugee population vulnerable to rent-seeking behaviour by Thai military personnel, political manipulation by the border Khmer Rouge, and recurrent forced relocation between camps and

4. The Rights of the Refugee are enshrined in Articles 1, 55 and 56 of the United Nations Charter, www.un.org/en/documents/charter/
5. Throughout the 1980s, Khao I Dang camp was the second largest Khmer city in the world (Robinson, 1998/2000: 71).

rebel zones on both sides of the national border.[6] By the late 1980s, however, the cold war had begun to thaw, and there was international momentum to resolve the Cambodian quagmire.

In April 1991, 14 member states of the United Nations and Cambodia's four warring factions signed the Paris Peace Agreement (PPA). Officially titled 'Agreement Concerning the Sovereignty, Independence, Territorial Integrity and Inviolability, Neutrality, and National Unity of Cambodia',[7] the PPA outlined a comprehensive solution for Cambodia's decades-long civil war and the region's refugee crisis. Under the authority of the United Nations Transitional Authority in Cambodia (UNTAC), Cambodia's national space was to be reassembled out of warring factions. The refugee populations living in Thai border camps were to be poured back into the container of the nation space, and verification of the removal of foreign forces (a euphemism for Vietnamese forces) was a paramount responsibility of the peacekeeping operation. In other words: national populations and boundaries were to be realigned and foreign forces expelled.[8]

On 21 November 1991, seven months after the signing of the PPA, the Thai Government, Cambodia's Supreme National Council and the Office of the United Nations High Commissioner for Refugees signed a tripartite memorandum, 'Relating to the Repatriation of Cambodian Refugees and Displaced Persons from Thailand', that definitively dissolved the contested refugee status of the border camp population:

> The contracting Parties shall cooperate with one another to insure that repatriation will be on a voluntary basis. *Where the contracting parties agree that*, with regard to the Cambodian refugees and displaced persons in the border camps in Thailand, *the circumstances that create the status of genuine refugee have ceased to exist, this principle will no longer be relevant.* (quoted, with emphasis, in Williams, 1997: 172)

By agreeing to ensure voluntary repatriation, these three political institutions assumed the authority to declare repatriation voluntary on behalf of individual refugees (ibid.). As repatriation was voluntary, the 'status of genuine refugee... ceased to exist', and their right to non-refoulement no longer held. Meanwhile, the Paris Peace Accord recognized the border population

---

6. For an in-depth discussion of the differences between camps and zones, as well as the circulation of refugees and displaced persons among them, see Robinson (1998/2000).

7. The Paris Peace Agreement begins with a preamble affirming the sanctity and mutually reinforcing tenets of sovereignty, freedom, human rights and security. See: http://www.usip.org/publications/peace-agreements-cambodia

8. The ambiguity around what constituted 'foreign forces' led the Khmer Rouge and their allies to insist that it referred to all ethnic Vietnamese in Cambodia. Jordans (1996: 138) writes, 'border forces attempted to unite Cambodia's fractured society on the basis of race, against Vietnamese occupation. Employing the common denominator of "race" meant every single ethnic Vietnamese in Cambodia — soldiers, fisher folk, migrants; men, women and children — were imagined to be integral cogs in the machinery of Hanoi's historical mission to "swallow" (*lep*) Cambodia'.

as refugees and, in so doing, assured them the right of self-determination in destination and of non-discrimination in resettlement within Cambodia (Robinson, 1998/2000: 74). In essence, then, displaced Cambodians became refugees as they crossed the national border (Eastmond, 2002: 5). Discursive contortions first trapped the border population in a state of limbo for more than a decade as displaced persons, and then returned them to Cambodian soil as refugees. Such shifts illustrate a biopolitics of sovereign repair where refugee status no longer attached to fixed bodies, territories or circumstances, but was rather shaped by national and transnational circulations and calculations.

INTERNATIONAL BODIES

Cambodia's protracted conflict served as a zone of experimentation for a renewed and expanded United Nations. The Paris Peace Accord mandated a transnational intervention in the name of sovereign reconstitution. Yet, as Ghosh wryly notes, 'in the contemporary world, sovereignty resides precisely where the UN's peacekeepers do not' (1994: 421).

UN Security-General Elect Boutros-Boutros Ghali sought to redefine the role of the United Nations in the rapidly shifting geopolitical context of the early 1990s. Ghali (1992: point 17) reaffirmed the centrality of state sovereignty in the post-cold war era, while asserting that global economic, discursive and environmental circulations had fundamentally reconfigured it:

> The foundation stone of this work is and must remain the State. Respect for its fundamental sovereignty and integrity are crucial to any common international progress. The time of absolute and exclusive sovereignty, however, has passed; its theory was never matched by reality. It is the task of leaders of States today to understand this and to find a balance between the needs of good internal governance and the requirements of an ever more interdependent world. Commerce, communications and environmental matters transcend administrative borders; but inside those borders is where individuals carry out the first order of their economic, political and social lives. The United Nations has not closed its door. Yet if every ethnic, religious or linguistic group claimed statehood, there would be no limit to fragmentation, and peace, security and economic well-being for all would become ever more difficult to achieve.

In an interconnected world, Ghali argued, state sovereignty is permeable (to supranational forces) and restricted (unlimited claims to self-rule threaten the peace, security and well-being of all). However, just as not all sovereign claims are equally valid, not all nations are equally permeable. Where, during the 1970s and 1980s, unprecedented numbers of refugees had resettled in countries of the global North, the 1990s saw a shift from a politics of refuge to a politics of repatriation (Hughes, 2009; Malkki, 1995) whereby 'former refugees [were] thus to be re-fitted as the missing parts into the disrupted and dis-membered national body' (Eastmond, 2002: 3). Third country resettlement gave way to first country return. The new humanitarian discourse of 'the right to return' was accompanied by romanticized notions of home and homecoming (Malkki, 1995). Radio UNTAC broadcasts and UNHCR pamphlets instructed refugees to take the cash option and 'go and settle with family'. Yet, for a great number of Cambodian refugees, 'family' and 'home' were deeply fraught concepts, mimetically tied to trauma, insecurity and deprivation (Thompson, 1993). The celebration of Cambodian refugees' right of return obscured the fact that for many, repatriation was, in fact, a further moment of displacement.

Within Cambodia, choice of destination was restricted by the scarcity of arable, mine-free land. Refugees were initially given three options: (A) 2 ha of agricultural land, (B) a plot of land for a house and building supplies, or (C) US$ 50 per adult and US$ 25 per child support.[9] However, it was immediately evident that there was insufficient available land within the Western provinces where the vast number of refugees elected to resettle. Thus, the cash option (Option C) was in many cases the only option (Williams, 1997: 174).[10] In practice, the refugee repatriation process entailed a slide from a guaranteed right against refoulement to the right to national return (which was also a command) and the right to self-determination therein — a right manifested in the (forced) option of a cash grant. Lack of self-determination was depoliticized through market mechanisms.

Cambodian refugees were overdetermined international bodies. Their circulation or internment was at each point a matter of geopolitical calculation. Put in terms of Gottesman's (2004: 12–13) riparian metaphor, 'the mightier the flow' of international forces, the more the refugee '[stood] as a symbol of Cambodian purity'.

BODIES AS TERRITORIES

The body is itself national territory at a fine scale. In lieu of control over national territory, refugee bodies constituted valuable territory for the resistance factions. The Khmer Rouge regime's rebuilding on the border received international support, in part, based on 'representation' of the sizeable refugee population (Reynell, 1989). Political recognition was also forthcoming: Democratic Kampuchea held the United Nations seat for Cambodia from 1979 to 1982, and continued to represent Cambodia within the United Nations as the head of the Coalition Government of Democratic Kampuchea until 1992. In the context of the Paris Peace Agreement, Khmer Rouge leadership sought to transmute international recognition (sovereignty as an external relation) into national authority (sovereignty as an internal relation)

---

9. All refugees received food aid for a year.
10. Williams (1997: 167) notes that, in the end, 88 per cent of refugees received a cash grant, while only 8 per cent received land and wood for building a house, and 3 per cent received farmland.

through controlled repatriation of the border refugee population. In other words, the Khmer Rouge sought reterritorialization through repatriation.

In the early 1980s and again in 1988, the Khmer Rouge engaged in selective, tactical repatriation as a means of national reterritorialization. Robinson (1998/2000: 75) highlights the following saying that circulated within camps under their control:

> *Those who go back first will sleep on cots*
> *Those who go back second will sleep on mats*
> *Those who go back third will sleep in the mud*
> *Those who go back last will sleep under the ground.*

In this saying, gradations of social standing were projected onto bodily relations in domestic space. While a homeowner sleeps on a cot, a servant or a boarder sleeps on a mat, a transient sleeps in the mud, and the dead sleep under the ground. The message is clear: to wait for a political solution is to risk landlessness or even death. Following the signing of the PPA in 1991, the Khmer Rouge sought to repatriate more refugees ahead of the UN's repatriation programme. This time, the Khmer Rouge promised families willing to repatriate under their timeline and within zones of their control up to 3 ha of land to clear and cultivate.[11] The regime again used fear of property scarcity among the camp populations, and played on what was arguably the most acute anxiety for refugees, namely that they would return to Cambodia after as many as thirteen years living in Thai border camps, landless (Refugee Policy Group, 1991: 30). As the material base of an agrarian economy and often the sole asset of the poor, access to land modulated the line between reintegration and ruin for returning refugees.[12]

Where the Khmer Rouge asserted sovereign claim over refugee bodies, they viewed foreign bodies within Cambodia as a direct threat to national sovereignty. Purity and contamination were central to Khmer Rouge statecraft and discourse (Hinton, 2002). During the Peace Process, their leadership entreated Khmers to rise up and cleanse the nation from the scourge

---

11. Information/Education Division, 24 July 1993, 'Aspects of life in the NADK rear-bases: Corridor 505 and Samlaut Sector (SW Battambang and Pursat)', UNTAC Information and Education Division papers.
12. UN authorities were aware of the dangers of extending this logic into the space of the nation state. One report cautioned:

> Return under factional control will have both humanitarian and political implications. Clustering of returnees in villages where they form a majority may lead to attempts to impose an administration independent of Phnom Penh and to reverse existing laws. This seems to be the KR goal in threatening to repatriate its camp populations independent of the UN plan, to zones currently under its control. Especially dangerous will be any attempt by military leaders or civilian refugees to seize homes and lands occupied by others since 1979. Return under factional control also may delay integration and create polarization into those who stayed and those who left for the border. (Refugee Policy Group, 1991: 32)

of the Vietnamese (Edwards and Swift, 1996).[13] Forces loyal to the Khmer Rouge committed a spate of murders and violent land grabs in the transitional period. On 10 March 1993, 33 ethnic Vietnamese citizens were massacred (including 15 women and 14 children), and 34 more wounded, in the floating village of Chong Kneas (Jordans, 1996: 139). In Kampong Chhnang, three families enlisted the help of Khmer Rouge soldiers to force off five other intruding families. The five families then claimed adjacent land, displacing other families in what became a chain reaction affecting 20 families (Teft, 1991: 5). In another case, people in Battambang burned over 100 homes belonging to ethnic Vietnamese families near Bek Chan airfield, and subsequently claimed their land.[14] In Phnom Penh, there were a number of grenade attacks against Vietnamese-owned businesses.[15] Khmer Rouge's radio mouthpiece, 'Voice of the Great National Union Front of Cambodia', celebrated these attacks, saying: 'if the people do not deal with [the Vietnamese] personally, Cambodians are certain to have no place to live'.[16] All told, nearly 200 ethnic Vietnamese Cambodians were murdered in the six months leading up to the UN-supervised elections of 1993 (Amnesty International, 1993: 6).

UNTAC officials found widespread acceptance of the basic tenets of Khmer Rouge's anti-Vietnamese propaganda among the border refugee population.[17] In 1991, UNHCR brought six refugees from Khao I Dang to see

---

13. The regime was long committed to the concept of 'permanent revolution', engaging the population in a ceaseless process of national purification through the rooting out of class enemies. Yet the most tangible enemy identified in Democratic Kampuchea's policies and propaganda was a racialized, rather than a class enemy. Those that the regime charged as spies, and cleansed from the revolutionary space of the nation, were said to have 'Khmer bodies but Vietnamese heads' (Gottesman, 2004: 161). This slippage from class to race recalls Foucault's argument:

    Whenever socialism has been forced to stress the problem of struggle, the struggle against the enemy, of the elimination of the enemy within capitalist society itself, and when, therefore, it has had to think about the physical confrontation with the class enemy in capitalist society, racism does raise its head, because it is the only way in which socialist thought, which is after all very much bound up with the themes of biopower, can rationalize the murder of its enemies. (Foucault et al., 2003: 262)

14. UNTAC Education and Information report on DK Radio, 29 January 1993. The reported violence occurred on 25 January in Battambang. The 'Voice of the Great National Union Front of Cambodia in Cambodia', the source on which UNTAC was reporting, is Khmer Rouge's Radio.

15. On the evening of 29 March 1993 there were attacks against three Vietnamese-run businesses, resulting in eight deaths and numerous casualties.

16. UNTAC Education and Information report and translation of 'Voice of the Great National Union Front of Cambodia' broadcast, 27 March 1993.

17. 'Report on Field Trip to Kompong Cham Province 18–15 January 1993', 28 January 1993. UNTAC Information Education Papers. See Edwards and Swift (1996) for a discussion of representations of 'others' by the Khmer Rouge and other factions.

at first hand the liberalization of the country, and the freedoms enjoyed by citizens. The expectation was that this would pique interest among camp residents for voluntary return. Instead, the visitors reported that there were Vietnamese everywhere — 'dressed as Cambodians and speaking fluent Khmer. They said that there was no freedom. They saw what they had been expecting to see' (Refugee Policy Group, 1991: 21). Popular belief in Vietnamese occupation and colonization was such that the lack of visible Vietnamese led them to determine not that the Vietnamese had left, but that they had become fully integrated and invisible.[18]

In the following transcription of a Khmer Rouge Senior Command meeting, the interplay of multiple biopolitical realms is striking. Senior officials expressed anxiety over waning sovereign power in the idiom of race, miasma, sexuality and nature:

> The Chinese have turned cold. Their situation is comparable to that of a boat, which is just about to reach the pier: they are killing the engine. The Thai don't seem to know what to do anymore. It's comparable to the foreign expression 'impuissance'. Alatas knows that this is the way the situation is evolving, but he has become impuissance. The Chinese also know what is going on, but are impuissance. Everyone knows the Yuon are all over Phnom Penh, but they've all become impuissance.

Yuon is a racially invective term for Vietnamese. That the Chinese 'are killing the engine', and that the Thai and Chinese are 'impuissance', refer to the Khmer Rouge's loss of geopolitical allies in the Peace Process. The transcription continues:

> First, the Yuon are in Cambodia without there being anyone to control them and so they will continue to be the masters. Second, the second level is called 'Yuonization' of the Cambodian people. Although it is true that more than one million Yuon nationals have taken up residence in the Eastern part of Cambodia, still only a few have come to take up residence in central and western Cambodia. These Yuon are just waiting for the moment when the Khmer Rouge[19] no longer have any punch and then both their army and their people will simply come right in.

> Therefore, the only way to cut through this muddy water is to put in some alum and stir things up. We've had experience of this already in Ta Ngok camp ... human beings in the camp were human beings belonging to us, but the committee was mischievous and didn't want them to come with us. However we conducted a battle to remove those scoundrels and we were able to seize the people.[20]

---

18. Information/Education Division, 24 July 1993, 'Aspects of life in the NADK rear-bases: Corridor 505 and Samlaut Sector (SW Battambang and Pursat)'. UNTAC Information and Education Division papers Section V: 'Obstacles to Returning Home'.
19. The UNTAC Education and Information Division translator of this meeting uses the term Khmer Rouge in their translation, though it is unlikely that the DK senior command would have used this term to describe themselves. The original Khmer language transcription is not available.
20. Transcription of a Khmer Rouge Senior Command meeting from February 1992. UNTAC Education and Information Papers. (Translation by UNTAC Education and Information Division.)

Where the first paragraph refers to the 'impotence' of the regime's allies, in the second paragraph the Khmer Rouge leadership warn of the Vietnamese-ization of the Cambodian people, and the third paragraph asserts a territorial claim over the refugee population. As it reads, 'human beings in the camp were human beings belonging to us'. In their discursive slippage between an external and internal enemy — from 'the Yuon are in Cambodia' to the 'Yuonization of the Cambodian population' we see the function of racism in creating a 'biopolitical-type relationship' between the life of one and the death of another (Foucault et al., 2003: 255). Having identified an internal enemy within the national body, the Khmer Rouge were then free to, in the words of their Senior Command, 'conduct a battle to remove those scoundrels [and] seize the people'.

THE WATER JAR IS FOR CATCHING WATER

In a meeting with the UNHCR head of refugee repatriation Shar Kibria in May 1989, the State of Cambodia's Prime Minister Hun Sen opened the meeting by saying, 'It seems there are five minutes left in a ten-year competition'.[21] By this he articulated both the historic conjuncture and the privileged place of refugee repatriation in it. The 'ten-year competition' was a reference to the decade-long impasse in which his Phnom Penh-based and Vietnamese-supported state had been militarily and geopolitically opposed by the internationally recognized Coalition Government of Democratic Kam-puchea state in exile.

Turning to the matter of refugee repatriation — the main topic of the meeting — Hun Sen added, 'For me there is no obstacle. As we say, the water jar is for catching water'.[22] As the Prime Minister of the state power that controlled the vast majority of Cambodian territory, yet lacked international sovereign recognition, Hun Sen was only too happy to facilitate resettlement for returnees. Ten years of state rule based in Phnom Penh put Hun Sen at the helm of a diffuse state apparatus with public authority from the group and village up to the provincial scale. However, Hun Sen's People's Republic of Kampuchea (PRK) state lacked both international political authority and legitimacy among the refugee population. Thus, hooking returnees into the weft and weave of state space, in the context of the UNTAC repatriation programme, manifested sovereign authority for his regime as both an internal and external relation.

The meeting between Hun Sen and Shar Kibria occurred just weeks af-ter the PRK had adopted a set of liberal reforms (which included a name change to the State of Cambodia). Arguably the most significant (and

---

21. Notes from 2 May 1989 meeting between Prime Minister Hun Sen and Shar Kibria, President of UNBRO and Director of ESCAP in Bangkok, PRK papers, NAC.
22. Ibid.

popular) among the changes was the introduction of a comprehensive land reform programme. Land reform is a powerful mechanism of mutual recognition between state authority and citizen, concretized through property relations (Lund, 2011). Cambodia's 1989 land reform predicated land allocation on existing settlement in 1989. In essence, this made land rights contemporaneous and coextensive with regime authority prior to the UN intervention and political plurality. The 1989 land reform initiated a process whereby residents applied to the State of Cambodia (SOC) for recognition of their claims. This process of application, in turn, engendered mutual recognition between claimant and SOC apparatus as *the* legitimate state authority in a moment of political uncertainty (Collins, 2016).

Refugees, meanwhile, were issued with identification cards and family books at the six temporary Refugee Processing Centres.[23] While the land reform formalized the settlement pattern that emerged in the 1980s — when the refugee population was in border camps — this did not necessarily preclude land claims of returnees. Rather, it established the terrain of negotiation, upon which returnees were invited to address their claims to property rights to SOC state officials.[24] Refugees returning voluntarily from the border prior to the UNTAC intervention were a special exception to the land law. A Circular 'Issuing Guidance on Land Management and Use Policy' states: 'Toward Cambodian Refugees — Cambodian people who stayed abroad, that return back into the country and other people who abandon the enemy line and return as repatriated people, we will offer free housing and farming land to the ability of each base organization'.[25] Such accommodation is an illustration of how, in the wake of rupture, political authority is constituted through the friction between solicitation, negotiation and contestation that bring the state apparatus and the population into an entanglement of mutual recognition (Lund, Introduction to this issue).

In 1992 most refugees took the Option C package and settled within the western provinces of Battambang, Siem Reap and Bantea Meanchey.[26] These provinces contained rich agricultural and fishing lands, and had the added benefit of being proximate to the Thai border in case it was again necessary to flee. In theory, SOC base authorities were not responsible for finding land for Option C refugees. However, in practice Option C refugees presented considerable challenges to national reconciliation and sovereign reconstitution. Vong South, the Representative of the Kandal Provincial

23. Council of Ministers Directive No. 97 SCHN.AV, 27 June 1992. Signed by Kong Somol, Deputy Director Representative Council of Ministers.
24. This point problematizes the oft-repeated claim that an 'implicit' goal of the land reform was to '[pre-empt] serious consideration of property restitution to Cambodian refugees and IDPs' (Williams, 2008: 40). I contend that understanding the land reform as primarily an instrument of exclusion radically undersells its significance.
25. Document 03SNn, 3 June 1989, State of Cambodia papers, NAC.
26. UMBRO Repatriation Plans, SOC papers, NAC.

People's Committee, wrote in a report on refugee resettlement to the Council
of Ministers:

> We still face some difficulty for Type C families. When they first return, they chose type
> C to live with siblings and parents but when they arrived in their native land they find that
> their siblings and parents have all died . . . . This is why they live without refuge, and some
> depend on the base authority and others claim public or private land causing chaos for the
> base authority.[27]

Central State of Cambodia authorities instructed local officials to find
suitable land for them regardless of their category. In a speech addressed
to Provincial District and Commune People Committee members in Phnom
Penh, the Deputy Director of the National Committee in charge of repatriation admonished the base authorities:

> Do not think that we do not have any responsibilities to returnees who choose Option C, on
> the contrary, we have to pay close attention to their situation since if they can't develop in
> 1993, our burden will become more and more. . . . I understand the difficulty in this, but I ask
> you to help the Royal Government in providing farmland and housing to returnees regardless
> of whether they are A, B or C option.[28]

Contrast the position taken above with that of the SOC's Council of Ministers
in the following case, in which 355 families, comprising 1,646 people from
the Site Two refugee camp, formed an 'Association' and requested repatriation as a collective to two adjoining communes.[29] The Cabinet Council of
Ministers summarily rejected this request. Their notes provide the following frank explanation: 'Keeping in mind the standing of the government,
we cannot build refugee camps within Cambodia'.[30] Not surprisingly, the
SOC would not reproduce zones of exception to their own authority within
Cambodian territory.

When, in late 1992, repatriation was well under way, the Deputy Director
of the Council of Ministers and the Director of the National Committee in
Charge of Repatriation provided the following instructions to Provincial and
City delegates:

> Our good work at this moment has shown the international community and expressed to
> repatriating families our Royal Government's honesty, and has strongly confirmed our com-
> mitment to '*freedom of election and human rights*', showing that the violations we were
> accused of in the past are now over. We ask you to strengthen your capacity to accommodate

---

27. Document No 010 RBA (rh), 'Inventory of refugee families that have been allocated land in
    Kandal Province up to January 31, 1993', 2 February 1993.
28. 'Solving the Land Problem for Repatriated People', speech in Banteay Meanchey Province
    to provincial and city delegates by HC Kong Samol, Deputy Director of Council of Ministers
    and Director of National Committee in charge of repatriation, no date.
29. Letter No. 1501 KBPS, 24 June 1992. The two adjoining communes were Roleap and
    Ansachambak in Krankor District, Pursat Province.
30. No. 1501 KBPS, Education Department's 'case filing notes' filed as 'Cabinet Council of
    Ministers Decision', 21 July 1992.

repatriated families who want to live in their hometown, particularly on their former land and farmland. If we can implement this, the party and the state will benefit in the estimation of reunited Khmer families.[31]

Here, refugee repatriation sits at the centre of a web of interferential sovereign relations: international legitimacy, human rights, democratic elections, land reform and family. The quotation illustrates how the SOC endeavoured to bolster its sovereign authority through a politics of mutual recognition and domestic repair.

It bears mentioning that the issuance of instructions from central State of Cambodia offices to provide land for refugees did not necessarily result in compliance. Orders from central SOC authorities to provide refugees with land often came into direct conflict with pre-existing claims, as well as with local authorities' own interests. For example, in June 1992 approximately 100 people of Koki Commune in Kien Svay District entered the compound of the Commune People's Committee office, 'demarcating the area, and dividing pieces of land between them to enable construction of houses'.[32] The file notes of the land dispute case record that the group was composed of 'twenty demobilized soldiers, five families of returnees and the others of unemployed and landless poor'.[33] Then there is a case in the same Commune, in which the Chief of the Land Committee rails against 46 'anarchists' who occupied 5,744 square metres of state property in Toul Thnoat village.[34] The Chief of the Land Committee notes in his statement that some of these 'devilish people' are repatriated people with category 'C'.[35] In a final example, 17 villagers of Chong Prek lodged a complaint against their Commune and District Committee Chiefs who, they allege, resold land to newcomers that had earlier been allocated to them. The villagers wrote, 'We do not agree with the local authority to divide [land] for constructing residences because all these lands are exploited by present living people every year for their living and if the state power is holding on like this it seems to slit open the throat of the people'.[36] These glimpses into contestation over land show how the recognition of one group's claim to property and belonging often entailed the usurpation of the claim of another.

The differential protection of populations and their property is particularly stark in terms of the experience of the ethnic Vietnamese population in this

31. 'Solving the Land Problem for Repatriated People', speech in Banteay Meanchey Province to provincial and city delegates by H.C. Kong Samol, Deputy Director of Council of Ministers and Director of National Committee in Charge of Repatriation, no date.
32. File 015/KSU, UNTAC Complaints files, NAC.
33. Ibid.
34. Report dated 19 November 1992, File 041/KSU, Box XX UNTAC Complaints Files, NAC.
35. File 041/KSU, Box XX UNTAC Complaints Files, NAC.
36. Ref: K/INV/24/92.

period. In a speech made before party, police and government officials in July of 1992, Prime Minister Hun Sen stated:

> In the future the [opposition] will find cause to fight with Vietnamese who are living in Cambodia, in order to provoke a demonstration [and] force the SOC police to protect Vietnamese instead of the nation. Therefore, Ministry of Police and all Province-Cities have to cooperate with UNTAC by letting UNTAC solve this problem. Our police do not protect Vietnamese [because] this is a human rights issue which is the responsibility of UNTAC.[37]

In the phrase, 'to protect Vietnamese instead of the nation', Hun Sen excised the Vietnamese population from the national body. In so doing, he articulated the function of racism to fragment the population so as to 'introduce a break into the domain of life that is under power's control' (Foucault et al., 2003: 254).

In December 1992, Hun Sen again made a racialized distinction among the refugee population. Invoking the metaphor of the home he instructed:

> For all the repatriated people, I will prepare for their arrival because I am the owner of the house. However, for returnees from Vietnam we have to be careful because they don't want to return into Cambodia, they wait for third country [resettlement], but now they have to return to Cambodia in order to go abroad. Repatriated people from Vietnam really want to live in Phnom Penh, and it is difficult for the Royal Government since they are not original Khmer, so if there are any political events, we request [UN]HCR to be fully responsible.[38]

Here, Hun Sen made a distinction between ethnic Khmer returnees, who would be governed as citizens, and ethnic Vietnamese returnees, who would be governed as global, but not national, humanitarian subjects. In both of the above statements Hun Sen distinguished between the sphere of international human rights and that of state protection. As such he confirmed Agamben's contention (1998: 133) that the separation of humanitarianism from politics follows directly from the original distinction — identified by Arendt — between the rights of man and the rights of the citizen (Arendt, 1968).

(RE)REFOULEMENT

In April 1993, Sadako Ogata, the head of the UNHCR, gave a speech in Phnom Penh in which she declared the end of the Indochinese refugee crisis. Nate Thayer (1995) noted at the time that had Ms Ogata turned around and

---

37. Document No. 1224 SCHN.SR. 'Notes of Cabinet Council of Ministers Meeting', 17 July 1992.
38. Document No. 133 KHN. 'Hearing between H.E. Hun Sen and Mr De Mello', UNHCR, Phnom Penh, 25 December 1992.

looked at the stretch of the Mekong River visible from her window, she would have been confronted with the falsity of that statement. On that day, and in the days and weeks that followed, a steady stream of fishing boats full of ethnic Vietnamese Cambodians travelled down that stretch of river towards the Vietnamese border (Thayer, 1995: 21). An estimated 20,000–30,000 ethnic Vietnamese Cambodians fled ethnic violence in the run-up to the 1993 elections (Jordans, 1996: 136–8). The UN assisted through 'Operation Safe Passage', effectively acting as armed escort that protected their bodies in exodus (though not in place).

Despite using the language of national repair and reconciliation, all state powers treated ethnic Vietnamese and ethnic Khmer differently with regards to their right to land and to return. In Cambodia in the late 1980s and early 1990s, who counted as a member of the nation (and thus needed to be incorporated for the nation to be whole) and who was deemed foreign (and thus could be expelled) was a function of racialized difference as much as citizenship or territory. This was made clear in August 1993, when an UNTAC Information and Education officer visited a camp of stranded refugees on the Vietnamese border, and filed the following report:

> There are currently about 200 families stranded at the CV3B border crossing point. Their applications to enter Cambodia have been flatly rejected without explanation by the Cambodian border authorities. These people are Cambodians of ethnic Vietnamese origin who fled Cambodia after violence and intimidation carried out against them during the pre-election period. The living situation of these refugees has reached a very tenuous point. They have exhausted their savings after several months of enforced non-productivity in Vietnam. Some will very soon be facing starvation. Refugees interviewed by the Information Officer unanimously and unequivocally stated their desire to return to Cambodia as soon as possible. This decision is primarily driven by a wish to return to what for them, and for generations of their ancestors, is home. (Jordans, 1993: np)

That the talismanic power of 'home' did not call forth an international intervention to ensure these refugees' right of return, as it had for their Khmer counterparts on the Thai border, illustrates that it was the differential sorting of the population into racialized categories, as well as the realignment of national population and territory, that contoured Cambodia's sovereign remaking.

The watery metaphors that coursed through the state discourse of the United Nations, the Khmer Rouge and the State of Cambodia naturalized particular bodies and circulations, and denaturalized others. Refoulement is a semantically dense concept. It means to push or force refugees back across a national border, while it also describes the process by which water is forced back into the channel of a river. In Cambodia's brief but intensive period of sovereign remaking, the humanitarian and the biophysical content of refoulement were intimately entwined.

REFERENCES

Agamben, G. (1998) *Homo Sacer: Sovereign Power and Bare Life*. Stanford, CA: Stanford University Press.

Agnew, J. (2005) 'Sovereignty Regimes: Territoriality and State Authority in Contemporary World Politics', *Annals of the Association of American Geographers* 95(2): 437–61.

Amnesty International (1993) 'Cambodia: Arbitrary Killings of Ethnic Vietnamese'. Amnesty International. www.amnesty.org/en/documents/asa23/005/1993/en/ (accessed 28 July 2016).

Arendt, H. (1968) *Imperialism: Part Two of the Origins of Totalitarianism*. Boston, MA: Houghton Mifflin Harcourt.

Berlant, L.G. (2011) *Cruel Optimism*. Durham, NC: Duke University Press.

Coleman, M. and K. Grove (2009) 'Biopolitics, Biopower and the Return of Sovereignty', *Environment and Planning D, Society and Space* 27(3): 489–507.

Collins, E. (2016) 'Postsocialist Informality: The Making of Owners, Squatters and State Rule in Phnom Penh, Cambodia (1989–1993)', *Environment and Planning A*. DOI: 10.1177/0308518X16658664

Eastmond, M. (2002) 'Reconstruction and the Politics of Homecoming: Repatriation of Refugees in Cambodia'. Working Paper No 1. Gothenburg: Department of Social Anthropology, Göteborg University.

Edwards, P. and J. Swift (1996) 'Imaging the Other in Cambodian Nationalist Discourse before and during the UNTAC Period', in J. Ledgerwood and S. Heder (eds) *Propaganda, Politics, and Violence in Cambodia. A Democratic Transition under United Nations Peace-Keeping*, pp. 50–72. New York: Routledge Press.

Evans, G. and K. Rowley (1990) *Red Brotherhood at War: Vietnam, Cambodia and Laos since 1975*. London: Verso.

Foucault, M., M. Bertani, A. Fontana, F. Ewald and D. Macey (2003) *Society Must Be Defended: Lectures at the Collège de France, 1975–1976 (Vol. 1)*. London: Macmillan.

Ghali, B. (1992) 'An Agenda for Peace, Preventive Diplomacy, Peacemaking and Peace-Keeping'. Report of the Secretary-General pursuant to the statement adopted by the Summit Meeting of the Security Council. www.cfr.org/peacekeeping/report-un-secretary-general-agenda-peace/p23439 (accessed 28 July 2016).

Ghosh, A. (1994) 'The Global Reservation: Notes toward an Ethnography of International Peacekeeping', *Cultural Anthropology* 9(3): 412–22.

Gottesman, E. (2004) *Cambodia after the Khmer Rouge: Inside the Politics of Nation Building*. New Haven, CT: Yale University Press.

Hinton, A.L. (2002) Purity and Contamination in the Cambodian Genocide', in J. Ledgerwood (ed.) *Cambodia Emerges from the Past: Eight Essays*, pp. 60–90. DeKalb, IL: Southeast Asia Publications.

Hughes, C. (2009) *Dependent Communities: Aid and Politics in Cambodia and East Timor*. Ithaca, NY: Cornell Southeast Asia Program.

Jackson, T. (1987) 'Just Waiting to Die? Cambodian Refugees in Thailand. Report of a Tour to the Thai–Cambodian Border and Subsequent Research'. Oxford: OXFAM House.

Jordans, J. (1993) 'Report on the Current Plight of Returning Cambodians of Ethnic Vietnamese Origin'. Unpublished UNTAC Report. Information and Education Division, United Nations Transitional Authority in Cambodia.

Jordans, J. (1996) 'Persecution of Cambodia's Ethnic Vietnamese Communities during and since the UNTAC Period', in S. Heder and J. Ledgerwood (eds) *Propaganda, Politics, and Violence in Cambodia. A Democratic Transition under United Nations Peace-Keeping*, pp. 134–58. New York: Routledge.

Kiernan, B. (2014) *The Pol Pot Regime: Race, Power, and Genocide in Cambodia under the Khmer Rouge, 1975–79*. New Haven, CT: Yale University Press.

Ledgerwood, J. and K. Un (2002) 'Introduction', in J. Ledgerwood (ed.) *Cambodia Emerges from the Past: Eight Essays*, pp. 1–15. DeKalb, IL: Southeast Asia Publications.

Lund, C. (2011) 'Fragmented Sovereignty: Land Reform and Dispossession in Laos', *Journal of Peasant Studies* 38(4): 885–905.

Malkki, L.H. (1995) 'Refugees and Exile: From "Refugee Studies" to the National Order of Things', *Annual Review of Anthropology* 24: 495–523.

Molyvann, V. (2003) *Modern Khmer Cities*. Phnom Penh: Reyum Press.

Ong, A. (2006) *Neoliberalism as Exception: Mutations in Citizenship and Sovereignty*. Durham, NC: Duke University Press.

Refugee Policy Group (1991) 'Cambodia: A Time for Return, Reconciliation and Reconstruction'. Washington, DC: Center for Policy Analysis and Research on Refugee Issues.

Reynell, J. (1989) *Political Pawns: Refugees on the Thai-Kampuchean Border*. Oxford: Refugee Studies Programme.

Robinson, C. (1998/2000) *Terms of Refuge: The Indochinese Exodus and the International Response*. London: ZED Books.

Teft, S. (1991) 'Cambodians Return to Tough Land Disputes', *The Christian Science Monitor* 21 November.

Terry, F. (2013) *Condemned to Repeat? The Paradox of Humanitarian Action*. Ithaca, NY: Cornell University Press.

Thayer, N. (1995) 'Wretched of the Earth', *Far Eastern Economic Review* 15 April.

Thompson, A. (1993) 'Oh Cambodia! Poems from the Border', *New Literary History* 24(3) 519–44.

Williams, B. (1997) 'Returning Home: The Repatriation of Cambodian Refugees', in M.W. Doyle, I. Johnstone and R.C. Orr (eds) *Keeping the Peace: Multidimensional UN Operations in Cambodia and El Salvador*, pp. 165–85. Cambridge: Cambridge University Press.

Williams, R. (2008) 'Stability, Justice, and Rights in the Wake of the Cold War: The Housing, Land, and Property Rights Legacy of the UN Transitional Authority in Cambodia', in S. Leckie (ed.) *Housing, Land, and Property Rights in Post-conflict United Nations and Other Peace Operations: A Comparative Survey and Proposal for Reform*, pp. 19–60. Cambridge: Cambridge University Press.

3

The Exemplary Citizen on the Exemplary Hill: The Production of Political Subjects in Contemporary Rural Rwanda

An Ansoms and Giuseppe D. Cioffo

INTRODUCTION

Since the tragic events of the 1994 genocide, Rwandan society has undergone a fast-paced wave of social and economic transformations, particularly after 2000. In a continent that for years has been associated with patrimonial and ineffective states (see other contributions in this special issue), the Rwandan example stands out for its efficient technocratic governance and for its impressive results in terms of development outcomes (for a discussion, see Ansoms and Rostagno, 2012). Twenty years after the genocide, Rwanda is a 'donor darling', lauded for its target-driven development model (applauded in various IMF reports), for the successful approach to improving its business environment (World Bank, 2015), and for its education and health care policies (see ODI, 2012; World Bank, 2011).

Such important results are seen as the product of a far-reaching and hierarchical system of governance put in place by the leadership of the Rwandan Patriotic Front (RPF), in power since the end of the 1994 genocide. On the one hand, the RPF governance is praised as an example of illuminated 'developmental patrimonialism' (Booth and Goloba-Mutebi, 2012). Referring to Khan's concept of developmental states in South-East Asia (Khan and Jomo, 2000), advocates of this school claim that the Rwandan case represents an important break with past histories of neo-patrimonialism in Africa. On the other hand, the RPF regime has been accused of 'cordoning off' political space, and of enforcing economic and political reforms without allowing public contestation or opposition (Reyntjens, 2013; Thomson, 2013). This has been coupled with state-organized political violence characterized by the imprisonment and disappearance of political activists, journalists and members of the government opposition (Prunier, 2009; Reyntjens, 2013).

What both critics and supporters of the Rwandan government acknowledge is that, since the RPF took power, it has been able to reform the state

The authors would like to thank the reviewers of an earlier draft of this chapter for their comments.

Rule and Rupture: State Formation through the Production of Property and Citizenship, First Edition.
Edited by Christian Lund and Michael Eilenberg.

effectively and to enforce control over its citizens. The country's reorganization is modelled according to *Vision 2020*, a manifesto elaborated at the
dawn of the new millennium with key ambitions for the reconstruction of
Rwanda (GoR, 2002). This political vision is enforced through a process of
social engineering, the restructuring of Rwandan society in line with a top-
down developmental envisioning of modernity (Ansoms, 2009; Reyntjens,
2013). Social mobilization for the implementation of that vision is achieved
through a system of governance that hierarchically links up different levels
of the local administration to central government's objectives.

Indeed, the skilful reforms of local governance implemented by the
Kagame administration have provided the country with an army of committed local administrators, tightly connected to the executive through performance contracts (known as *imihigo* in Kinyarwanda). Local leaders and
administrators are part of a 'technocratic and depoliticized' governance
apparatus (Chemouni, 2014), from the administrative cell unit, to village
(*umidugudu*), sector and district levels, all the way up to the central government (see also Ingelaere, 2014). Through this apparatus, policies are implemented and the Rwandan population is mobilized for an extensive range of
activities through 'sensitization' sessions, and an array of regulations, fines
and commitments to local authorities. The Rwandan post-genocide state
achieves policy adherence and implementation through its presence at virtu-
ally every level of society (Purdekova, 2011). This allows state structures to
link the distribution of access to resources with the creation of 'governable'
political subjects.

Existing scholarly literature on post-genocide Rwanda has described the
functioning of this dense and far-reaching state apparatus in the domain of
reconciliation and reconstruction policies. Thomson (2013), for example, has
shown how unity and reconciliation policies have facilitated political control
by the RPF-led state machine, while allowing for swift implementation of
policy objectives. Purdekova (2012) speaks of the state's ambition to shape
a 'governable subject', 'one that is both docile (non-contrary, accepting,
responsive) and easily organized (visible, readable, accessible, traceable,
orderly)' (Purdekova, 2012: 361). This literature thus illustrates how the
top-down imposition of policy objectives goes hand in hand with the state's
efforts to generate political subjects who are able to engage successfully
with government policies.

In this chapter, we argue that political subjectivity is also constructed
through the government's rural development policies in Rwanda. As most
of the Rwandan population lives and works in rural areas, the policies reor-
ganizing space and production patterns in rural areas contribute profoundly
to the production of Rwandans as political subjects, and in turn constitute
and consolidate state authority. In the first part of this chapter, we define
the concepts of 'subject' and 'political subjectivity' and we look at the way
in which the current literature has engaged with the production of political
subjectivity in Rwanda. In the second part, we highlight the role of rural policies in the shaping of political subjectivity through the conceptualization of

'exemplary citizenry'. In the third part, we present two empirical examples of how concrete state policies produce subjects, and how these subjects politically engage with or react to state policies. In our conclusion, we problematize the creation of 'exemplary citizenry', and point to the importance of the often hidden political nature of collective action in rural Rwanda.[1]

THE MAKING OF POLITICAL SUBJECTS

Before we proceed with the contextual and empirical discussion, it is crucial to define 'political subjects' and the production of 'political subjectivity'. In this chapter a 'subject' is understood 'in its double sense, i.e. both an object of domination and an active agent, in relation to forms of government' (Blundo and Le Meur, 2009: 10). On the one hand, subjects are at the receiving end of a relationship, which presents a power imbalance (domination). However, at the same time, they are agents who utilize their own resources and ingenuity to influence the outcomes of these 'forms of government'. Seen through the lens of public policy implementation, 'subjects' are policy recipients as well as 'active co-producers of this policy'. In this sense, subjectivity is political in so far as subjects actively manage to influence the modes of governmentality that contribute to the production of 'subjects, goods and services through the definition of representational boundaries and practical fields of actions' (ibid.: 29).

The double sense of 'subject' as presented by Blundo and Le Meur (2009) directs our attention to two important features of subject making. First, the subject-producing process is intertwined with forms of governance and governmentality that 'weave domination and subjectivation in a common framework' (ibid.: 11). Indeed, 'political authority is (re-)produced through its successful exercise over an issue in relation to social actors [subjects] that are affected by it' (see Christian Lund's Introduction to this special issue). As a result, the production of subjects cannot be de-linked from dynamics of state formation, a topic that is recurrent in the literature on post-genocide Rwanda (Purdekova, 2012; Thomson, 2013). Second, subject making occurs through the production and distribution of 'goods and services', the immediate objects of policy implementation; but it also depends upon the 'rhetorical level of discursive practices' (Blundo and Le Meur, 2009: 14, 11). In this chapter we are not only looking at the production of subjects in the process of state formation, but also at the discourses, actions and practices that make such subjectivities 'political'.

---

1. The empirical materials in this chapter are the product of different phases of fieldwork by the authors. Since 2004, Ansoms has been engaged in longitudinal qualitative research in six villages in the Southern Province of Rwanda (part in collaboration with Jude Murison). In 2013 and 2014, Cioffo conducted mixed quantitative and qualitative research in two districts of the Northern Province. Both authors engaged in collaborative research in 2013, in both the Southern and Northern Provinces.

This question is particularly relevant for Rwanda, as a lively academic debate is ongoing on whether forms of non-participation in, or active boycott of, public policies may represent forms of 'political resistance'. As mentioned by Lund (Introduction to this special issue), 'visibility' is a basic condition for the recognition of individual and collective rights. What does it then mean to choose to remain invisible? Is 'staying at the sidelines' of public space and engagement an act of subtle political resistance, or should it rather be framed as a short-sighted, instrumental tactic to ensure survival? Thomson (2013), for example, interprets local non-participation in public policies as acts of 'hidden' or 'everyday resistance', a notion that builds on Scott's (1985) concept of *infrapolitics*. Thomson defines 'everyday resistance' as 'any subtle, indirect, and nonconfrontational act that makes daily life more sustainable in the light of the strong and centralized power of the [state]' (Thomson, 2013: 132). This view, however, is called into question by Palmer (2014), who warns against 'seeing resistance everywhere and reading it into all types of negotiations and contestations' (ibid.: 242). Palmer criticizes Thomson's approach for over-interpreting local-level boycotts or non-participation as acts of political resistance, rather than choices motivated by momentary necessity, needs, or economic conditions. According to Palmer, the question is thus whether engagement in or resistance to public policy is motivated by individual considerations to maximize the chance of survival; or whether it deliberately reinforces or challenges dominant forms of governance. In short, do actions, moved by necessity or worldly interests, carry a political weight? Or are they just ways of coping with structural conditions of life in a poor country?

In order to answer this question, we need to take a momentary step back to define the analytical elements of what frames individual subjectivity as 'political'. For this purpose, we need to conceptualize both politics and action. Arendt's *The Human Condition* (1958) is particularly relevant to this discussion. Arendt engages with the question of what defines humans as subjects of a political body and as active participants within that body — either through validated participation or through opposition. According to Arendt, there are three basic activities of human life that are fundamental to the existence and reproduction of people across cultures, societies and time: labour, work and action. *Labour* is defined as the set of activities performed to sustain one's bodily life. Cultivation for household consumption, for example, is a form of labour. Labour can be performed individually or in a group, or one may control and profit from other people's labour. *Work* is defined as the set of activities oriented towards the creation of a product that is not necessary for immediate subsistence, such as manufactured goods or works of art. Work responds to men and women's longing for immortality, one's will to assert oneself in the world through the act of making. As a result, work is an essentially human and lonely activity. Both labour and work are, for Arendt, pre-political activities. *Action* is what defines men and women as part of a political body. Action may take the form of speech and thought, and it is only possible collectively. Action is the only human activity that relates to people for what they are, without the intermediary of the worldly things that are necessary for both labour and work. The only precondition for action is the presence of a plurality of individuals: '[W]hile all aspects of human condition are somehow related to politics, this plurality is specifically the condition — not only the condition *sine qua non*, but the condition *per quam* — of all political life' (Arendt, 1958: 7).

In order to be political, the activities we present throughout the following case studies must thus belong to the realm of Arendt's notion of *action* and not only to those of *labour* or *work*. According to Arendt, the chief feature of *action* — the mark of the political — is *speech*. Speech accompanies action, and unveils the political nature of it. Arendt warns us that 'most words and deeds are about some worldly objective reality *in addition* to being a disclosure of the acting and speaking agent' (Arendt, 1958: 180, emphasis added). In fact, the political meaning of those 'words and deeds' may be concealed in what Scott (1985) frames as 'hidden transcripts', only appearing in the public sphere in extremely disguised ways. Arendt points to the importance of identifying the potential political meanings of words and deeds that are seemingly limited to the non-political world of *labour* and *work*. According to Arendt, 'even the most "objective" intercourse, the physical, worldly in-between, is overlaid and, as it were, overgrown with an altogether different in-between which consists of deeds and words and owes its origins exclusively to men acting and speaking directly to one another', an in-between that becomes inherently political (Arendt, 1958: 183).

This notion of *action* is relevant to the discussion of what defines *political subjectivity*. In this chapter, we shall focus mainly on the shaping of political subjectivity as a result of opposition to public authority. We focus on cases where subjects engage in political action *vis-à-vis* the state apparatus, to reflect upon what makes resistance *political*. For Palmer (2014), political action has to take the form of 'active political protest', carried out in some self-assessing and necessarily outwardly evident form (see Figure 1). We argue, however, that *action* is often a matter of navigating social relations in a controlled social environment, in which space for political contestation may be extremely reduced. Palmer's approach, in fact, fails to grasp the more subtle ways in which power relations structure rural life in contemporary Rwanda. As we may understand from Arendt, political action does not always come in a self-asserting, publicly identifiable way. Bayart's (1981: 63) illustration of popular modes of political action (*modes populaires d'action politique*) appears to be relevant to the present discussion, because such modes of political action often take place in the space of the 'ambivalent, the allusive, the evasive'. For Bayart, 'to neglect' the political quality of popular action is to accept a-critically the monolithic claims of political power by the state while ignoring the 'polytheistic' forms of social organizations that define contemporary African societies. It is in this light that Thomson's rich illustration of the subtlety of 'everyday forms of resistance' is an important

Figure 1. A Continuum of Resistance

Coping Strategies Individual acts of policy violation aimed at survival	
Deliberate violation Individual acts of deliberately policy violation (element of pride in violating)	
Collective conscience Individual acts of policy violation with implicit support from others	Political action
Collective hidden acts Collective discourse of policy violation remaining part of the hidden transcript	
Infrapolitics (Scott, 1985) Collective discourse of policy violation reaching out to the public sphere in disguised ways	
Visible Political Action Organized discourse performed in public that pursues particular policy change	
Broad Political Action Organized acts performed in public that pursue broad political change	

contribution that makes a better account of the complexity of political life in Rwanda.

For Thomson (2013), political action takes place from the point where deliberate policy violation occurs in order to ensure survival against the odds. She points to the ways in which such political action may become collective. 'Strategic and purposeful' everyday acts of resistance — according to Thomson — are also expressions of political action (see Figure 1). However, we have already concluded that political action requires the existence of a shared, common consciousness about action (*speech*) in order for the 'coping strategy' to take on its truly political meaning. This shared consciousness may take the form of a very explicit discourse expressed within the public sphere; but it may also be extremely subtle — even without or beyond words — and difficult to detect by an outsider's eye. In fact, in the light of our empirical materials, we suggest viewing political action in Rwanda as placed on a continuum that goes from individual responses to material needs towards overt political action (see Figure 1). It is important to remark that this is a simplification of much more fluid real-life dynamics that cause individuals to move constantly on this continuum. In other words, *action* (read: 'political action') takes place in the 'space of appearance' among a plurality of subjects. The only condition for it to happen and to make subjectivity truly political is for it to be apparent and real to others, even if that may be in very subtle ways, and even if those others are a very limited group. Before we turn to the empirical material, we provide an appraisal of the complex of policies that will be the object of our case studies.

STATE-ORCHESTRATED REORGANIZATION OF SPACE AND PRODUCTION

The organization of public and productive space in Rwanda is emblematic of the way in which the country is managed. Routinely, new researchers and visitors are taken by surprise by the tidiness of Kigali's roads and gardens. The capital city of Rwanda stands as an example in urbanism and city planning, and has been widely acclaimed as a success story by international organizations. Manirakiza and Ansoms (2014) illustrate how the process of orderly reorganization of city space is continuously spreading from the centre towards poorer neighbourhoods in peri-urban areas. Purdekova (2012: 355) highlights how 'actions and wider symbolic registers attached to cleaning and cleansing, as well as other social themes, come to inform and mould a broader field: a unique form of governance' which acts through social ordering and control. However, the control and organization of public space is a prominent feature of social life not only in the capital city, but increasingly also in the countryside.

   The organization of rural public space and rural life seems paramount to the realization of the RPF governance project. The notion of 'exemplary citizenry' is used for those who insert themselves into the authorities' re-engineering project. A key instrument in the creation of an exemplary citizenry is the *imidugudu* villagization policy. When it was started in 1996, this policy focused on refugee resettlement. However, it evolved towards a broader strategy forcefully relocating the traditionally scattered Rwandan dwellings into centralized and easily accessible villages. Whereas in the initial stage (1997–9) donors actively funded the policy, the coercive relocation of non-refugee households catalysed international attention at the beginning of the 2000s (Des Forges, 2005; Human Rights Watch, 2001). This led to a retreat of funding and a scaling-down of the policy, replacing coercive relocation of settled households with enforced centralization of newly established households. New households are obliged to build their houses within the boundaries of the village site as specified by local authorities (for a discussion, see Ansoms and Murison, 2013).

The organization of space in legible settlements that may be 'governed' easily by the political centre is not a new phenomenon in African history. The most famous examples include villagization in Ethiopia during the 1980s, and the Tanzanian *ujamaa* experience under Julius Nyeryere's leadership (Scott, 1999). Also in the Rwandan context, reorganization of space occurred before 1994, with the creation of *paysannats* under the Habyarimana government (Newbury and Newbury, 2000; Verwimp, 2013). Scott (1999) analysed in detail how such examples of state-driven resettlement and habitat organization pivot around the need for the state to govern populations, and to discipline rural production in order to foster economic accumulation. Lund (see Introduction) highlights how territorialization does not merely represent a '[restructuring] of physical space, [but also of] the social and political perception of it', and how this represents a structuration of citizenship.

The reorganization of rural space is also very evident in the post-genocide restructuring of the state administration system, introduced in 2004 and adapted in 2006. The reform created six levels: the national level, the province level (four provinces plus the City of Kigali), the district level (30 districts), the sector (*imirenge*) level (416 sectors), the cell (*akagari*) level (2,150 cells), and the village level (*umudugudu*, plural *imidugudu*) (14,975 villages). Local administration is characterized by a mechanism of upward accountability through performance contracts that tie administrators' careers, and local-level policy objectives, to the government agenda (Ansoms and Rostagno, 2012; Ingelaere, 2014; Thomson, 2013).

Decentralized organs of governance, and in particular the district and sector offices, are crucial implementers of rural policy in two ways. First, the executive secretaries of Rwanda's 30 districts, directed by the district mayor, are the 'operative managers' of the national development projects. Sector and cell agronomists, acting in coordination with the sector executive secretary and the district agronomist, oversee the reception and implementation of national policies by farmers. Second, these administrative divisions also structure political and social life. The local bodies of government organize a range of social activities and public duties that vary from public community work (*umuganda*), to public gatherings in the frame of the unity and reconciliation policy, to sensitization campaigns explaining public policies.

A word-frequency study carried out by Ingelaere (2014) on more than 300 life stories from rural Rwandans shows that 'authority' is the third most recurrent word mentioned during interviews, following 'children' and 'land'. Ingelaere (ibid.) points to the presence and reach of Rwanda's central administration at every level of the social space in rural areas. One of the consequences of such a tightly controlled and upward-facing administration system is the 'de-politicization of local politics' (Chemouni, 2014: 253). Rather than democratic structures that represent local issues and contribute to the formation of national-level policy, local administration appears in Rwanda as an efficient and responsive apparatus for the achievement of centrally set policy objectives.

This top-down state apparatus also facilitates — in parallel with the reorganization of rural public space — a redesigning of the productive space. The Rwandan government has embarked upon an ambitious mission to reshape farming practices in line with its ambition to initiate a Green Revolution in the Rwandan countryside (see Ansoms, 2009; Ansoms et al., 2014; Cioffo, 2014; Cioffo et al., 2016). The policy package aims at extending a commercial monoculture model through centrally organized and coordinated crop production schemes. The model is based upon a profound rearrangement of productive space obtained through land consolidation and the distribution of productive inputs. The legal and political framework that facilitates the policy objectives is already firmly in place. The land law — approved by the Rwandan parliament in 2005 and amended in 2013 — sets out the formal conditions for a land titling system. Article 25 ties land access rights to 'productive use', a notion that is left vague. The subsequently elaborated Crop Intensification Programme asserts a strategy of land use consolidation, concentrating on the development of six commercial crops throughout Rwanda. State authorities limit the variety of crops that may be grown on particular parcels through a series of social and legal devices (see Cioffo, 2014; Cioffo et al. 2016). In practice, the legal framework ties land rights to participation in the development scheme of agricultural modernization.

As farmers are required to create economic surplus in line with national objectives, they are pushed firmly to change their social and economic terms of reference. Moreover, the recognition of their *citizenship* depends upon their ability to conform to the image of the productive, commercially oriented farmer. This notion of citizenship is quite explicitly defended in several presidential speeches: 'If we can utilize the resources that God has given us to good effect, we can eradicate poverty. ... We would like to urgently appeal to the Rwandese people to work. As the Bible says, "he who does not work should not eat"' (Kagame, 2000). The reorganization of rural space and the process of redefining citizenship have become ways to restructure social relations of property and citizenship (see Introduction).

In short, Rwandan farmers are required to change their ways of farming and are obliged to settle within reconfigured patterns of rural habitat. However, as highlighted in the previous section, farmers do not blindly internalize nationally designed policy objectives, particularly when policies do not match local agro-ecological specificities or farmers' livelihood needs. Frustration and anger provide grievances around which individual and collective action takes place. The two cases presented below illustrate how the political subjectivity of farmers is triggered through their resistance to space-reorganizing policies. Farmers' claims contribute to the formation of 'unacceptable' political subjectivities that clash with the model of 'exemplary citizenship'.

NEGOTIATING *AGASOZI NDATWA*

The first case discusses the consequences of imposed crop cultivation schemes on consolidated land. The village of Remera[2] is situated in a rural sector of the Northern Province of Rwanda. Remera is situated at high altitude and about 20 km from the nearest district town, and the quality of the connecting road is very poor. Before the genocide, the village was spread over two hills. When the *imidugudu* villagization policy was implemented in 1996, most families were obliged to move into grouped settlements on top of the two hills. Before agrarian modernization policies were applied in 2008/9, farmers mainly cultivated sorghum, beans and potatoes on the hills; and white cabbage, carrots and tomatoes in the marshlands.

However, with the introduction of the Crop Intensification Programme (CIP) in 2008/9, sorghum production was no longer allowed on selected 'consolidated' sites. Sorghum is a traditional crop excluded from the CIP, and agronomists regard it as a low-value crop belonging to subsistence farming. From then on, crop production on consolidated land focused on wheat and beans during the first agricultural season, and on beans and potatoes during the following season. The consolidated sites in which modern agriculture is practised are called *agasozi ndatwa*, literally meaning 'the hill which is nice to see' or 'the hill that we show off with pride'. Farmers cultivating land in the *agasozi ndatwa* must grow the crops chosen for the area. In the case of Remera these were wheat, maize and beans. Non-compliance is punished through fines, imprisonment, and even the possible loss of land rights (on the basis of Land Law's article 25).

However, local producers soon noticed that Remera's soils were not suited for wheat production and many farmers knew this in advance. However, they were confronted by a local authority structure that was firmly determined to implement the policy guidelines. The issue was raised several times in various focus groups. A female teacher explained:

> Normally the ideas should come from the farmers; it should not come from the top to the bottom . . . . They should not come with papers on which there is written that on these hectares you should do these crops. We do not have those hectares, and even if we had them, you cannot decide what we are going to cultivate, really.[3]

In addition to the fact that wheat was not suited to the local agro-ecological conditions, the region was confronted with an unpredictable rainy season and a particularly hot dry season. At the end of the year, wheat harvests were predictably meagre. As one focus group participant — with land inserted in the land consolidation scheme — put it: 'The problem is that the soil is not

---

2. Fictional name.
3. Focus group with *inyangamugayo*, Northern Province, July 2014.

the same. They can tell us to do wheat . . . but in my plots wheat does not grow, so I do not earn even a franc. This is the problem'.[4]

By the next season, in 2010, the village authorities were summoned by the district to transform the whole of Remera into an *umudugudu ndatwa*, an 'exemplary village' where the land consolidation programme is implemented over the whole surface of the village. Normally, only part of the village's land is chosen for the *agasozi ndatwa*, which is also often the most fertile land.[5] However, when classified as an *umudugudu ndatwa*, the whole village is bound by strictly controlled agricultural production schemes. Given the poor harvest of wheat and maize during the previous season, Remera's villagers were very worried. Some focus group participants tried to frame their reluctance to cultivate wheat as a matter of lack of means: 'Not all people have the same money, or can choose the same crop. You may not have the money to buy that seed'. Others, however, pointed clearly to the fact that the authorities had made the wrong choice:

> People who do the planning [crop assignment] should not say: 'On this surface you are going to do wheat'. If they do this, they are forcing us to do wheat where wheat is not productive, even if we use fertilizer. You will see that wheat is not productive on those soils, so my suggestion would be that they do the planning according to the soil we have in the village.[6]

In Buhoro, a neighbouring village of Remera confronted with the same problem, farmers had restarted sorghum production against the sector authorities' directives, but with the permission of the local village chief. Farmers in Remera soon started following their neighbours' example. When confronted with the widespread violation of centrally imposed policy guidelines, local authorities at various levels in the administrative chain reacted differently. District and sector authorities, on the one hand, imposed rigorous policy adherence. Village and — to a lesser extent — cell authorities, however, were often faced with the same problems as their fellow villagers. Some of them tried to pass on information about the problematic aspects of the policy to the higher levels in the administration. As the village chief of Buhoro put it: 'In the meeting [with sector authorities] I really tried to say [what] did not work in the consolidated region. . . . As they did not have any help that they could give us, they just stood silent'.[7] Nevertheless, this input was ignored and decisions were implemented from the top down:

---

4. Focus group with poor farmers, Northern Province, July 2014.
5. Information provided by farmers both in focus groups and individual interviews, as well as by local authorities, during fieldwork carried out in 2013 and 2014. Also see Cioffo (2014).
6. Focus group with *inyangamugayo*, Northern Province, July 2014.
7. Village chief, Northern Region, Rwanda. Focus group with village authorities, 21 July 2014.

'The policy was decided at a high level ... they said, for example, in this sector you will do maize and wheat. They do not consider that even if you are in the same cell we can all have different soils, even in the same *umudugudu*.[8] Up until the end of the first agricultural season in 2013, fines and imprisonments were quite widespread in the sector in response to policy violation.

Cultivation of sorghum and other non-allowed crops continued nonetheless. Whereas initially non-compliance was an individual coping response to the meagre harvests on consolidated land, it transformed into a collective strategy challenging the policy guidelines (Cioffo, 2014; Cioffo et al., 2016). The common experience of the violation of policy guidelines resulted in the emergence of a shared discourse about the inappropriateness of the imposed crop cultivation schemes. By May 2013, more and more farmers were violating the official policy. Moreover, the village chiefs of both Remera and Buhoro increasingly tolerated the transgressions, and transgressed themselves.[9] Farmers started 'crying out' in favour of being able to plant sorghum. The case even caught the attention of a national newspaper (see Ishimwe, 2013). Figure 2 details the various stages of resistance to *Agasozi Ndatwa*, scaling up to political action.

Three elements emerge from this case. First, it points to how Rwandan authorities have instrumentalized the notion of 'exemplary citizenship' as dependent upon farmers' alignment to official rural policy guidelines. Policy makers even scaled up the notion of 'exemplary citizenship' from the individual level to the village level, where land rights and the 'exemplary citizen' status depended on adherence to government policy. This illustrates the way in which struggles over property and citizenship are closely interrelated in the shaping of political authority. Second, the case illustrates how farmers are both objects of domination (through locally implemented policy guidelines and systems of punishment) as well as active agents who shape the process of policy implementation. Finally, individual action to respond to immediate practical challenges gradually surpassed the domain of the private. The experience of conscious transgression was shared by a multitude of subjects, which in turn resulted in the articulation of a common discourse. The production of such discourse challenged policy guidelines, initially in more disguised ways, but eventually quite openly. In fact, action and speech moved from a response to immediate circumstances, to openly asking more general questions who takes decisions on policy implementation? How were these decisions taken? Why were we [the farmers] not involved in this process?

---

8. Focus group with village authorities, Northern Province, Rwanda, 24 July 2014.
9. Individual interviews with farmers in Remera and Buhoro 2013; focus groups in Remera and Buhoro in 2014.

Figure 2. The Continuum of Resistance in Negotiating Agasozi Ndatwa

Continuum of Resistance	Negotiating *Agasozi Ndatwa*
Coping strategies Individual acts of policy violation aimed at survival	Individuals cultivate sorghum for household consumption in a hidden way to survive.
Deliberate violation Individual acts of deliberately policy violation (element of pride in violating)	Individuals cultivate sorghum for household consumption in a hidden way out of a principled position, considering sorghum as an important part of their livelihood.
Collective conscience Individual acts of policy violation with implicit support from others	Individuals cultivate sorghum as an individual resistance strategy. The act is reinforced by validation through implicit support from others (neighbours in most cases). No explicit coordination.
Collective hidden acts Collective discourse of policy violation remaining part of the hidden transcript	Many people in the village cultivate sorghum, resulting in the emergence of a common discourse that justifies policy transgression at a collective level.
Infrapolitics Collective discourse of policy violation reaching out to the public sphere in disguised ways	Sorghum cultivation becomes known to local authorities; collective protest reaches out to the public sphere but in disguised ways.
Visible political action Organized discourse performed in public that pursues policy change	Collective protest reaches out to the public sphere in more open ways (media, for example), co-opting local authorities in the negotiation with the higher-level officials.
Broad political action Organized acts performed in public that pursue abstract political aims	Resistance at broader level against land consolidation, monocropping and forced commercialization of production.

SMUGGLING CASSAVA

The second case analyses farmers' reactions to the enforced marketization of agricultural production. Kinazi cassava factory is a processing plant in Ruhango district (Southern Province). During our research stay in 2011, when the cassava factory was still under construction, participants in a focus group held in an area near the factory spoke of it as a source of hope for economic development. The factory was supposed to have a processing capacity of 250 tonnes of raw cassava per day to produce 60 tonnes of cassava flour (Sabiiti, 2011). People were genuinely convinced that the nearness of the factory would improve their chances of negotiating good prices for their cassava harvest. The Kinazi factory was officially inaugurated in April 2012. On that occasion, President Kagame 'called on the area residents to make the most of the processing plant to empower themselves economically. He said that while in the past, cassava was just eaten raw, roasted or boiled, the new factory comes with value addition, which should make their products competitive on the international market' (Musoni, 2012). A year earlier, the CEO of the Rwanda Development Bank — Jack Kayonga — claimed that 'the factory will increase the residents' income and provide a market for the local cassava farmers' (Sabiiti, 2011).

However, hope soon withered after the opening. A focus group participant reported:

> When we noticed the construction of the factory, we were happy that development was to come to our region. But the first thing they did was to prohibit us to cultivate sorghum. And we just told you that the little sorghum they let us cultivate gave such a high production the last season. Then, at the moment we started to deliver the cassava to the factory, we noticed that the price was very low. We thought that the factory would mean 'development' but it has made us go down instead of making us grow. We are not happy with that factory stuff.[10]

According to another farmer, 'Normally, cassava was our crop. We earned a lot of money. But the factory pushed us to do even more but gives a very low price'.[11] At the time of our research in 2013 the price paid by the factory to farmers for their cassava varied between 40 and 60 RWF/kg for fresh cassava. Farmers lamented the price paid by the factory to be less than the price on the local market, which varied between 100 RWF/kg at harvest season, and 200 RWF/kg. These prices refer to cassava which has been treated (soaked, dried and peeled) by the farmers themselves, while the factory only purchases fresh cassava.

Disappointed by the limited price offered, farmers turned to alternative strategies — to the production of other crops, for example. This was problematic for the Rwandan authorities. 'For sure, the factory gives a low price', a focus group participant explained. 'But as we knew this, we got out of cassava production, and rather cultivated another crop that brought us more money, because we did not earn well at the factory. But a big constraint was that the government did not allow us to do anything other than cassava, because the factory needs its capacity, and that is why we had to produce'. Another confirmed that 'Cultivating cassava is an obligation. At the moment the factory was built, they told us that it has to receive at least 600 kg per day. If not, the factory makes losses. Since then, it is obligatory [in this region] to cultivate cassava [and sell it to the factory]'.[12]

An alternative strategy was to not sell one's cassava to the factory, but to search for alternative options. At the time of our research (September 2013), the factory was not producing at its full capacity. By June 2013, *The New Times Rwanda* reported a processing capacity of 120 tonnes of raw cassava per day on the basis of a 20-hour daily operation, of which, at that time, only 40 per cent was being utilized. Corroborating this, farmers mentioned that the factory was always searching for cassava. But as one participant in our focus group explained: 'It is not that we produce little [cassava], but the price is low so we try to keep as much as possible in our own hands. If they would increase the price, the factory could even have a surplus that it could

---

10. Focus group with local cassava producers, Kinazi sector, September 2013.
11. Focus group with local cassava producers, Kinazi sector, September 2013.
12. Focus group with local cassava producers, Kinazi sector, September 2013.

not treat'.[13] In fact, farmers who did not sell their product to the factory were fully aware of the implications of their actions for factory production levels. They were also aware of the fact that refusal to sell to the factory had become so widespread that the authorities realized what was going on.

This led to a forceful reaction from the authorities. To counter the sale of cassava to buyers other than the factory, all of the household equipment necessary to dry cassava was destroyed. One interviewee explained: 'When the factory came, they gave an order that no one could treat cassava. Those who had basins to soak it had to destroy them. Today this [activity] is no longer permitted'.[14] In another focus group, a participant confirmed that, 'All the soaking equipment has been destroyed, as the factory gave the order to destroy it'. But he acknowledged that, 'People who do it [treat cassava themselves] do it in small quantities in barrels. But you really cannot do it openly'.[15] Later in the interview, our participants revealed how they dry their cassava on their roofs, or on quickly removable sheets that they hide behind the house. This was done for smaller quantities that, when transformed into cassava flour, were mainly destined for household consumption.

Farmers also developed inventive strategies to sell their cassava to alternative trade chains on a larger scale. Such illegal cassava trade had to be carried out in secret. A rather subtle way was to sell raw cassava to local traders who would take it to a region where the factory did not dominate the trade chain: 'There are traders who do this and take the harvest, dry it, and sell it to the market which is further away from the factory'. A participant in another group confirmed this: 'The traders of the region who have money buy up [our harvest], dry it, and sell it in Kigali. . . . They do not pay per kilo, but they buy up an entire plot. They buy the cassava that is ready [to be harvested]'.[16]

Over time, this kind of trade became more and more organized and, as a result, also more obvious in the public sphere. This trend was confirmed when traders from abroad came to buy up cassava on a massive scale. Several focus groups mentioned that traders were coming from Cyangugu (near the Congolese border, and far from our research setting). A participant noted that this trade 'occurs *en cachette*, the buses are charged during the night and they leave in the morning'. For another, 'Everyone knows this secret, because we live here'. The 'secret' became more and more open. 'There are cheaters everywhere', a participant confessed, 'and given that I know that, I had my go with it. These traders come at noon and then

---

13. Focus group with local cassava producers, Kinazi sector, September 2013.
14. In the region of the study, farmers used to treat cassava tubers in the household in order to produce cassava flour. This is normally done by peeling the tubers, soaking them in water in a basin or a hole in the ground, and then drying them in the sun on a rack or on the ground.
15. Focus group with local cassava producers, Kinazi sector, September 2013.
16. Focus group with local cassava producers, Kinazi sector, September 2013.

we sell our harvest. We put them on the truck with sheeting on top. And then they leave very quickly to bring that to DRC'. While farmers went through the motions of concealment, the massive quantities disappearing from the local market were certainly noticed by the authorities. A focus group participant explained that, 'Even the cellule and sector chiefs are aware of this. The secretary of the sector knows the truth because he knows that the price at the factory is low'.[17] An admission to the press by the plant manager, Robert Runazi, shows that he was indeed aware that farmers were selling their produce to neighbouring countries such as the DRC and Burundi (Ishimwe, 2013).

When we asked how the agronomists at the level of the cellule and the sector reacted when confronted with the low production quantities offered to the factory, the answer was plain: 'These agronomists are from the region. They know the situation. And they too have to eat cassava flour. So they cannot punish the people directly'.[18] Resistance to official policy prescriptions had become more and more open, up to a point where the case was publicly discussed in the Rwandan press. It became a news item in the government-controlled *The New Times*, and on national television. Farmers expressed their dissent in an increasingly open way. Figure 3 illustrates this.

As with the previous case, several conclusions can be drawn. First, this case provides an illustration of how the discourse of 'exemplary citizenship' was employed to reshape property relations — in this case not property as land but property as the harvest generated by the land. The discourses of high-level authorities presented the factory at its launch as a chance for empowerment, a gateway to increased revenue and to international competitiveness. The local population was called on to perform as 'exemplary' smallholders, using this opportunity for their own development. Second, the case highlights how the making of political subjectivity depends upon the development of a common *speech* that frames the *action* of farmers (in Arendt's terms). Such *action* — when taken up collectively — may rapidly result in a coherent 'hidden transcript' (Scott, 1985) capable of breaking out into the public sphere. Nevertheless, the case also illustrates how farmers remain prudent in the formulation of their dissent. Whereas *visible political action* to confront the low factory prices was in this case quite apparent, expressions of *broad political action* calling into question the broader agrarian commercialization policies of the Rwandan government remained limited. Farmers were very aware that the seeming openness from the authorities' side to discuss the price issue in public could turn against them in the near future. 'We know that the days of a thief are 40', a farmer said, quoting a Swahili proverb invoking a dangerous situation that cannot

17. Focus group with local cassava producers, Kinazi sector, September 2013.
18. Focus group with local cassava producers, Kinazi sector, September 2013.

Figure 3. The Continuum of Political Action in Smuggling Cassava

Continuum of Resistance as Political Action	Negotiating *Agasozi Ndatwa*
Coping strategies Individual acts of policy violation aimed at survival	Individuals keep their cassava production for household consumption, and cultivate other crops, in order to cope with low prices.
Deliberate violation Individual acts of deliberate policy violation (element of pride in violating)	Individuals keep their cassava production for household consumption and/or local sales on hidden markets, to cope with low prices and out of a principled position that the factory should bring development and benefit local producers.
Collective conscience Individual acts of policy violation with implicit support from others	Individuals keep their cassava for local sales but with implicit support from neighbours who know and do not reveal this to the authorities.
Collective hidden acts Collective discourse of policy violation remaining part of the hidden transcript	Many people participate in alternative cassava trade. Active engagement from several members of the community ensures that the activity stays hidden.
Infrapolitics Collective discourse of policy violation reaching out to the public sphere in disguised ways	The authorities start noticing that local farmers are selling their cassava to alternative trade chains. On the producers' side, a façade discourse of 'harvests being poor' is created and reproduced in order to perform compliance with policy guidelines.
Visible political action Organized discourse performed in public that pursues policy change	Collective protest reaches out to the public sphere in more open ways, co-opting local authorities and the media in the negotiation with the higher-level authorities for higher prices.
Broad political action Organized acts performed in public that pursue abstract political aims	Resistance at broader level against power disequilibria of farmers in centrally-imposed trade chains.

continue forever. 'We know that one day this will be over, and that we will get 30 years in prison if they catch us'.[19]

SUBJECT MAKING AND EVERYDAY POLITICS

Narratives of statehood and development in Rwanda tend to unfold along opposite lines. Critiques of the post-genocide Rwandan state highlight the lack of public space for political expression. Advocates of the post-genocide regime bring to the fore its results in terms of technocratic governance, economic development and the provision of public goods. To move beyond the opposition between the two streams of literature, we call for a more nuanced reading of the necessary reconfiguration of property and citizenship that

19. Focus group with local cassava producers, Kinazi sector, September 2013.

state building mobilizes. We highlight three elements that, taken together, may provide a better understanding of the structural tensions between the articulation of political claims and subjectivity, on the one hand, and the consolidation of the post-genocide Rwandan state on the other.

First, we challenge the idea of the Rwandan post-genocide state as a coherent, monolithic structure through which decisions flow unhindered from the top to the bottom. In both our case studies, the post-genocide state apparatus is not unresponsive to pressures exerted by claims from the bottom. In fact, in both cases, public authority represents the coercive arm of the state, but also an opportunity for articulating claims around access to resources. Lower levels of public administration are subjected to pressure from two sides. They are closely connected to the central government through performance contracts; as such they are implementers of public policy and bearers of public authority. On the other hand, they do respond to local grievances, at times cautiously pushing for recognition of local claims at higher levels of the administration. At the same time, this receptivity of lower-tier public administration to citizens' claims is not free from risk. Accepting the legitimacy of locally articulated grievances implies that local-level authorities, at least partially, admit the failure of the national modernization project. In the case of the Kinazi cassava factory, the strategy to deliberately turn a blind eye to illegitimate cassava trade brought to public view the image of impoverished cassava producers, countering the government's media narrative of successful modern farming.

Second, the contestation of public policy paves the way for the production of *speech* and *action*, and the emergence of collective claims around the control over resources. The image of the 'modern exemplary farmer' is contested through the organized, intended violation of policy guidelines. While these actions may be seen as a purely strategic response to material conditions of poverty, they 'are also the expression, the alibi of something else that defines a *position* of the people within global society and *vis-à-vis* state institutions' (Dozon, 1977, quoted in Bayart, 1981: 59). Farmers who cannot and do not want to fit within the commercial model are incapable of performing within the boundaries of 'exemplary citizenship'.

Interestingly, this discourse is also — partly — adopted by farmers themselves. In both our case studies we gathered accounts of farmers declaring themselves as 'unfit' for government policies. The poorest farmers referred to themselves as 'the poor' or 'the peasants' (*abahinzi*) as opposed to the authorities (*ibozy*, a Kinyarwanda derivation of the English 'boss'). While *abahinzi* belong to the realm of reproduction and survival, *ibozy* belong to that of decision making and modern production. It is often perceived by farmers that 'this government does not like the poor',[20] and that policies and economic strategies are formulated without taking into consideration

---

20. Conversation with women farmers, 2013.

the rationalities of subsistence farmers (see Ansoms, 2009; Cioffo, 2014; Thomson, 2013). However, the fact that the poorest Rwandan farmers may define themselves as 'powerless' does not impede *action* altogether. Although powerlessness is the structural condition imposed on Rwandan farmers, the very nature of power means that it cannot be accumulated or stored, but inevitably circulates (Arendt, 1958). In fact, *action* to contravene policy guidelines does not only aim at redefining struggles over property, but also culminates in the emergence of a commonly shared *speech*.

Finally, the tension between subject making and state building seems to be a constitutive element of the post-genocide political community. As we have seen, the government's capacity to reach out and exert control over the local representatives of public authority (through the *imihigo* performance contracts, for example) makes it difficult for farmers to bring their shared *speech* to the public space. In fact, the discourse produced by farmers rarely enters the public domain in a confrontational way. It rather becomes 'the secret that everyone knows',[21] eventually entering the public sphere in disguised ways. In turn, the confinement of contestations to non-public (but not private either) forms of *infrapolitics* (Scott, 1985) further exacerbates the government's need for social control. In this way, public authority and political subjectivity (even when antagonistic) are decisively and necessarily mutually constituted, in so far as the emergence of action and its accompanying speech are the response to the hardship of rural life *and* to the government's effort to trigger social transformation. It is through this dialectical movement that 'power, accumulation and common sense' (Bayart, 1981: 72) are negotiated. Importantly, increased control may hinder the emergence of political claims to the public, but can hardly respond to them. It is in a non-public — but not private either — 'space of freedom' (Arendt, 1985) that *speech* becomes an outspoken illustration of farmers' political subjectivity.

The emergence of such a space remains specific to social circumstances. Although its borders may vary, they rarely openly cross the frontier of public state power (Bayart, 1981). The creation of specific political subjectivities and the emergence and consolidation of the Rwandan post-genocide state are twin historical specificities, formed through mutual interactions and struggles over the distribution and access to productive resources. For farmers to develop a publicly articulated discourse would mean a further step into public confrontation. However, farmers' boycott and resistance do not have the mere character of the 'worldly': they do pivot on worldly objectives and coping strategies, but they also evolve to encompass a common point of view placed at the interaction between the perception farmers have of themselves, the rearrangement of space and production, and the dominant modes of governance in post-genocide Rwanda. To neglect this point is to fail to grasp the dialectical interaction between state consolidation and the

---

21. An expression often used in focus groups both in Remera and Kinazi.

emergence of grassroots, often-disorganized forms of political contestation. For the government, accepting public contestation on such matters would mean to question the very ideal-type of the 'exemplary citizen', in which a consistent part of the national project of the post-genocide state is rooted. The control over property and citizenship is not merely a *conditio sine qua non* of state power in Rwanda; it turns out to be a *conditio per quam*.

REFERENCES

Ansoms, A. (2009) 'Re-engineering Rural Society. The Visions and Ambitions of the Rwandan Elite', *African Affairs* 108(431): 289–309.

Ansoms, A. and J. Murison (2013) 'Formalizing the Informal in Rwanda: From Artisanal to Modern Brick and Tile Ovens', in I. Hillenkamp, F. Lapeyre and A. Lemaître (eds) *Securing Livelihoods: Informal Economy Practices and Institutions*, pp. 235–53. Oxford: Oxford University Press.

Ansoms, A. and D. Rostagno (2012) 'Rwanda's Vision 2020 Halfway Through: What the Eye does not See', *Review of African Political Economy* 39(133): 427–50.

Ansoms, A., G. Cioffo, C. Huggins and J. Murison (2014) 'The Reorganisation of Rural Space in Rwanda: Habitat Concentration, Land Consolidation, and Collective Marshland Cultivation', in A. Ansoms and T. Hilhorst (eds) *Losing your Land: Dispossession in the Great Lakes*, pp. 163–85. Woodbridge: James Currey.

Arendt, H. (1958) *The Human Condition*. Chicago, IL: University of Chicago Press.

Bayart, J.F. (1981) 'Le politique par le bas en Afrique noire. Questions de méthode' ['Grassroots Politics in Black Africa. Methodological Questions'], *Politique Africaine* 1(1): 53–82.

Blundo, G. and P-Y. Le Meur (2009) *The Governance of Daily Life in Africa. Ethnographic Explorations of Public and Collective Service*. Leiden: Brill.

Booth, D. and F. Golooba-Mutebi (2012) 'Development Patrimonialism? The Case of Rwanda', *African Affairs* 111(444): 379–403.

Chemouni, B. (2014) 'Explaining the Design of the Rwandan Decentralization: Elite Vulnerability and the Territorial Repartition of Power', *Journal of East African Studies* 8(2): 246–62.

Cioffo, G.D. (2014) 'Les petits agriculteurs face à la modernisation rurale dans la Province du Nord du Rwanda: Consolidation de l'usage des terres, distribution d'intrants améliorés et sécurité alimentaire' ['Smallholder Farmers and Rural Modernization in the Northern Province of Rwanda: Land Consolidation, Improved Input Distribution and Food Security'], in F. Reyntjens et al. (eds) *L'Afrique des Grands Lacs: Annuaire 2014–2015* [*Great Lakes Africa: Yearbook 2014–2015*], pp. 427–54. Paris: L'Harmattan.

Cioffo, G.D., A. Ansoms and J. Murison (2016) 'Modernizing Agriculture through a "New" Green Revolution: The Limits of the Crop Intensification Programme in Rwanda', *Review of African Political Economy* 43(148): 277–93.

Des Forges, A. (2005) 'Land in Rwanda, Winnowing out the Chaff', in F. Reyntjens and S. Marysse (eds) *L'Afrique des Grands Lacs: Annuaire 2005–2006* [*Great Lakes Africa: Yearbook 2005–2006*], pp. 353–71. Paris: L'Harmattan.

Dozon, J.P. (1977) 'Transformation et reproduction d'une société rurale africaine dans le cadre d'une économie de plantation. Le cas du Bété de la région de Gagnoa' ['Transformation and Reproduction of a Rural African Society in the Framework of Plantation Economy. The Case of Bété in the Gagnoa Region'] in ORSTOM (ed.) *Essais sur la reproduction de formations sociales dominées* [*Essays on the Reproduction of Subordinated Social Formations*], pp. 16–17. Paris: Travaux et Documents de l'ORSTOM (Office de la recherche scientifique et technique outre-mer; Office for Technical and Scientific Research in Overseas Domains).

GoR (2002) *Rwanda Vision 2020*. Kigali: Government of Rwanda.

Human Rights Watch (2001) *Uprooting the Rural Poor in Rwanda*. New York: Human Rights Watch.

Ingelaere, B. (2014) 'What's on a Peasant's Mind? Experiencing RPF State Reach and Over-reach in Post-genocide Rwanda (2000–10)', *Journal of East African Studies* 8(2): 214–30.

Ishimwe, T. (2013) 'Shortage of Cassava Leaves Kinazi Plant Operating at 40% of Capacity', *The New Times Rwanda* 3 June. www.newtimes.co.rw/section/article/2013-06-03/66375/ (accessed August 2016).

Kagame, P. (2000) 'Address to the Nation by H.E. Paul Kagame on his Inauguration as President of the Republic of Rwanda', 22 April. www.gov.rw/government/president/speeches

Khan, M.H. and K.S. Jomo (2000) *Rents, Rent-seeking and Economic Development. Theory and Evidence in Asia*. Cambridge: Cambridge University Press.

Manirakiza, V. and A. Ansoms (2014) '"Modernizing Kigali": The Struggle for Space in the Rwandan Urban Context', in A. Ansoms and T. Hilhorst (eds) *Losing your Land: Dispossession in the Great Lakes*, pp. 186–203. Woodbridge: James Currey.

Musoni, E. (2012) 'Rwf6b Cassava Factory Opens', *The New Times Rwanda* 17 April. www.newtimes.co.rw/section/article/2012-04-17/51762/ (accessed August 2016).

Newbury, C. and D. Newbury (2000) 'Bringing the Peasants Back In. Agrarian Themes in the Construction and Corrosion of Statist Historiography in Rwanda', *The American Historical Review* 105(3): 832–77.

ODI (2012) 'Delivering Maternal Health. Why is Rwanda Doing Better than Malawi, Niger and Uganda?'. ODI Briefing Paper. London: Overseas Development Institute. www.odi.org/publications/3848-odi-briefing-papers (accessed March 2015).

Palmer, N. (2014) 'Re-examining Resistance in Post-Genocide Rwanda', *Journal of East African Studies* 8(2): 231–45.

Prunier, G. (2009) *From Genocide to Continental War. The 'Congolese' Conflict and the Crisis of Contemporary Africa*. London: Hurst & Company.

Purdekova, A. (2011), '"Even If I Am Not Here, There Are So Many Eyes": Surveillance and State Reach in Rwanda', *Journal of Modern African Studies* 49(3): 475–97.

Purdekova, A. (2012) 'Rendering Rwanda Governable: Order, Containment and Cleansing in the Rationality of Post-genocide Rule', in F. Reyntjens et al. (eds) *L'Afrique des Grands Lacs: Annuaire, 2012–2013 [Great Lakes Africa: Yearbook 2012–2013]*, pp. 355–80. Paris: L'Harmattan.

Reyntjens, F. (2013) *Political Governance in Post-genocide Rwanda*. Cambridge: Cambridge University Press.

Sabiiti, D. (2011) 'New Cassava Factory Nears Completion', *The New Times Rwanda* 28 March. www.newtimes.co.rw/section/article/2011-03-28/29679/ (accessed August 2016).

Scott, J. (1985) *Weapons of the Weak: Everyday Forms of Peasant Resistance*. New Haven, CT: Yale University Press.

Scott, J. (1999) *Seeing Like a State. How Certain Schemes to Improve the Human Condition Have Failed*. New Haven, CT: Yale University Press.

Thomson, S. (2013) *Whispering Truth to Power: Everyday Resistance to Reconciliation in Postgenocide Rwanda*. Madison, WI: University of Wisconsin Press.

Verwimp, P. (2013) *Peasants in Power. The Political Economy of Development and Genocide in Rwanda*. New York: Springer.

World Bank (2011) 'Toward Quality Enhancement and Achievement of Universal Nine Year Basic Education: An Education System in Transition, A Nation in Transition'. Rwanda Education Country Status Report. Washington, CD: World Bank. https://openknowledge.worldbank.org/handle/10986/2733 (accessed March 2015).

World Bank (2015) 'Doing Business 2015: Going Beyond Efficiency'. Washington, DC: World Bank. www.doingbusiness.org/reports (accessed March 2015).

4

Making Territory: War, Post-war and the Entangled Scales of Contested Forest Governance in Mid-Western Nepal

Sarah Byrne, Andrea J. Nightingale and Benedikt Korf

INTRODUCTION

'If we are working for conservation, we have no one to fear' (Gansnu forest user).

Nepal is a particularly relevant context in which to analyse how authority is produced under conditions of repeated ruptures in rule. The country experienced a series of revolutions, a civil war (1996–2006), and a recurrently contested process of state (trans-)formation that increasingly is being defined around ethnicity and territory. However, ruptures as exceptional events in 'national' politics do not necessarily work through to local politics, where more ongoing, continuous processes of both contestation and conservation around local resource use may persist amidst a turbulent political landscape at other political scales. Dichotomizing rupture and continuity therefore has analytical limits. We suggest that in many situations characterized by significant and long-standing contention over political power, rupture and continuity should be thought of in 'both-and' terms; rupture *and* continuity may be co-present, albeit on different scales of politics, which are nevertheless entangled and affect each other. While rupture may offer 'open moments' (Lund, Introduction to this issue), it may equally foreclose those. Continuous practices of claiming authority and rights in the shadow of those ruptures may equally shape the spaces and practices of states, citizens and property *in the making*. In a reflection on the historiography of rupture and repair in South Asia, Yogesh Raj (2013: 6) has argued that 'all ruptures trigger unprecedented and vigorous attempts to regain what the affected people think

We would like to express our thanks to the Gansnu forest users who generously shared their time, experience and insights, and to Gitta Shrestha and Subita Pradhan who provided fieldwork assistance. Conversations with Bharat Pokharel and Rony Emmenegger have helped to shape our analysis, as have comments from the editors of this special issue and two anonymous reviewers. The financial support of the Swiss National Science Foundation (grant numbers 100013_124459/1 and 100017_124459) is gratefully acknowledged, as is the support of a British Academy International Partnership and Mobility Award (2012–16).

of as the state of normalcy'. These two struggles — to seize the opportunity of the 'open moment' and to return to the status quo — should be thought through together.

Unpacking the process of making territory is central to this analysis, a process we understand as not simply the backdrop for state formation, but as a key constituent of it (Reeves, 2011). Territory is not something that a state construes, 'governmentalizes' and achieves (or not). It is, we claim, 'made' through an amalgam of territorializing practices that a variety of state and non-state actors devise, but it nevertheless produces a state 'effect' (Mitchell, 1991). We focus on the spatial and territorial dimensions of ruptured and continuous rule, particularly attempts to 'repair' ruptures, and the claims for recognition of political and resource use rights that emerge as a result. Making territory, we suggest, is the effect of the entanglement of different territorial politics and practices. These include both processes of claiming authority or rule over material spaces, and the relationships between people and resources that emerge within those spaces. We understand territory as constituting a claimed and bounded social space (Peluso and Lund, 2011) and territorialization as a process that produces particular 'bundles of powers' (Ribot and Peluso, 2003). We show how certain forms of territorial practices — particularly claiming citizenship and resource rights — both produce and are produced by an 'entangled landscape' (Moore, 2005) of differently bounded and situated spatial practices of claims making.

This contribution explores processes of making territory, states and citizens through a case study of a contested forest in the Nepalese hills, linking this particular conflict to broader patterns of political contestation including the civil war, post-war 'transition', and an ongoing federalization process — all part of what we call Nepal's 'entangled scales' of politics. The case study spans the reorganization of district borders in 1961 that sparked the original dispute about who should have authority over the forest, through to the ongoing debate over the division of territory and powers in Nepal's new federal structure. We analyse the rupture and realignment of contentious claims to political authority by the Forest Department, Maoist rebels, district officials and local notables, amongst others, and the continuities of group-level negotiations pertaining to formalizing forest access claims amidst these competing political authority holders. Building on an in-depth analysis of a case study particularly rich in entangled territorial politics, our conceptualization of 'making territory' is possibly even more salient in Nepal's present juncture, as administrative borders are redrawn and territories reshaped in the highly contested process of federalization. The detailed description of entangled territorial politics we provide here shows that even if ruptures such as war and post-war political configurations unsettle and reshuffle the territories of rule, claims to political and resource rights endure (and significant efforts are made to maintain them),[1] demonstrating how territories, states and citizens are in a constant state of being made.

Community Forest User Groups (CFUGs)[2] are important players in the struggle to make territory, both because of the resources at their disposal and their ability to function effectively in contexts where other political actors, including representatives of the state, are less effective. Due to the rather complex nature of their authority over forest property, CFUGs are a potent medium for establishing the legitimacy and practices of territorial claims. CFUGs possess financial resources (from the sale of forest produce) and also control access to basic livelihood resources (fodder, litter, fuelwood). They therefore 'rule' over a significant local resource, which attracts the interest of many political intermediaries. Even for those who are less dependent on simple access to the forest, there is a significant interest in forest governance authority, for example for purposes of political profiling, building up leadership experience, or deciding how the CFUG fund will be spent. In this sense, the stakes of governing a territory as a community forest are different from those for other kinds of land. We should expect then, that political ruptures would have fundamental effects on the workings and rulings of these organizations. And yet, many CFUGs have continued to function (although many also have not) throughout the turbulent periods of war and post-war transition (Nightingale and Sharma, 2014).

Our study of fragmented and contradictory rule and the dynamic nature of state–citizen relations resonates with a strong tradition of Nepalese and South Asian literature that analyses the state–citizen–forest relationship and the imposition of order (and its resistance) on both people and forests through different forms of territorialization and governmentality.[3] While much of this literature has emphasized the power and ordering effects of

---

1. While our main focus here is on rupture and continuity in terms of territorial politics, it should be noted that this is imbricated in multiple other ongoing socio-economic and political transformations (on the topic of change, see Nightingale and Rankin, 2014; de Sales, 2011; Zharkevich, 2014). On post-war politics more generally, see the contributors to von Einsiedel et al. (2012) as well as Byrne and Klem (2015); Jha (2014); Lawoti (2014).
2. CFUGs are officially registered community-based organizations that are mandated by the Government of Nepal with responsibility for managing parcels of forestland. Crucially, however, the bundle of rights accorded to CFUGs does not include ownership, a right that remains with the state (Acharya et al., 2008). In 1978, the government of Nepal started to decentralize forest management rights, first granting limited rights to local governments. Local governments managed forests based on their political jurisdiction, with little regard for the extent of the forest itself or forest use patterns. This was changed with the 1993 Forest Act, which launched the community forestry programme. Over the last two decades, a significant proportion of forests used by communities in accessible areas of Nepal's mid-hills have been 'handed over' to user groups.
3. See, among many others, Agarwal (2005); Blaikie and Springate-Baginski (2007); Campbell (2005); Guha (1989); Nightingale and Ojha (2013); Ojha et al. (2008); Sivaramakrishnan (2000); Tarnowski (2002).

forest governmentality, our spatial analysis unpacks the overlapping and entangled 'governable spaces' (Watts, 2003) that have sedimented over years
of rupture and continuity. We analyse how these continuities and ruptures
have mapped into local processes of territorialization and forest governance,
and probe the implications for citizenship claims. Our analysis resonates
with work that has studied the negotiations of disputed political authority
over territory among rebels, state and other claimants, and the processes of
contestation and accommodation entailed in local struggles over resource
access.[4] In order to understand these dynamics we analyse concrete practices of meaning making, bordering, recognition and authority claiming at
different scales (on scale and forestry, see Ahlborg and Nightingale, 2012).

The analysis which follows is guided by three propositions. First, and
paradoxically, both territory (as a specific set of rules governing access to
forests, among other things) and citizenship rights can be quite stable even
when the political landscape itself is highly fractured, contentious, and experiencing sequences of ruptures and uncertainty. Second, territorialization is
a multi-sited process and constitutes a multitude of political spaces. Where
these spaces intersect, negotiation of their different borders and authorities
gives meaning to such categories as 'citizen', 'forest' and 'state'.[5] Third,
the relationship between citizens and state in territory-making processes is
not simply a dialectic of expansion and resistance. Citizens and groups of
citizens have their own territorial strategies, which may resist those of different state authorities, but may also adapt to, imitate or reinforce them. In
some cases, people's own territorialization strategies can also be bids to gain
explicit recognition by the state (see also Lund, Introduction to this issue).
The boundary-making process inherent in territorialization can thus produce
both state and state-like effects (Mitchell, 1991). We see this clearly when
we probe border making and claims to property and belonging at different
scales. We are therefore using property and claims to belonging as specific
lenses that give us insight into these political dynamics.

MAKING TERRITORY: CONCEPTUAL PROPOSITIONS

In order to conceptualize how property and citizenship claims become entangled in the continuities and ruptures of contested authorities and territorialization practices, we draw on Vandergeest and Peluso's landmark study from
Thailand (1995). In this work, Vandergeest and Peluso analysed the internal
territorialization of state power and its relation to the allocation of rights

---

4. For example, Gellner (2013); Korf (2005); Korf and Fünfgeld (2006); Shah (2007); Suykens
   (2010); Vandekerckhove (2011).
5. We could add 'market' to this list as processes of market formation and relations are also
   important in making territory. However, the intersection of market dynamics with the political
   relationships that we focus on is far too complex to be given adequate treatment here.

to access and use of natural resources. Their analysis suggests the gradual expansion of state power and authority into places and fields that had not previously been regulated by the state, according to a relatively coherent overall vision of controlling people and nature (see also Scott, 1998). Analyses of counter-territorial practices that resist state expansion complement our understanding of the contested nature of such processes (see, for example, Campbell, 2007; Corson, 2011; Holmes, 2014; Isager and Ivarsson, 2002).

In this chapter, we are particularly interested in the 'entangled landscape' (Moore, 2005) — that territory consists of multi-layered or multidimensional spatial (re-)organization of political authority and bundles of rights and abilities to access forest areas. Territorialization is not simply an expansion (and resistance) of state territorialization in one plane (see also Roth, 2007). Rather, it is a multi-dimensional operation that serves to produce borders, authorities and different forms of property and citizenship. We are interested in how territorialization processes create spaces in which government officials and ordinary people collude and compete over how and where state borders are asserted, and how people can make claims upon the state as citizens. We would like to emphasize three aspects in particular: the entanglement of different scales of claims making; the co-emergence of citizenship and the resource itself in territorialization processes; and the state effects of territorialization.

It is paramount to understand 'the configuration, the entanglement and interplay of these multiple "governable spaces" in a given locality and at a given time' (Korf et al., 2010: 389). Vandergeest and Peluso recognize that government agencies often have to reclassify and remap to account for the ways in which people have crossed earlier paper boundaries. Their analysis, however, does not extend to accounting for how different layers of reclassifications sediment over time (new ones do not simply replace old ones) and how different and even contradictory classifications can exist in the same place. Not only do different registers of spatial claims making coexist in the same site, but they are also implicated in mutual co-production. In developing this argument, we hope to better account for the 'verticality' of territory (Delaney, 2005: 31; see also Braun, 2000) and to show how the diversity of registers in which governance authority is claimed by different actors leads to the production of space (territory) as 'stretched out social relations' which serve to mutually transform both space and society (Massey, 1992). In other words, how they serve to transform property and citizenship.

As Lund points out in his Introduction, by differentiating rights to natural resources, territorialization contributes to the structuration of citizenship. Here we would add that by differentiating rights to natural resources, territorialization also contributes to the transformation of the resource itself. The political and natural landscapes are mutually productive (Castree and Braun, 2001; Nightingale, 2006). As Paasi (1996: 26) writes, 'landscapes are always socially constructed, they are built around dominant social institutions and are ordered by their power. Landscapes are coded by society and several coexisting codes are in a complex way linked to different spheres of life e.g. social, political, cultural, or economic. As a result, subjects and landscapes are constantly transforming each other'. The recognition of different resource use rights, and authorization of different resource use practices that are key to territorial contestations, can have a significant impact on the shape of the resource itself. Examples include the conversion of forestland to agricultural land, harvesting different types of resources, and even burning forests.[6]

Territorialization as a process to demarcate spatial borders is not only about distinguishing who has rights to use what kinds of resources within those borders, but indeed about definitions of rights-bearing subjects.[7] Such an analysis highlights how questions of citizenship and belonging are important, and how territory is the effect of struggles between different actors operating at different scales and their claims to articulate rights over space and resources. Sivaramakrishnan (2000: 448), for example, shows that 'cadastral surveys, censuses, land reforms, and commercial forestry have historically worked, as JFM [Joint Forest Management] is doing now, to instigate land use changes that redefine the village community in ways that have pitted village against village'. Further, Paasi (1996: 28) suggests that making territories is always a struggle about the right to propose new definitions of different kinds of bounded categories: 'the question of the production/reproduction of various social distinctions and identities is also essential in the case of spatial demarcations'. For example, as we shall show in detail later in this chapter, the definition of what 'community' entails can become contingent and changeable, subject to negotiation and boundary management. Following Peluso and Lund (2011), we understand 'community' as a collectivity pursuing a collaborative claim to territory.

Our case study of a forest that appears 'stuck' between a variety of overlapping and mutually exclusive claims to managerial authority demonstrates how competing territorialization practices nevertheless produce state(-like) effects. These are not simple imitations, but rather reflect strategic tacking between resisting and reproducing state power by different kinds of people, and they therefore serve to trouble a simple separation of state and society. Mitchell argues that state formation should be understood as an effect of various mundane processes including spatial organization, and that this process of rearranging social and natural environments demonstrates state power (Mitchell, 1991, 2002; see also, Harris, 2012). In other words, as Neumann

---

6. On the suppression of seasonal burning under community forestry, see Nightingale (2005). On the burning of forests as a form of resistance, see Agarwal (2005). Our evidence suggests that some CFUGs stopped harvesting timber during the war to protest Maoist/state double taxation (see also Nightingale and Sharma, 2014). However, other researchers have reported cases of forests being burned by the army to literally and figuratively 'smoke out' Maoists and punish villagers (for example, Shneiderman and Turin, 2010).
7. On the work of claiming and maintaining boundaries, see Lamb (2014) and Reeves (2011, 2014).

suggests, 'proprietary claims and the process of mapping, bounding, containing, and controlling nature and citizenry are what make a state a state. States come into being through these claims and the assertion of control over territory, resources, and people' (Neumann, 2004: 185). Thus, it is not only states and their organs and apparatus that make territory and re-inscribe their power into the landscape; citizens and groups of citizens, political brokers and other types of actors do this as well. In the process of making territory, they often bring about state 'effects', and it is in this sense that we see state formation and citizenship as entangled with territorialization. Negotiations of authority and the recognition of political and resource access rights and property relations more broadly are carried out through interactions between these rearrangements at different scales.

MAKING TERRITORY: THE EMPIRICAL CASE

Our theorization of making territory as an entangled landscape of claims to rights, authority and recognition emerges from a very particular empirical puzzle that we encountered during our research in mid-Western Nepal. Regarding this puzzle, one of our interviewees jokingly warned: 'the history of Gansnu is long and it may take days to understand' (Gansnu forest user).

It was one of those 'ethnographic moments' that make one rethink the empirical situation and its theoretical interpretation. Sarah Byrne and her research assistant had started fieldwork in the mid-western hill district of Salyan in 2011 with the intention of exploring CFUG strategies for 'living between' the army/police and Maoist rebels during Nepal's decade-long civil war.[8] To learn more about the war-time strategies and tactics of CFUGs for negotiating authority over forest resources, and in particular access to forest resources, Byrne was directed to a CFUG located at the border between Salyan and Rolpa districts. This CFUG was considered a 'model CFUG' in terms of its performance and resilience in general, and especially during the war years. With their investments in replanting, their detailed record keeping, their well-organized forest monitoring and work plan, their investments in other community and infrastructure development initiatives, this indeed seemed to be an exemplary CFUG.

During the visit, however, the forested landscape on the opposite slope posed a different question. Where this group had invested so much into replanting, the hill opposite was covered with a very lush forest. Why would people invest so much in plantation and rehabilitation, as they had done in the 'model' CFUG, when there was this very rich forest — Gansnu forest —

---

8. This chapter is based on interviews and participant observation conducted with and among Gansnu forest users during several visits to the area between 2011 and 2013. Interviews were also conducted with district level authorities and other informants in the district headquarters, as well as in Kathmandu. Gansnu is a pseudonym.

right on their doorstep? They did so, the CFUG members explained, because the newly planted forest was 'theirs', whereas the rich older forest still belonged to the District Forest Office and 'they' were not supposed to use it. In a context such as the mid-hills of Nepal, where the management of huge swathes of forest land has been handed over to local communities, finding a forest in an accessible area that has not yet been handed over is somewhat anomalous.[9] In this locality, the situation had been complicated by the border between the districts of Salyan and Rolpa. Running right through Gansnu forest, the border draws into question who exactly constitutes 'the community' that can decide about forest access in the context of community forestry. In other words: territorial borders dissected the forested landscape, and they did so on several scales, including those of district borders and those of the borders between private land holding and state forest.

This was what we considered our empirical puzzle: why did Gansnu forest not yet belong to 'the community' (whatever its borders might be) in a neighbourhood with several functional CFUGs? This puzzle leads us to the following observation: although the political landscape in Nepal has seen many ruptures and dramatic changes both of political boundaries and rulers, these ruptures have not resolved the question of who is entitled to receive benefits from this particular forest. Whereas the natural landscape has gradually changed through the drawing and redrawing of different borders, particularly that between public forestland and private agricultural land, significant political ruptures have not disrupted the continuity of disputed claims over forest property rights (see also Zurick, 1989). The ruptures have only adapted the practices and discourses through which consistent claims to recognition of these rights are made.

In the following sections we discuss the wider (in a spatial and temporal sense) territorial politics that frame these practices and discourses to claim recognition of forest property rights in order to illuminate how such entanglements are constitutive of state formation and public authority. We distinguish three kinds of territorializing practices that invoke different scales. First, we trace the politics of administrative bordering, including its continuity and contestation during times of civil war with competing governing authorities in place. Second, we outline the forest-related territory-claiming practices deployed by different categories of forest users. Third, we show how encroachment and claiming of land for individual use is a form of territorial practice. These three layers (or scales) are entangled — that is, they

---

9. However, it is certainly not unique. During our fieldwork, we were made aware of a handful of other cases around the borders of Salyan district, for example (interviews with Salyan DFO and Khalanga-based NGO). Further, as noted above, the ongoing process of federalization is likely to make such issues even more salient — not only the location of the borders themselves but the distribution of powers across them. Forests appear on both the provincial 'own' list as well as the 'concurrent list' of the 2015 constitution, meaning that both federal and provincial governments have a claim to forest governance authority.

Figure 1. The Districts of Salyan and Rolpa in Mid-Western Nepal

influence and shape each other, in terms of rule, rupture and continuity. The pertinent question for our analysis is therefore whether or not — and in which ways — a rupture in rule in one layer affects the rules of the game in another, in terms of legitimately claiming resources and citizenship, and demarcating boundaries.

Our case study is located in a border area between the districts of Salyan and Rolpa (see Figure 1), where three different local government units and three different electoral districts meet. Salyan and Rolpa are two ethnically diverse districts in Nepal's mid-western hills, one of the most disadvantaged regions in Nepal that has experienced weak state penetration and a reliance on governance through local 'big men' (Whelpton, 2005) and strong person-alized political networks (Ramirez, 2004). The region also has a long history of radical politics dating back to the mid-twentieth century (Cailmail, 2009; Ogura, 2007), and in the 1990s became a centre of the decade-long Maoist rebellion. The border is marked by the forest that traverses it, as well as a small market/village, the outer reaches of which encroach on the forest. In the market there are a couple of tea shops, and shops selling agricultural supplies, medicine and non-perishable goods. People from both districts use this market, which is accessible by a dirt road from Salyan's district head-quarters Khalanga (the connecting road was constructed in 2005). Liwang, the district headquarter of Rolpa, is not accessible by road from this place but can be reached by foot in one day. The main political parties are all present here and the area on the Salyan side of the border is well known for producing district-level political leaders. People living in the settlements around the border are mostly from the relatively less disadvantaged social groups, including ethnic minorities, and the extent of literacy, access to safe drinking water, and other measures of well-being are relatively high for the districts.

Territorial Politics 1: District Re-bordering

District border(ing) politics is a layer of territorialization that (at present) is both undefined and highly contested, given the political stalemate on the national level, where demarcation of sub-national administrative entities and their boundaries has been highly controversial. This is also the case in Gansnu forest, which is situated on the border between the two districts of Salyan and Rolpa. In this section we analyse how overlapping territorial claims have been produced, contested and legitimated, and ask what their dis/continuities can tell us about the importance of place-based notions of political belonging and citizenship. We highlight how citizens are engaged in territory-claiming practices in the form of political lobbying across scales, having recourse to judicial review over property registration, and moving to access a public service. The territorial configurations of electoral constituencies, public service delivery, private landholdings and war-time Maoist People's Governments, among others, are at stake in these territorial politics of district re-bordering.

In order to explore the production of Salyan and Rolpa district territories, it is useful to distinguish three key and relatively recent periods. These are: the redrawing of district borders that took place in 1975; the overlapping state and rebel governments in place during most of the civil war (1996–2006); and the ongoing discussions (since 2008) over the shape of a future federal Nepal. In the first period, the interests of local political leaders proved to be highly significant in shaping how actors at local, district and national levels mobilized property claims. In 1961–2 the government of Nepal undertook a nationwide 're-districting' process establishing the current 75 districts, including the district of Rolpa (which was carved out from neighbouring Pyuthan and Salyan). A second re-districting in 1975 again changed the boundaries, while maintaining the same number of districts. Ostensibly this was to create smaller districts and improve access to public services. A Royal Proclamation (*Raj patra*) was issued that documented which localities were to be moved from one district to another, but this led to disputes over precisely where the border should lie.[10]

In the 1975 re-districting process, two issues were at stake. These were the location of Rolpa's district headquarters and the location of the border between the two districts. Powerful leaders lobbied to have the district headquarters of Rolpa placed in the locality of Gansnu forest. The district capital of the neighbouring district of Rukum had already been shifted in 1973 after competition between political families (Ogura, 2007), so there was a precedent with which people were familiar. However, other leaders lobbied more successfully for another locality called Liwang, one that is

---

10. Photocopies of the Proclamation were carefully preserved by our informants, but are getting old and are difficult to read in some parts. Attempts to find the original in archives in Kathmandu were not successful.

more central to Rolpa district as a whole (interviews with Gansnu forest users; Salyan District Forest Office; Khalanga-based historian). Thus the area around Gansnu, which was a sufficiently important place to be under consideration as a district headquarters, remained stuck in a border area, politically peripheral to both Salyan and Rolpa. While significant political capital remained with the area's leaders, the locus of decision making as well as investment in infrastructure shifted elsewhere.

Having failed to attract the district headquarters, the local leaders were successful in moving the district border (interviews with Gansnu forest users; Salyan District Forest Office; Khalanga-based historian). They were able to ensure that some localities were moved from Rolpa into neighbouring Salyan district, which moved the district border to the east. Political leaders from both sides of the current border suggested that the placement of the border at this time was based on political interests: ensuring that powerful political families were in separate electoral constituencies meant that they did not have to compete against each other for election to the national parliament. As a result of this territorial politics, Gansnu forest was located at the intersections of national electoral constituencies as well as the district borders.[11] It thus marks the meeting/dividing point of three different national electoral constituencies, in which the citizenship right of voting is exercised, as well as serving to shape local political authority significantly.

During the civil war, the second of our three periods, the area around Gansnu forest was again subject to a rescaling of political authority. The Nepalese state, in the form of public officials, police and security apparatus, as well as the 'people's government' (*jana sarkar*) established by the Maoist rebels, mobilized competing claims to political authority in the area. By 2003, Kiyoko Ogura found that *jana sarkar* were established in 43 out of the 47 local government units of Salyan (2007: 461). The existing district borders remained salient (or at least this one did) for both state and Maoist governance. Inhabitants on the Salyan side of the border, for example, were governed by a different chain of command than those on the Rolpa side.

Because Rolpa and neighbouring Rukum were their 'base areas', the Maoists considered borders like the one between Rolpa and Salyan important for security reasons. Maoists were especially concerned that information about their numbers and movements did not travel outside of the base area, and therefore discouraged people on the Rolpa side from talking to their neighbours in Salyan. Thus, in effect, Maoist everyday governance took place within the territory of the existing districts and local government units, and this served to demarcate the Maoists' base area in the minds of local inhabitants. However, the whole area was also considered part of the ethnicity-based Magarant Autonomous Region declared by the Maoists in

11. For a fascinating account of the process of producing and attempting to align electoral constituencies, administrative districts and census districts, see Kansakar (1977).

2004 in a move intended to rescale and reframe the basis of district-level authority in the region (Lecomte-Tilouine, 2004; Ogura, 2007, 2008; de Sales, 2007).[12] In a more abstract sense, the retention of the Rolpa–Salyan border, combined with their ethnicity-based approach to belonging, served to inscribe which citizens were considered 'core' within the new *jana sarkar*, and which were more peripheral.

After 2006, with the signing of the Comprehensive Peace Agreement, the third period of district re-bordering began. This period was characterized by uncertainty about the territorial governance of Nepal: national-level negotiations about transforming Nepal into a federal state started in 2008 and in 2015 the Constituent Assembly promulgated a new, federal constitution. At the time of writing (early 2016), the delimitation of federal units foreseen in the constitution was being both contested and negotiated, and its implementation appeared unclear. The 2015 constitution defined a seven-province model and distributed the districts among these provinces, splitting three current districts. This is important to the issue of the border conflict around Gansnu forest. Our respondents expected that the current (at the time of the fieldwork in 2011–13) district border would have much less salience in the future, as the whole area was expected to be part of the same new province. Thus, Byrne was assured, the 'issue about where to register the forest cannot be decided at the moment. But it does not matter because in a couple of years this border will not matter anymore and we won't have to decide in which district to register the CFUG' (Gansnu forest user). Political boundaries created a resource management problem, but they were also expected to make the management issue disappear again. In contrast to these expectations, however, the delimitation of provinces proposed in the new 2015 constitution reinforces this particular border, as the border between the proposed 'Province 5' and 'Province 6' divides Salyan and Rolpa.

The rescaling of political borders and its effects on property and citizenship rights is still highly contested. Throughout the ruptures in rule, the issue at stake remains fundamentally tied to territorially based property and citizenship rights: who has the right to access and govern the forest and where do citizens belong? This can be seen in two circumstances — one historical, one contemporary. The first, historical, circumstance concerns a decoupling of the territorial borders of property (land ownership) from those of citizenship (entitlement to state services). When the land survey took place in Salyan in 1981, everyone in the territory of Salyan district was required to register their land and was issued with a title documenting this. Some families who maintained claims to land property on both sides of the new district border 'were prevented' from registering their land. Effectively, registering

12. The production of ethnic territories both by the Maoists during the war and in the post-war debates about how to define new federal units (one proposal is for ethnic federalism) is highly relevant but not analysed here. See, for example, Shneiderman and Tillin (2015). On the importance of territory for the Maoist project see Parvati (2005).

the land in Salyan would have shifted the district border back slightly east again, and would have linked the concerned families' citizenship, access to public services and electoral constituency to Salyan. One of these families took their case all the way to the Supreme Court of Nepal to demand that their land be registered in Salyan. The court found that they did not live in Salyan, but in Rolpa (confirming that the new district border would stand). However, in an unusual compromise, the court ruled that the families could keep their citizenship registration in Salyan (for voting, public services and other such purposes) but that their land would have to be registered in Rolpa. This verdict meant that these families were supposed to pay land taxes in Rolpa and access public services in Salyan. The state seemed to recognize at the time that it had to let its citizens 'belong' in the places with which they felt some association, and yet it also wanted to ensure that the lines on the map stayed in their 'proper' place. The war-time Maoist People's Governments were similarly concerned with keeping the border in its 'proper' place, and reportedly forced the reluctant Rolpalis to sign a paper saying that they were from Rolpa and would refrain from using public services in Salyan (Gansnu forest users). This was part of the Maoists' strategy to use ethnicity and geographical belonging as political categories to establish authority over territory.

The other, contemporary, circumstance concerns the redrawing of internal administrative boundaries to create provinces, and the regrouping of districts within them as laid out in the 2015 Constitution. This reordering raises contentious questions about community, citizenship, territory and authority (as is evidenced by the widespread and violent protests with which the new constitution was received in southern Nepal). A re-districting proposal that would have divided Salyan swiftly generated tensions in the district; for three to four days, 'people called for a "single Salyan" [*akhanda Salyan* in Nepali]' (Saferworld, 2013: 39). While the situation eventually calmed down and the main political parties stated that they had not proposed dividing the district, similar incidents reported in other parts of the country (for example, Surkhet in 2015) indicated that this was not an isolated case, but rather reflected contestations over the underlying principles of federalism by different groups of people. Furthermore, this incident resonates with concerns raised by some of our informants about ending up in a new province that 'belongs' to another ethnic group (Gansnu forest users), which relates also to tensions of longer standing between ethnic groups in the region (Ogura, 2007).

In this section we have traced a series of territorializing practices employed by state organs, state officials and citizens in relation to the border of the districts of Salyan and Rolpa. These practices evolved around struggles over access to place-related citizenship rights such as voting (electoral constituencies, location of the district headquarters) and property regimes (location of registered property). While the state reserves the right to delimit its internal units of governance, politically active citizens engage in border making (and claiming property rights) as well — for example, through attempts to mobilize political influence, through a court case, or by floating proposals for dividing the district. Interestingly, the revolutionary Maoist People's Governments replicated these very same territorial borders during the war: there was no territorial rupture in that sense. However, the Maoists added an additional layer of ethnically defined political units: a practice of rescaling borders, and a recognition of the ethnic (as opposed to place-based) basis of belonging that has important implications in today's debates on federalism. Thus — through their participation in making the borders of districts, electoral constituencies, war-time People's Governments, and future federal units — a group of citizens has been engaged in an ongoing negotiation with governmental and other political actors over the shape of the political landscape and the resultant linkages between territories, property and citizenship rights.

Territorial Politics 2: Forest-related Territory-claiming Practices

In this section, we analyse forest governance practices, where the state-like effects of territorializing practices resulting from citizen actions are becoming most visible. We highlight the ways in which 'community' members claimed rights to forest property and the authority to govern by establishing the community forest as a bounded and meaningful social space with a particular bundle of powers.

Conflicts over the territory of community forests have not been uncommon in rural Nepal, particularly during the process of establishing new CFUGs in the 1990s (see Yadav et al., 2003). Usually these conflicts are about either the exact territorial borders of the forest in question — when the relationship between outdated and incomprehensible cadastral maps and the situation on the ground is contested — or entitlement to membership of the group, in which the main issue is the extent to which seasonal forest users (pastoralists) are included alongside everyday forest users. Generally these conflicts are resolved at the time of handing over the forest. However, there are a number of cases, like Gansnu, that remain unresolved and conflictual. Furthermore, as Nepal moves forward with the massive redrawing, re-scaling and redistributing project that is federalization, disputes about who has what governance authority over what territory will doubtless proliferate.

Here, we study a particular situation of state absence (the state was unable or unwilling to govern Gansnu forest effectively), in which citizens intervened to define the bundle of rights governing forest use. The users claimed they were practising conservation with greater credibility than the state itself, thereby '[territorializing] like a state' (Vaccaro, 2005: 6). In this case, citizens were not waiting to be 'invited' by the government to assume authority over forests (as would be the 'correct' practice), but actively promoted these claims by speaking to the government in its own language. In so doing, this group of forest users both sought recognition (to become an official community forest user group) and bolstered their claim to forest governance authority by mimicking government practices of forest conservation, albeit as an 'unofficial' CFUG (an institutional entity without formal government recognition).

This interpretation needs to be placed in context. The people living around Gansnu forest were active members of other CFUGs in the area. Gansnu is a relatively valuable forest — not necessarily in terms of timber, but in terms of non-timber forest products and basic subsistence needs such as fuelwood and fodder, medicinal herbs and water — making it attractive to CFUG governance. Furthermore, in Salyan and Rolpa districts, between one half and two thirds of forestland has been handed over to 'communities' within the powerful implementation process of community forest management. So, why not Gansnu?

In Gansnu, we were told that the forest could not be handed over because of a disagreement over who could claim property rights to it. The great majority of the forestland was considered to be in what is now Rolpa district, and the great majority of the traditional users live in what is now Salyan district. According to official legislation, there was no problem for forest users from Salyan to be members of a community forest located and registered in Rolpa, as official policy does not consider district borders as central in defining forest users.[13] However, the forest users themselves perceived this to be a problem. Their problem was that officially the forest would need to be registered in one or other district; users on either side of the border feared exclusion should the forest be registered in the other district. Some informants therefore claimed that the core problem was a lack of trust between users located in different districts (Gansnu forest users). The scale at which local users felt secure in claiming property rights, then, seemed to reflect the official system prior to the 1990s under which local governments managed forests and the relevant territorial scale was that of the local government, as one informant suggested (interview with Kathmandu-based community forestry advocate). Thus, the interesting dynamic, in the case of Gansnu, is that forest users contest the proper scale for forest governance authority, even while simple access could be ensured (at least legally).

In view of the unresolved political questions of district borders and belonging (citizenship), local resource users formed an 'unofficial' community forest user group. The main purpose of the group is to provide a space in which issues of forest governance can be discussed, and to maintain a claim by the communities to legitimate authority over what otherwise is government management (in which communities have no say). The group has been functioning over the past 30 years (with the exception of the latter years of the war). It mirrors or imitates official groups in several ways, but is not

---

13. The Master Plan for the Forestry Sector of 1988, the Forest Act of 1993, and the Forest Regulations of 1995 give the legal and regulatory frame for community forestry.

registered with the District Forest Office (DFO) of either district. Nevertheless, the people are all members of other official CFUGs and therefore know the basic working procedures and rules. For some years the user group has been a joint one, mostly when it was under the leadership of someone from Rolpa. At the time of Byrne's last visit (March 2013), a joint 'unofficial' CFUG was in operation, with a chairperson from Rolpa and secretary and treasurer from Salyan.

These resource users thereby asserted the function of conserving the forest resource, as the DFOs of both Rolpa and Salyan claimed not to have enough staff to supervise the forests under their responsibility effectively. Conservation thus functioned as a property practice (von Benda-Beckmann et al., 2006). Categorically, it served to align the forest users with the government's policies aiming to conserve forestland and wildlife and to prevent deforestation. In concrete terms, the practice of conservation instigated by the unofficial CFUG delimited — on its own initiative — a particular bundle of access rights. In this case, the user group was doing the job of the DFO, and claimed to be doing it more effectively than the DFO, thereby legitimating their property claims in terms of access.

This discourse of conservation was repeatedly and extensively employed by all of our informants. It was explicitly cited as the reason for establishing an 'unofficial' CFUG, as a local leader noted: 'People had started destroying the forest. But others — we — decided that we should protect the forest because we are all users, even if the forest belongs to the government. The committee ran smoothly for 12 years, but after that could not run because of political power games' (Gansnu forest users). Further, the 'unofficial' Gansnu CFUG actually calls itself the 'Gansnu Forest Conservation Committee' and addressed an official letter of complaint to the DFOs of Salyan and Rolpa in this name. With the subject line 'Call for justice', this letter accuses three named individuals of 'illegitimate forest destruction' and threatening the forest guard (letter to the DFOs of Salyan and Rolpa, dated 05.02.2067 in the Nepali calendar). While their knowledge of Byrne's former affiliation with a community forestry programme may have influenced why this topic was constantly raised, we were very struck by the forest users' discursive and practical commitments to conservation.

It is thus by exercising territorial control over spaces, and over the relationships between people and resources that emerge within those spaces, that social organizations (in this case the CFUG) exhibit state effects. Although the unofficial CFUG did not have an operational plan or a constitution — which are required of official CFUGs — it did impose a series of rules. These rules were similar to those imposed in neighbouring CFUGs, and while they were not written down, they were clearly well understood, as almost everyone we asked gave the same account. In order to help enforce these rules, the forest users constituting the unofficial CFUG had employed a local resident as forest guard for 22 years, paid through contributions from the forest users. According to the forest guard, his tasks were to stop people from cutting timber, hunting animals (deer), grazing animals, and collecting herbs. Local people often raised the fact that they were employing the forest guard as a sign that they were serious about conservation. The community had no authority to impose these rules, as it was government property and the DFO was in charge of managing and protecting it. The DFO of Salyan (three individuals held the post of DFO in the 2.5 year span in which field-work for this chapter was conducted) generally tolerated these practices as long as the community was acting in the interests of conservation. The re-spondents from Salyan often voiced their conservation credentials and their seriousness about its implementation as a reason why they should have the authority to manage the forest. Here we see how forest conservation is not only an invention of the international environmentalist community, but also a specific indigenous practice consisting of myriad diverse and sophisticated local initiatives that are conservationist and at least partially effective in the sustainable management of local natural resources (Müller-Böker, 1991; Zurick, 1990).

In fact, conservation practices are being used to *make territory* by attempt-ing to bound Gansnu forest differently and define the bundle of use rights available. These practices have ranged from the laissez-faire approach of the DFO, to the proactive approach of forest users employing a forest guard for a forest to which they had no official property rights. The community adopted many of the practices and discourses of community forestry poli-cies, in particular the emphasis on conservation and good governance, in the service of their own territorializing strategy. Though they may appear like fully 'environmentalized' subjects (Agarwal, 2005), we suggest rather that the community was 'territorializing like a state', precisely to make a claim to a state-controlled resource in the language of a state-sponsored programme. The mimicking of the practices and discourses of community forestry was thus a territorial strategy to ensure *de facto*, if not *de jure*, continued rights to access and use Gansnu forest. The discourse of conservation was more prominently expressed on the Salyan side of the border, which had a weaker claim based on where the border was delimited at the time of research. This discourse served here primarily to shore up claims to territorial authority and to (re)shape state–citizen relations.

Territorial Politics 3: Encroachment and the Politics of Recognition

Property categories and taxation are other important dimensions through which citizen–state relations are negotiated. Conflicts over individual land-use practices, in particular around the conversion of forestland to farmland, are a potent domain: within it, citizens claim rights and territory is produced. In this particular context, the dynamics of a series of political ruptures complicate matters as land-use patterns that may have been recognized under one regime are brought into question under its successor. We will illustrate this by looking at *ailani* land, which is public land privately occupied and not registered.[14] These transformative processes highlight different — and sometimes contradictory — interests within what we have been calling a community.

The struggle for recognition of customary land use is key to *ailani*. *Ailani* has long been practised in the area around Gansnu and informants described it as being quite a normal land-use practice (Gansnu forest users). However, it had become a contested issue in two ways. First, during the war, the Maoists demanded tax from *ailani* land, saying that if people were using public land they should pay for it. They charged a certain amount per *ropani* (unit of land measurement), although the figures we were given varied somewhat (and they may also have varied in practice). Some people were able to resist them and negotiate their way out of paying. Those who paid were issued with a certificate to document the transaction, which served to legitimate and recognize the occupation of that land. The *ailani* system was thus made official by the Maoist war-time government, but its legitimacy disappeared when that government disappeared at the end of the war. The new Nepali government did not recognize land registrations carried out by these war-time governments. Transparency about what happened to the funds paid, how much additional forest encroachment the Maoists legitimized, and the extent to which the documentation of tax payments is still valid as a confirmation of use rights, all remain highly sensitive issues (see also de Sales, 2013).

The term 'encroachment' signposts the second contentious issue: what for some was a more or less acceptable traditional and widespread practice (and legitimized through the Maoist taxation), seemed to others an unacceptable, illicit act. Several informants recounted incidents of alleged violence, for example when some 40 self-appointed 'forest defenders' confronted a small group of women who were cutting grass and aggressively confiscated their knives, baskets and other material (Gansnu forest users). Precisely when and how *ailani* was considered to have turned into encroachment was unclear, but it seemed some forest users believed that certain people had taken over too much of their neighbouring forestland. A little expansion of land was considered to be common practice, but at a certain point some people had, in their neighbours' view, become greedy.

The question here is who provides or refuses recognition for *ailani* practices, and whether recognition varies across different categories of people. Indeed, some informants were adamant that forest could not be registered as a community forest until these war-time forest encroachments were

---

14. *Ailani* refers to a situation in which the land user does not have the official legal right to use the land, but is generally understood to have some kind of customary or traditional usufruct rights. The general pattern is that a farmer who owns a particular piece of registered land gradually expands by taking over nearby areas if they are unregistered or public land. Alternatively, at the time of land registration, people might have registered less land than they were actually using.

documented and addressed. They considered the establishment of totally new plots of farmland within the forest as a clear case of encroachment, and pointed out to us some cleared islands in the middle of the forest to demonstrate their disapproval. As the DFOs in both districts were taking a hands-off stance (justifying their caution by citing a lack of capacity to monitor properly, for example), groups of forest users had taken it upon themselves to police this issue. The forest users we spoke to on both sides of the district border decried the extent of deforestation during the war years when the unofficial Gansnu CFUG had stopped functioning after threats to its leaders by the Maoist authorities (Gansnu forest users). The Maoists' system of taxation had encouraged and legitimized the encroachment, pushing up the high rate of forestland conversion during the war. This made efforts to turn back or reduce encroachment after the war politically sensitive.

The contentious question of *ailani* thus indicates how territorial practices at one scale are often intertwined with territorial practices at other scales. Conservation credentials were used as a practice to legitimize claims to forest governance authority and, at the same time, served to demarcate various forms of property and belonging. In this particular case, claims to have the right to 'police' encroachment became intertwined with the legacy of territorial practices imposed/allowed by the Maoists during the war, the failure of the state officials to implement regulations, and the conservation rhetoric of an unofficial CFUG that gained organizational strength after the war. These struggles over the recognition of *ailani* practices indicate how territorializing practices become entangled with authority and citizenship claims. Through the ruptures in forest and *ailani* governance perpetuated by the war, continuities in practices of conservation and claims to belonging remained. It is inadequate to assume that the openings provided by the war were simply accepted and institutionalized, or that in the post-war setting new claims to *ailani* land were categorically dismissed. The openings served to reshape the property–citizen relation and such reconfigurations are never smooth or uncontested.

MAKING TERRITORY

In this chapter we have described three different scales within which property rights and authority over a contested forest located on the border between Salyan and Rolpa districts in mid-western Nepal were demarcated. Our argument has been that while political ruptures caused by the war and post-war dynamics unsettle and reshuffle the political terrain, claims to political and resource rights endure, even if the language and form of the claim are adapted. These claims are embedded within existing political jurisdictions but, at the same time, actors at different scales lay claims to property and citizenship rights by working across jurisdictional scales. It is within this broad understanding that the words of the informant quoted at the outset have something to tell us: 'If we are working for conservation, we have no one to fear'. Conservation became one among a number of tactical narratives to effectuate claims to forest territory amidst the turmoil of a highly unstable political landscape. User-group members successfully claimed property rights over that forest territory in a fragmented political landscape of competing authority claimants (government and Maoist rebels) and shifting political constellations at different scales (changing district borders, changes in governance regimes attached to the forest). The important point is that they did this by claiming to produce 'good' territory that matched the state's ambitions.

Our case points to the importance of recognizing that citizens have their own strategies and integrating this insight into our analyses of territorialization. An exploration of property rights to a forest sitting on the border between two districts has helped to show that the relationship between citizens and states in processes of territorialization is not simply the dialectic of expansion and resistance, but rather is complicated by a series of discontinuous strategies on both sides. Territorialization practices serve to produce state effects, both by being domains wherein authority over forest property and district borders are contested, and also by highlighting the muddy tracts of citizenship claims. These claims are entangled in jurisdiction over land taxation, conservation landscapes, and encroachment on forests that are technically the property of the government. In our analysis, we have traced out a series of processes through which 'state', 'citizen' and 'forest' as rights objects are mutually produced through acts of territorialization. In so doing, we have highlighted how concrete practices of meaning making, bordering, recognition, and authority claiming produce authority within political and natural landscapes.

What also emerges from this analysis is how a rupture in rule at one scale has remarkably little effect on the terms of claiming property and access rights and demarcating boundaries at other scales. Instead, forest users maintain their access and property claims across a variegated, ruptured and contested landscape of competing political authorities with ever-changing configurations due to national political ruptures. They assert citizenship rights by demanding access to services in sites that make most sense for them geographically, but this kind of territorial claim is simultaneously resisted by the national state that wants to protect the integrity of its jurisdiction over land. Citizens thus find themselves sitting within an entangled landscape of property, territory, access and rights that does not map cleanly onto the political jurisdictional borders surrounding them. This complex mapping illuminates some of the terrains within which claims to belonging are being contested in Nepal today. While ethnicity is currently paramount in shaping national-level federalism debates, at the local scale we find more complex entanglements of territory, property and identities that are bound up in both national political ruptures (federalism) and historically embedded practices and claims (*ailani*, community forestry, and district borders).

Political ruptures expose these entanglements and make them more visible, thereby providing the empirical material for a reading of territorialization as 'making territory' outside the formal confines of the state. In the current context, understanding these fractured and multi-sited moments of territorialization and state formation are absolutely crucial to an analysis of Nepal's contested politics.

Seeing territorialization as an expanding frontier of state territory into forestlands, resisted in various ways by local communities, is therefore simply not sufficient. Making territory is rather a co-production: it takes place at a variety of scales and constitutes a multitude of political spaces. Territory is an effect of the socio-political relations of multiple claimants with their desires and struggles for citizenship and recognition, and multiple authority holders. Where these spaces intersect, negotiation of their different boundaries and differently composed relationships between rights and authority gives meaning to such categories as 'citizen', 'forest' and 'state'. It is in this sense that territorializing practices are foundational to state formation. They show the messy and complex practices through which authority is claimed and legitimated, citizenship rights are asserted and defined, and property rights quite literally transform landscapes and resources. Territorialization is more than a state project, and at the same time effectuates a state 'effect'. In a broader political landscape of rupture, discontinuities and turmoil, these territorial effects are always fragile and preliminary in their achievements. And yet these preliminary achievements in particular sites can endure over a long period of time and serve to demarcate citizens, resources and authority.

REFERENCES

Acharya, K.P., J. Adhikari and D.R. Khanal (2008) 'Forest Tenure Regimes and their Impact on Livelihoods in Nepal', *Journal of Forest and Livelihood* 7(1): 6–18.

Agarwal, A. (2005) *Environmentality: Technologies of Government and the Making of Subjects.* Durham, NC and London: Duke University Press.

Ahlborg, H. and A.J. Nightingale (2012) 'Mismatch between Scales of Knowledge in Nepalese Forestry: Epistemology, Power, and Policy Implications', *Ecology and Society* 17(4): 16.

von Benda-Beckmann, F., K. von Benda-Beckmann and M.G. Wiber (2006) 'The Properties of Property', in F. von Benda-Beckmann, K. von Benda-Beckmann and M.G. Wiber (eds) *Changing Properties of Property*, pp. 1–39. New York and Oxford: Berghahn Books.

Blaikie, P. and O. Springate-Baginski (eds) (2007) *Forests, People and Power: The Political Ecology of Reform in South Asia.* London: Earthscan.

Braun, B. (2000) 'Producing Vertical Territory: Geology and Governmentality in Late Victorian Canada', *Cultural Geographies* 7(1): 7–46.

Byrne, S. and B. Klem (2015) 'Constructing Legitimacy in Post-war Transition: The Return of "Normal" Politics in Nepal and Sri Lanka?', *Geoforum* 66: 224–33.

Cailmail, B. (2009) 'A History of Nepalese Maoism since its Foundation by Mohan Bikram Singh', *European Bulletin of Himalayan Studies* 33–34(2008–2009): 11–38.

Campbell, B. (2005) 'Nature's Discontents in Nepal', *Conservation and Society* 3(2): 323–53.

Campbell, B. (2007) 'Resisting the Environmentalist State', in D.N. Gellner (ed.) *Resistance and the State: Nepalese Experiences*, pp. 83–112. New York: Berghahn Books.

Castree, N. and B. Braun (2001) *Social Nature: Theory, Practice, and Politics*. Oxford and Malden, MA: Blackwell Publishers.

Corson, C. (2011) 'Territorialization, Enclosure and Neoliberalism: Non-state Influence in Struggles over Madagascar's Forests', *Journal of Peasant Studies* 38(4): 703–26.

Delaney, D. (2005) *Territory: A Short Introduction*. Malden, MA: Blackwell Publishing.

von Einsiedel, S., D.M. Malone and S. Pradhan (eds) (2012) *Nepal in Transition: From People's War to Fragile Peace*. Cambridge: Cambridge University Press.

Gellner, D.N. (ed.) (2013) *Borderland Lives in Northern South Asia*. Durham, NC: Duke University Press.

Guha, R. (1989) *The Unquiet Woods: Ecological Change and Peasant Resistance in the Himalaya*. Berkeley and Los Angeles, CA: University of California Press.

Harris, L.M. (2012) 'State as Socionatural Effect: Variable and Emergent Geographies of the State in Southeastern Turkey', *Comparative Studies of South Asia, Africa and the Middle East* 32(1): 25–39.

Holmes, G. (2014) 'Defining the Forest, Defending the Forest: Political Ecology, Territoriality, and Resistance to a Protected Area in the Dominican Republic', *Geoforum* 53: 1–10.

Isager, L. and S. Ivarsson (2002) 'Contesting Landscapes in Thailand: Tree Ordination as Counter-territorialization', *Critical Asian Studies* 34(3): 395–417.

Jha, P. (2014) *Battles of the New Republic: A Contemporary History of Nepal*. Delhi: Aleph.

Kansakar, V.B.S. (1977) 'Population Censuses of Nepal and the Problems of Data Analysis'. Kathmandu: Centre for Economic Development and Administration, Tribhuvan University.

Korf, B. (2005) 'Rethinking the Greed–Grievance Nexus: Property Rights and the Political Economy of War in Sri Lanka', *Journal of Peace Research* 42(2): 201–17.

Korf, B. and H. Fünfgeld (2006) 'War and the Commons: Assessing the Changing Politics of Violence, Access and Entitlements in Sri Lanka', *Geoforum* 37(3): 391–403.

Korf, B., M. Engeler and T. Hagmann (2010) 'The Geography of Warscape', *Third World Quarterly* 31(3): 385–99.

Lamb, V. (2014) '"Where is the Border?" Villagers, Environmental Consultants and the "Work" of the Thai–Burma Border', *Political Geography* 40: 1–12.

Lawoti, M. (2014) 'Reform and Resistance in Nepal', *Journal of Democracy* 25(2): 131–45.

Lecomte-Tilouine, M. (2004) 'Ethnic Demands within Maoism: Questions of Magar Territorial Autonomy, Nationality and Class', in M. Hutt (ed.) *Himalayan People's War: Nepal's Maoist Rebellion*, pp. 112–35. Bloomington, IN: Indiana University Press.

Massey, D. (1992) 'Politics and Space/Time', *New Left Review* I/196: 65–84.

Mitchell, T. (1991) 'The Limits of the State: Beyond Statist Approaches and their Critics', *The American Political Science Review* 85(1): 77–96.

Mitchell, T. (2002) *Rule of Experts: Egypt, Techno-politics, Modernity*. Berkeley and Los Angeles, CA: University of California Press.

Moore, D.S. (2005) *Suffering for Territory: Race, Place and Power in Zimbabwe*. Durham, NC and London: Duke University Press.

Müller-Böker, U. (1991) 'Knowledge and Evaluation of the Environment in Traditional Societies of Nepal', *Mountain Research and Development* 11(2): 101–14.

Neumann, R. (2004) 'Nature–State–Territory: Towards a Critical Theorization of Conservation Enclosures', in R. Peet and M. Watts (eds) *Liberation Ecologies: Environment, Development and Social Movements* (2nd edn.), pp. 179–99. London: Routledge.

Nightingale, A.J. (2005) '"The Experts Taught Us All We Know": Professionalisation and Knowledge in Nepalese Community Forestry', *Antipode* 37(3): 581–604.

Nightingale, A. (2006) 'The Nature of Gender: Work, Gender, and Environment', *Environment and Planning D: Society and Space* 24(2): 165–85.

Nightingale, A.J. and H.R. Ojha (2013) 'Rethinking Power and Authority: Symbolic Violence and Subjectivity in Nepal's Terai Forests', *Development and Change* 44(1): 29–51.

Nightingale, A. and K. Rankin (2014) 'Political Transformations: Collaborative Feminist Scholarship in Nepal', *Himalaya, the Journal of the Association for Nepal and Himalayan Studies* 34(1): 105–17.

Nightingale, A. and J. Sharma (2014) 'Conflict Resilience among Community Forestry User Groups: Experiences in Nepal', *Disasters* 38(3): 517–39.

Ogura, K. (2007) 'Maoists, People and the State as Seen from Rolpa and Rukum', in H. Ishii, D.N. Gellner and K. Nawa (eds) *Political and Social Transformations in North India and Nepal (Social Dynamics in Northern South Asia, volume 2)*, pp. 437–75. Delhi: Manohar.

Ogura, K. (2008) 'Maoist People's Governments 2001–2005: The Power in Wartime', in D.N. Gellner and K. Hachhethu (eds) *Local Democracy in South Asia: Microprocesses of Democratisation in Nepal and its Neighbours*, pp. 175–231. Delhi: Sage.

Ojha, H.R., N.P. Timsina, C. Kumar, M.R. Banjade and B. Belcher (2008) *Communities, Forests and Governance: Policy and Institutional Innovations from Nepal*. Delhi: Adroit.

Paasi, A. (1996) *Territories, Boundaries and Consciousness: The Changing Geographies of the Finnish–Russian Border*. Chichester: Wiley.

Parvati Yami, H. (2005) 'People's Power in Nepal', *Monthly Review: An Independent Socialist Magazine* 57(6). http://monthlyreview.org/2005/11/01/peoples-power-in-nepal/

Peluso, N.L. and C. Lund (2011) 'New Frontiers of Land Control: Introduction', *Journal of Peasant Studies* 38(4): 667–81.

Raj, Y. (2013) 'Ruptures and Repairs: A New Vantage in South Asian Historiography', in Y. Raj (ed.) *Ruptures and Repairs in South Asia: Historical Perspectives*, pp. 1–20. Kathmandu: Martin Chautari.

Ramirez, P. (2004) 'Maoism in Nepal: Towards a Comparative Perspective', in M. Hutt (ed.) *Himalayan 'People's War': Nepal's Maoist Rebellion*, pp. 225–42. London: Hurst & Company.

Reeves, M. (2011) 'Fixing the Border: On the Affective Life of the State in Southern Kyrgyzstan', *Environment and Planning D: Society and Space* 29(5): 905–23.

Reeves, M. (2014) *Border Work: Spatial Lives of the State in Rural Central Asia*. Ithaca, NY: Cornell University Press.

Ribot, J.C. and N.L. Peluso (2003) 'A Theory of Access', *Rural Sociology* 68(2): 153–81.

Roth, R. (2007) 'Two-dimensional Maps in Multi-dimensional Worlds: A Case of Community-based Mapping in Northern Thailand', *Geoforum* 38(1): 49–59.

Saferworld (2013) 'Rapid Conflict Assessment: A Snapshot of Conflicts, Tensions and Insecurity in Eight Selected Districts in Nepal's Far West and Mid-West Regions'. Kathmandu: Pact, Sajhedari Bikaas Program.

de Sales, A. (2007) 'The Kham Magar Country: Between Ethnic Claims and Maoism', in D.N. Gellner (ed.) *Resistance and the State: Nepalese Experiences*, pp. 326–57. New York and Oxford: Berghahn Books.

de Sales, A. (2011) 'Time, Identity and Historical Change in the Hills of Nepal', *European Bulletin of Himalayan Studies* 39: 106–26.

de Sales, A. (2013) 'Thabang: The Crucible of Revolution', in M. Lecomte-Tilouine (ed.) *Revolution in Nepal: An Athropological and Historical Approach to the People's War*, pp. 164–211. Delhi: Oxford Unversity Press.

Scott, J. C. (1998) *Seeing Like a State: How Certain Schemes to Improve the Human Condition Have Failed*. New Haven, CT: Yale University Press.

Shah, A. (2007) '"Keeping the State Away": Democracy, Politics and the State in India's Jharkhand', *Journal of the Royal Anthropological Institute* 13: 129–45.

Shneiderman, S. and L. Tillin (2015) 'Restructuring States, Restructuring Ethnicity: Looking across Disciplinary Boundaries at Federal Futures in India and Nepal', *Modern Asian Studies* 49(01): 1–39.

Shneiderman, S. and M. Turin (2010) 'Negotiating Nepal's Two Polities: A View from Dolakha', in P. Manandhar and D. Seddon (eds) *In Hope and Fear: Living through the People's War in Nepal*, pp. 200–13. Delhi: Adroit.

Sivaramakrishnan, K. (2000) 'Crafting the Public Sphere in the Forests of West Bengal: Democracy, Development and Political Action', *American Ethnologist* 27(2): 431–61.

Suykens, B. (2010) 'Diffuse Authority in the Beedi Commodity Chain: Naxalite and State Governance in Tribal Telangana, India', *Development and Change* 41(1): 153–78.

Tarnowski, C. (2002) 'Forest Places, Political Spaces: The Social Implications of Community Forestry in Nepal'. PhD Thesis, University of Georgia.

Vaccaro, I. (2005) 'Property Mosaic and State-making: Governmentality, Expropriation and Conservation in the Pyrenees', *Journal of Ecological Anthropology* 9(1): 4–19.

Vandekerckhove, N. (2011) 'The State, the Rebel and the Chief: Public Authority and Land Disputes in Assam, India', *Development and Change* 42(3): 759–79.

Vandergeest, P. and N.L. Peluso (1995) 'Territorialization and State Power in Thailand', *Theory and Society* 24(3): 385–426.

Watts, M. (2003) 'Development and Governmentality', *Singapore Journal of Tropical Geography* 24(1): 6–34.

Whelpton, J. (2005) *A History of Nepal*. Cambridge: Cambridge University Press.

Yadav, N.P., O.P. Dev, O. Springate-Baginski and J. Soussan (2003) 'Forest Management and Utilization under Community Forestry', *Journal of Forest and Livelihood* 3(1): 37–50.

Zharkevich, I. (2014) '"Changing Times": War and Social Transformation in Mid-Western Nepal'. PhD Thesis, University of Oxford.

Zurick, D.N. (1989) 'Historical Links between Settlement, Ecology, and Politics in the Mountains of West Nepal', *Human Ecology* 17(2): 229–55.

Zurick, D.N. (1990) 'Traditional Knowledge and Conservation as a Basis for Development in a West Nepal Village', *Mountain Research and Development* 10(1): 23–33.

5

Violence Entrepreneurs, Law and Authority in Colombia

Jacobo Grajales

INTRODUCTION

I met Luis on a sunny morning in a coffee shop in downtown Santa Marta.[1] He was a community leader from the Los Fundadores neighbourhood, a slum that had swelled in the mid-1990s to a population of 10,000, mostly due to the arrival of internal refugees, *desplazados*. After a coffee or two, Luis invited me to follow him in his daily routine as a community leader. I accepted gratefully, pleased to live what I expected to be an ethnographically rich experience. First we met Jaime, who worked for the General Inspector's office and was in charge of the assistance policy for internal refugees as well as other human rights issues. We spent nearly an hour in his office, talking about an ongoing case of violent land grabbing that had affected people from Luis's organization. Jaime told us an investigation was trying to establish the strategies used by businessmen linked to paramilitary groups to legalize violently seized property. The next meeting took us to a foreign NGO office, where Luis had to arrange some details concerning the next cycle of workshops for community leaders. They were focused on the use of judicial tools for the protection of peasants' property rights on abandoned plots. After a quick lunch, I accompanied Luis to a meeting with members of his organization. It was an important day, as they were expecting the arrival of a local politician. This man had promised his support in the diverse judicial procedures for the recognition of property rights. I knew him by reputation, as his political mentor had been found guilty of supporting paramilitary groups. According to the trial judges, the terms of his mentor's deal with the paramilitaries covered both electoral alliances and bureaucratic intervention. The political influence of paramilitaries had been instrumental in the cycle of violent eviction and land grabbing that local people had endured. Some of these dispossessed peasants were members of Luis's organization. It all felt

I would like to thank Christian Lund, Michael Eilenberg, Yves-Pol Hemonin and the anonymous reviewers for their helpful comments on earlier versions of this contribution. This chapter also benefited from lively discussions held at the *Ancrages politiques* seminar, organized by Jean-Louis Briquet, Marie Vannetzel and Romain Le Cour Grandmaison.

1. The names of interviewees have been fictionalized so as to protect their identities.

very awkward and contradictory; after the meeting I bashfully expressed my incomprehension to Luis. He seemed amused. 'He is a powerful man', he told me. 'He will help us with bureaucratic stuff. Hopefully, if everyone here votes as they should, we will gain an ally, and the *paracos* (paramilitaries) will leave us alone'.[2]

The above account invites us to carry out an assessment of the relation between the struggle for rights and resources and the formation of political authority. My analysis is relevant to a body of scholarship that explores these links (Lund, 2006; Sikor and Lund, 2009), and refers to current debates on the link between institutional competition and the production of citizenship and political subjectivity (Comaroff and Comaroff, 2008; Gayer, 2014; Hansen and Stepputat, 2009; Jaffe, 2013). These processes are traced during a moment of rupture in the political order which offers favourable conditions for the observation of everyday processes of state formation (Lund, Introduction to this issue).

Like several Colombian regions, the Magdalena Province (*departamento*) experienced, from the mid-2000s, a deep rupture in the local forms of political authority. The demobilization of paramilitary groups and the criminal procedures brought against local politicians resulted in a reconfiguration of patronage networks and state intervention. In some ways, this rupture has led to a centralization of the political game and a nationalization of local political spaces. New rights specifically related to compensation for the victims of paramilitary groups have been recognized by the central government.

However, this process has not led to a reconfiguration of politics following the standards of legal-rational authority and good governance. From the point of view of the *desplazados* and their organizations, the new situation is characterized by a multi-level game, where the pursuit of recognition via official institutions is not in contradiction with the necessity of gaining the protection of local politicians, members of collusive networks associated with convicted individuals and new armed groups, the heirs to the paramilitary militias. Despite political rupture, old forms of authority persist and continue to determine local politics. While the existence of newly empowered legal arenas opens the way to new rights and offers new grounds for their enforcement, the salience of official institutions has not led to a marginalization of unofficial spaces of power. An examination of the local setting reveals a complex entanglement of legal and illegal practices in the exercise of authority that cannot be considered as a failure in state building. Rather, it should be seen as an instance of the 'vulgarization of power' (Berman and Lonsdale, 1992: 5), a manifestation of the ability of individuals and social groups to use institutions to further their own interests.

This contribution is based on the case of Magdalena. First, I provide an analysis of the formation of political authority both before and after

---

2. Field notes, Santa Marta, March 2009.

the reconfiguration of local power in Magdalena. This is followed by an examination of the production of new political subjectivities in a time of rupture.[3]

RUPTURE AND RECONFIGURATION OF THE LOCAL ORDER

For decades, local order in Magdalena was defined by the collusive relations between politicians and what can be referred to as 'violence entrepreneurs' (Volkov, 2002). This order was disturbed by the intervention of central state authorities which led to prosecutions aimed at dominant local elites. In spite of this intervention, local political authority has not been entirely reconfigured around the new principles of law and rational-bureaucratic central power. Some politicians have been able to retain their political influence in spite of criminal convictions, mostly by placing their relatives in key positions within the local administration. Moreover, if paramilitary groups went through profound changes after their official demobilization, their former members continue to be active in the political and economic sphere, and play a central role in the control of local communities. This section will trace the reconfiguration of local authority in order to gain insight into the mechanisms that led to a situation of overlapping authorities that is marked by new forms of state intervention and the reconfiguration of violent entrepreneurship. Access to land appears as one indicator of a reconfiguration of local power. Paramilitary rule had been marked by plunder and dispossession, both of which were based on the use of violence and the mobilization of political and administrative alliances (Grajales, 2013). As the state was supposed to recover direct jurisdiction over the territory, an ambitious policy of land restitution was adopted. Yet, as will be argued throughout this chapter, access to property is still determined by the capacity of individuals to navigate both statutory institutions and political networks linked to violence entrepreneurs.

The Paramilitary Local Order

In Magdalena, the first violence entrepreneurs, initially dedicated to the protection and regulation of the drug economy, can be traced back to a booming marijuana industry in the 1970s. Their engagement in the repression of political movements, and also labour and peasant organizations, was linked to the transformation of the dynamics of internal conflict in Colombia which involved the politicization of criminal actors, the criminalization of

---

3. This contribution draws on field research carried out in 2009 and 2011 in different parts of Magdalena, which formed part of my doctoral research on the links between paramilitary groups and the state, published as Grajales (2016a).

the state's repressive forces and practices, and the radicalization of social conflicts linked to land property and land control.[4]

The first violence entrepreneurs to adopt a counter-insurgent orientation were the Giraldo and the Rojas clans, respectively active on the northern and western slopes of the Sierra Nevada de Santa Marta, a coastal mountain range that rises 5,700 metres above the shores of the Caribbean Sea. Both groups had their origins in the contentious social context of the marijuana — and later cocaine — boom, and established strong links with the economic and political elites of the province.

Hernán Giraldo, the patriarch of one of these families, has acknowledged his participation in the murder of political and community leaders from the mid-1980s, a time when left-wing parties and grassroots movements started to be regarded as a threat to the hegemony of installed political entrepreneurs. Judicial investigations into his political allies have also shown that he acted as a political broker, exchanging the votes of peasants living in his zones of influence for the support of regional politicians.

At the turn of the century, Giraldo's local power was challenged by the arrival of a new paramilitary group. The AUC (Autodefensas Unidas de Colombia — United Self-defence Group of Colombia) backed a national confederation of paramilitary groups (Cubides, 2005). Although not initially hostile to local paramilitaries, AUC leaders soon made their intentions clear: to integrate Giraldo's group into their own network. Giraldo was ultimately forced into compliance, and his group became a part of the 'northern block', a paramilitary army led by the now infamous Jorge Cuarenta, which was officially part of the AUC although it was politically and financially independent.

Elsewhere in Colombia, diverse dynamics led to a similar result. In most cases, paramilitaries participated in local politics, supporting their own candidates as mayors and governors, as well as members of municipal and provincial councils (Romero, 2007). While some of these political allies were newcomers, most of them were well-established politicians who successfully negotiated their support. Their upper hand in local politics provided paramilitary groups with the possibility of placing loyal associates in parliamentary positions, where they could influence legislative debates and nominate the heads of executive agencies and public investments in local projects. Paramilitary commanders also reaped huge profits from their participation in politics. Through the creation of shell companies, or with the complicity of existing firms, a share (or the whole) of public contracts was redistributed to the paramilitary network, enriching politicians, civil servants and other accomplices. The diversion of public funds could lead to elaborate schemes; in Magdalena, the collection of local taxes and electricity bills was

---

4. A different account of the origins of paramilitary groups can be found in Romero (2003). In the case of Magdalena, I engage with the work of Renán-Rodríguez (2007) and Zúñiga (2007).

privatized, and the firm in charge of the collection was controlled by one of Jorge Cuarenta's lieutenants. Criminal investigations have shown that around 20 per cent of the money collected had been diverted into the paramilitary 'economy' (Martínez and Molinares, 2008).

Paramilitary control over a territory frequently led to violent forms of land grabbing. However, violence was not enough; their political and bureaucratic networks played a key part in their strategy to acquire land (Restrepo Echeverri and Franco Restrepo, 2011). With this support, they obtained property titles for land that had been forcibly abandoned by its owners. The complexity of property rights in Colombian rural areas, where legal ownership of the land is an exception and most peasants merely enjoy tenancy rights, further facilitated this strategy (Barbosa et al., 2007; Reyes, 2009). In Magdalena, several cases of active bureaucratic assistance in land grabbing have been identified. In cases from the town of Chivolo, documented thanks to peasant and NGO mobilization and judicial intervention, beneficiaries of land reform programmes, who had received property titles during the 1980s and 1990s, were dispossessed by the same state agency that had been in charge of land allocation. It was the task of INCORA (Instituto colombiano de la reforma agraria — Colombian Institute for Land Reform) to redistribute under-exploited land. Yet, when paramilitary groups grabbed land that belonged to agrarian reform beneficiaries, the same agency legally certified that the plots had been abandoned by their owners, something that was contrary to the land allocation agreement. Consequently, regular owners lost their property titles, which were reallocated by INCORA to family members or frontmen of paramilitary members and commanders.

Research into these matters is only possible because of the radical rupture in political power in these areas, brought about by the demobilization of paramilitary groups. Both field and documentary research have been strongly dependent on the possibility of moving around freely (even if not completely securely) in places such as Magdalena, and obtaining access to the cascade of judicial investigations against former paramilitary allies. The next section provides some insight into this period of rupture and the reconfiguration of political and criminal networks.

Disruption of Local Powers

A few weeks after the newly elected president Alvaro Uribe took office in August 2002, secret meetings were held between representatives of the government and paramilitary commanders. The discussions led to the signing of the Ralito Agreement in July 2003, which marked the official beginning of negotiations aimed at the demobilization of paramilitary groups.[5] The process was profoundly disrupted by the paramilitaries who saw the

5. This episode is analysed in detail in Grajales (2016b).

demobilization as an easy way to legalize their assets, thereby escaping criminal prosecution in the United States. However, justices of the Constitutional Court and Supreme Court rapidly became an unavoidable obstacle to the government's intention to grant generous amnesty to former paramilitaries. Even Congress, though dominated by the presidential majority, was divided between those who supported the 'benevolent' treatment of demobilizing paramilitaries and those who criticized the government's bill in the name of human rights, justice for paramilitary victims and constitutional principles (Lecombe, 2014).

As the prospect of quick and profitable negotiations diminished, paramilitary commanders tried to pressurize the government. Some of their middlemen, who had never laid down their weapons, started to become more visible, bringing back the threat of rearmament and even insurrection against the state. As the process had already led to the voluntary confinement of paramilitary leaders, the latter used compromising information about their links with politics as leverage. From late 2006, information and evidence about these collusive alliances were leaked to the press, thus confirming rumours that had been circulating for over a year. Moreover, the publicity given to these links, and the political scandal that followed, strengthened judicial investigations that were already pending.

As these prosecutions became politically explosive, they were taken before the Supreme Court, which had legal jurisdiction over the cases against members of parliament and high civil servants. The Supreme Court's intervention disabled the usual legal obstruction and circumvention strategies, and led to the collapse of political alliances. Such a fluid conjuncture led to more than 200 investigations against MPs, and hundreds of governors, mayors and local officials were also convicted.

Yet the paramilitary commanders' pressure on the government did not have the expected result. As a way of neutralizing the disruptive potential of both compromising revelations and militia rearmament, President Uribe extradited 14 paramilitary commanders to the US in May 2008, where they are currently being held on drug-trafficking charges. This move was severely criticized by the Supreme Court and human rights organizations, who saw it as a way of covering a disturbing truth.

A new rupture followed, with the election of President Juan Manuel Santos (2010–present). One of his first actions was the introduction of the Land and Victims Bill, which was presented as a means to end the cycle of violence and dispossession that marks Colombia's contemporary history. This offered an opportunity to reformulate the links between citizenship and property at the local level, especially in peripheral areas such as Magdalena. One of the objectives of the law is the restitution of several million hectares of land that were violently grabbed by paramilitary groups, thus favouring the return of internally displaced people to the rural areas. Even though the resources allocated to such an endeavour do not reflect the complexity of the issues surrounding land and violence in Colombia, this decision was a turning point in public policy regarding forced displacement and land grabbing (Vargas-Reina, 2014).

Violence and Politics Today

Political power held by local politicians and paramilitary groups did not vanish entirely behind the impressive intervention of central justice institutions. Both armed and political networks were reconfigured and adapted to the new situation. The relations between violence, crime and politics were also reshuffled. The recognition on which citizenship and property depend remains connected to these forms of unofficial authority, but the hybridity of the new order — the various fluctuating elements determining recognition — has yet to be clarified. It is clearly difficult and hazardous to study a very recent context determined by clandestine links and hidden strategies, but some hypotheses can be offered on the basis of known data and recent scholarly research.

The extradition of some paramilitary leaders in 2008 accelerated the fragmentation of the existing armed groups. Their chiefs, mostly former lieutenants of those who were extradited, became autonomous criminal actors, placed in a situation of violent competition (Ávila and Nuñez, 2008; Restrepo Echeverri, 2010). This new context also favoured the emergence of new leadership. In northern Magdalena, Hernán Giraldo's extradition was followed by a war involving rival factions headed by two of his sons. In need of new allies, Giraldo's heirs called for the support of criminal entrepreneurs from other regions, contributing to the escalation of violent struggle over this territory.

Demobilization, accompanied by state repression leading to the arrest and death of old leaders, created opportunities for younger, less experienced violence entrepreneurs. Sociologist William Renán-Rodríguez has studied typical trajectories, such as the story of Dagoberto Maldonado. Initially part of the rank and file under Giraldo's rule, Maldonado became the chief of one of the rival groups associated with the patriarch's sons, a gang known as the Paisas (Massé et al., 2010). According to Renán-Rodríguez (2007), the emergence of these new chiefs went hand in hand with their dependence on translocal criminal networks which linked drug traffickers and violence entrepreneurs throughout Colombia (and even Venezuela). These networks provided emergent chiefs with the necessary resources to participate in a highly conflictive criminal competition.

The Bacrim (an acronym for *bandas criminales*, criminal gangs), as these groups are called by the press and the Colombian government, are associated with diverse actors in the drugs trade to whom they provide protection of coca plantations, drug production and transportation. They engage in cocaine and marijuana production, but do not generally control the entire economic cycle. They are also invested in other sectors of the illegal economy, such as gasoline smuggling, subcontracted homicides and prostitution. In several Santa Marta neighbourhoods, Bacrim control retail drug dealing, either directly or by co-opting smaller gangs. Moreover, the Santa Marta central market shopkeepers seem to be subjected to their racket, as recurrent acts of violence against unwilling payers demonstrate.

These armed groups are agents of social control in everyday life. In the Los Fundadores shanty town, groceries, bus drivers and hairdressers pay a 'tax' for Bacrim 'protection'. The informal economy seems to be controlled in a more direct manner. Illegal motorcycles providing individual transportation, known as *mototaxis*, are often controlled by the Bacrim. They are not only business-oriented but also provide intelligence to the criminal network. Moreover, the local head of the disarmament, demobilization and reintegration (DDR) agency admitted that most drivers of *mototaxis* are former paramilitaries, some of whom bought their motorcycles thanks to DDR subsidies (allowances provided by the state to demobilized paramilitaries).[6] Racketeering and illegal business generally combine financial aims and social control. For instance, the ascent of Bacrims in Los Fundadores was, according to local inhabitants, accompanied by the emergence of a particularly usurious money-lending scheme. The *paga diario* ('pay every day') consists in lending small amounts of money and collecting interest every day. The general daily rate was 10 per cent in 2009 and 2011. Needless to say, failure to pay would lead to corporal punishment, and sometimes even death.[7]

According to official inquiries and journalistic research, the initial fluidity of Bacrim started stabilizing from 2009 (Corporación Nuevo Arco Iris, 2010; Massé et al., 2010). Smaller and weaker groups disappeared and were replaced by more sophisticated criminal organizations. In Magdalena, two main networks emerged, respectively known as the Urabeños and the Paisas. These organizations are capable of blatant demonstrations of territorial and social control. One episode exemplifies this capacity. In January 2012, after a police operation led to the death of Juan de Dios Úsuga, one of the group's leaders, his brother Dairo ordered an 'armed strike' (*paro armado*) in all the zones of influence of the group; this action was aimed at capturing the attention of provincial and national authorities, as a demonstration of the Urabeños' authority over local communities. In Magdalena the 'strike' was generally followed, as trade and transportation shut down for 48 hours on 4–5 January 2012.

While statutory institutions now claim to have full monopoly on the enforcement of property rights, the access of peasants and *desplazados* to their land continues to be subject to violence and threats. In Magdalena, individuals and peasant organizations have denounced the obstacles *desplazados*

---

6. Interview, Santa Marta, March 2009.
7. Lukas Jaramillo-Escobar (2011) makes the same observation in his study of the Nelson Mandela shanty town in Cartagena.

seeking to return to their land still confront in the aftermath of AUC's demobilization. In the case of Chivolo, mentioned above, tentative returns started in the middle of 2007. From January 2008, peasant leaders started reporting threats against their lives to the Ombudsman bureau (Defensoría del pueblo). They accused local landlords, who had presumably acted as frontmen for Jorge Cuarenta, of being the source of the threats. One of these men, Saúl Severini, is under criminal investigation for conspiracy to commit murder. In 2010 peasant leaders reported the presence of armed men in the countryside, purportedly members of the gang of Omar Montero, also known as Codazzi, a former AUC lieutenant. They also accused Augusto Castro, a businessman and the brother of a former MP who had been convicted for his alliance with paramilitaries, of being a central actor in the land-grabbing strategy. Criminal investigations have shown that Castro crafted complex financial schemes to introduce grabbed land into global markets. Thanks to his brother's political support, he obtained subsidies from Corpomagdalena, the provincial environment agency, as well as a contract for timber production with French multinational ONFI, in 2006. Both Castro and Codazzi are currently behind bars. The former was captured in October 2012 and the latter was extradited from Venezuela in July 2014.

The reconfiguration of these violence entrepreneurs coincided with changes in political networks. In Magdalena, most of the established political entrepreneurs were convicted for their links with paramilitary groups. Former governor Trino Luna was found guilty of criminal conspiracy and is currently under investigation for the murder of one of his political rivals. Almost all the MPs elected after the 2002 and 2006 elections have been convicted. But criminal convictions have not affected the political capital of all of the major actors in the same way. The rich families of Santa Marta, who had controlled the key political positions for decades, lost a share of their capital. Convicted political figures tried, rather unsuccessfully, to transfer their power to members of their families. However, former governor Luna, despite being in prison, became one of the key actors of the local political scene. He managed to install his private secretary, Omar Diazgranados, in the governor's seat. During the 2010 legislative elections, Luna's support was instrumental in the election to the senate of his former legal adviser. Luna's capital even resisted further judicial pursuits. In 2011, Diazgranados was dismissed from the governor's position by the Inspector General's office on embezzlement charges; nevertheless, Luna and his allies piloted the election of a 24-year-old member of the provincial assembly as governor of Magdalena in October 2011. In the same elections, mayors were elected despite pending judicial prosecution in several Magdalena towns.

All over the country, the links between the Bacrim and the politicians who inherited their political power from the allies of the paramilitaries have been denounced. These countless accusations have led to a single indictment, in the case of the Guajira governor Kiko Gómez, who is accused by the Attorney General's office of having conspired with a local Bacrim leader to murder three of his local rivals. Today, in the absence of further judicial inquiries, it is impossible to assess the extent and the mechanisms of these new collusive networks. Yet, as Colombian local governments (*municipios*) enjoy great autonomy both in financial and security matters, alliances with mayors and local officials are vital to criminal and armed actors (Valencia, 2009). In fact, the implementation of security policies is largely dependent on local actors. Mayors are supposed to monitor security and report to the national police and the army. Law enforcement operations are communicated to a provincial security council, where the governor is represented. In consequence, links between armed actors and local politicians are probably one of the most effective strategies for evading law enforcement.

Under such conditions, political order appears fluid and contingent. The recent intervention of central institutions in favour of the rights of *desplazados*, especially through the land restitution policy, is undoubtedly a novelty. Yet such a new institutional framework does not necessarily subvert the relation between the legal and the illegal, or the official and the unofficial. The overlapping of statutory and clandestine forms of authority is not necessarily a temporary situation, bound to bring forth either chaos or legal 'normality'. It is more likely to be, as Laurent Gayer argues, a situation of 'fluctuating, tensile equilibrium', which 'may accommodate a significant level of competition over the means of coercion' (Gayer, 2014: 12). For more than two decades in Magdalena, political authority, citizenship and access to property were determined by the close alliances that existed between violence entrepreneurs and politicians. The intervention of the central state can thus be viewed as a centralization of power, although the initial intentions of the government should not be overstressed. The fragmentation of the paramilitaries' power structures can be attributed to complex interactions between DDR policies, judicial inquiries and security matters — not a centralized endeavour to monopolize violence. Throughout, the intervention of the state reconfigured local political authority, but it did not marginalize the economic and political role of violence. The next section explores the ways in which these changing forms of authority interact with agency and political subjectivity.

TOWARDS A NEW ORDER?

How can we reconcile these opposing views of politics, one marked by the reinforcement of the rule of law and the other by the reconfiguration of forms of violent and unofficial political authority? This section will examine the ways in which statutory and unofficial forms of authority belong to the same institutional landscape. As we consider public authority as the result of the recognition of a specific institution's capacity to qualify and enforce different forms of property and citizenship rights (Lund, 2006; Sikor and Lund, 2009), the study of rights-claiming processes provides insight into the practical ways in which statutory institutions and illegal violent authorities are related.

Bringing Back the Law

The first time I met Alberto in Bogotá, he was quite suspicious about our meeting. I had contacted him through a human rights NGO, whose name I hoped and expected would serve as an endorsement. Support from such NGOs was certainly the reason why he accepted a meeting with me. However, times were not conducive to free speech, and they were especially unfavourable when I asked Alberto to inform me about the investigations his organization had been conducting into the links of politicians and INCORA officials to paramilitaries and violent land grabbing. This was in 2009, when denunciations of this kind were publicly stigmatized by President Uribe himself as serving the guerrilla cause, a life-threatening accusation.[8]

Two years later, when I met Alberto again, he set up a meeting with Omar, the leader of a peasant community from Chivolo in central Magdalena. Alberto's organization, an NGO named ILSA (Instituto latinoamericano para una sociedad y un derecho alternativos — Latin American Institute for an Alternative Society and an Alternative Law) was taking the community's case to court. Members of Omar's organization had been victims of forced displacement and land grabbing perpetrated under orders from Jorge Cuarenta. Although they enjoyed property titles to their plots, they had been dispossessed by a combination of legal schemes and the complicity of local notaries and INCORA officials. Omar's case was one of the few land-grabbing incidents selected by the judiciary and the government that illustrate the combination of legal and illegal strategies used in land grabbing, and the evident responsibility of the state.[9]

The considerable differences in the circumstances of these two meetings correspond to profound changes in political opportunities, linking legal action, rights claiming and access to land. A month before the second meeting, the Supreme Court had ordered INCODER (Instituto colombiano de desarrollo rural — Colombian Institute for Rural Development), previously known as INCORA, to revoke 36 title deeds that had been granted to Jorge Cuarenta's frontmen in Chivolo. The Court's sentence acknowledged the fact that land grabbing had been facilitated by the intervention of INCORA, thus endorsing the claim that had been made for several years by peasant organizations and supporting NGOs like ILSA. The ruling also ordered the Attorney General's office to investigate the criminal responsibilities of IN-CORA officials. At the time of writing this chapter, José Fernando Mercado Polo, former head of INCORA in Magdalena, had pleaded guilty to charges of criminal conspiracy, and admitted participation in Cuarenta's land grabbing scheme. Other INCORA executives were subsequently prosecuted on similar charges.

---

8. Field notes, Bogota, March 2009.
9. Field notes, Bogota, February 2011.

The Court's intervention contributed to the process of constructing land grabbing as a public problem. The activities of 'human rights entrepreneurs', such as ILSA and other NGOs, have been crucial to this process. More discreet institutions, such as those in charge of social policies for *desplazados*, also played a role in the construction and framing of the problem (Estrada and Rodríguez, 2014). In October 2010, the Ministry of Agriculture announced the selection of 149 cases considered to be 'emblematic' and requiring administrative investigations: of those cases, 89 were situated in Magdalena. The main reason these cases received official attention was the role the bureaucratic allies of paramilitary groups played in the legalization of land grabbing. The government intended to concentrate its administrative and financial resources on cases where the responsibility of state officials was directly involved.

Such a calculation was partially due to the international mobilization of NGOs in land-grabbing cases in Colombia. The case of the black communities of the Lower Atrato Valley had marked a rupture in the judicialization of land grabbing in Colombia (Grajales, 2015; Rolland, 2012). Following the intervention of a Colombian NGO, Justicia y Paz, the Inter-American Court of Human Rights recognized that these communities had been victims of forced displacement and land grabbing, and that paramilitary groups and their corporate allies had benefited from military support. The international intervention triggered a series of inquiries by Colombian institutions. Between 2005 and 2006, the Inspector General's office and INCODER recognized the link between forced displacement, land grabbing and agribusiness. The Inspector General even considered that 'land grabbing, dispossession and plundering [were] part of a "counter agrarian reform" mostly perpetrated by paramilitary groups in alliance with corporate actors' (Procuraduría General de la Nación, 2006: 156).

Land conflicts and land restitution issues have occupied a dominant position on the political agenda of the government since 2010. Since the beginning of peace talks with the FARC guerrillas in 2012, the government has presented the land restitution policy as indisputable proof of its solid commitment to peace building. However, there have been deep disagreements about the meaning and the scope of this new policy since its inception. For Uprimny and Sánchez (2010) two competing interpretations of this policy were expressed from the beginning of the debates. The first, referred to as 'thin restitution', stresses the reinforcement of the rule of law, the marginalization of criminal actors and the clarification of property rights. Such reforms are seen as part and parcel of a good governance paradigm, which is compatible with the commodification of land and the industrialization of agrarian production. The second, 'thick restitution', holds that land policies should address fundamental issues such as the concentration of land and natural resources, the lack of recognition of specific peasant rights, and the promotion of alternative agrarian models. If scholars and peasant movements understand the Land and Victims Law as corresponding to a 'thin' model, it is too soon to assess correctly the consequences of the implementation of this policy.

Violence against peasant movements has also been considered a public problem. In 2012, President Santos stated that a 'land cartel' had been formed, composed of criminal actors, former paramilitaries and their frontmen. Their objective, Santos said, was to obstruct the implementation of the land restitution policy by threatening peasant organizations. The names of 15 people were released to the press, and rewards were promised for information leading to their capture. Several of these individuals, including Codazzi and Castro (above) have already been captured. However, this does not mean that the Colombian police have managed to dismantle a centralized criminal organization. On the one hand, the image of a 'land cartel' was certainly a political construction destined to capture the attention of the media and public opinion. As is generally the case when criminal 'organizations' come under the spotlight, political actors and security professionals tended to exaggerate the structured character of what typically are fluid networks (Briquet and Favarel-Garrigues, 2010; Sommier, 1998). Studies of Bacrim's violence against peasant organizations conclude that these conflicts are determined by very diverse types of local alliances between large landowners, violence entrepreneurs and agribusiness firms (Massé and Camargo, 2013). Violence entrepreneurs are part of complex networks connecting legal and illegal economic actors and politicians (Giraldo-Ramírez, 2011; Giraldo-Ramírez and Muñoz-Mora, 2012). Repression against peasant organizations is not determined by a criminal structure that would pursue a centralized agenda, but more prosaically by the fact that the rupture in local political orders has not precluded the use of violence as a repertoire in the competition for resources and political power.

An enormous gap remains between the resources allocated to land restitution policies and the consequences of armed conflict. Between 2012 and 2013, the newly created Land Restitution Agency (Unidad de restitución de tierras) received more than 3,700 claims pertaining to Magdalena. In December 2013, 248 of these claims were taken before the Santa Marta special land restitution courts (juzgado especializado en restitución de tierras), of which 54 per cent were approved. Although the agency publicized and advertised these numbers, they remain quite modest in the light of the number of victims of armed conflict. Indeed, between 2000 and 2008, the state's database of internal displacement registered 294,664 people in Magdalena (Unidad para la Atención y Reparación Integral a las Víctimas, 2013). According to a study by the University of Magdalena, two-thirds of the province's *desplazados* were peasants, with either a legal title deed or a tenancy right (Barbosa et al., 2007) to land from which they were forcibly displaced.

This state of affairs creates new obstacles for rights recognition which are linked to the social characteristics of claimants. As the Chivolo example mentioned above shows, the possibility of success of collective action is strongly dependent on the definition of land grabbing cases as politically sensitive, and on the intervention of high judiciary authorities. Both the judicial and the political construction of the urgency of a few land-grabbing cases are strongly linked to the capacity of peasant activists to obtain the support of NGOs specialized in legal advocacy. The effectiveness of collective action is also linked to the extent to which the case meets legal criteria. Uppermost is evidently the existence of title deeds; yet a history of ongoing relations between the land claimant and diverse institutions of 'rural development', such as INCORA/INCODER or the Rural Development Bank (Banco agrario) can also be instrumental in the definition of a land-grab case as fitting the restitution criteria. In consequence, state intervention primarily benefits people who already had access to modalities of rights protection and who were already, in some sense, 'clients' of the state. In this way, the restitution policy reproduces forms of inequality that find their origins in past policies such as agrarian reform and modernization programmes. It also reproduces the forms of (in)visibilization that stem from the same policies, as institutions and bureaucracies are more likely to 'see' those who correspond to the image of individual peasant entrepreneurs enjoying legal property over a determined plot.

Subjectivity and Authority

What about all the others, namely those who are less likely to be prioritized in the application of these policies? Furthermore, what about all the social needs that exceed the scope of land restitution and redistribution: money, housing, food? Internally displaced people have become the target of both social stigma (frequently labelled as guerrilla supporters) and a diverse range of social policies (Gómez, 2012). Yet, the implementation of these social policies is strongly dependent on the *desplazados'* capacity to associate with patronage networks. Moreover, as has been argued above, life in shanty towns, where these internal refugees live, is controlled by armed groups, usually former paramilitaries. As a result, social claims must be expressed in ways that would not be considered hostile by armed actors.

This does not mean that the *desplazados* I met rejected the legitimacy of statutory institutions or that they were unable to criticize bureaucrats, politicians and violence entrepreneurs. They were more likely to have developed the skills to navigate these diverse social spaces, adopting the appropriate language and repertoire of action. Applying these skills can be viewed as a type of social navigation (Vigh, 2006).[10] Individuals navigate statutory institutions, mobilizing a civic and lawful rationale, while simultaneously

---

10. While I will not engage theoretically with the very rich elaborations of Henrik Vigh, I share his critique of the purely stylistic usages of this notion. According to Vigh, 'social navigation' is not simply a 'metaphor for practice', but aims at providing a 'point of departure for a reworking of the relationship between agency and social forces ... in volatile environments' (Vigh, 2009: 419, 433). As such, it appears particularly pertinent for the study of social settings such as civil wars, post-conflict or 'no peace, no war' situations.

building, maintaining and helping to reproduce linkages with unofficial networks, in search of brokerage and protection. This metaphor does not come down to an ontology of a rational actor capable of planning and calculation. Social navigation is less about strategy than about tactics (de Certeau, 1984); it is less about calculation than about the capacity to interpret and to adapt to changing social circumstances (Vigh, 2006). It is not only about a situated and limited rationality, but also about a *habitus* shaped by social trajectories. An analysis of social navigation coincides with the findings of a study of Colombian *desplazados* conducted by Agier (2000). The study concludes that the existence of multiple authorities leads people to acquire a fine-grained knowledge of actors and interests at stake and to develop tactics of seeking patronage, given that such a course is deemed inevitable. Social navigation is thus constitutive of the formation of political subjectivities that cannot be reduced to passive patron–client relations but which do not correspond to a moral economy of liberal citizenship either.

Desplazados are thus confronted with overlapping forms of authority. Their capacity to navigate leads them to formulate a diversity of claims pertaining to citizenship and property. Yet a closer look at their everyday tactics of survival demonstrates one of the conclusions of this issue, namely 'that competition over jurisdiction is not simply a question of crass confrontation but equally one of clever collusion' (Lund, Introduction to this issue).

The example of Luis, mentioned at the beginning of this chapter, illustrates the link between social navigation, subjectivity and the formation of political authority. When I met him, he had just created a new *desplazado* organization. His vocation as an activist was linked to his social trajectory and his political background. Luis had fled from Pivijay, a violence-ridden town 150 km (but more than five hours) south of Santa Marta. Paramilitaries had accused him of being sympathetic to the ELN guerrillas, and threatened to kill him if he did not leave.

He was very proud of his past as a young activist with ANUC (Asociación nacional de usuarios campesinos — National Association of Users of State Agricultural Services), a corporatist organization that became the largest peasant confederation in the country in the 1970s. His background as an activist had provided him with a variety of organizational skills. Luis knew how to write a *tutela* (plea for protection of fundamental rights); he had learnt to interact with rural development actors and to obtain subsidies and credit. As a peasant activist he had met domestic and foreign development professionals, and was pleased to be able to say that he had succeeded in setting up a farming project with the help of the FAO. He had become a 'development broker' (Olivier de Sardan et al., 2000).

Luis originally came to Santa Marta traumatized by his experience of forced displacement. He joined a *desplazado* association that collectively negotiated subsidies with the state to satisfy basic needs, and tried to survive

selling avocados in the street. When I interviewed him, he was extremely
critical of his first experience as a member of such an organization:

> The leader of the first foundation I went to [*fundación* is one of the terms commonly used
> to refer to non-profit and grassroots organizations in Colombia] had no political perspective,
> no sense of identity or solidarity . . . Plus, he was not an honest man. He wanted to have as
> many people as possible with him, but only because each of us had to pay a monthly fee.
> More people, more money! And each time someone got a subsidy, whether for housing, for
> a project, or so on, he got his share![11]

Despite these criticisms, the trajectory Luis followed to become a leader
corresponds with his capacity to navigate both the field of statutory institutions, producing a discourse of moral rectitude and compliance with the
law, and the field of patronage. Asked why he decided to create his own
organization, he told me:

> I was sick of the corruption and immobility of X. But I did not feel ready to start a foundation
> of my own. One day, when I was at INCODER I met David; I knew him from a project
> back in Pivijay. He was in charge of rural subsidies for *desplazados*. He told me: 'If you
> create your own foundation, I will help you, we have a new programme, there is money for
> you to distribute among your people, and elections are coming'. So I understood he wanted
> me to gather *desplazado* votes for him. Actually not for him, for X who was a senator and
> controlled bureaucratic positions in INCODER. I saw a good opportunity and I went for it![12]

Luis's role as a broker demonstrates the types of collusion that exist between different types of authority. In fact, *desplazados*' struggle for recognition is dependent on their capacity to succeed at a series of assessment
operations (Mora-Gámez, 2013), as well as to obtain the support of a political network. In both cases, brokers like Luis play a pivotal role. They
act as translators — introducing newcomers to bureaucratic language and
procedures — and endorsers — providing a social guarantee of the veracity
of the *desplazado*'s account. They are regarded as fulfilling a useful role
by both rights claimants and bureaucrats. Furthermore, brokers have expert
knowledge of the diverse procedures to follow in order to obtain social
aid and micro-credit from local, national and international organizations.
They are fluent in the bureaucratic language of these institutions, which
bestows upon them a certain kind of credibility regarding the use of funds,
project management skills and other qualitative assessment aspects, such
as a gender-conscious approach and potential for individual empowerment.
The latter are qualitative indicators that state and NGO officials often regard
as indicative of the potential of beneficiaries to become autonomous.

Mastering these social skills is a necessary but not a sufficient condition
for anyone seeking to become a fully established client of the state's social
programmes. The recognition of a *desplazado* organization as a credible

11. Interview, Santa Marta, March 2009.
12. Interview, Santa Marta, March 2009.

partner of statutory institutions often requires the intervention of a political figure. Luis and David's meeting in INCORA illustrates that officers in these institutions are also members of a political network. These agents owe their position to the 'recommendation' of a politician. In exchange, they are in charge of recruiting supporters for political meetings and of gathering votes for elections. In this endeavour, they are highly dependent on people like Luis, who are directly in contact with the beneficiaries of social programmes. Luis felt he had managed to obtain the 'confidence' of several political figures (mostly town councillors) because he was recognized as being capable of mobilizing his troops on election days.

Furthermore, the relationship with politicians and their patronage networks — such as David's — is also a strategy of protection for individuals who live in dangerous environments where social claims can be perceived as subverting the social order. For Luis and other leaders I met, political activism had to be conducted 'on the edge', mostly in relation to land conflicts. Several members of Luis's organization were claiming for state recognition of their abandoned plots. Yet they had received threats from a local landlord who was using the land for pastures and — as peasants thought — would be negotiating the allocation of a legal title deed with INCODER. Luis had filed a legal complaint and was requesting special protection of the plots on behalf of claimants. He had gathered a large number of documents and statements in order to support the claim of legitimate tenancy rights. He also received legal counselling from a foreign NGO that specialized in peasant and *desplazado* rights. At the same time, he was trying to obtain David's help to reach his political patron, an influential senator; Luis thought political support would expedite the process. Furthermore, he was convinced that being identified with a powerful man and his political network would protect him and his people. When I asked him what kind of protection a politician could provide, he told me: 'It is simple, he is a paramilitary ally. Those guys work for him, as I do; they gather votes for him, as I do; they even financed his last campaign. If they know we all work for the same man they will leave us alone'.[13]

Subjectivity is the product of images and identities generated by the state, such as 'victim' or 'internally displaced person'. These identities are compatible with the repertoire of intermediation. Institutions in charge of social policies define *desplazados* as 'entrepreneurs of aid' and 'actors of their own inclusion'. Their capacity for autonomy, displayed through the establishment of social organizations involved in the distribution and administration of social assistance, is regarded as a sign of their capacity for 'self-help'. Public institutions, along with NGOs that participate in the implementation of social policies, interpret everyday practices of social navigation as signifying this capacity. The episode this chapter opens with, the meeting between Luis and

---

13. Field notes, Santa Marta, March 2009.

Jaime at the Inspector General's office, illustrates this argument. When Luis raised his concerns about the security issues that might hinder the potential of some members of his foundation to return to their land, Jaime answered: 'I can help you with the legal paperwork but I cannot ask the police to stay night and day at your friend's house. They [peasants] cannot go back that easily (*como si nada*). They have to get the go-ahead from the armed groups. But you know what to do, your politician friend might be able to help'. Then he looked at me and said: 'This is why I like this guy [Luis]. Some *desplazados* keep waiting for the state to come and give them security, food and shelter. He is not like that. He is a *berraco* [resourceful man]. He doesn't sit and wait for things to drop down from heaven [*que las cosas le caigan del cielo*], he goes for them'.[14]

Aid professionals do not consider political intermediation as an illegitimate practice, but rather as an indicator that allows them to distinguish between 'active' and 'passive' clients. This self-image of resourcefulness and astuteness (*berraquera, malicia*) that is advanced by peasant leaders but also by bureaucrats and political brokers, reflects the importance my interlocutors attribute to moral values that are common among peasants from Magdalena (and other Colombian regions), who often see themselves as 'pioneers' or 'colonizers' of new agrarian frontiers. The emphasis placed on self-reliance and the capacity to overcome the challenges of life echoes the moral economy of peasant communities in peripheral areas of recent occupation. Consequently, political brokerage is not seen as contradictory to an appeal to statutory institutions for recognition and support. It belongs to a varied repertoire of intermediation and 'arena shopping' where seeking the support of an NGO and a politician's patronage at the same time is not incompatible but sometimes even mutually reinforcing.

CONCLUSION

The description of the structure of official and unofficial local powers and the practices of social navigation that characterize rights claiming provides us with a better understanding of the formation of political authority and the recognition of property and citizenship rights in Colombia.

An analysis of a historical period that encompasses conflict and post-conflict periods helps us to arrive at a more nuanced understanding of social order than the one that is often assumed by political actors and policy analysts. The Colombian case shows that violent local orders are not simply swept away by a new institutional framework that is based in rational-bureaucratic institutions and the rule of law. Everyday practices of rights claiming illustrate in a concrete manner the types of relations that can exist

---

14. Field notes, Santa Marta, March 2009.

between statutory institutions and unofficial forms of local power. An approach that focuses on the perspective of the rights claimants also provides a better understanding of the kind of political subjectivities that are created under circumstances of overlapping political authorities. Their claims to rights and resources are indicative of complex processes of state formation where, as Sikor and Lund (2009) observe, the recognition of rights and the acknowledgement of the state's authority to grant those rights are mutually constitutive.

Accordingly, unofficial and even criminal powers do not necessarily pose a threat to the authority of the state. Not only do they participate in the practical functioning of politics and policy implementation, but they also reinforce the idea of the state as somehow being 'above' society (Ferguson and Gupta, 2002). In this way, they are the homage that vice pays to virtue.

REFERENCES

Agier, M. (2000) 'Perte de lieux, dénuement et urbanisation: les desplazados de Colombie' ['Lost Places, Bareness and Urbanization: The Desplazados of Colombia'], *Autrepart* 14: 91–105.

Ávila, A. and M. Nuñez (2008) 'Expansión territorial y alianzas tácticas' ['Territorial Expansion and Tactical Alliances'], *Arcanos* 14: 52–61.

Barbosa, J., W. Renán-Rodríguez and W. Suárez (2007) 'La propiedad rural en el Magdalena 1970-2004 y algunas relaciones con el desplazamiento forzado' ['Rural Property in Magdalena 1970–2004 and Some Links with Forced Displacement']. Unpublished Report, University of Magdalena.

Berman, B. and J. Lonsdale (1992) *Unhappy Valley. Conflict in Kenya and Africa: State and Class.* Portsmouth, NH: James Currey.

Briquet, J.-L. and G. Favarel-Garrigues (eds) (2010) *Organized Crime and States: The Hidden Face of Politics.* Basingstoke: Palgrave Macmillan.

de Certeau, M. (1984) *The Practice of Everyday Life.* Berkeley, CA: University of California Press.

Comaroff, J. and J.L. Comaroff (2008) 'Law and Disorder in the Postcolony: An Introduction', in J. Comaroff and J.L. Comaroff (eds) *Law and Disorder in the Postcolony*, pp. 1–56. Chicago, IL: University of Chicago Press.

Corporación Nuevo Arco Iris (2010) 'El declive de la Seguridad democrática' ['The Demise of Democratic Security'], Special Issue *Arcanos* 15: 2–93.

Cubides, F. (2005) *Burocracias armadas [Armed Bureaucracies].* Bogotá: Norma.

Estrada, M. del R. and N.M. Rodríguez (2014) 'La política de tierras para la población desplazada 2001–2011: de la protección a la restitución' ['Land Policy for Forcibly Displaced People 2001–2011: From Protection to Restitution'], *Estudios Socio-Jurídicos* 16(1): 75–119.

Ferguson, J. and A. Gupta (2002) 'Spatializing States: Toward an Ethnography of Neoliberal Governmentality', *American Ethnologist* 29(4): 981–1002.

Gayer, L. (2014) *Karachi: Ordered Disorder and the Struggle for the City.* London: Hurst.

Giraldo-Ramírez, J. (ed.) (2011) *Economía criminal en Antioquia: narcotráfico [Criminal Economy in Antioquia: Drug Trafficking].* Medellín: EAFIT.

Giraldo-Ramírez, J. and J.-C. Muñoz-Mora (2012) *Informalidad e ilegalidad en la explotación del oro y la madera en Antioquia [Informality and Illegality in Gold and Timber Exploitation in Antioquia].* Medellín: EAFIT.

Gómez, L. (2012) 'Le déplacement forcé par la violence en Colombie: émergence, réinscription et transformations d'une nouvelle catégorie de l'action publique' ['Forced Displacement in Colombia: Emergence, Transformation and Reinscription of a Public Problem']. PhD dissertation, Sciences Po, Paris.

Grajales, J. (2013) 'State Involvement, Land Grabbing and Counter-Insurgency in Colombia', *Development and Change* 44(2): 211–32.

Grajales, J. (2015) 'Land Grabbing, Legal Contention and Institutional Change in Colombia', *Journal of Peasant Studies* 42(3–4): 541–60.

Grajales, J. (2016a) *Gouverner dans la violence. Le paramilitarisme en Colombie [Governing in the Midst of Violence. Paramilitary Politics in Colombia]*. Paris: Karthala.

Grajales, J. (2016b) 'Quand les juges s'en mêlent. Le rôle de la justice dans la démobilisation des groupes paramilitaires en Colombie' ['When the Judges Get Involved. The Role of Courts in the Demobilization of Paramilitary Groups in Colombia'], *Critique Internationale* 70: 117–36.

Hansen, T.B. and F. Stepputat (2009) *Sovereign Bodies: Citizens, Migrants, and States in the Postcolonial World*. Princeton, NJ: Princeton University Press.

Jaffe, R. (2013) 'The Hybrid State: Crime and Citizenship in Urban Jamaica', *American Ethnologist* 40(4): 734–48.

Jaramillo-Escobar, L. (2011) 'Orden en tiempos paramilitares: Violencia, política y lucro en un barrio del caribe colombiano' ['Order in Paramilitary Times: Violence, Politics and Profit in a Colombian Caribbean Neighbourhood'], *Desafíos* 23(2): 123–48.

Lecombe, D. (2014) '"Nous sommes tous en faveur des victimes". La diffusion de la justice transitionnelle en Colombie' ['"We Are All in Favour of the Victims": The Diffusion of Transitional Justice in Colombia']. Paris: Institut Universitaire Varenne, LGDJ.

Lund, C. (2006) 'Twilight Institutions: Public Authority and Local Politics in Africa', *Development and Change* 37(4): 685–705.

Martínez, T. and C. Molinares (2008) 'Sucedió en la república independiente de la Sombrerona' ['It Happened in the Sombrerona's Independent Republic'], *Verdad Abierta* 16 December.

Massé, F. and J. Camargo (2013) 'Actores armados ilegales y procesos de restitución y reclamación de tierras' ['Illegal Armed Actors and Processes of Land Claiming and Restitution']. Toledo: CITpax.

Massé, F., J. Munevar, E. Alvarez, and W. Renán-Rodríguez (2010) 'Parte II: área de DDR' ['Part II: The Scope of DDR'], in Observatorio internacional *DDR: Ley de Justicia y Paz [DDR: Justice and Peace Law]* 'Tercer informe' ['Third Report'], pp. 59–130. Toledo: CITpax.

Mora-Gámez, F.A. (2013) 'Reconocer a los reclamantes: sobre el Registro Único de Víctimas en Colombia como ensamblado sociotécnico' ['Recognizing Claimants: the Unified Victims Register in Colombia as a Socio-Technical Assembly], *IM-Pertinente* 1(1): 11–32.

Olivier de Sardan, J.-P., J.-P. Chauveau and T. Biershenk (eds) (2000) *Courtiers en développement: les villages africains en quête de projets [Development Brokers: African Villages in Search of Projects]*. Paris: Karthala-APAD.

Procuraduría General de la Nación (2006) 'Proyecto control preventivo y seguimiento a las políticas públicas en materia de reinserción y desmovilización' ['Project on Preventive Control and Monitoring to Public Policies on Reinsertion and Demobilization']. Bogotá: Government of Colombia.

Renán-Rodríguez, W. (2007) 'Contextualización del desplazamiento en el departamento del Magdalena y Santa Marta (1997–2007)' ['Contextualization of Forced Displacement in Magdalena and Santa Marta (1997–2007)']. Unpublished report, University of Magdalena.

Restrepo Echeverri, J.D. (2010) 'Estructuras paramilitares desmovilizadas en Medellín: de la unificación de la criminalidad a la fragmentación violenta' ['Demobilized Paramilitary Structures in Medellin: From United Crime to Violent Fragmentation'], *Arcanos* 15: 64–77.

Restrepo Echeverri, J.D. and V.L. Franco Restrepo (2011) 'La toma de la tierra: lógicas de guerra y acumulación en el Bajo Atrato' ['Land Grabbing: Logics of War and Accumulation in Bajo Atrato'], in M. Romero (ed.) *La economía de los paramilitares [The Paramilitaries' Economy]*, pp. 269–410. Bogotá: Random House Mondatori.

Reyes, A. (2009) *Guerreros y campesinos. El despojo de la tierra en Colombia [Warriors and Peasants. Land Plundering in Colombia]*. Bogotá: FESCOL/Norma.

Rolland, S. (2012) 'Mobilisation de résistance au conflit armé dans le Nord-Ouest de la Colombie' ['Mobilizing and Resisting Armed Conflict in Northwestern Colombia'], in R. Bazenguissa-Ganga and S. Makki (eds) *Sociétés en guerres. Ethnographie des mobilisations violentes [Societies at War. Ethnographies of Violent Mobilizations]*, pp. 145–65. Paris: Editions de la MSH.

Romero, M. (2003) 'Reform and Reaction. Paramilitary Groups in Contemporary Colombia', in D.E. Davis and A. Pereira (eds) *Irregular Armed Forces and their Role in Politics and State Formation*, pp. 178–208. Cambridge: Cambridge University Press.

Romero, M. (ed.) (2007) *Parapolítica. La ruta de la expansión paramilitar y los acuerdos políticos [Parapolitics. The Route of Paramilitary Expansion and Political Agreements]*. Bogotá: Corporacion Nuevo Arco Iris.

Sikor, T. and C. Lund (2009) 'Access and Property: A Question of Power and Authority', *Development and Change* 40(1): 1–22.

Sommier, I. (1998) *Les mafias [Mafias]*. Paris: Montchrestien.

Unidad para la Atención y Reparación Integral a las Víctimas [Office for Victims' Attention and Full Reparation] (2013) 'Informe nacional de desplazamiento forzado en Colombia (1985–2012)' ['National Report on Forced Displacement in Colombia (1985–2012)']. Bogotá: Government of Colombia.

Uprimny-Yepes, R. and N.C. Sánchez (2010) 'Los dilemas de la restitución de tierras en Colombia' ['Land Restitution Dilemmas in Colombia'], *Estudios Socio-Jurídicos* 12(2): 305–42.

Valencia, L. (2009) 'Municipio y violencia paramilitar en Colombia 1984–2008' ['Municipality and Paramilitary Violence in Colombia 1984–2008'], in F. Velásquez (ed.) *Las otras caras del poder. Territorio, conflicto y gestión pública en municipios colombianos [The Other Faces of Power. Territory, Conflict, and Public Management in Colombia]*, pp. 121–78. Bogotá: Foro Nacional por Colombia - GTZ.

Vargas-Reina, J. (2014) 'Análisis comparativo de los diseños institucionales que regulan la participación de las víctimas en Colombia: antes y después de la Ley 1448 de 2012' ['Comparative Analysis of Institutional Settings for Victims' Participation: Before and After Law 1448 of 2002'], *Estudios Socio-Jurídicos* 16(1): 165–206.

Vigh, H. (2006) *Navigating Terrains of War: Youth and Soldiering in Guinea-Bissau*. Oxford: Berghahn Books.

Vigh, H. (2009) 'Motion Squared: A Second Look at the Concept of Social Navigation', *Anthropological Theory* 9(4): 419–38.

Volkov, V. (2002) *Violent Entrepreneurs. The Use of Force in the Making of Russian Capitalism*. Ithaca, NY: Cornell University Press.

Zuñiga, P. (2007) 'Ilegalidad, control local y paramilitares en el Magdalena' ['Ilegality, Local Control and Paramilitaries in Magdalena'], in *Parapolítica, La ruta de la expansión paramilitar y los acuerdos políticos [Parapolitics. The Route of Paramilitary Expansion and Political Agreements]*, pp. 285–322. Bogotá: Corporación Arco Iris.

6

Occupied! Property, Citizenship and Peasant Movements in Rural Java

Christian Lund and Noer Fauzi Rachman

INTRODUCTION

Land occupation sounds as simple as it is radical. You move on to land held by others and announce, 'This is ours now!'. In fact, while it is radical, land occupation is not simple at all. In recent decades, land ownership and control have been significantly challenged in most parts of Indonesia. Not only have new groups of land users occupied land from which they were formerly excluded; the institutions to which these people are beholden for their land are also new. During the late 1990s, agrarian protests became ever more frequent as the Suharto regime (the New Order, 1966–98) spiralled into decline and finally collapsed. From 1998, different social organizations, groups and movements formed in a period of political transformation (the so-called *Reformasi*). The fall of the Suharto regime opened a path for democratization and a series of decentralization reforms which provided increased autonomy to local government. This appeared to offer opportunities to transform society, including agrarian structures. Land occupations by smallholders accompanied the protests.[1] They seized — from state forests or private and government plantations — land which had often been farmed by smallholders before coming under the control of Dutch colonial authorities and plantations. The land occupations were controversial. On the one hand,

This chapter is based on two two-month periods of fieldwork in 2012 and 2013, as well as Rachman's previous work in the area. We owe a debt of gratitude to the local communities who took us in and patiently explained their histories to us. For sad and obvious reasons, they must remain anonymous. Many people have helped us to improve the text. Especially, we wish to thank Michael Eilenberg, Nancy Lee Peluso, Duncan McDuie-Ra, Jason Cons, Erin Collins, Christian Lentz, Jonathan Padwe, Zach Anderson, Mike Dwyer, and Reece Jones for challenging questions and suggestions, and the journal's anonymous referees for constructive comments. We wish to acknowledge financial support from the Danish Social Science Research Council.

1. The terminology in this field can be tortuous. We opt for a simple model. A 'farmer' farms. A 'smallholder' is a farmer of a relatively small plot of land, and a 'peasant' is a smallholder in a particular class position *vis-à-vis* capital and labour. In this text we refer to the movement as a peasant movement because this is how the movement refers to itself in English, and because it is a particular class project. We generally refer to its active members as smallholders because their class position is in flux and their relations to bodies of authority are in the making.

Rule and Rupture: State Formation through the Production of Property and Citizenship, First Edition. Edited by Christian Lund and Michael Eilenberg.

they were condoned and even hailed by popular movements as the realization of the long-awaited land reform which was embedded in the Basic Agrarian Law from 1960 but never fully implemented (see Bachriadi and Wiradi, 2011). On the other hand, forest and plantation owners, as well as local government institutions, frequently condemned the occupations as theft. Whether occupation was 'reclaiming' of lost land or 'theft' is one issue. Another, underlying, issue is how this fundamentally challenged and re-worked the social relations of property and citizenship and, thereby, political authority.

This chapter analyses the reworking of property and citizenship relations in areas of land occupation on Java following the decline of an authoritarian regime in Indonesia. We focus especially on the role of social movements in this process and how different social relations intermesh with and succeed one another to produce new relations of property, citizenship and authority, which should never be treated as finished products — they are always in the making (Lund, Introduction to this issue). We engage the processes through which property, citizenship and authority are produced, fabricated or some-times conjured up, and the dynamics through which they are reproduced, challenged, undermined and possibly eliminated. We attempt to do this while remaining mindful of the uncertainty experienced by the protagonists themselves.

In the following sections, we first sketch our conceptual framework, then analyse how governing institutions in Indonesia have dispossessed different groups of people, and how the categorization of property and citizenship has structured exclusion in rural Java. We outline the configuration of recognition and misrecognition of property and political and economic identity claims that effectively entitle actors to possess land. In the process, we show how established categories and entitlements are destabilized, and how public authority itself is put on the line.

THE CONCEPTUAL FRAMEWORK OF PROPERTY, CITIZENSHIP AND AUTHORITY

Property and citizenship are often dealt with as two distinct concerns and different fields of inquiry. However, as stated in the Introduction to this issue, people often engage with both concerns simultaneously. Property and citizen-ship are fundamentally relational, and intimately related to public authority in their constitution. They share the same essential element: recognition. By property we understand a legitimized claim to objects of value sanctioned by some form of relevant political authority (MacPherson, 1978; Rose, 1994; Sikor and Lund, 2009). Struggles for property rights can therefore be seen as struggles for the recognition of a wide variety of rights to access resources in various ways. Citizenship we understand as meaningful membership of an organized political body. Struggles for citizenship are, generally, struggles for the recognition of the very right to have rights in this body politic (Arendt, 1948/1979; Lund, 2011a, 2011b; Somers, 2008). Formal national citizenship is just one of several configurations of socially constructed collective subjectivities. For most people, different political bodies are relevant for different aspects of life.

The colonization of what became Indonesia represented a dramatic and violent re-ordering of property and political subjectivity. Colonial agents — governments and private companies in various combinations — dispossessed colonial subjects and constituted new property regimes. In so doing, they established new subject categories and various degrees of (dis-)enfranchisement of people in their new dominions. While independence and revolution held promise of fundamental change, many colonial patterns of exclusionary property and subject formation were preserved — some even extended — under President Sukarno and especially President Suharto. Sukarno's rule (1947–65) traversed revolution, nationalization ('Indonesianization') of property, and efforts at land reform, but it rested on authoritarian 'guided democracy' and racially differentiated citizenship. Suharto's regime, known as the New Order, emerged through massacres that targeted hundreds of thousands of citizens who were alleged to be 'communist'. The New Order consolidated the government's control over land and resources in strong and close alliances with private capital.[2]

Even when the impetus from governments on property making and subject making is very strong, however, we argue that authority is mutually constitutive in relation to both property and citizenship. Rights and authority are co-produced. Processes of recognition of claims to land and other resources, and of political identity with various entitlements, simultaneously invest the institution that provides such recognition with recognition of its authority to do so. Struggles over property and citizenship are, therefore, as much about the idea, scope and constitution of authority as about access to resources and membership (see the Introduction to this issue).

This mutual constitution of rights and authority takes place in many institutional settings. Thus governance is not reserved for statutory institutions alone, and the ability to govern may reside in institutions other than in formal government. In other words, it is not only government institutions that have state effects. Claims to rights are therefore ways to invoke public authority

2. For the purposes of a book chapter, it is necessary to reduce the complexity of Indonesia's modern history to a few lines; this is acceptable only because so much literature exists. For analyses of Sukarno's rule through the years of revolution, liberal parliamentarianism and authoritarian (so-called 'guided') democracy, with differentiated and curtailed citizenship rights to Indonesians of Chinese extraction, see inter alia Hefner (1990); Lev (2000); McTurnan Kahin (1953/2003); Rachman (2011); Ricklefs (1993); Vickers (2005). For an analysis of the massacres in the 1960s and the shifts in policy making and enforcement — and relations between the armed forces and the leading political party, Golkar — during the Suharto years, see for example Anderson (1998); Farid (2005); Huizer (1974); Kammen and McGregor (2012); Lindsey (2008); Ryter (1998); Slater (2010); White (2016).

and governing capacity in different institutions, be they statutory or not. A claim to authority through the categorization of property and citizenship is a way to acquire and exercise state quality. It is a claim to 'state' (Lund, 2006; see also Introduction to this issue). In Indonesia this includes customary (*adat*) institutions, but also institutions with a shorter history such as non-governmental organizations (NGOs) and social and political movements. They may claim to be 'non-state', yet, in practice, they govern and control political subjectivities, resources and space.

By following the actual relationships, the historical and contingent shifts, the multiple logics and the tensions between them in our two case studies of occupation, we will uncover how property and citizenship have come about, and how public authority in these domains has been produced as a consequence (Lund, 2014).

RECENT HISTORY OF PROPERTY AND CITIZENSHIP IN JAVA

The dynamics of the mutual constitution of property, citizenship and authority shape the trajectory of Indonesian land politics. With a special focus on rural West Java, this section examines the recent historical context of the decline of the authoritarian New Order, the contemporary history of political pluralism and pressure for social change, and some of the institutional ramifications.

From Colonialism to the New Order

The period from colonization to the heyday of the New Order saw several tectonic shifts in terms of property and citizenship, and the authority to govern in rural Java. Colonial classifications of people endowed individuals with rights to resources or disenfranchised them. During that era, the colonial government usurped the land of Indonesia by force and with the help of obliging local leaders. By giving priority to Dutch civil law, other forms of property based on custom were conveniently rendered legally invisible by the colonial government whenever Dutch interests in land were at stake.[3]

With independence in 1945, new relationships of property and citizenship could be established and old ones reworked. The Basic Agrarian Law (1960) promised land reform, whereby the Indonesian rural population would become politically and legally visible. This law (which is, in principle, still in force today) firmly establishes state control over the country's land resources; central features in the legislation include land distribution and

---

3. Again, there is a rich literature on this: see for example Breman (1983, 2015); van Doorn and Hendrix (1983); Furnivall (1939, 1948); Gordon (2010); Hoadley (1994); Onghokham (2003); Sato (1994); Silean and Smark (2006); Svensson (1991).

a ceiling on landholdings. The legislation is complex and not without contradictions; it has always been subject to competing interpretations. Moreover, government authority over land was split between competing ministries and departments, and the most significant land-controlling government agencies (with jurisdiction over forest and plantation land) recognized property claims from companies with these interests. The Sukarno government emphasized the land distribution element of the law. Land occupations in the early 1960s — mostly driven by the Indonesian Communist Party — were an attempt to solicit the government's active recognition of smallholder land claims.

These efforts to secure land rights were cut short by the coup d'état in 1965 and General Suharto's authoritarian New Order regime. This regime emphasized the element of state control in the law. During the New Order, Suharto developed state-owned plantation companies like PT Perhutani that controlled all major teak plantations in Java. Outside Java, plantations were granted to companies run by Suharto's cronies. In this period, patronage politics and top-down control over land allocation and concessions were central in the establishment of an alliance between a property-owning elite and a government backed by the army. The New Order orchestrated persecution of known and alleged communists. In the name of restoring security and order, an intense propaganda campaign to dehumanize the Communist Party legitimated murder and arrests on a massive scale.[4] The many farmers who had moved onto Dutch property after independence, in anticipation of land reform, were forced out. They were not only dispossessed of land rights; for people labelled as communists, even the right to have rights was effectively expunged. This persecution was largely organized and carried out by paramilitary and civilian organizations encouraged, equipped and protected by the army (Centre for Village Studies, 1990; Farid, 2005: 4; Huizer, 1974; Kammen and McGregor, 2012; Ryter, 1998). For many years, 'land reform' was equated with a 'communist agenda',[5] and the political category of 'communist' came to imply total exclusion.

The New Order government never actually repealed the Basic Agrarian Law. However, it fundamentally changed its orientation and used it to dispossess landholders by re-categorizing their political identity as communist, by delegitimizing their claims, and by removing them with force. Under the New Order, the Basic Agrarian Law looked very similar to the colonial *Domeinverklaring* which gave decisive control over property to the state. Toward the end of the New Order era, land returned to the political agenda through various actors. A large number of organizations, NGOs and movements began to carve out political space in the increasingly pluralist context

---

4. According to Farid (2005: 8), 'An estimated half a million persons were killed and a million and a half were indefinitely detained as political prisoners. The families of such prisoners lived with the constant threat of harassment'. See also Huizer (1974).
5. Land reform only re-entered the government vocabulary in 2006 (Slaats et al., 2009).

(Bachriadi et al., 2013; Li, 2000; Lucas and Warren, 2003, 2013; Peluso et al., 2008). During the same period, land occupations began to occur once again on Java and elsewhere in Indonesia. Farmers occupied land in plantations and forests from which they claimed to have been evicted earlier. Many of these plantations had been Dutch-owned during the colonial era, and had already been taken over by farmers once before, in the 1950s and 1960s. In West Java the occupations came about as a result of interaction between community leaders and student and other activists. They challenged the ownership and control of the land by the plantations which had been established since the mid-1960s.

Reformasi and the SPP

A large number of peasant unions appeared in the 1990s; many were federated in the Indonesia Peasant Union Federation (Federasi Serikat Tani Indonesia). In West Java, the Sundanese Peasant's Movement (SPP) emerged gradually in the 1990s. The social basis of the organization lay among the landless and smallholders in association with urban activists and students, who also began to form unions around that time. The main tactic was land occupations of State Forest Corporation or plantation land, and in this they echoed the 'unilateral operations' of the Indonesian Communist Party in the early 1960s (Rachman, 2011: 9). The idea was that originally the land had belonged to smallholders, who had been dispossessed by colonial and post-colonial government policies for the benefit of private and government companies. This may explain why, once evicted, smallholders and their descendants have returned to the same locations time and again. For many, the claim is on what they see as their specific land; it is not an abstract claim on just any land. SPP was seen as a political force to be reckoned with by the Garut, Tasikmalaya and Ciamis district governments and the National Land Agency (Bachriadi, 2010: 291–319; Rachman, 2011, 2016).

For good reasons, there are no comprehensive membership lists for SPP, although membership cards were issued. Moreover, 'membership' or adherence was qualified by 'active participation' rather than by payment of a membership fee (see below). Different sources estimate SPP to have numbered anywhere between 25,000 and 700,000 people (Aji, 2005: 42; Andéer and Jelmin, 2004: 27): numbers may also have fluctuated over time. SPP appears to be firmly rooted in some 50 villages, where 30–50 land occupations of different sizes have been organized.

The political atmosphere was positive toward land reform in the first years after *Reformasi* and decentralization. A speech by President Abdurrahman Wahid in 2000 epitomized the turn of the tide, as he argued that it was not appropriate to accuse people of stealing land, because 'in fact, the plantations have stolen the people's land'. He continued: 'some 40 per cent of plantation land should be distributed to cultivators who need it. Moreover, people could even hold shares in the plantation itself' (quoted in Fauzi and Bachriadi, 2006: 19). During the 2000s, movements like SPP encouraged and organized land occupations while urging government institutions and politicians at different levels to validate the cause of occupiers and recognize the legitimacy of their demands (Rachman, 2011: 10). As Lucas and Warren explain:

> These 'reclaiming' actions included occupation of plantation estates, golf courses, and ne-
> glected 'sleeping land' acquired by investors for speculative purposes. In East Java alone,
> according to Legal Aid Foundation sources, there were more than fifty actions by dispos-
> sessed farmers reclaiming disputed lands. At Jenggawah ... local people occupied the estate
> [a former Dutch plantation covering more than 3,000 hectares], after a decade-long strug-
> gle. In North Sumatra, two thousand farmers demanded the return of 100,000 hectares of
> plantation land controlled by a state company. (Lucas and Warren, 2003: 88–90)

In Garut, Tasikmalaya and Ciamis districts, some 14,000 families occupied 9,000 ha of land in 41 locations in early 2003 (Afiff et al., 2005: 4). During this period, the State Forest Corporation, plantation owners, and armed forces violently opposed occupations. Corporate landholders and occupying smallholders engaged in many confrontations throughout Java — some more violent than others, and some very violent indeed. The occupations remained modest in relation to the extensive territory of the districts, but as a challenge to the existing order they were very significant. To the thousands of occupying farmers, they were dramatic, transformative events.

Land occupations involved several aspects, not least competition over ter-minology. In 1998, a plantation owner in Cilawu in West Java engaged an Islamic national celebrity preacher, Zainuddin MZ, to give a speech denounc-ing land occupation on religious grounds. In a passionate performance, he described land occupation as theft, or land looting (*penjarahan*), and there-fore a sin. Immediately after the speech, the vice-president of SPP — who was also imam of a mosque in Garut — called together the imams of the sub-district of Cilawa for a debate. The result was a counter-declaration to be pronounced in all mosques at the following Friday prayer. The declaration recognized theft as sin. Yet, the land occupations by smallholders were not to be seen as theft, the clergy argued, but rather as repossession (*reklaiming*) of land, which had initially been stolen from the people by the Dutch and subsequently 'fenced' to plantation owners. In this light, repossessing the land by occupation actually meant absolving the plantation owners of their sins of theft. Land occupation, therefore, represented new livelihood options through legitimate repossession of property, as well as a good deed. The irony was not lost on people, yet the significance of the semantics was more than word play. Labelling the operation with the language of an ethics that was understood and respected by ordinary folk removed it from a simple question of legality.

Land occupations did not concern questions of land access alone; they had a wider implication for property and territorial control. SPP managed to have many of its members elected to the newly established village councils.

They thereby played a political part in Indonesia's new government institutions. However, SPP also established elements characteristic of autonomous governing institutions. As noted above, members of the movement did not simply take out a 'subscription': active participation and mobilization were the salt of SPP membership. The readiness to act was the 'membership fee', or 'tax', that they paid, which then enabled them to rely on the reciprocal protection of their own land claims by SPP's mobilization of fellow members in times of need. When an eviction was looming, SPP would mobilize all its members, and thousands would go to the occupied plantation in question. This averted many forced removals. While this mutual recognition of occupants' land claims and SPP's authority to command members' presence did not entail a financial exchange, the cost of participation incurred by mobilized smallholders was not negligible. In addition to the danger of violence and arrests, the costs of transport, food and absence from one's own farm were sometimes a considerable burden on a tight budget.

Finally, while land acquired through such occupation was not subject to an actual cadastral registration, imitations of formal registration of plots in occupied areas were not unusual. The format of the ledgers of the National Land Agency was copied, and the occupying smallholders kept the books. Names, locations, crops and membership history were recorded. Paperwork was filled out in order to apply to the National Land Agency for recognition of ownership. The process of registering the land with the National Land Agency was often not carried through, however. Various explanations for this were offered in interviews with SPP members and cadres. One was hostility on the part of the National Land Agency. A more convoluted version was that SPP cadres would explain to the members that procedures for land registration had been engaged, but because of some new appointments in the National Land Agency, the whole procedure had to start over. Some members suggested that SPP was in fact stalling the process. As a result, SPP members remained beholden to the movement for their land, as they were kept from establishing property relations as mutual recognition of claims to land and authority with Indonesian statutory institutions. The property rights produced in this relationship between successful squatters and an active movement were circumscribed. In the ideology of SPP, it was important that land was not a commodity to be transacted and accumulated in capitalist dynamics. As a consequence, land transactions within occupied areas were, in principle, limited. Land could be bequeathed to heirs but could not be subdivided, rented, mortgaged or sold. Thus beholden to SPP, smallholders could farm the land, but not transact it. When people actually did, tensions would emerge, and the question of what institution guaranteed such transacted land rights would arise.

Adherence to the movement meant that small conflicts between occupying smallholders were dealt with by SPP cadres. In fact, card-carrying members of SPP would proudly brag to us how their membership gave them not only land: members enjoyed a status which meant they would no longer be physically harassed by police and others at the market, and people could even wriggle their way out of the odd fine for a traffic violation by producing an SPP card or claiming to be 'citizens of SPP'. Contrary to the situation during the Suharto years, police, foresters and even the officers of the State Forest Corporation acknowledged that they had, in practice, less effective jurisdiction in areas with a strong SPP presence and less jurisdiction over the movement's members. SPP could even make it difficult for people *not* to be members in an occupied area.

SPP had a sovereign moment in the areas where it had a strong membership base. It controlled land allocation in these pockets; it defined and enforced rules of land tenure; it taxed and protected people in its occupations; it created a school; and it successfully established a terminology that combined the radical seizure of property and authority with the propriety of an honourable Muslim life. Land occupations and the relations between movement and members were not without tensions, however. While SPP defined and enforced new property relations, statutory institutions remained in the imaginary of occupying smallholders as desired institutions with the power of legitimizing as well as recognizing their claims to land. Different occupations all had their distinct trajectories, but cases studies of two emblematic examples from the southern part of 'occupied' West Java will invoke the broader picture.[6]

TWO OCCUPATIONS

Banjaranyar

In Banjaranyar, a village in Ciamis district, current land occupations mark the latest in a long series of shifts in land control. The area around the village was a 348 ha, Dutch-owned rubber plantation.[7] People in the area were very active in the colonial resistance, and with the flight of the Dutch in 1942 the local population, including plantation workers, moved onto the land and began to cultivate it. At independence and the definitive departure of the Dutch, all plantation buildings and material were set ablaze, and the rubber trees were uprooted.

In 1960, after the adoption of the Basic Agrarian Law, the area was to be distributed through a land reform programme that included the entire

---

6. Data on the two cases were collected through interviews and access to SPP village archives.
7. According to Swart's (1911) report on rubber companies in the Netherlands East Indies, the plantation was owned by Bandjarsarie (Java) Rubber Company, Limited. The tenure of the plantation was held on a Netherlands Indian Government lease (*erfpacht*) that would expire in 1975. For a map of the plantation, see van Diessen and Ormeling (2003: 255).

348 ha.[8] In 1963, a local government leader challenged the land reform plan and the smallholders' occupation of the land; he applied instead for a plantation lease to convert and renew the colonial lease. The dispute went to the Agrarian Court (also known as the Land Reform Court) but no settlement was reached. In 1970, the system of Agrarian Courts was dissolved (see von Benda-Beckmann and von Benda-Beckmann, 2014: 112). At the time, intense political conflicts were raging, mainly between communists and nationalists on the left, and the army (with support from Islamic parties) on the right.

In 1965, after the coup that brought the army and Suharto to power, Banjaranyar was targeted in the anti-communist purge, like thousands of other villages in Java.[9] The land was effectively 'freed up'. Smallholders were evicted; some were arrested; their houses in the plantation area were destroyed; and land was handed over to a private plantation company with a 30-year lease. From 1967, the village was categorized as a forced-labour camp; prisoners were forced to work on the plantation without pay. Some of the area was farmed with paddy rice, and the political prisoners were given plots to farm on the condition that 80 per cent of the harvest went to the local military commander. The surviving prisoners were freed in 1979 — the same year in which thousands of prisoners were released from the notorious Buru prison island. However, for years after their release they had to report to the police every month, their ID cards were stamped with 'ET' — 'Ex-TaPol' or former political prisoner — and they and their children were barred from holding government jobs.[10] Only in 1999, with President Habibie's general amnesty, did the 'Ex-TaPol' stigma cease to be seared into their public identities.

---

8. The plantation was not included in the nationalization programme of the Sukarno government, which established state-owned plantation companies in 1959.

9. While thousands of alleged communists were killed throughout Indonesia by the army, by Islamist militias, and by *preman* (semi-official political gangsters), an order made by the West Java army commander *not* to kill communists saved the lives of hundreds of villagers in Banjaranyar.

10. 'Before being freed [political prisoners] had to sign a declaration that they would not demand compensation. Despite a government order to return their possessions, in reality nobody has successfully reclaimed their books, land and homes.... Ex-Tapols were not permitted:

   • To work in any form of government service, nor in any state-owned corporation, strategic industry, political party, or news media. They were not permitted to become a minister in any religion, a teacher, village head, lawyer, or puppeteer (*dalang*);
   • To vote or be elected;
   • To obtain a passport and travel overseas, even for medical treatment (some allowance was made for those going to Mecca on pilgrimage);
   • To choose where to live or to move house freely;
   • To obtain credit from the bank, even when they fulfilled other requirements;
   • To receive the pensions to which they are entitled from their former employers when they were sacked in 1965' (van Klinken, 1999: 17).

After their release from the forced-labour camp, villagers attempted another occupation in 1986, but they were immediately evicted. At the downfall of Suharto and the end of the New Order in 1998, villagers formed a committee and went to the new district administration to get the land back. The answer was somewhat ambiguous; people could rebuild their houses on the plantation land, but they were 'not to bother the plantation' (*tidak mengganggu perusahaan*). By the end of 2003, however, local inhabitants had seized 160 ha of plantation land, and the committee became a recognized local chapter of the SPP.

Faced by smallholder membership of SPP, the plantation company embarked on a new strategy. Instead of resorting to violent evictions, it entered into negotiations with the land occupants. In the end, local smallholders were to retain some 69 ha of the 160 ha they had occupied, which had not been actively farmed by the plantation company. The company would sign over the land for 'land reform' so that the National Land Agency could take steps to issue land certificates to the smallholders. In return, they were to give up the remaining 91 ha of occupied land, leaving a total of 215 ha for the plantation. They did so, for a time. However, much of the plantation land was, in fact, not used as a plantation. The plantation company rented out around 100 ha to smallholders for a fee of Rp. 100,000 (about US$ 10) per 1,400 m² and eight days of labour per year plus 30 per cent of the harvest. Such arrangements — sub-letting leased land — were not legal but were, and remained, quite common.[11] The final 115 ha were used for rubber and worked by plantation workers. They lived on the plantation lands in two small settlements.

As for the occupied 69 ha, it was decided by SPP that all members should have a share in it, and the association began to map and divide the land. As a consequence, each plot was a mere 1,000–2,000 m². People used their plots for building houses with a garden. In 2004, the community of occupants applied to the National Land Agency for land titling of the 69 ha, with the help of SPP. After some six months of field investigations, the National Land Agency issued land certificates for more than 500 plots. However, land certificates were not given directly to the land occupants, but were handed to the local chapter of SPP to distribute to its members. SPP organized a meticulous ceremony. Each landholder — generally a family — presented itself to the chairman of SPP for an interview. Four questions were asked and answers were recorded. People were asked to: (1) account for the history of their land in the village; (2) give evidence of their participation in the land struggle; (3) explain the meaning of the land certificate; and (4) explain what they felt about receiving the certificate.[12] This was a very intense ordeal, and

---

11. Smallholders received receipts from the company for the rent they paid.
12. Delivery of the certificate took 31 days. The transcripts of each interview are between two and five typed pages long. Most of the histories trace alternating eviction and occupation for three generations. (Material in private possession.)

left people in no doubt about the importance of SPP's role in authorizing their land access.[13] To receive papers for the land was one thing, but the fact that the documents bore no indication of their Ex-TaPol status, was quite another. With the land certificates they were now fully enfranchised, tax-paying citizens beholden to the government of Indonesia for the (admittedly, tiny) plot of land they had occupied.

After obtaining certificates on the 69 ha, a second phase of occupation was initiated in Banjaranyar in 2008. SPP members occupied another 150 ha of land. Of these, 65 ha represented simple defections on the part of those leasing land directly from the plantation company: SPP members had encouraged these tenants to suspend their payment to the company and join their organization. SPP threatened to report the plantation's illegal practice of sub-letting leased land to farmers to the National Land Agency. This would jeopardize any hopes of renewal of the lease.[14] By 2012, the plantation company had ceased to charge rent for the land.

The change from a tenancy arrangement with the company to landholding guaranteed by SPP was very significant for the villagers. Certificates were not issued for any land beyond the initial 69 ha. No government institution recognized the smallholders' possession of this land as legal or legitimate, leaving the smallholders beholden solely to the SPP. It had established a land register in which the landholding of each member was listed, its location indicated, and the payment of the SPP membership fee recorded. Each member paid Rp. 3,000 per year per 1,400 m^2 of land held. In addition, each family contributed Rp. 10,000 if there was an SPP activity such as a meeting to which the organization needed to send a representative. Finally, ad hoc contributions could be required. Support for SPP was not unanimous among the land occupants. Some farmers had occupied land alongside the SPP members and were farming it in the same manner, but they did not mobilize to protect other squatters from eviction at the behest of SPP. SPP leadership frowned upon this free-riding and let it be known to the plantation company that selected and targeted evictions would not be opposed by the movement. This SPP practice of disassociating itself from certain occupants left the latter exposed and put pressure on them to join the SPP.

The democratic and decentralized political system that emerged after the fall of Suharto offered new possibilities for local politics. Thus, the village of Banjaranyar elected an SPP member as village head in 2008. When a new school was built in 2010, it was situated on the plantation company's leased land: the village head had negotiated with the company and eventually convinced it to write a letter granting land to the school project. The

---

13. We did not hear of anyone who was refused land, but the procedure would have discouraged those with slim chances from making a claim.
14. This was not an idle threat. As for many of the plantation companies, the duration of the original lease was 35 years. This meant that many leases expired around 2000 and in the years following. Some companies had not taken care to renew them, and were themselves technically squatting on the land.

company's legal right to transfer leased land like this was quite uncertain, and the wording of the letter quite opaque. However, the fact remained that village infrastructure, which facilitated settlement within the disputed area, had been constructed. In the event of a future further subdivision of the village, this increased the chances that the area around the school would form a new centre.

The history of land conflicts in Banjaranyar is long. It extends over at least three or four generations and alternates between government control — either directly or through concessions to plantations — and control by villagers themselves. Mostly, this control was structured through the SPP. Villagers' membership of SPP gave them land and simultaneously gave SPP authority. This period included several significant moments. First, when the initial occupation of 160 ha was reduced to 69 ha, the path to obtaining certificates issued by the Indonesian government was opened. While depending on SPP's protection and committing themselves to its actions, smallholders sought recognition from government institutions as well. By applying for land rights, people attempted to make themselves visible to the National Land Agency, anticipating acknowledgement of their claim. By obtaining land certificates from the National Land Agency, smallholders held property with legal recognition from the Indonesian government. They were thus beholden to the government for this property and, most importantly for the people of Banjaranyar, they had been elevated to full citizenship by that token. They were no longer Ex-TaPol with curtailed civil rights. The recognition of property rights by the Indonesian government went hand-in-hand with obtaining recognition as full, uncompromised citizens of Indonesia. In this light, the size of the individual plots mattered little.

For the remaining 150 ha, different dynamics of recognition emerged. Here, the smallholders remained beholden to SPP, and SPP had not been delegated the authority to control this land. It was not property that gave access to citizenship, but the reverse. It was their membership of SPP — effectively a form of citizenship — that entitled people to a piece of land recognized as theirs by this organization. The SPP's efforts seemed to prepare for the re-categorization of the occupied land from 'plantation land' to 'land for land reform', ideally paving the way for the government's recognition of the farmers' property rights. At the time of writing, in 2016, it remains to be seen whether SPP will actually relinquish its authority over land by transferring it to the National Land Agency, and whether the Agency will recognize the occupants' claims as rights.

Harumandala

Harumandala is a village in Pangandaran district.[15] The village consists of several sub-villages or *kampungs*, and is located within a steeply sloped

---

15. In 2013, Ciamis district was divided into two: Ciamis and Pangandaran districts.

130   *Christian Lund and Noer Fauzi Rachman*

landscape. After independence, the area saw many armed confrontations between the Indonesian army and the Islamic movement. The confrontations died down around 1961. The area was formally under the territorial authority of the Provincial Forestry Service of West Java, and the entire area was classified as 'forest'. However, most of the area was populated with villages and kampungs. Generally, people were farming paddy rice on terraces, as well as different crops on forest plots (trees, fruits, vegetables, spices, etc.). In practice, people could clear land for paddy rice farming and other activities without much interference from the authorities. No legal rights ensured people's access to land, but the Provincial Forestry Service tolerated farming and people regarded the land as their own.

In 1978, all the forestland controlled by the Provincial Forestry Service in West Java — close to 1 million ha — was transferred to the State Forestry Corporation, which had previously operated only in Central and East Java.[16] As a parastatal institution with its own uniformed 'forest police', and as a part of an authoritarian regime, the State Forest Corporation was inaccessible to ordinary people seeking to argue their case or negotiate. The Corporation established boundaries to create teak and mahogany plantations in the area, clearing the area of any farmed fields that might be in the way. Then, it started to act as a government landlord, charging rent for the fields people cultivated within the area. The State Forest Corporation officials appointed individual villagers as rent collectors and gave them rent-free land in return. The rent consisted of 33 per cent of the villagers' rice production: these farmers thus became tenants of the Corporation, and in the process consolidated its land control. There was no legal basis for this rent, and it was never registered as official income of the company. Illegal logging activities increased steeply after 2001, with teak and mahogany as the targeted species in Ciamis district. Accusations and counter-accusations between villagers and the Corporation were frequent. The villagers claimed that the Corporation and police officers were colluding with loggers, who also hired villagers to work for a daily wage, while the State Forest Corporation, on the other hand, accused the SPP of being behind the illegal logging.

In 2006, the villagers created a local chapter of SPP, and some 186 people joined. During training sessions farmers were told that the Forest Corporation's collection of rent was illegal, and actions toward land reform could be launched in the area by occupying land the Corporation claimed to control. Forestland was never earmarked for land reform, however, so SPP cadres may have overstated the opportunities in their attempt to galvanize support. The first move, nonetheless, was to refuse to pay rent to the State Forest

---

16. On historical aspects of the State Forest Corporation (SFC) in relation to the government and village communities, see Peluso (1992) and Rachman (2011: 27–36). After including West Java forest land, 'the territory controlled by the SFC mirrored that controlled by the Dutch Forest Service in Java except for enclaves of forest land disputed by peasants placed there by the Japanese or occupying the land since the revolution' (Peluso, 1992: 125).

Corporation. Instead, people paid Rp. 10,000 per month to SPP, and turned their presence into a land occupation. Some villagers were summoned to the Forest Corporation office where they were interrogated and accused of logging in the area, but the occupation continued. Information about the occupation reached the West Java police commander and the Corporation director in Jakarta. They decided to re-establish the Corporation's control over the occupied forestlands by launching a forest security operation funded by the Ministry of Forestry. The operation was preceded by a joint reconnaissance for forest security control conducted in March 2008.[17] The State Forest Corporation provided the reconnaissance team with a detailed map that indicated 'forest security disturbances'. The team reported that approximately 290 ha of forestland were occupied by nearly 1,600 villagers from four villages within Cigugur sub-district. A detailed report from Forest Unit 89 stated that permanent crops such as cocoa, vegetables, herbs and wood species, as well as a small mosque, nine houses, several monitoring posts, and an SPP office were located on the occupied lands.[18]

Three months after this reconnaissance report, the West Java Police, the Ministry of Forestry and the State Forest Corporation launched a forest security operation. This was a joint effort to combat illegal logging and timber trade, the first of five policies prioritized by the Ministry of Forestry for 2005–9. The main objectives of the operation were to re-establish control of the state forestland and to evict the people occupying it. The operation invoked the military terms, Security Operation (*Operasi Keamanan*) and Dangerous Area (*Daerah Rawan*), echoing the Suharto era. Similarly, the use of terms like 'illegal loggers', 'illegal occupiers', 'subversive', and 'anti-state' established an association between these activities and organized crime.

Officers from the State Forest Corporation and the Provincial Police in Bandung came to Harumandala and its six kampungs. More than 300 police officers set up camp in the local soccer field and began to prepare the evictions. The operation was initiated by a ceremony, in which the police commander, the head of the Corporation's forest police, and representatives from the local government Forestry and Plantation Unit went through the objectives of the operation — namely, to find evidence of illegal logging, to evict illegal occupants and destroy their farms, and to remove any illegal

---

17. The team was composed of officials from the District Military Office, West Java Police Office, West Java Civil Police Office, the National Land Agency's West Java Office, West Java Forest Office, and the State Forest Corporation. The team was assigned on the basis of a decision by the West Java Governor, No. 552.02/Kep.560-Binprod/2007 (Surat Keputusan Gubernur Jawa Barat Nomor 552.02/Kep.560-Binprod/2007 tentang Tim Pengamanan dan Penanganan Gangguan Keamanan Hutan Negara dan Perkebunan Besar).
18. Material in private possession.

construction from the area.[19] First, the police and the Corporation officers made house-to-house searches for timber.[20] Then, fields were ravaged and houses were burnt to the ground. Some houses were left standing, but the police marked them with chalk, 'This house must be destroyed by yourself' (*Harus dibongkar sendiri*), or 'This house and land is not yours but the property of the state' (*Rumah dan tanah ini bukan milik kamu tapi milik Negara*). Finally, the police forced the villagers to sign a statement in which they renounced their membership of SPP and declared they would never join again. During the operation, some 10 villagers were arrested and subsequently sentenced for 'destruction of forest by illegal occupation'. They all spent between one and two years in jail.

After the police operation, people resumed the cultivation of their plots within the area but moved to kampungs outside of the State Forest Corporation area for a couple of years. By 2010, people began to move back to the abandoned kampung of Pasir Pilar within the Corporation-controlled area. People reconstructed their houses, and within six months some 34 families had re-established themselves in the kampung. The local SPP chapter drew up a map of the area, registering each plot and its owner.[21]

The State Forest Corporation contacted the settlement, but now with a new approach. They announced a planting ceremony of mahogany trees and invited villagers to witness. An area was cleared and 1,000 seedlings were planted in rows. Each row was publicly named after a government institution. Thus, the first row was named, 'the row of the provincial governor', the next, 'the row of the police commander', 'the row of the Indonesian army', and so on. The intention, no doubt, was to impress upon the people of the area that these resources belonged to and were under the protection of the entire government structure of Indonesia. The State Forest Corporation had the whole episode filmed.[22] The following night, however, all 1,000 mahogany seedlings were uprooted. A few days later, the Corporation agents returned to mete out punishment for the destruction of the plants. In the fighting and commotion that followed, Corporation agents destroyed the local mosque. This provoked people from Pasir Pilar and other kampungs to go to the local

19. Curiously, the Bandung-based NGO, Council for Forest Salvation, also participated. No doubt its presence represented 'civil society'.
20. It is not possible to establish whether villagers were indeed involved in logging trees planted by the Corporation or whether, as villagers claim, this logging was part of an everyday routine of Corporation staff in collusion with police and local gangs. Villagers did cut trees, but claimed them to be 'their own', and not planted by the Corporation. The fact that some sawmills processing the illegally logged timber were owned and run by police officers did not make the picture any clearer.
21. SPP in Ciamis had organized training sessions in cartography and mapping for all activists, and a small group from Harumandala had participated.
22. The Corporation film crew also wanted to document the local smallholders destroying their own crops, but the smallholders refused.

police in Cigugur to complain about the wanton destruction of the religious edifice. The presence of several hundred angry farmers seemed to make an impression on the police, who promised to investigate. Although nothing ever came of the investigation, the situation calmed down; people remained in their kampungs on the disputed land; they resumed farming their plots and rice fields, and they continued not to pay rent to the State Forest Corporation. They were not beholden to the Corporation or the Indonesian government for their land rights. Instead, they held land thanks to 'the republic' of SPP, with the opportunities and dangers this implied.

As people moved from Cikares and other kampungs outside of the Corporation area and back into the kampung of Pasir Pilar, they asked the official local territorial administration — the Village Office — for new ID cards that would reflect this change. This was done. By that token, Pasir Pilar became an official kampung, situated within the area that the State Forest Corporation claimed to control as forest. Moreover, as people registered to vote for the 2014 elections, officials from the sub-district would visit all houses and place an official government sticker on the door with the name of the voter, and place of residence — their new official kampung.

The system of payment to SPP remained provisory, but with the small-holders' return to the contested lands in 2010, all kampungs of Harumandala also began to contribute to the Village Office to the tune of Rp. 1,000,000 annually. At first, the Village Office, its mayor, and its elected parliamen-tarians were reluctant to receive the funds. They were unsure if they were entitled to them, and what accepting them would entail, but after some ne-gotiation the Village Government of Harumandala accepted the contribution at a public ceremony.[23] While still perceived as illegal occupants by the State Forest Corporation, smallholders were also beginning to be seen as tax-paying, voting, registered, Indonesian citizens. The contributions were not from individual members but from SPP, and people generally saw the 'contribution' as related to the issue of land. This 'contribution' established a new substantive relationship between landholders and the formal struc-tures of the Indonesian government at its lowest level, the Village Office. It remains unclear what this new relationship represents. One might argue that this relationship not only established the SPP landholders as owners of property in the eyes of the Village Office; it also established the Village Of-fice as a public authority on questions of property in land that was classified as forest. As the smallholders made claims to resources, they also bestowed state quality on the Village Office by attributing to it the authority to validate land claims. This may, eventually, put the Village Office in competition with other statutory institutions.

---

23. All the local chapters of SPP we visited in October–November 2013 that had occupied State Forest Corporation land told similar stories of donations to village governments.

DISCUSSION AND CONCLUSION

The confrontation between governments, powerful landholders, and more or
less organized rural masses has been driving agrarian change in Indonesia
throughout its modern history. The upheavals following the end of the New
Order are thus not the first but simply the latest in a series of dramatic claims
following political ruptures and new possibilities.

Land occupations of the past 20 years were defined as illegal by government, yet occupying the land enabled the peasant movement to gain political
and legal visibility. By forming an organization, people resisted and averted
evictions, and access to land for the smallholder went through the movement rather than through the recognition of a right by statutory government.
SPP mapped space, distributed land, collected tax, resolved disputes, and
provided other services; thereby it took on the mantle of a governing institution. SPP also worked to exclude non-members, and the transfer of control
to statutory institutions seemed not to be very urgent. The movement har-
nessed and organized discontent, protest and interest in the twilight between
contentious and routine politics, between being a movement embodying a
'collective will' and an organization with bureaucratic and service operations
for its members, and hints of institutional logics. Even if SPP cadres saw
themselves as distinctly outside of government, they defined and enforced
collectively binding rules and effectively exhibited 'state quality'. Hence,
just as government institutions may be stakeholders *as well as* authorizers,
social movements may authorize *as well as* represent interests.

The recent land occupations through peasant movements also articulated
social identity. Active membership and readiness to be mobilized for more
than one's 'own' plot of land defined the relationship. This was crucial, as
legalization of land occupations remained rudimentary, and such possession was rarely recognized as property by government institutions. In fact,
discrediting land occupations through criminalization and labelling by government remained the norm. It is not easy to see a pattern in the reactions
of statutory institutions to land occupations. They ranged from opposition,
through tolerance, to acceptance and approval. In a situation of rupture, government institutions, as much as other institutions, seemed to be searching
for a long-term tenable position.

The struggles over land challenged more than the existing land rights;
they challenged and suspended government's very authority to define them.
This produced a sovereign moment for the peasant movement. The SPP was
not beholden to government for the land it controlled. Rather, it had established a new relationship of mutual recognition with its members, the local
smallholders. The SPP recognized their claims to land on the basis of active
adherence, and the smallholders, in turn, recognized the movement's capacity to recognize and defend these claims as rights. SPP members recognized
the movement's state quality and authority to govern. This quality formed

through land struggles at the rupture of the New Order. This relationship effectively produced property, even if the Indonesian government did not recognize it.

Rule has never been uncompromised in rural West Java, and for the occupied areas, this is especially true. Order and resistance have been woven into one another as competing actors have tried different combinations of force, legitimation and governance. The actual occupations of land — by government agencies and corporations, or movements and farmers — depended on their respective ability to dig in their heels, and evict or exclude rival claimants. The military force and hired muscle used against organized smallholders in large numbers was a decisive first step towards control of space. In one of the cases analysed above, a plantation company ceded its land; in the other, government claims in the form of the State Forest Corporation's demand for rent failed to prevail. Instead, the social relationship between smallholders and the SPP was the dominant structuring dynamic of resource control in these spaces. Whether the mutual recognition will be consolidated politically, legally and institutionally over time is an open question. The smallholders walked a fine line. They adhered to the movement to secure the collective protection of their settlement and their property. Yet, in anticipation of recognition, they also continued to engage with statutory institutions with demands for land registration, or with ostentatious tax payment to hesitant local governments — institutions to which hitherto they had remained barely visible citizens without even the right to have rights.

REFERENCES

Afiff, S., N. Fauzi, G. Hart, L. Ntsebeza and N.L. Peluso (2005) *Redefining Agrarian Power. Resurgent Agrarian Movements in West Java, Indonesia.* Berkeley, CA: Center for Southeast Asia Studies, University of California Berkeley.

Aji, G.B. (2005) *Tanah untuk Penggarap. Pengalaman Serikat Petani Pasundan Menggarap Lahan-lahan Perkebunan dan Kehutanan* [*Land to the Tiller. SPP's Experience in Occupying and Cultivating Plantation and Forest Land*]. Bogor: Pustaka Latin.

Andéer, L. and K. Jelmin (2004) 'Peasants' Resistance in a Global Context. A Two-Case Study of Solidarity within the Transnational Peasant Movement'. BSc Thesis, Uppsala University, Department of Government.

Anderson, B. (1998) *The Spectre of Comparisons. Nationalism, Southeast Asia and the World.* London: Verso.

Arendt, H. (1948/1979) *The Origins of Totalitarianism.* New York: Harcourt, Brace, Janovich.

Bachriadi, D. (2010) 'Between Discourse and Action. Agrarian Reform and Rural Social Movements in Indonesia Post-1965'. PhD Thesis, The Flinders Asia Centre School of International Studies, Flinders University, Adelaide.

Bachriadi, D. and G. Wiradi (2011) *Six Decades of Inequality. Land Tenure Problems in Indonesia.* Bandung: Agrarian Resource Centre.

Bachriadi, D., A. Lucas and C. Warren (2013) 'The Agrarian Movement and Emerging Political Constellations', in A. Lucas and C. Warren (eds) *Land for the People: The State and Agrarian Conflict in Indonesia,* pp. 308–71. Columbus, OH: Ohio University Press.

von Benda-Beckmann, F. and K. von Benda-Beckmann (2014) *Political and Legal Transformations of an Indonesian Polity. The Nagari from Colonialism to Decentralisation*. Cambridge: Cambridge University Press.

Breman, J. (1983) *Control of Land and Labour in Colonial Java*. Leiden: Foris.

Breman, J. (2015) *Mobilizing Labour for the Global Coffee Market. Profits from an Unfree Work Regime in Colonial Java*. Amsterdam: Amsterdam University Press.

Centre for Village Studies (Gadjah Mada University) (1990) 'Rural Violence in Klaten and Banyuwangi', in R. Cribb (ed.) *The Indonesian Killings 1965–1966*, pp. 120–57. Clayton: Monash University, Centre for Southeast Asian Studies.

van Diessen, J.R. and F.J. Ormeling (2003) *Grote Atlas van Nederlands Oost-Indië* [*Atlas of the Dutch East Indies*]. Utrecht: Koninklijk Nederlands Aardrijkskundig Genootschap/Royal Dutch Geographical Society Advisory Committee.

van Doorn J. and W.J. Hendrix (1983) 'The Emergence of a Dependent Economy. Consequences of the Opening Up of West Priangan, Java, to the Process of Modernization'. CASP Paper no. 9. Rotterdam: Erasmus University Rotterdam.

Farid, H. (2005) 'Indonesia's Original Sin. Mass Killings and Capitalist Expansion, 1965–66', *Inter-Asia Cultural Studies* 6(1): 3–16.

Fauzi, N. and D. Bachriadi (2006) 'The Resurgence of Agrarian Movements in Indonesia. Scholar-Activists, Popular Education and Peasant Mobilization'. Paper presented at the conference 'Land, Poverty, Social Justice and Development', Institute of Social Studies, The Hague (9–14 January).

Furnivall, S. (1939) *Netherlands India: A Study of Plural Economy*. Cambridge: Cambridge University Press.

Furnivall, S. (1948) *Colonial Policy and Practice. A Comparative Study of Burma and Netherlands India*. Cambridge: Cambridge University Press.

Gordon, A. (2010) 'Netherlands East Indies: The Large Colonial Surplus of Indonesia, 1878–1939', *Journal of Contemporary Asia* 40(3): 425–43.

Hefner, R.W. (1990) *The Political Economy of Mountain Java*. Berkeley, CA: University of California Press.

Hoadley, M. (1994) *Selective Judicial Competence. The Cirebon-Priangan Legal Administration, 1680–1792*. Ithaca, NY: Cornell Southeast Asia Program.

Huizer, G. (1974) 'Peasant Rebellion and Land Reform in Indonesia', *Review of Indonesian and Malayan Affairs* 8: 81–138.

Kammen, D. and K. McGregor (2012) 'The Contours of Mass Violence in Indonesia, 1965–68', in D. Kammen and K. McGregor (eds) *The Contours of Mass Violence in Indonesia, 1965–68*, pp. 1–14. Singapore: National University of Singapore; Copenhagen: Nordic Institute of Asian Studies.

van Klinken, H. (1999) 'Coming Out', *Inside Indonesia* 58 (April–June): 16–17.

Lev, D. (2000) *Legal Evolution and Political Authority in Indonesia. Selected Essays*. The Hague: Kluwer Law International.

Li, T.M. (2000) 'Articulating Indigenous Identity in Indonesia. Resource Politics and the Tribal Slot', *Comparative Studies in Society and History* 4(1): 149–79.

Lindsey, T. (ed.) (2008) *Indonesia. Law and Society*. Annandale: The Federation Press.

Lucas, A. and C. Warren (2003) 'The State, the People, and their Mediators: The Struggle over Agrarian Law Reform in Post-New Order Indonesia', *Indonesia* 76: 87–126.

Lucas, A. and C. Warren (eds) (2013) *Land for the People: The State and Agrarian Conflict in Indonesia*. Columbus, OH: Ohio University Press.

Lund, C. (2006) 'Twilight Institutions. Public Authority and Local Politics in Africa', *Development and Change* 37(4): 685–705.

Lund, C. (2011a) 'Fragmented Sovereignty. Land Reform and Dispossession in Laos', *Journal of Peasant Studies* 38(4): 885–905.

Lund, C. (2011b) 'Property and Citizenship. Conceptually Connecting Land Rights and Belonging in Africa', *Africa Spectrum* 46(3): 71–5.

Lund, C. (2014) 'Of What Is this a Case? Analytical Movements in Qualitative Social Science Research', *Human Organization* 73(3): 224–34.

MacPherson, C.B. (1978) *Property: Mainstream and Critical Positions*. Oxford: Basil Blackwell.

McTurnan Kahin, G. (1953/2003) *Nationalism and Revolution in Indonesia*. Ithaca, NY: Cornell Southeast Asia Program.

Onghokham (2003) *The Thugs, the Curtain Thief, and the Sugar Lord. Power, Politics and Culture in Colonial Java*. Jakarta: Metaphor Publishing.

Peluso, N.L. (1992) *Rich Forests, Poor People. Resource Control and Resistance in Java*. Berkeley, CA: University of California Press.

Peluso, N.L., S. Afiff and N.F. Rachman (2008) 'Claiming the Grounds for Reform. Agrarian and Environmental Movements in Indonesia', *Journal of Agrarian Change* 8(2–3): 377–407.

Rachman, N.F. (2011) 'The Resurgence of Land Reform Policy and Agrarian Movements in Indonesia'. PhD Thesis, University of California, Berkeley.

Rachman, N.F. (2016) *Land Reform dan Gerakan Agraria Indonesia* [*The Resurgence of Land Reform Policy and Agrarian Movements in Indonesia*]. Yogyakarta: Insist Press.

Ricklefs, M.C. (1993) *A History of Modern Indonesia since c. 1300*. Stanford, CA: Stanford University Press.

Rose, C. (1994) *Property and Persuasion. Essays on the History, Theory and Rhetoric of Ownership*. Boulder, CO: Westview Press.

Ryter, L. (1998) 'Pemuda Pancasila: The Last Loyalist Free Men of Suharto's Order', *Indonesia* 66: 43–73.

Sato, S. (1994) *War, Nationalism and Peasants: Java under the Japanese Occupation 1942–1945*. Sydney: Allen and Unwin.

Sikor, T. and C. Lund (2009) 'Access and Property: A Question of Power and Authority', *Development and Change* 40(1): 1–22.

Silean, P. and C.J. Smark (2006) 'The "Culture System" in Dutch Indonesia 1830–1870: How Rawls's Original Position Ethics Were Violated', *The Business Review, Cambridge* 6(1): 1–8.

Slaats, H., E. Rajagukguk, N. Elmiyah and A. Safik (2009) 'Land Law in Indonesia', in J. Ubink, A. Hoekema and W. Assies (eds) *Legalising Land Rights. Local Practices, State Responses and Tenure Security in Africa, Asia and Latin America*, pp. 493–526. Leiden: Leiden University Press.

Slater, D. (2010) 'Altering Authoritarianism. Institutional Complexity and Autocratic Agency in Indonesia', in J. Mahoney and K. Thelen (eds) *Explaining Institutional Change. Ambiguity, Agency and Power*, pp. 132–67. Cambridge: Cambridge University Press.

Somers, M. (2008) *Genealogies of Citizenship. Markets, Statelessness, and the Right to Have Rights*. Cambridge: Cambridge University Press.

Svensson, T. (1991) *State Bureaucracy and Capitalism in Rural West Java. Local Gentry versus Peasant Entrepreneurs in Priangan in the 19th and 20th Century*. NIAS Report no. 1. Copenhagen: Nordic Institute of Asian Studies.

Swart, A.G.N. (1911) 'Rubber Companies in the Netherland East Indies'. Compiled for the Netherlands Commission for the International Rubber Exhibition in London. Amsterdam: J.H. De Bussy.

Vickers, A. (2005) *A History of Modern Indonesia*. Cambridge: Cambridge University Press.

White, B. (2016) 'Remembering the Indonesian Peasants' Front and Plantation Workers' Union (1945–66)', *Journal of Peasant Studies* 43(1): 1–16.

7

A State of Fragmentation: Enacting Sovereignty and Citizenship at the Edge of the Indonesian State

Michael Eilenberg

INTRODUCTION

The Indonesian decentralization reforms have been portrayed as among the most radical worldwide and have reshuffled political authority and resource access throughout the archipelago. After the fall of the authoritarian regime of President Suharto in 1998, regional autonomy became the prime focus of the subsequent 'reform' governments and new legislation resulted in a series of so-called democratization reforms that provided district governments with increased autonomy over local political and economic matters. The rapid decentralization process and the promotion of increased district autonomy was, among other things, an attempt by the new post-Suharto governments to prevent large-scale secessionist movements by reallocating resources and political authority to the nation's neglected and dissatisfied outer regions. Those regions had, during the Suharto era, experienced large-scale, state-controlled resource extraction regimes without the benefits of economic development and political representation (Duncan, 2007; Fox et al., 2005; Resosudarmo, 2004). The founders of the decentralization process thus hoped that increased regional autonomy would forestall acts of separatism that might culminate in the territorial collapse of Indonesia (Aspinall and Fealy, 2003). The reshuffling of authority has driven previously marginalized groups in underdeveloped districts to stake formal claims to political representation and valuable natural resources — a process most pronounced in Indonesia's resource-rich outer regions like the borderlands of West Kalimantan (Eilenberg, 2012a; McCarthy, 2004; Moeliono et al., 2009; Wadley and Eilenberg, 2005; Wollenberg et al., 2006).

For centuries, the West Kalimantan border communities have been seen as a national security threat because of their strong cross-border ties and economic transactions with the neighbouring Malaysian state of Sarawak. It is not uncommon, for example, for border residents to hold dual-citizen

I thank Christian Lund and Heri Valentinus and two anonymous reviewers for comments. Tanjungpura University, Pontianak, provided academic sponsorship for field research, with permission from the Indonesian Institute of Sciences (LIPI) and the Indonesian Ministry of Research and Technology (RISTEK), Jakarta. The conclusions drawn here are not necessarily those of the above agencies, but the responsibility of the author alone.

documents, both Indonesian and Malaysian, although this violates both Indonesian law and the country's sovereignty. Such documents are used to engage in transnational labour migration and to maintain connections with kin across the border in Malaysia (Eilenberg and Wadley, 2009).

Along the border the main currency is the Malaysian ringgit, and the majority of school children attend schools across the border in Malaysia, where curricula offer them little knowledge of Indonesian national history or politics (*Harian Berkat*, 2009).

However, since the onset of decentralization, the successive reform governments have increased their focus on the nation's lawless borderlands as regions in dire need of development and a strong state presence (Bappenas, 2004, 2006, 2010; BNPP, 2011). As the head of the provincial border development agency put it: 'The border area has not yet been properly socialized into the nation. The dominant merchant trading is carried in foreign currency and moreover, our citizens at the border are more familiar with the leaders of our neighbours compared to those of their own country' (*Equator News*, 2005).

Post-Suharto, numerous news reports touching upon the issue of national loyalty among the West Kalimantan borderland population appeared in the national press, expressed in headlines such as 'Communities Living along the Kalimantan-Sarawak Border Are Still Isolated within their Own Country' (*Kompas*, 2000). Such a depiction highlights isolation, underdevelopment and cross-border ethnicity as the main reasons for cross-border solidarity and subsequent lack of national consciousness. Another headline in the main provincial newspaper claimed that, 'The Border Citizens Still Rely on Malaysia' (*Pontianak Post*, 2005). Numerous news headlines depicting the nation's borderlands as lawless and beyond the state's control triggered a national debate on the inability of the central government to uphold the territorial sovereignty of the nation. The resource-rich Indonesian borderlands provide an exceptionally important site for investigating these paradoxes of sovereignty and citizenship, the changing dynamics of state–periphery relations, and the kind of governance that Indonesia has experienced since decentralization. For decades, the ethnic border population has been viewed with suspicion by the central government in Jakarta because of its close historical relationship and cross-border networks. People have often been labelled as unruly citizens, if citizens at all, and thus largely excluded from the right to development.

This chapter explores how the creative practices of the border population in the district of Kapuas Hulu simultaneously transform, challenge and accommodate the notion of the 'sovereign state' and the idea of citizenship by juggling the power relations between the centre and periphery. States are often unable to make their claims stick or to assert a sense of collective identity in remote borderlands that lack infrastructure and have sparse populations, which tend to have flexible loyalties towards the two bordering nation states (Donnan and Wilson, 2010; Horstmann and Wadley, 2006; van

Schendel and de Maaker, 2014). In these locations, the issue of sovereignty is a vexed question at best. Defined territorially, sovereignty is the principle of recognition of what is both internal and external to states: domestic authority and international recognition (Bartelson, 1995). Yet while the bounded sovereign state remains the foundation of the modern political system, its analytical relevance in a world in which political authority over economy and society transcends the territorial boundaries of states has been called into question (Agnew, 2005; Dunn and Cons, 2014; Ong, 2006; Wissenburg, 2008). The classical definition of sovereignty, which presupposes a strong 'unitary' state imposing unlimited control on a clearly defined territory, is widely questioned by scholars who have taken up the challenge of conceptualizing the state as fragmented and constituted by a disparate series of effects. As Jones argues, sovereign power 'is better conceptualized as multifaceted, partial, and conflicted' (Jones, 2012: 687). Here, *de facto* state sovereignty is far messier than its classical definitions suggest, and the existence of nested, overlapping and competing sovereignties within and across borders is increasingly recognized (Hansen and Stepputat, 2006; Lund, 2011; Peluso and Lund, 2011).

In the Indonesian case, the fragmented character of the archipelago state became especially obvious in the reform period after the collapse of the patrimonial regime of President Suharto. The reform period and the power vacuum in the years after Suharto instigated a fierce scramble for resources (property) and authority between government institutions, regional administrative divisions and political elites. The new political openings that emerged out of the massive decentralization process suddenly created new possibilities for the enactment of sovereignty locally, regionally and within national politics, according active citizens the ability to define rights and privileges in the Indonesian state project — something severely restricted under the previous authoritarian regime.[1]

In what follows, I shall introduce the case of Kapuas Hulu and discuss the local impact of national decentralization reforms. This is followed by an analysis of a local autonomy movement and its attempt to carve out a new administrative district from the mother district of Kapuas Hulu. The chapter highlights the intricate process of claim making and identity politics involved in the process of district splitting on the border. It analyses how property and political representation are negotiated by appropriating government rhetoric of national sovereignty, good citizenship and development. It concludes by considering how large political ruptures — Indonesian regime change,

---

1. This chapter is based on 30 months of field research conducted in the Kapuas Hulu district, West Kalimantan in the period 2002–16. For a fuller account, see Eilenberg (2012a). Interviews were carried out with a wide array of local and national actors ranging from state officials, politicians, NGOs, entrepreneurs and local elites (village heads and tribal heads) to local community members. Interviews and observations were triangulated with data from government and NGO reports and newspaper clippings.

decentralization reforms and subsequent increased regional autonomy — have created new opportunities to claim property and citizenship on the border.

THE CASE OF KAPUAS HULU

We do not want the central government to think 'danger'; and 'what are the politics of the border people in creating a district?'. We are Indonesian. We continue to love Indonesia. However, what we want is change and advancement in the border area. That is our argument and motivation behind a new Border District.[2]

Since the onset of decentralization reforms in 1999, ethnic elites have struggled to create small zones of autonomy along the Indonesian territorial border in remote upland districts of the West Kalimantan Province, bordering the Malaysian state of Sarawak (see map of Borneo, Figure 1). The case of the Kapuas Hulu district epitomizes how political rupture — from highly centralized authoritarian rule to increased regional autonomy — has enabled elite members of local society to make new claims to citizenship and control over local natural resources and territory. However, while administrative decentralization reforms provided new opportunities for political aspiration among elite sections of local society, most inhabitants of rural communities became increasingly excluded from access to land and the benefits of the new political arrangements. As Nordholt and van Klinken (2007: 1) remind us, 'a shift from centralized to a decentralized government is not synonymous with a shift from authoritarian to democratic rule'. By analysing an ongoing claim for regional autonomy in the district of Kapuas Hulu, this contribution illustrates how local elites within the legal (but fuzzy) framework of administrative decentralization reforms attempt to create their own administrative district. The 'state' is understood creatively and national loyalties are claimed at the state edges by appropriating the state rhetoric of development and good citizenship.

The district of Kapuas Hulu encompasses 29,842 km^2 (20 per cent of West Kalimantan) and is divided into no fewer than 23 sub-districts, with a total population of only 236,136. It is situated in the northernmost corner of the province, more than 700 km from the provincial capital, the coastal city of Pontianak (BPS-KB, 2011; BPS-KH, 2014). To the north, the district shares an international border with Sarawak, Malaysia; to the east, it borders the Indonesian provinces of Central Kalimantan and East Kalimantan. This chapter focuses specifically on the border autonomy movement headed by an organization known as the Committee for the Establishment of the North Border District (Panitia Pembentukan Kabupaten Perbatasan Utara, PPKPU), that

---

2. Interview, member of autonomy movement, Putussibau, 13 March 2007.

Figure 1. Map of Borneo

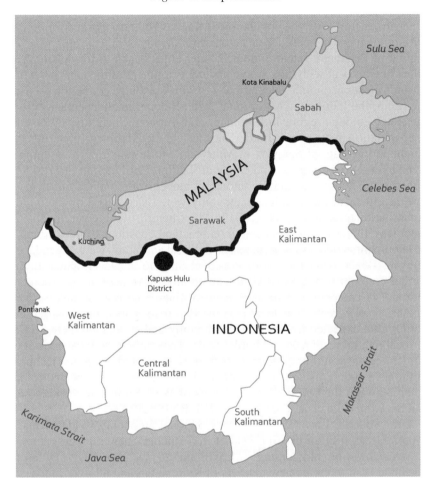

grew out of the five sub-districts of Batang Lupar, Embaloh Hulu, Badau, Empanang and Puring Kencana in 2000. The five sub-districts (covering approximately 6,296 km² or 22 per cent of the Kapuas Hulu district) make up the largest stretch of territory along the international border with Malaysia within the 'mother' district. According to district government statistics, the population of the five border districts reached 20,500 in 2013 (BPS-KH, 2014).³

---

3. According to the PPKPU, however, the population in the five sub-districts was estimated to have reached approximately 37,000 back in 2007 (PPKPU, 2007).

Administrative Fragmentation

Since the early 1990s, the population of Kapuas Hulu has pushed for border development and increased local autonomy. Already during the authoritarian regime of President Suharto, ethnic border elites began to formulate ideas about how to deal with the chronic underdevelopment of the area and work towards closer economic integration — besides resource extraction — with the rest of the Indonesian nation state. After Indonesian independence from the Dutch colonial regime in 1949, the socio-economic activities of the ethnic population in the remote borderlands were directed primarily towards the neighbouring state of Sarawak in Malaysia, whose proximity was emphasized by a shared language and ethnic affiliation. Until the fall of President Suharto, this loosely organized autonomy movement remained rather inactive, as efforts to increase local autonomy were discouraged by the highly authoritarian regime (Eilenberg, 2012a). The rhetoric of this emerging movement was, therefore, mostly centred on practical questions of infrastructure development, while issues of increased political autonomy were downplayed (Kuyah, 1992). After the fall of President Suharto, however, and with the formal creation of the PPKPU, the autonomy movement gained momentum and re-emerged as a local response to increased outside involvement in what were perceived as local matters. By creating their own district, the border elite expected to boost local autonomy and strengthen their control of local natural resources and border trade. They anticipated that control of border access would become an important political and economic resource in the near future, as enhanced commercial exchange was expected to develop between the two bordering regions of West Kalimantan (Indonesia) and Sarawak (Malaysia) (Bappenas, 2010; BNPP, 2011).

After Suharto, Law No. 22/1999 on regional autonomy suddenly made it possible to split an existing district into smaller ones, a process known as *pemekaran*, or 'blossoming' (McWilliam, 2011).[4] The 1999 law led to a general rush to create new districts in Kalimantan and all over Indonesia (Booth, 2011; Firman, 2009; Fitrani et al., 2005; Kimura, 2007; Vel, 2007). For example, in West Kalimantan in 1999 the large border district of Sambas was split into the Sambas and Bengkayang districts and, in East Kalimantan, the resource-rich border district of Bulungan was split into Bulungan, Malinau and Nunukan districts (Tanasaldy, 2007; Wollenberg et al., 2006). Later, in 2012, that district, together with the Tana Tidunk and Tarakan districts, was transformed into the new province of North Kalimantan (*Jakarta Globe*, 2012).

---

4. *Pemekaran* refers not only to the splitting of districts but also to other levels of administrative fragmentation like the creation of new provinces, sub-districts, villages and hamlets (Kimura, 2013).

Popularly portrayed as a bottom-up process in which citizens could gain a larger degree of empowerment and transparency in local government matters, regional proliferation became immensely popular in Indonesia. The number of districts rose dramatically from 298 in 1999 (Firman, 2013) to 415 in 2014 (KDNRI, 2014). However, Law No. 22/1999, which was drawn up hastily in the early days of decentralization, has since been revised and superseded by more restrictive laws (No. 32/2004 and No. 78/2007). Among other things, these raised the minimum number of sub-districts to be included in a new district from three to five. Tighter structural regulation was an attempt to slow down the process of district blossoming. Undoubtedly, the economic incentive of large financial transfers from central government to support new districts — and lucrative positions in the new administrations — has been an important motive for local elites who promote *pemekaran*. The decentralization laws stipulate that new districts will receive subsidies in the form of both general allocation funds and special allocation funds from the central government. In many cases, the driving force behind *pemekaran* was the urge to gain authority over various valuable resources rather than the establishment of more accountable local governments (McWilliam, 2011; Pisani, 2014; Roth, 2007).

Identity Politics and Ethnicity (Mobilizing Ethnic Sentiments)

The members of the PPKPU movement discussed in this chapter were primarily ethnic Iban, who are all part of a small but prominent ethnic elite group of customary leaders, village headmen, members of the district assembly and district government officials. The Iban make up the largest section of the population in the five sub-districts discussed, while the two other ethnic groups, the Maloh and Malay, make up a small minority.[5] The Maloh and Malay support the movement, but because of their minority status, they are less influential, which creates a certain amount of inter-ethnic distrust. Sections of the Maloh and Malay communities see the PPKPU movement as primarily an Iban project with the purpose of capturing political power and natural resources in the proposed new district.[6] However, such ethnic distrust is partly unspoken in order for the movement to appear strong and united. PPKPU members on both sides of the divide constantly promote ethnic unity and downplay ethnicity as less relevant by focusing on the chronic underdevelopment of the region and their shared 'borderland identity' (Eilenberg

5. Compared to the Maloh and Malay, the Iban have strong cross-border ethnic ties with the Iban in Sarawak, where they make up the largest single ethnic group.
6. There has been a long history of inter-ethnic confrontation and conflict over access to land and resources dating back to the colonial period, involving the Iban and, especially, the Maloh (King, 1976).

and Wadley, 2009). Despite this inter-ethnic rivalry, the various groups re-
alize that, for the PPKPU to succeed with the *pemekaran* process, the five
sub-districts must at least officially appear as one 'border community'. Such
concerns, therefore, remain veiled, even as tension continues to build along
accentuated ethnic lines.

Nevertheless, despite attempts by the PPKPU to ignore ethnicity, the issue
is an important one. For example, during local meetings, some younger
Iban participants made jokes about the movement being the 'Free Iban
Movement', or GIM (Gerakan Iban Merdeka), seeing it primarily as a
movement for Iban revitalization and sovereignty. The reference here is to
the armed guerrilla movements in Sumatra and Papua — the 'Free Aceh
Movement' or GAM (Gerakan Aceh Merdeka) in North Sumatra and the
'Free Papua Movement' (Gerakan Papua Merdeka) in West Papua. Among
some members, such jokes express the dream of promoting Iban Adat
(traditional) authority and reclaiming sovereignty over what they perceive
as their traditional territory, which is now claimed by other ethnic groups.
Later in the same meetings, Iban members changed the acronym GIM to
GBM (Gerakan Bersama Maju) or 'Jointly We Prosper Movement', and
thus downplayed the issue of ethnicity (Eilenberg, 2012a). In other parts of
Indonesia, *pemekaran* is often carried out along ethnic lines, which has, in
many cases, resulted in violent conflicts (Aspinall, 2011; Duncan, 2007; Vel,
2007).

The PPKPU movement is using the experience of the split of other border
districts in the province, especially the subdivision of the Sambas district
into the Bengkayang and Sambas districts in 1999.[7] The head of the PPKPU
movement is a highly educated Iban (originally from the Kapaus Hulu
district) who holds an influential government position as head of a district-
level office in the Bengkayang district. Having a front row seat from which
to observe the success of these new districts and the complicated political
processes that *pemekaran* demands, he, together with a small group of other
well-off men, initiated the PPKPU movement. The PPKPU further fed into
a larger alliance of border communities known as the Forum for Border
Community Care,[8] positioned in the provincial capital, Pontianak. This forum was created in 2004 with the purpose of lobbying for and promoting the
overall development of the border regions of West Kalimantan; its members
are from all the ethnic groups living along the entire length of the border.
Until 2013 the head of FPMP was a prominent Iban from the district of
Kapuas Hulu. The PPKPU has used the forum mainly as a meeting place for
consolidating new alliances, especially with provincial government officials
and politicians.

---

7. Law No. 10/1999.
8. Forum Peduli Masyarakat Perbatasan Kalimantan Barat (FPMP).

District Blossoming on the Border

In April 2006, approximately 100 people representing the five districts met with members of the district assembly in the district capital, Putussibau. The representatives were greeted positively, and the assembly subsequently issued a letter of decree supporting the formation of a new district in the border area (KepDPRD, 2006). In addition, after numerous meetings and discussions, in early March 2007 representatives and supporters from the five districts (approximately 400 people) met with the Kapuas Hulu district head at an official gathering in the district office in Putussibau.The PPKPU boldly proclaimed their proposed new district as the North Border District (Kabupaten Perbatasan Utara). At the same time, they presented a final report of several hundred pages containing the legally stipulated requirements for a new district and the signatures of all of the local (elite) supporters (*Equator News*, 2007a). This report, which emphasized the considerable potential of the border area and its current underdevelopment, was the outcome of an unofficial feasibility study carried out by the PPKPU in cooperation with a Jakarta-based NGO (PPKPU, 2007).

In the period between 2004 and 2007, the PPKPU had carried out an extensive lobbying campaign. In February 2006, it sent out its first formal letter of aspiration to the district head, presenting the plan for a new district. Then, in 2007, the PPKPU attempted to precipitate the *pemekaran* process (*Equator News*, 2007b). Mindful of failed efforts and bitter disappointment in the past, the PPKPU was eager to push this initiative through. Early in the presidency of Megawati (2001–4), the same border elite had applied to the central government to be recognized as a Special Authority Region (Otorita Daerah Khusus) and, thereby, receive favourable conditions such as free border trade and a higher degree of political autonomy. According to the PPKPU, a letter of decree that would have granted special authority to the border area was being prepared. Then, in 2004, a new president was elected, and the decree was postponed. During the Megawati presidency, the government had prepared a development strategy for the Kalimantan border region, and, according to the PPKPU, the change in central administration turned out to be a significant setback for the lobbying efforts of the border movement at the time, as old allies in the administration were replaced (Bappenas, 2003). Now, in a 2007 statement outlining the urgency of the current campaign, a PPKPU member said: 'We need to push forward now and keep going. We cannot wait for official approval from the district office. Government regulations, as they look today, may be different tomorrow so we need to act while there is still an opportunity'.[9]

The huge popularity of *pemekaran* throughout Indonesia has put an immense strain on the central government's resources and budget, while

9. Interview, Badau, 20 March 2007.

outcomes in the form of improved services for the majority of people have, so far, been meagre. Meanwhile, corruption and nepotism have reportedly increased, a development that the central government largely blames on self-interested regional elites (Bappenas and UNDP, 2008). Such accusations have fostered widespread protest from provincial and district assembly members, who accuse the central government of being arrogant and lacking commitment to the development of the outer regions and the reallocation of promised economic benefits from the centre to its margins.

Mimicking State Rhetoric of Citizenship and Sovereignty

The first step in the *pemekaran* process, as stipulated in the government laws and regulations, is a demonstration of the viability of a proposed new district and a justification of the need for its creation. As indicated by the name, the North Border District, the PPKPU clearly specified the common ground and key resources of the five districts involved. Despite its vast natural resources, the border area, after more than 60 years of Indonesian independence, is still categorized as a region of extreme poverty and isolation (*daerah terting-gal*) with insufficient infrastructure, health services and education facilities (Agustiar, 2008; BNPP, 2011; KNPDT, 2007). As proclaimed by PPKPU participants during an August 2006 borderland 'awareness-raising' meeting held to discuss the local advantages of splitting the district: 'It has now been 63 years since we became an independent nation, but our roads are still yellow [dirt] and at night, our lamps are still dark. Is this the result of independence?'. A chorus of voices from the crowd replied, 'We still live in misery and poverty. Development has left us behind' (PPKPU, 2007: 206).

The main argument put forward for splitting the Kapuas Hulu district was its sheer size and lack of capacity to develop its outer districts. The PPKPU stressed that the 'mother' district of Kapuas Hulu was too large, and past and current district administrations had not succeeded in developing the border area compared to other areas in the district and thus providing the rewards of citizenship to the local population. As a result, they said, the border people were forced to act by themselves if any changes were to take place: 'Until now the border communities have just been a tool of central government in extracting natural resources, that is why the community wants their own autonomy, to take control by themselves, and at least have their own district'.[10]

Other strategies adopted by the PPKPU for cultivating central government goodwill and support for their cause included applying the central government rhetoric of sovereignty and development, and emphasizing the role of border inhabitants as loyal citizens. The members constantly presented the

---

10. Interview, Lanjak, 1 March 2007.

creation of a new border district as a local effort to preserve the unitary state of the Republic of Indonesia (Negara Kesatuan Republik Indonesia). They announced that enhanced political and economic autonomy would prevent acts of separatism among the border communities and nurture good citizens. Furthermore, the border district would become the new, bright, outward face of Indonesia towards Malaysia and, most importantly, would improve national defence, guarantee security and prevent illegal activities (*Equator News*, 2006).

Throughout the *pemekaran* process, the PPKPU were quick to disavow past public so-called 'illegal' activities in the border area and to depict such activities as the last resort of desperate people, solely in response to a long-standing economic disparity along the border (*Equator News*, 2011). For example, in the period 2000–05, the five districts were the scene of large-scale timber smuggling across the border to Malaysia, drawing immense national and international attention (Wadley and Eilenberg, 2005). Local press estimated that every month timber worth US$ 1 million was smuggled across the border to Malaysia by timber barons in cooperation with border communities (*Media Indonesia*, 2004; *Sinar Harapan*, 2004; *Suara Pembaruan*, 2004). During that time, state presence in the borderland was largely neutralized by large-scale political instability and administrative rupture within central government. Local border elites were quick to take advantage of this political vacuum and began extracting local forest resources with assistance from their Malaysian cross-border connections, circumventing central government institutions. This short period of semi-autonomy sustained by cross-border timber smuggling allowed the local economy to flourish and reinforced the local dictum that the border communities were better off taking matters into their own hands. However, the timber boom ended abruptly in 2005 when a strengthened central government reasserted its authority through military force in the border region (Eilenberg, 2012b). According to the PPKPU, the only way to prevent further illegal activities and enhance national loyalty was to involve border communities in developing the area through engagement in local-level politics and economic affairs.

Autonomy and Secessionist Aspirations

Officially, the PPKPU may have proclaimed their strong national loyalty in local news media, but during the heated debates in closed local meetings, becoming part of Malaysia was often mentioned as a final option. The Iban border population generally accepted their status as Indonesian citizens, and everybody knew that secession was impossible. However, the threat clearly indicated the preparedness of the PPKPU to play the 'border card' in political negotiations with the district and central governments. Fear of local separatism has often been expressed by central government as a possible future outcome of the special borderland circumstances of underdevelopment and cross-border connections (*Harian Berkat*, 2009; *Kompas*, 2001; *Kompas*, 2003). As an excited Iban supporter of district splitting announced: 'We will just join Malaysia. We will organize training over there and rebel. We will still try the nice way first but if official procedures turn out to be unworkable, well, what can we do?'.[11]

During the Dutch colonial period in what is known today as Indonesian West Kalimantan, the ruler of Sarawak (Malaysia) at the time — the British Raja Brooke offered the Iban border population the opportunity to secede to Sarawak, although such offers never resulted in concrete action. Throughout the Dutch colonial presence in the border area, the border communities were seen as unreliable and rebellious citizens. One major contributing factor was a long history of movement, applicable particularly to trade and warfare, that did not recognize arbitrary state borders. The border population strategically took advantage of the artificial line dividing the Dutch and British territories. One legacy of Dutch attempts to subdue these recalcitrant subjects and extend colonial administrative discipline to the unruly border areas is a pronounced local suspicion towards state authority among the majority of the border population (Wadley, 2004). A British colonial administrator, referring to the border-dwelling Iban, was of the view that 'Persons who find it politic to hurriedly shift from one side of the border to the other can hardly be considered as valuable citizens of either State'.[12] Furthermore, in the last days of Dutch colonialism and just after Indonesian independence, ideas of a Pan-Dayak identity were emerging in Kalimantan (Dayak is an umbrella term for all the indigenous populations on the island of Borneo). For example, in 1945 leaders from both sides of the border met to discuss ideas of separatism and the possible role the Iban might play in an independent Pan-Dayak state (Wadley, 1998). The Iban, like many border people, have long considered themselves as extrinsic to any large national entity; for them, central government often materializes as a confining authority that restricts their everyday practices and spatial mobility. They often reason that the distant provincial and national centres do not comprehend the special and shifting circumstances of life in the borderland that are expressed in a high degree of spatial flexibility.

The historic cross-border relations and ongoing, mostly rhetorical support from small segments of the Iban population in Sarawak, Malaysia, boosted local confidence. As one PPKPU member commented during a local meeting, 'We can make things very difficult for them [district and provincial officials]' — referring to former acts of vigilantism and to the existence of close ties to similar ethnic groups in Sarawak. The border populations are notorious for acting on their own when they feel that the government system

11. Interview, Lanjak, 21 March 2007.
12. British colonial administrator quoted in 'Report from Assistant Resident A.A. Burgdorffer, 2 December 1914, Verbaal 20 Augustus 1915 No. 41, Ministerie van Koloniën'.

is unjust and not operating in accordance with the special circumstances of life along the border (Eilenberg, 2011). Despite such statements, the PPKPU always stressed that everything they did would have to conform to the law, and that they should not attempt to win independence through armed struggle like Aceh in North Sumatra or the independence movement in West Papua. No attempt should be made to disturb the stability of the border. However, on the question of what might happen if the border communities were not given increased autonomy and their own district, a customary leader answered:

> If the border area is not allowed to emerge as a new district by the central or local government, I am afraid that many of the communities would lose their faith in the unity of the nation and want to separate themselves or break away to Malaysia. If you ask the community, 99 per cent would prefer to be under the political control of Malaysia, and that would put the unity of the nation in danger. Well, older people like us try to protect the unity of the Indonesian nation by suggesting the creation of a new district instead of separatism.[13]

As Kimura argues, regional proliferation in Indonesia is often 'less about a region seeking to isolate itself from the state and more about new and different kinds of access and relationships between center and region' (Kimura, 2013: 86). The PPKPU was constantly walking a fine line in seeking to enhance the region's autonomy without detaching it from national membership. In 2012, the PPKPU decided to change the name of the proposed new district from the more contested and politicized North Border District to Banua Landjak District (*Tribun Pontianak*, 2013a, 2013b). This was done in order to send a message of national loyalty to the central government and indicate their deep territorial and emotional attachment to the region. 'Banua' could be translated as 'My homeland/fatherland' and 'Landjak' is the name of the major trading town in the five sub-districts (*Sinar Harapan*, 2013). The PPKPU were acutely aware of central government plans to increase its authority in the unruly borderlands through a military build-up, and did not want the proposed district to appear recalcitrant by overplaying the separatist card. However, the issue of separatism, with its orientation towards Malaysia, is frequently flagged by communities along the Kalimantan–Malaysia border (approximately 2,000 km long) in order to attract central government and public attention to chronic underdevelopment (*Berita Satu*, 2014; *Harian Berkat*, 2009). The name change to Banua Landjak was thus a complex attempt to emphasize their historical claims to customary lands and simultaneously their loyalty to the nation.[14] History plays an important role in ethnic consolidation in the border area and Iban committee members constantly highlighted the importance of origin and ancestry in authorizing claims to land and territory.

13. Interview, Embaloh Hulu, 13 June 2007.
14. Interviews, Lanjak, Badau, and Pontianak, December 2013.

Claiming Territory and Natural Resources

The district head of Kapuas Hulu initially appeared to be supportive of the idea of a new district, attending meetings and personally donating funds to the PPKPU (*Akcaya*, 2007). Nevertheless, he also seemed to be deliberately stalling the process. Like the district heads of other resource-rich districts, he has, since the onset of decentralization, consolidated his power and support through income from natural resources. Informal interviews with district government officials in Putussibau produce a picture of a general, although not publicly expressed, worry within the district office that the mother district risks losing major income from strategic resources, such as timber, minerals, plantation development, and the future lucrative border trade, if it is split. The decentralization laws further require the mother district to support the new district economically for the first few years before the new district receives its own fiscal transfers from the central government. The creation of the new border district could further isolate the mother district, which is already the most remote district in the province. If the new district is created, the mother district will be geographically (and possibly economically) isolated in the northernmost corner of the province. The sheer distance to the provincial capital, more than 700 km, makes border access highly important for the local economy; Sarawak economic centres across the border are much closer than the provincial capital and road access is easy (Wadley, 2000). According to a PPKPU member, the main reason for the district head to stall the district-splitting process was to maintain and consolidate his control of the resource-rich border region:

> Now we are actually able to fulfil the requirements for creating a new district put forward by central government, but the mother district seems to be hesitant about letting us go. It keeps holding on to our tail. There is too much potential so they cannot let go and let the new district emerge. I think if Putussibau lets the border area become a district, Putussibau will die.[15]

During the campaign for the 2005 district election (*Pilkada*), the district head was re-elected by promising the five border sub-districts greater autonomy on local economic issues and general infrastructure development.[16] Since the revision of the law on regional autonomy in 2004, district heads have been voted into office by direct popular elections and not, as before, by the district legislative assembly. District heads are therefore more dependent on popular support than before when it comes to re-election (Buehler, 2007). Outright rejection of a new border district could make dealings along the border more difficult and possibly mean loss of support from the border

---

15. Interview, Badau, 19 March 2007.
16. Several Iban and Maloh inhabitants interviewed in the border sub-districts expressed their lack of confidence in the district head; being a Malayu, they believed he was more accommodating towards the needs of the Malayu than those of the Iban and Maloh border population in the district.

population on whom the district head is partly dependent in upholding a minimal amount of authority in this remote part of Kapuas Hulu. During this period, the district office has managed to keep the most critical voices at bay by contributing minor funding for the border movement while at the same time prolonging the bureaucratic process involved in the split.

Transnational networks add to the complexity of this case. During the many local meetings about the new border district, the PPKPU invited several Malaysian 'investors' from across the border. It was envisaged that a possible new district should cooperate closely with private business partners within the oil palm and rubber industry across the border in Sarawak, and develop large plantations along the border under the control of local communities. Many of these 'investors' were closely connected with individual PPKPU members through kinship ties and were deeply involved in the logging boom that ended in 2005. Economic support from wealthy Malaysians could end up being a key factor in realizing the establishment of the new district. Even more importantly, cross-border resources make the new district more autonomous and, thus, less dependent on central government politics and financial support (Eilenberg, 2012a). As indicated by a local executive, 'If we already had a new district here, many smart people from Malaysia would come and invest their money in plantations and so on. There are plenty of them waiting across the border. But for now, they do not want to come, as they do not trust the government'.[17] Several members of the PPKPU announced that they would not allow any outside companies to enter local forestlands without prior agreements with local communities. As stipulated by a customary leader in a 2007 interview: 'Many companies want to enter the area and open oil palm plantations, but we have not yet given our consent. We will wait until we have gained official authority over the area'.[18]

These comments are symptomatic of the widespread mistrust of government authorities and of the conviction of the border communities that they would be better off handling things themselves. However, these local cross-border negotiations were placed under strain in 2007 when the district government (with support from central government and the military) allocated large tracts of land for plantation development within the five border sub-districts to the Sinar Mas Group, Indonesia's largest palm oil producer (Yuliani et al., 2010). Until that time the Kapuas Hulu district had not been directly affected by agrarian change taking place in the lower parts of the province. However, in 2005–6 the district government — encouraged by central government and with a view to providing an alternative to timber extraction — began negotiating with private palm oil companies to open up the district for large-scale plantation development. After the fall of Suharto the reform government loosened its grip on the plantation sector and introduced more market-oriented agribusiness arrangements, facilitating private

---

17. Interview, Lanjak, 1 August 2007.
18. Interview, Lanjak, 28 March 2007.

investment. This central state withdrawal of direct involvement, and the ces-
sion to local governments of greater authority to take control of the issuing
of plantation permits, has dramatically increased the expansion of oil palm
plantations in West Kalimantan (Potter, 2011).

Internally, within the PPKPU, this move by the district government to
develop the border region was seen as an attempt to strengthen district authority over the rebellious sub-districts by claiming authority over land and
resources.[19] Despite large-scale protests by the PPKPU and local customary leaders, Sinar Mas quickly began converting large tracts of land into
oil palm plantations maintained by imported migrant workers from outside
the province (*Kompas*, 2011). In 2007 alone, the district government issued
no fewer than 21 plantation licences for the conversion of approximately
360,000 hectares of land. However, because of poor spatial planning and a
lack of clear regulation, these plantation concessions often overlapped with
locally claimed customary forestlands, triggering company–community conflicts. Weak law enforcement led to communities pushing forward with complaints, encouraging acts of vigilantism against the oil palm companies. The
non-transparent and intricate process of gaining permits made it extremely
difficult for local communities with customary claims on forests to appraise
the legality of permits issued to companies. Among the border population,
very few have formal legal titles to their land and they are therefore vulnerable to encroachment from plantation companies (*Borneo Tribune*, 2008).[20]

DISCUSSION AND CONCLUSION

During a field visit in May to June 2016, the PPKPU was still awaiting a
formal response to their request for a new district. The outcome seemed
as uncertain as ever and was highly dependent on rapid political changes
taking place locally and nationally. The future of the *pemekaran* process
very much depended on the goodwill of key politicians in Jakarta and of
local government administrative heads, like the district head and governor,
who have their own, often divergent, political agendas for the border area.
As remarked by a customary leader in a 2016 interview: 'Before and during
elections they [the president, governor and district head] are enthusiastic
about supporting our movement for a new district, but when votes are cast
they lose interest and continue to prolong the process. It seems like the
political (national and local) elite are using our cause for vote fishing'.[21]

Since 2005, the district head of Kapuas Hulu, together with four other
district heads, has been involved in yet another *pemekaran* process. These

---

19. Interview, Pontianak, 3 March 2011.
20. Most local land falls under various forms of customary land ownership, and over centuries
    has been passed from generation to generation through intricate systems of rights (Wadley,
    1997).
21. Interview, Lanjak, 26 May 2016.

five district heads wish to split from the current province of West Kalimantan and create a new province, Kapuas Raya, and all available district resources seemed directed towards carrying out this grand plan for a new province (*Jakarta Post*, 2013; *Kalimantan Review*, 2008). Further, during an interview in late 2007, the head of the provincial legislative assembly in the provincial capital, Pontianak, expressed strong doubts as to whether a new border district would have any chance of being approved at the central level. According to him, one of the major hurdles was the low population density. With only about 20–30,000 inhabitants, the proposed border district would be too sparsely populated to survive on its own. He estimated that it might take another five to ten years before the border population could be ready to manage its own district. This observation was contested vigorously by PPKPU members and local academics, who argued that in the past the border population had shown their ability to manage local affairs and cross-border trade, and that taxes from the large palm oil companies and future mining operations (bauxite and coal) would provide plenty of income to support the proposed district. The argument of the PPKPU that a new district would be viable was later supported by an assessment study carried out by the Research Institute of the University of Tanjungpura in Pontianak (*Borneo Tribune*, 2012).

In the heated debate about the viability of the many new districts in Indonesia, national and regional commentators have suggested that the central government should prioritize the establishment of new districts and provinces in regions with special needs such as underdeveloped and sensitive state border areas (*Haluan Kepri*, 2013; *Media Indonesia*, 2014; *Tempo*, 2012). This, they argue, would be in line with one of the original ideas behind decentralization, namely that of facilitating and ensuring national unity and preventing separatism (*Kompas*, 2007). However, the central government has been hesitant and vague regarding the possibility for new districts in the border regions. Its plans for the borderlands will not necessarily involve an increase in local autonomy, but are more likely to foster the reclaiming of central authority over these resource-rich peripheral regions (Eilenberg, 2014). Between 2009 and 2012, a moratorium was imposed on regional expansion through *pemekaran*, although on several occasions the House of Representatives (DPR) has ceded to local pressure to open new administrative regions (Aspinall, 2013). For example, in October 2013 the Provincial Legislative Council (DPRD) in West Kalimantan approved the creation of the proposed border district of Banua Landjak (*Sinar Harapan*, 2013) and, in March 2014, the border district was endorsed by the Regional Representative Council (DPD-RI) in Jakarta (DPD-RI, 2014; *Sinar Harapan*, 2014b).

However, such approvals and endorsements do not necessarily reflect the views of the central government in Jakarta, which has not ceased to express reservations about the rapidity with which authority and funds are being transferred to the districts. The centre argues that the local results are mixed and often lead to communal conflict, while the benefits for ordinary citizens are less obvious. Critics claim that the uncontrolled formation of new districts creates jurisdictional fragmentation, encouraging rampant rent seeking among political elites (Bappenas and UNDP, 2008; *Jakarta Post*, 2012; *Tempo*, 2013). Since early 2014 the central government has agreed to engage in discussions with the House of Representatives concerning an overall draft proposal for the creation of 65 new autonomous regions (*Daerah Otonomi Baru* or DOB) — the border district discussed in this chapter is mentioned as one of two new proposed districts in West Kalimantan (*Sinar Harapan*, 2014a, 2014b).[22] However, at the same time as negotiations over possible new autonomous regions are taking place, central government is drafting a bill that will grant it the authority to take back power from corrupt regional leaders and closely regulate the process of establishing new autonomous regions (*Jakarta Post*, 2014).

Whatever the future success or failure of the PPKPU movement in creating a new district, the border communities will continue to exploit the openings presented by the decentralization reforms and the duality of life along the border in order to negotiate political authority, take control of local natural resources and claim the rights of national membership. As McWilliam (2011: 165) argues, 'For all its stumbling inefficiencies, administrative proliferation provides multiple new avenues for integrating and enclosing the scattered and still loosely-governed peripheries into the regulatory ambit of the unitary state'.

This chapter has set out to explain how border communities in Kapuas Hulu, like many other marginal populations in post-independence Indonesia, have struggled for recognition and membership (citizenship) in the Indonesian nation state. Such struggles have more often than not centred on claims to rights over natural resources (property) — a campaign by peripheral citizens who during the authoritarian regime of Suharto had been discouraged, restricted and subdued. Overall, the *pemekaran* case demonstrates how the immense political rupture and administrative fragmentation following the fall of Suharto created new opportunities for local claim making over matters of property and citizenship at the edge of the Indonesian state. It suggests a complex relationship between state authority and regional autonomy that helps shed light on the often ambivalent relationship between citizenship and state sovereignty. This chapter demonstrates the complexity of relations between local communities, local elites and the various levels of government in negotiating authority over natural resources and customary territory in a period of rupture and fragmentation. These observations help remind us of the fractured character of state sovereignty in these marginal regions comprising multiple and overlapping cores of autonomy, and of how competing loyalties and identities (ethnic, national, regional, cross-border) are negotiated on a daily basis.

---

22. The draft proposal or bill is referred to as the 65 RUU-DOB (65 Rancangan Undang-Undang Daerah Otonomi Baru).

REFERENCES

Agnew, J. (2005) 'Sovereignty Regimes: Territoriality and State Authority in Contemporary World Politics', *Annals of the Association of American Geographers* 95(2): 437–61.

Agustiar, D.R. (2008) 'Presiden anggap perbatasan beranda depan negara' ['The President Considers the Border as the Front Porch of the State'], *Tempo Interaktif* 15 August.

Akcaya (2007) 'Bupati dukung pemekaran Kabupaten Perbatasan Utara Kapuas Hulu' ['The District Head Supports the Proliferation of the North Border District in Kapuas Hulu'], *Akcaya* 9 March.

Aspinall, E. (2011) 'Democratization and Ethnic Politics in Indonesia: Nine Theses', *Journal of East Asian Studies* 11(2): 289–319.

Aspinall, E. (2013) 'A Nation in Fragments', *Critical Asian Studies* 45(1): 27–54.

Aspinall, E. and G. Fealy (2003) 'Introduction: Decentralisation, Democratisation and the Rise of the Local', in E. Aspinall and G. Fealy (eds) *Local Power and Politics in Indonesia: Decentralisation & Democratisation*, pp. 1–11. Singapore: Institute of Southeast Asian Studies.

Bappenas (2003) 'Strategi dan model pengembangan wilayah perbatasan Kalimantan' ['Strategy and Development Model for the Kalimantan Border Region']. Jakarta: Kementerian Perencanaan Pembangunan Nasional, Badan Perencanaan Pembangunan Nasional.

Bappenas (2004) 'Kawasan perbatasan: Kebijakan dan strategi nasional pengelolaan kawasan perbatasan antarnegara di Indonesia' ['Border Areas: Policy and National Strategy on the Management of Border Areas in Indonesia']. Jakarta: Kementerian Perencanaan Pembangunan Nasional, Badan Perencanaan Pembangunan Nasional.

Bappenas (2006) 'Laporan akir: Evaluasi kebijakan perencanaan program pengembangan wilayah perbatasan' ['Final Report: Evaluation of the Planning Policy Development Program in Border Regions']. Jakarta: Kementerian Perencanaan Pembangunan Nasional, Badan Perencanaan Pembangunan Nasional.

Bappenas (2010) 'Dinamika pembangunan kawasan perbatasan negara' ['The Dynamics of Development in Border Areas'], *Bulletin Kawasan, Bappenas* 24: 1–29.

Bappenas and UNDP (2008) 'Evaluation of the Proliferation of Administrative Regions in Indonesia, 2001–2007'. Jakarta: Bappenas.

Bartelson, J. (1995) *A Genealogy of Sovereignty*. Cambridge: Cambridge University Press.

Berita Satu (2014) 'Jokowi–JK berkomitmen bangun wilayah perbatasan' ['Jokowi-JK are Committed to Develop Border Regions'], *Berita Satu* 29 November.

BNPP (2011) 'Desain besar pengelolaan batas wilayah negara dan kawasan perbatasan tahun 2011–2025' ['The Great Design of the Management of State Borders and Border Regions from 2011–2025']. Jakarta: Kementerian Perencanaan Pembangunan Nasional, Badan Nasional Pengelola Perbatasan.

Booth, A. (2011) 'Splitting, Splitting and Splitting Again: A Brief History of the Development of Regional Government in Indonesia since Independence', *Bijdragen tot de Taal-, Land- en Volkenkunde* 167(1): 31–59.

Borneo Tribune (2008) 'Tanah di perbatasan belum bersertifikat' ['Land on the Border Has Not Been Certified'], *Borneo Tribune* 25 September.

Borneo Tribune (2012) 'Penelitian pemekaran Banua Landjak murni dana masyarakat' ['Research on the Proliferation of Banua Landjak is Purely Based on Public Funds'], *Borneo Tribune* 29 February.

BPS-KB (2011) 'Propinsi Kalimantan Barat dalam angka' ['The Province of West Kalimantan in Figures']. Pontianak: Badan Pusat Statistik, Propinsi Kalimantan Barat.

BPS-KH (2014) 'Kabupaten Kapuas Hulu dalam angka' ['The District of Kapuas Hulu in Figures']. Putussibau: Badan Pusat Statistik, Kabupaten Kapuas Hulu.

Buehler, M. (2007) 'Local Elite Reconfiguration in Post-New Order Indonesia: The 2005 Elections of District Government Heads in South Sulawesi', *Review of Indonesian and Malaysian Affairs* 41(1): 119–47.

Donnan, H. and T.M. Wilson (eds) (2010) *Borderlands: Ethnographic Approaches to Security, Power and Identity*. Lanham, MD: University Press of America.

DPD-RI (2014) 'Laporan perkembangan pelaksanaan tugas alat kelengkapan dan pengesahan Keputusan DPD RI' ['Progress Report on the Implementation of Fittings and Ratifications of the House of Regional Representatives RI Decision']. Dewan Perwakilan Daerah Republik Indonesia, 7 March.

Duncan, C.R. (2007) 'Mixed Outcomes: The Impact of Regional Autonomy and Decentralization on Indigenous Ethnic Minorities in Indonesia', *Development and Change* 38(4): 711–33.

Dunn, E.C. and J. Cons (2014) 'Aleatory Sovereignty and the Rule of Sensitive Spaces', *Antipode* 46(1): 92–109.

Eilenberg, M. (2011) 'Flouting the Law: Vigilante Justice and Regional Autonomy on the Indonesian Border', *Austrian Journal of South East Asian Studies* 4(2): 237–53.

Eilenberg, M. (2012a) *At the Edges of States: Dynamics of State Formation in the Indonesian Borderlands*. Leiden: KITLV Press.

Eilenberg, M. (2012b) 'The Confession of a Timber Baron: Patterns of Patronage on the Indonesian–Malaysian Border', *Identities: Global Studies in Culture and Power* 9(2): 149–67.

Eilenberg, M. (2014) 'Frontier Constellations: Agrarian Expansion and Sovereignty on the Indonesian–Malaysian Border', *The Journal of Peasant Studies* 41(2): 157–82.

Eilenberg, M. and R.L. Wadley (2009) 'Borderland Livelihood Strategies: The Socio-economic Significance of Ethnicity in Cross-border Labour Migration, West Kalimantan, Indonesia', *Asia Pacific Viewpoint* 50(1): 58–73.

Equator News (2005) 'Membangun perbatasan, mensejahterakan masyarakat lokal' ['Develop the Border, the Welfare of the Local Community'], *Equator News* 6 December.

Equator News (2006) 'Kabupaten perbatasan, upaya pertahankan NKRI' ['The Border District, Efforts to Defend the Homeland'], *Equator News* 28 July.

Equator News (2007a) 'Masyarakat sepakati nama Kabupaten Perbatasan Utara' ['The Community Agreed on the Name North Border District'], *Equator News* 10 March.

Equator News (2007b) 'Pemekaran kabupaten upaya menyerap aspirasi masyarakat' ['The Proliferation of the District is the Effort of Community Aspirations'], *Equator News* 13 November.

Equator News (2011) 'Kabupaten Kapuas Hulu layak dimekarkan' ['Subdividing the District of Kapuas Hulu is Feasible'], *Equator News* 4 August.

Firman, T. (2009) 'Decentralization Reform and Local-government Proliferation in Indonesia: Towards a Fragmentation of Regional Development', *Review of Urban & Regional Development Studies* 21(2–3): 143–57.

Firman, T. (2013) 'Territorial Splits (Pemekaran Daerah) in Decentralising Indonesia, 2000–2012: Local Development Drivers or Hindrance?', *Space and Polity* 17(2): 180–96.

Fitrani, F., B. Hofman and K. Kaiser (2005) 'Unity in Diversity? The Creation of New Local Governments in a Decentralising Indonesia', *Bulletin of Indonesian Economic Studies* 41(1): 57–79.

Fox, J.J., D.S. Adhuri and I.A. Pradnja (2005) 'Unfinished Edifice or Pandora's Box? Decentralisation and Resource Management in Indonesia', in B.P. Resosudarmo (ed.) *The Politics and Economics of Indonesia's Natural Resources*, pp. 92–108. Singapore: Institute of Southeast Asian Studies (ISEAS).

Haluan Kepri (2013) 'Pemekaran kabupaten di wilayah perbatasan jadi perioritas' ['The Proliferation of Districts in the Border Area is a Priority'], *Haluan Kepri* 20 April.

Hansen, T.B. and F. Stepputat (2006) 'Sovereignity Revisited', *Annual Review of Anthropology* 35(1): 295–315.

Harian Berkat (2009) 'Puring Kencana bergabung Malaysia?' ['Will Puring Kencana Join Malaysia?'], *Harian Berkat* 6 March.

Horstmann, A. and R.L. Wadley (2006) 'Centering the Margin in Southeast Asia', in A. Horstmann and R.L. Wadley (eds) *Centering the Margin: Agency and Narrative in Southeast Asian Borderlands*, pp. 1–24. New York: Berghahn Books.

Jakarta Globe (2012) 'House Agrees on Creation of Indonesia's 34th Province: "North Kalimantan"', *Jakarta Globe* 22 October.

Jakarta Post (2012) 'How Many Provinces Does Indonesia Need?', *Jakarta Post* 20 April.

Jakarta Post (2013) 'Plan to Establish Kapuas Raya Province Draws Mixed Reactions', *Jakarta Post* 14 November.

Jakarta Post (2014) 'Bill Gives Power Back to Jakarta', *Jakarta Post* 24 September.

Jones, R. (2012) 'Spaces of Refusal: Rethinking Sovereign Power and Resistance at the Border', *Annals of the Association of American Geographers* 102(3): 685–99.

Kalimantan Review (2008) 'Pembentukan Provinsi Kapuas Raya' ['The Establishment of the Kapuas Raya Province'], *Kalimantan Review* 7 March.

KDNRI (2014) 'Pembentukan Daerah-Daerah Otonom di Indonesia Sampai Dengan Tahun 2014' ['The Establishment of Autonomous Regions in Indonesia up until 2014']. Jakarta: Kementerian Dalam Negeri Republik Indonesia.

KepDPRD (2006) 'Persetujuan pembentukan Kabupaten Sentarum dan Kabupaten di Wilayah Perbatasan Kabupaten Kapuas Hulu ['Approval of the Formation of the Sentarum District and a District in the Border Region of Kapuas Hulu']. Keputusan Dewan Perwakilan Rakyat Daerah Kabupaten Kapuas Hulu, No. 8. Putussibau: Kabupaten Kapuas Hulu.

Kimura, E. (2007) 'Marginality and Opportunity in the Periphery: The Emergence of Gorontalo Province in North Sulawesi', *Indonesia* 84: 71–95.

Kimura, E. (2013) *Political Change and Territoriality in Indonesia: Provincial Proliferation.* New York: Routledge.

King, V.T. (1976) 'Some Aspects of Iban-Maloh contact in West Kalimantan', *Indonesia* 21: 85–114.

KNPDT (2007) 'Rencana aksi nasional pembangunan daerah tertinggal tahun 2007–2009' ['National Action Plan for the Development of Disadvantaged Areas, 2007–2009']. Jakarta: Kementerian Negara Pembangunan Daerah Tertinggal.

Kompas (2000) 'Masyarakat perbatasan Kalimantan-Sarawak terasing di negerinya sendiri' ['Communities Living along the Kalimantan-Sarawak Border Are Still Isolated within their Own Country'], *Kompas* 7 August.

Kompas (2001) 'Masyarakat perbatasan RI-Malaysia terasing di negeri sendiri' ['Communities Living along the Indonesian-Malaysian Border are still Isolated within their own Country'], *Kompas* 8 October.

Kompas (2003) 'Indonesia bangsaku, ringgit uangku' ['Indonesia Is My Nation, Ringgit Is My Money'], *Kompas* 21 March.

Kompas (2007) 'Pemekaran wilayah perbatasan jadi prioritas' ['Proliferation in the Border Region is a Priority'], *Kompas* 11 September.

Kompas (2011) '200.000 Ha Sawit Malaysia di Perbatasan Indonesia' ['200,000 Hectares of Malaysian Oil Palm Plantations in the Indonesian Border Area'], *Kompas* 19 October.

Kuyah, F. (1992) 'Pengaruh pembangunan terhadap peningkatan masyarakat perbatasan kabupaten Kapuas Hulu' ['The Impact of Development on the Improvement of the Kapuas Hulu District Communities']. Lokaraya Hukum dan Pembangunan Masyarakat Perbatasan Kabupaten Kapuas Hulu, Lanjak (5–7 December).

Lund, C. (2011) 'Fragmented Sovereignty: Land Reform and Dispossession in Laos', *Journal of Peasant Studies* 38(4): 885–905.

McCarthy, J.F. (2004) 'Changing to Gray: Decentralization and the Emergence of Volatile Socio-legal Configurations in Central Kalimantan, Indonesia', *World Development* 32(7): 1199–223.

McWilliam, A. (2011) 'Marginal Governance in the Time of Pemekaran: Case Studies from Sulawesi and West Papua', *Asian Journal of Social Science* 39(2): 150–70.

Media Indonesia (2004) 'Belum ada fakta gangster Malaysia kuasai perbatasan' ['There Are Still No Facts about the Malaysian Gangster Controlling the Border'], *Media Indonesia* 25 April.

Media Indonesia (2014) 'Pemberdayaan perbatasan dengan pemekaran khusus' ['Empowering the Border with Special District Proliferation'], *Media Indonesia* 24 November.
Moeliono, M., E. Wollenberg and G. Limberg (eds) (2009) *The Decentralization of Forest Governance: Politics, Economics and the Fight for Control of Forest in Indonesian Borneo*. London: Earthscan.
Nordholt, H.S. and G. van Klinken (2007) 'Introduction', in H.S. Nordholt and G. van Klinken (eds) *Renegotiating Boundaries: Local Politics in Post-Suharto Indonesia*, pp. 1–29. Leiden: KITVL Press.
Ong, A. (2006) *Neoliberalism as Exception: Mutations in Citizenship and Sovereignty*. Durham, NC: Duke University Press.
Peluso, N.L. and C. Lund (2011) 'New Frontiers of Land Control: Introduction', *Journal of Peasant Studies* 38(4): 667–81.
Pisani, E. (2014) 'Indonesia in Pieces: The Downside of Decentralization', *Foreign Affairs* July/August.
Pontianak Post (2005) 'Warga perbatasan masih harapkan Malaysia' ['The Border Citizens Still Rely on Malaysia'], *Pontianak Post* 24 May.
Potter, L. (2011) 'Agrarian Transitions in Kalimantan: Characteristics, Limitations and Accommodations', in R.D. Koninck, S. Bernard and J.-F. Bissonnette (eds) *Borneo Transformed: Agricultural Expansion on the Southeast Asian Frontier*, pp. 152–202. Singapore: NUS Press.
PPKPU (2007) 'Gambaran umum kelayakan pemekaran pembentukan Kabupaten Perbatasan Utara di Kapuas Hulu, Kalimantan Barat' ['General Overview of the Feasibility of the Subdivision of the North Border District in Kapuas Hulu, West Kalimantan']. Pontianak/Jakarta: Panitia Pembentukan Kabupaten Perbatasan Utara (PPKPU) dengan Lembaga Kajian Pemerintahan Daerah dan Pembangunan Indonesia (LKPDPI).
Resosudarmo, I.A.P. (2004) 'Closer to People and Trees: Will Decentralisation Work for the People and the Forests of Indonesia?', *European Journal of Development Research* 16(1): 110–32.
Roth, D. (2007) 'Many Governors, No Province: The Struggle for a Province in the Luwu-Tana Toraja Area in South Sulawesi', in H.S. Nordholt and G. van Klinken (eds) *Renegotiating Boundaries: Local Politics in Post-Suharto Indonesia*, pp. 121–47. Leiden: KITVL Press.
van Schendel, W. and E. de Maaker (2014) 'Asian Borderlands: Introducing their Permeability, Strategic Uses and Meanings', *Journal of Borderlands Studies* 29(1): 3–9.
Sinar Harapan (2004) '"Gangster" bersenjata Malaysia dilarporkan kuasai perbatasan' ['General Overview of the Feasibility of the Subdivision of the North Border District in Kapuas Hulu, West Kalimantan'], *Sinar Harapan* 22 April.
Sinar Harapan (2013) 'Disetujui Pembentukan Kabupaten Banua Landjak' ['The Formation of the Banua Landjak District is Approved'], *Sinar Harapan* 30 October.
Sinar Harapan (2014a) 'DPR bahas dua DOB di Kalbar' ['The House of Representatives Discuss Two New Autonomous Areas in West Kalimantan'], *Sinar Harapan* 24 September.
Sinar Harapan (2014b) 'Pemekaran bersamaan Provinsi Kapuas Raya sulit terealisasi' ['The Simultaneous Proliferation of the Kapuas Raya Province is Difficult to Implement'], *Sinar Harapan* 10 March.
Suara Pembaruan (2004) 'Mafia Malaysia babat hutan di perbatasan Kalbar', ['Malaysian Mafia Destroy the Forest on the West Kalimantan Border'], *Suara Pembaruan* 22 April.
Tanasaldy, T. (2007) 'Ethnic Identity Politics in West Kalimantan', in H.S. Nordholt and G. van Klinken (eds) *Renegotiating Boundaries: Local Politics in Post-Suharto Indonesia*, pp. 349–71. Leiden: KITVL Press.
Tempo (2012) 'Ryaas: Sebaiknya Pemekaran di Daerah Perbatasan' ['Ryaas: Proliferation Should Take Place in Border Regions'], *Tempo* 7 April.
Tempo (2013) 'Govt Declines Formation of New Regions', *Tempo* 11 September.
Tribun Pontianak (2013a) 'Banua Landjak terdiri lima Kecamatan' ['Banua Landjak Consists of Five Sub-districts'], *Tribun Pontianak* 29 October.

Tribun Pontianak (2013b) 'DPRD paripurnakan Kabupaten Banua Landjak pemekaran Kapuas Hulu' ['The Provincial Parliament Completes the Subdivision of the Banua Landjak District from the Kapuas Hulu District'], *Tribun Pontianak* 29 October.

Vel, J. (2007) 'Campaigning for a New District in West Sumba', in H.S. Nordholt and G. van Klinken (eds) *Renegotiating Boundaries: Local Politics in Post-Suharto Indonesia*, pp. 91–119. Leiden: KITVL Press.

Wadley, R.L. (1997) 'Variation and Changing Tradition in Iban Land Tenure', *Borneo Research Bulletin* 28: 98–108.

Wadley, R.L. (1998) 'The Road to Change in the Kapuas Hulu Borderlands: Jalan Lintas Utara', *Borneo Research Bulletin* 29: 71–94.

Wadley, R.L. (2000) 'Transnational Circular Labour Migration in Northwestern Borneo', *Revue Européenne des Migrations Internationales* 16(1): 127–49.

Wadley, R.L. (2004) 'Punitive Expeditions and Divine Revenge: Oral and Colonial Histories of Rebellion and Pacification in Western Borneo, 1886–1902', *Ethnohistory* 51(3): 609–36.

Wadley, R.L. and M. Eilenberg (2005) 'Autonomy, Identity, and "Illegal" Logging in the Borderland of West Kalimantan, Indonesia', *Asia Pacific Journal of Anthropology* 6(1): 19–34.

Wissenburg, M. (2008) *Political Pluralism and the State: Beyond Sovereignty*. London and New York: Routledge.

Wollenberg, E. et al. (2006) 'Between State and Society: Local Governance of Forests in Malinau, Indonesia', *Forest Policy and Economics* 8(4): 421–33.

Yuliani, E.L. et al. (2010) 'Biofuel Policies and their Impact on Local People and Biodiversity: A Case Study from Danau Sentarum', *Borneo Research Bulletin* 41: 109–44.

8

The Construction of the 'Self' in Conflicts around Land in Contemporary Tarabuco (Bolivia)

Verónica Calvo

INTRODUCTION

The municipality of Tarabuco is located 64 km from the city of Sucre, the constitutional capital of the plurinational state of Bolivia. Situated in Yamparaez province in the department of Chuquisaca, Tarabuco was formerly an 'Indian settlement',[1] a jurisdiction administered by two authorities representing two overlapping social orders: the *Kuraka* (Superior) native authority of the Republic of Indians, and the *Corregidor*, the authority of the Republic of Spaniards. The settlement was established by the colonial administration of Viceroy Toledo between 1573 and 1578. Currently, the municipality has 19,000 inhabitants.[2] The majority of Tarabuco's population is monolingual in Quechua; less than half the population speaks both Spanish and Quechua. The main town (also called Tarabuco) has a population of around 2,000, with the rest of the population spread among the 73 rural communities found throughout the municipality.

Tarabuco features three principal forms of social and political organization: peasants' syndicates,[3] neighbourhood assemblies and indigenous communities known as 'native' (*orígenes*) or *ayllus*.[4] The Tarabuco Peasants'

The author would like to thank the anonymous reviewers and the journal's editorial team for their constructive comments that greatly contributed to improving the final version of the chapter. She would also like to thank Christian Lund and Michael Eilenberg, the guest editors of this special issue, for their support during the process. Her sincerest thanks are extended to Jacobo Grajales, Stellio Rolland and Ricardo Cavalcanti for their generous comments on the first drafts.

1. *Reducción de Indios* in Spanish.
2. Based on preliminary figures from the most recent population census, which took place in November 2012.
3. 'Peasant' in the Bolivian context makes reference to a social class that emerged with the National Revolution in 1952. It refers to smallholders who are organized in syndical structures. It is also the word used by the actors to refer to themselves.
4. The term *ayllu* means 'family' in Quechua. Nowadays, it refers to the idea of a native indigenous community. Several studies in Andean ethnohistory conjectured that before the colonial period, ayllus were lordships organized in kin groups, geographically distributed on 'vertical archipelagos' to ensure access to several ecological zones (Murra, 1978; Rowe, 1946). Under the colonial administration, the ayllus were constrained in acquiring land titles, which

Rule and Rupture: State Formation through the Production of Property and Citizenship, First Edition. Edited by Christian Lund and Michael Eilenberg.
Chapters © 2017 by The Institute of Social Studies. Book compilation © 2017 John Wiley & Sons Ltd.

Syndical Association is the largest social organization in the municipality in terms of the number of member communities — 66 out of 73 communities, or 80 per cent of the municipality's population. The association is affiliated at the national level with the Unified Syndical Confederation of Peasants of Bolivia (CSUTCB). In 1997 this national organization became the core of a complex synergy between different social movements which led to the creation of the Instrument for the Sovereignty of the Peoples, the political platform of Evo Morales at the 2005 elections. The remaining seven rural communities are not affiliated with the peasants' syndicate, but form part of the Yampara Nation, for which the organizational structure at the national level is the National Council of Ayllus and *Markas* of Qullasuyu (CONAMAQ). Finally, the neighbourhood assemblies represent the system of social organization of the inhabitants of Tarabuco, the capital of the municipality; they are also the second largest organization in the municipality in terms of resident membership. They are linked at the departmental level by the Neighbourhood Assemblies Federation.

Since the approval, via a popular referendum in 2009, of the process of conversion towards indigenous autonomy, a major conflict has developed between these three social organizations, in particular between the leaders of the Tarabuco Syndical Association and the native authorities of the seven ayllus of the Yampara Nation. According to the Autonomy and Decentralization Framework Law, the structure of the new autonomous indigenous government and the system for electing the authorities must be regulated by a statute of autonomy, the drafting of which was entrusted to a deliberative assembly consisting of locally elected representatives of the three social organizations. The drafting of the statute of autonomy is in fact an exercise in self-definition and the establishment of a shared local history, a 'culture' to which all participants must subscribe in order to enjoy the benefits of autonomy: self-governance and the possibility of administering, at least partially, the region and its resources. Peasant Native Indigenous Autonomies (AIOC),[5] as stipulated in Articles 289 and 296 of the Constitution, and more precisely in Articles 42 and 51 of the Autonomy and Decentralization Framework Law, can only apply to the peoples and nations of Bolivia whose 'existence predates the colonial era', who are 'indigenous, native or rural', and who share 'a common territory, culture,

---

transformed the ayllu into a territory-based unit of production and communal landholding (Platt, 1984; Rivera Cusicanqui, 2010). Andean intellectuals and indigenous activists describe the current ayllu as a social and political organization inherited from the Inca period (Choque and Mamani, 2001: 207). Scholars (Fabricant, 2010; Weismantel, 2006) argue that this as an appropriation by activists who oppose the dominance of neoliberalism and advance political and economic alternatives. The memory of the ayllu, partially reinvented, is thus employed in political and territorial claims, and illustrates the 'multivocality of the *ayllu*' (Ouweneel, 2003: 82).

5. *Autonomía Indígena Originaria Campesina* in Spanish.

history, languages, organizations, and particular legal, political, social, and economic institutions'.

An ethnographic examination of the meetings of the assembly tasked with drafting the statute of autonomy — an arena of fierce debate, mainly between representatives of the ayllus and the syndicate — and the identification of different conditions in the production of the self reveals the difficulty that the inhabitants of Tarabuco face in their attempt to create a common category with which every member may establish an affective or emotional connection. In fact, the creation of an AIOC in Tarabuco has raised the question: 'Who are we?'. The inhabitants of Tarabuco, in particular the leaders of social organizations, are seeking to answer this question through the construction of an identity involving the mobilization of elements of *tarabuqueña* society. This has led to the establishment of several distinct types of ethos that clash at a local level, with each side attempting to impose a set of criteria that have to be met in order to belong to a future *tarabuqueña* society and gain access to certain material resources.

At stake in this conflict, therefore, are the values and principles that the new system of autonomy in Tarabuco is to embrace. Among both the syndicate-affiliated communities and the ayllus, these distinct values and principles are formulated by drawing on a common frame of reference: the relationship to the land. This relationship is linked to the largely shared history and social customs of the members of the two organizations. However, these are reformulated and placed in competition by means of two discourses that are radically opposed to each other. Values, principles and desires are projected onto the land, a major resource for both groups. Indeed, the conditions of belonging to one or other membership group are based on different conceptions of personhood that are strongly linked to systems of land ownership and rules of appropriation (Strang and Busse, 2011). Different 'technologies of the self' (Foucault, 1994a) and distinct standards of behaviour in relation to others and in relation to the land lay the groundwork for a moral economy. This notion will help us not only to identify the different forms of economic behaviour in Tarabuco (Polanyi, 1944/1983) but also to grasp the way in which these values are used and reformulated in the relationship of force and conflict that prevails between the social organizations in the local arena (Siméant, 2010; Thompson, 1971).

This chapter analyses these conflicts in the light of the ways of life and being that are being constructed, making use of the notion of 'subjectivation' (Foucault, 1994a, 1994b) or the production of the self, which in this case is linked to the relationship to the land. This approach enables us to move beyond an interpretation of the conflict in terms of rational choice, or strategies of power accumulation. The latter often results in a superficial analysis of relationships of forces and conflicts, as it does not take into account, for example, that the so-called 'memory of the ayllu' is the product of complex subjectivation processes involving a reinterpretation of inherited historical norms and principles of self-behaviour. Furthermore, the chapter aims to overcome the pitfalls of an identity-based approach, avoiding both the notion of a fluid identity — which a constructivist approach is predisposed to, stripping the term of any analytical usefulness — and a reifying essentialism that is just as unhelpful (Bayart, 1996; Brubaker, 2001). Examining this phenomenon — the production of subjectivity — will demonstrate that individuals react to the imperative of identification triggered by the indigenous autonomy system, not through strategic manipulation but rather via a complex and active construction of the self that is influenced by relationships of power.

THE AGRARIAN HISTORY OF TARABUCO, FROM THE *HACIENDA* TO THE RURAL WORKERS' SYNDICATE

In the sixteenth century, Viceroy Toledo turned the Tarabuco region — then known as Señorío Yampara — into an 'Indian settlement' which, as noted above, was administered by two different authorities: the native authority of the Republic of Indians, the Kuraka, and the Corregidor, the authority of the colonial administration. The colonial authority relied on the traditional legitimacy of the Kuraka in order to exploit the local workforce by exacting tribute labour 'payments' or *Mita*.[6] The legitimacy accorded to the Kuraka by the indigenous population was based on its ability to redistribute material and symbolic resources in accordance with the Andean logic of reciprocity (Murra, 1978: 50–120). The Kuraka was an ideal mediator between colonial ways of thinking and the indigenous world of meanings. He was the representative of an ordered space for the redistribution of the forces and energies of the world, and tasked with the formulation of a reciprocal pact between the tribute labour supplied by the indigenous population and the conditions of land occupation in the post-conquest era of colonial administration (Platt, 1982). He was therefore a key player in the particular moral economy (Thompson, 1971) of the colonial era.

This social and economic order was maintained until the last quarter of the nineteenth century, when the *hacienda* (a *latifundia* system based on large-scale landowning) was dramatically expanded, following a sharp increase in the 'commercialization of the land' (Platt, 1984). The expansion of the hacienda regime led to the spread of a particular farming system — that of renting land to the indigenous population. In exchange for usufruct of the land, these indigenous tenants were required to pay a small sum of money representing their rent and, most importantly, give up a large portion of their harvest to the owner of the hacienda. In addition, they were required to carry out domestic tasks and organize the transport of crops without receiving any remuneration for such work (Langer, 1987).

---

6. The Potosi *Mita* is the term for the forced labour that the indigenous population was required to carry out in the Potosi mines, and was a kind of tribute to the Spanish crown.

The historical archives at the National Agrarian Reform Institute for the Tarabuco region reveal a surprising fact: at the beginning of the twentieth century, all cultivable land was in the hands of local tenants. Only a small proportion of the land was directly controlled and worked by the owners of the haciendas (Cavalcanti-Schiel, 2013: 79; Langer, 1987). However, for the 'indigenous tenants' on the hacienda, the logic of reciprocity between them and the guarantor of material and immaterial resource redistribution prevailed. According to this Andean tradition, which can be traced back to the Inca period, the *hacendados* (large-scale landowners) had the responsibility to turn the main seasons of agricultural work into festivals. During harvesting season, the owners would offer workers *chicha*,[7] food, tobacco and coca leaves, and they would bring in bands of musicians. The harvest festival was a custom that involved a redistribution that was material, but also symbolic given its ritualistic character (Langer, 1987). Failure to respect this pact of reciprocity could lead to a confrontation in court. The moral economy marked by reciprocity that was characteristic of the colonial era was therefore reinvented by the owners of the hacienda, enabling them to maintain a relationship of subjugation by consent.

However, by the early twentieth century, the terms of the pact of reciprocity that existed between the indigenous population and landowners within the social order of the hacienda had been shaken. This was due to the excessive greed of the owners and the failure to recognize the legitimacy of the indigenous population's symbolic order and needs. The collapse of this delicate balance between the two parties paved the way for the National Revolution of 1952. Initiated by the Revolutionary Nationalist Movement (MNR) and heavily influenced by a Marxist view of history, the revolution of 1952 foresaw the coming of a worker-peasant class that would transcend ethnic divisions. One of the first measures taken by the new regime, led by President Paz Estenssoro, was the enactment of an Agrarian Reform that sought to dismantle the hacienda system and redistribute land to those who were working it — the indigenous tenants, who from then on were categorized as rural workers.

The dismantling of the former haciendas was a long and costly process. The current composition of rural communities was only established in the 1960s, and their territorial base was largely created from scratch. By the time the Agrarian Reform was initiated in 1953 the ancestral indigenous social system of the ayllus had almost disappeared, having been absorbed by the hacienda system. There was almost no trace of their territorial boundaries (Rivera Cusicanqui, 2010). The National Agrarian Reform Institute thus redistributed the land that had been worked by indigenous tenants, in the process creating small-scale landowners and a *minifundio* (smallholding)

---

7. Alcoholic beverage made using fermented maize; chicha is usually drunk in a ritualized manner.

system. Along with their villas or main homes, hacienda owners were only allowed to retain plots under their direct control; in this way these former landlords, too, became small-scale landowners.

Another type of property was preserved by the new administration, namely the 'Indian territories' or 'rustic land'. The colonial administration had maintained the so-called 'indigenous land', namely those territories that had been occupied by indigenous people since time immemorial and that were not part of the haciendas. The Agrarian Reform thus generated 'non-transferability and consolidation' proceedings relating to these rare cases of Indian territories. However, these were only initiated much later, between 1963 and 1973 (Cavalcanti-Schiel, 2013: 74–90). Meanwhile, both greed and extreme enthusiasm to acquire these new plots of land led to numerous conflicts between indigenous rural workers from the former hacienda and the indigenous-native people who inhabited the 'Indian territories'. Indigenous-native families were required to join the peasants' syndicate in order to receive their property titles. The agrarian syndicate was effectively the only institution that granted these titles and decided on the allocation of plots through procedures involving agrarian juries. However, the 'non-transferability' proceedings that applied to former indigenous territories did not imply the recognition of a pre-existing social organization. Indeed, it was as though the arrival of agrarian syndicalism meant that history had begun again from year nought. In most cases, permanent property titles were only allocated very belatedly, after the 1963–73 period.

The role of the syndicate was not limited to granting property titles, however. It also acted as principal mediator within the new social order inaugurated by the 1952 revolution. The syndicate, like the Kurakas of the colonial era and the hacendado of the nineteenth century, enjoyed legitimacy in the eyes of rural communities because it succeeded in abolishing the hacienda system and enabled the creation of smallholder communities. The syndicate was also the only entity able to stand up to the legal manoeuvring of the hacendados. In a sense the rural workers' syndicate, under the new corporatist-syndical state system installed in the wake of the 1952 revolution, was the new guarantor of the terms of reciprocity and redistribution (Rivera Cusicanqui, 2010: 147).

Today the legal procedure for land allocation regulated by law No. 1715 of 1996, and its amendments of 2006, is still overseen by the National Agrarian Reform Institute, and known as a 'restructuring procedure for regulating property titles and boundaries'.[8] The purpose of these procedures is to manage property titles on the basis of earlier agrarian trials, the effective use of land and contracts for the purchase and sale of land. The most recent nationwide property title regulation campaign was initially planned for the period 2007–13, but it is still in progress.

---

8. In Spanish, *proceso de saneamiento*.

In the Tarabuco territory, the 2014 procedure for regulating property boundaries was preceded by a conflict within the ayllus communities. The vast majority of these communities had obtained legal personality as communities that are part of the indigenous Yampara people, and have since declared their desire to switch to a new system of collective land ownership. This system, known as Native Community Land (TCO), has been provided for in law since 1995. Since the adoption of the new constitution in 2010, it has been known as Rural Native Indigenous Territory (TIOC). However, for a territory to be recognized as a TIOC, the landowners inhabiting it must legally renounce their individual property titles and execute an act for the reconstitution of ancestral territory, thus switching to a system of collective land ownership. It is therefore not simply a choice between different forms of land tenure or property; it is also a choice between different institutions. On the one hand there is the TIOC, which is new and invokes notions of ancient forms of ownership and membership, and on the other, there is the syndicalist movement, which has protected the land rights of its individual members.

This project has encountered strong resistance from certain inhabitants of the ayllu communities who have opted to join the syndicate in order to keep their individual property titles (Mischkamayu community). Elsewhere, in certain syndicate-affiliated communities located close to an ayllu community, the creation of a TIOC has raised fears of land being 'stolen' during the procedure. We shall return to this later.

THE 'ECONOMIC LIFE'[9] OF THE LAND IN TARABUCO MUNICIPALITY

Nearly all territory of the Tarabuco municipality is situated at an altitude of between 3,100 and 3,400 metres. The territory therefore mainly consists of high plains with scarce water resources and temperatures that vary between a summer high of 27°C and a winter low of −6°C. Only in a small portion of the territory, in the northeast of the municipality, does the landscape feature valleys. The vast majority of Tarabuco's inhabitants are single-crop farmers. The most commonly grown crops are tubers (various types of potato), cereals, wheat, barley, corn, quinoa and grain. Some communities have implemented artificial irrigation systems, using small dams, that enable them to grow products normally found in the valleys, such as tomatoes, oranges, apples and herbs (oregano, parsley, coriander). This agriculture is complemented by livestock farming, which usually consists only of domestic livestock (sheep, goats, horses, cattle) used in particular for agricultural work such as ploughing (bullocks) or threshing (horses). Farm produce is sold at a local market. Only a small portion is distributed outside of the territory, in

---

9. Phrase borrowed from Polanyi (1944/1983: 87).

particular barley, which is sold at larger markets in Sucre and other cities. The main local outlet for the area's produce is Tarabuco market, held every Sunday in the municipality's main town of the same name.

However, in Tarabuco, monetary exchange is only one of four 'principles of behaviour' (Polanyi, 1944/1983: 92) for economic activity in the territory. Tarabuco agricultural market, known as the 'farmers' market', features two parallel systems of trade: monetary exchange and bartering. The bartering process occurs between farmers from the high plains and those from the valleys. They exchange high-altitude crops (various types of tuber, barley) for products from the temperate valley areas (in particular, various fruits). In Tarabuco, the local market economy is only one way in which the population's needs are met. The other three models described by Karl Polanyi can also be observed: redistribution (of goods and services), the reciprocity inherited from a pre-existing Andean symbolic logic, described above, and the autarky characteristic of the *oikos* or domestic administration, in which production is for one's own benefit (Polanyi, 1944/1983: 99).

Agricultural work, for example, is not exclusively based on a wage system. As observed, customary rules are followed according to which farm labour is remunerated beyond the payment of a wage or *jornal*. During the harvest period, owners of plots of land often hire farm workers, known as *jornaleros*, in order to ensure that the harvest work is completed in good time. These jornaleros earn between 45 Bs and 60 Bs a day, depending on their task. However, in addition to their wage, the jornaleros receive other forms of remuneration for their work. Throughout the season, the owner's wife oversees the harvest and provides the workers with breakfast, lunch, an afternoon snack and dinner. The value of the workforce is therefore not exclusively determined by the jornal. This food-based payment appears to form part of a broader conception of work (Harris, 2010). We may reasonably assert that agricultural work, more than market goods, is viewed by the inhabitants of Tarabuco as a form of energy that cannot be matched by the payment of a wage dependent on the labour market. This energy must not be reduced to a mere economic relationship of monetary exchange. The agricultural workforce therefore finds itself partially embedded (Polanyi, 1944/1983: 104) in a wider reciprocal relationship that places agricultural work and tasks within a social environment, with its own particular elements of meaning.

The jornaleros are often very demanding regarding the food given to them. They explicitly request food that they do not normally consume, prepared from crops that they do not grow on their own plots of land (often they are also smallholders). Most of the jornaleros grow corn and wheat on their land, usually to be consumed domestically (the autarkic model). They are not able to consume other products such as rice or pasta, given their high cost.

These customary practices linked to the harvest are an indication of another much older practice that still exists among some inhabitants of Tarabuco.

This is *mink'a* or *ayni* (two terms used interchangeably by the inhabitants of Tarabuco):[10] the harvest festival that was practised under the hacienda system, but with a history reaching back to the Inca Empire. Mink'a is a system under which the community's labourers are summoned to work on a piece of land throughout the harvesting period without receiving any economic remuneration for their work. However, food, alcoholic beverages (often chicha), coca and tobacco — along with a group of musicians — are provided to sustain them throughout the harvesting season. The duration of the mink'a can vary from a few days to a few weeks. As one interviewee explained:

> The mink'a is generally conducted during the harvest period. The workers are offered food and drink, and festivities are organized. In the evening in the countryside, you must have seen houses in the community all lit up, with music playing. Well, then you can be sure they're practising mink'a. . . . Mink'a is practised indiscriminately, both by those with a lot of money and those with none, because it's a custom, not a requirement. But it's true that mink'a means the harvest is finished a lot quicker, since there are so many of them. In reality, it's also a way of gathering people in order to finish the harvest as soon as possible.[11]

This extract from an interview with a crop farmer in the town of Tarabuco provides insight into mink'a as a social and ritual practice. It coexists with the labour market but is aligned with the model of reciprocity. A person who decides to gather people to conduct a mink'a invariably agrees to a pact of reciprocity between his or her community and the workers that are to provide help during the harvest period. The pact includes a responsibility to provide his or her workforce if any other member of the community decides to organize a mink'a. However, the person is not engaging in a subsistence ethic (Scott, 1976). As this interview extract shows, the mink'a is practised by both well-to-do farmers and the poor. The pact of reciprocity implied by participating in a mink'a further serves to perpetuate the bonds of cooperation and mutual assistance between families that are also united by kinship and political alliances.

The economic life (Polanyi, 1944/1983) surrounding the land and farm work in Tarabuco is therefore partly *embedded*: in order to provide for themselves, people rely on social and ritual practices, on an economic life that is grounded in specific values and traditional practices that are a part of the social environment. However, as we have seen, exchanges also take place that are characteristic of a market economy and labour market. The economic world here is one that is undergoing a gradual process of *disembedding*. These two dynamics coexist and indicate different types of economic

---

10. However, the word ayni refers to an individual reciprocal practice. Mink'a implies a group of workers, whereas ayni occurs between two individuals.
11. Interview, Tarabuco, 8 April 2013.

logic, revealing the heterogeneous nature of the competing economic be-
haviours (Roitman, 2000). As a Tarabuco farmer explained:

> During any agricultural activity, whether or not you are practising mink'a, you have to give
> the workers, in addition to their wage, a breakfast — usually bread with a hot drink, then
> a plate of food straight afterwards. Then there's lunch, which is soup and a main dish, and
> dinner, consisting of the same thing. I'm no longer able to practise mink'a and don't have
> the time to organize all that, and also I don't want to inflict all that cooking on my wife. So I
> pay the jornales — it's simpler.[12]

Rather than seeing the economy and tradition in opposition, then, we
should examine the nature of economic life on the land in Tarabuco. This
economic life is based on social practices such as those of reciprocity and
redistribution, which existed long before the colonial era. This economy of
the land is 'moral' to the extent that it is founded in a traditional legitimacy, yet it is one that is partly reinvented (Fassin, 2009). These practices
are thus the product of an integration of norms and duties, the meaning of
which is now being debated afresh at local level by competing syndicate
and ayllu members. An analysis of this discourse reveals how elements of
local history and ritual social practices are being reformulated, revealing the
conflictual nature of political subjectivation, which occurs within various
practical spaces of identification, in this case related to land. The elabora-
tion of a moral economy allows us to qualify and disqualify manners of
formulating new rights, ways and means of belonging in different configurations of power relationships.

THE INHERENTLY CONFLICTUAL NATURE OF THE PROCESS OF
LAND-BASED POLITICAL SUBJECTIVATION IN TARABUCO

The establishment of a Rural Native Indigenous Territory (TIOC) in Tarabuco
is one of the developments that best illustrates the construction of different
conceptions of inhabited space: land versus territory. In Tarabuco, the ayllu
communities obtained this legal change to property titles in order to reform
their territory which they associate with memories of 'rustic land' or 'native
territories' — the territories, mentioned earlier, that were self-administered
by natives, and not incorporated into the hacienda system.

   For members of the syndicate, retaining individual ownership of land is
non-negotiable. Historically, individual ownership is the foundational element upon which their syndical organization has relied, and it was the means
by which they were liberated from subjugation in the past. With the memory
of the hacienda regime still fresh in their minds, most Tarabuco communities
continue to perceive the agrarian syndicate as the only mediating institution
capable of instituting a 'fair' system for the allocation and redistribution of

---

12. Interview, Tarabuco, 8 April 2013.

resources. This is why some ayllu communities, notably the Mischkamayu community, have preferred to join the syndicate for fear of losing their land in the process of establishing the TIOC, and the recent procedure of regulating property titles and boundaries. However, it is precisely this mediating role of material redistribution that the ayllus organization has sought to challenge since ayllus were reconstituted in 2003. An interviewee explained the situation as follows:

> For example, this TIOC business, it's not designed to give everyone the same thing, the same amount of land; they keep the boundaries of their plots as they are now. It's not designed to redistribute land equally, it's for joining forces on the political level, for saying that they are one person. From that point of view, personally it makes me think of the old hacienda, where all the land was controlled by a single authority. . . .
>
> We're a syndicate. They're like the *caporales*, by which I mean exploiters, thieves who take what you own, who want to steal what's yours. They want to steal from you in the name of the community. For example, if I buy a hectare for my children in the area where they live, they'll want to keep the hectare for the community. And that's not good: I want to buy a plot of land for my children, not for them to keep it. And if I didn't have any children, I'd give my land to the syndicate, because the syndicate is Bolivia, and the ayllus are like the United States.[13]

Like the syndicalists, the leaders of the ayllus are drawn to the socio-historical relationships of mediation and reciprocity. Seeking to become the new mediators, they emphasize values and principles different to those defended by the syndicate. As one ayllu leader stated:

> The syndicate manipulated the Mishkamayu community with all this talk of projects, that's how they convinced them to renounce the ayllu and affiliate themselves with the syndicate instead. But once we are able to secure our own projects, then things will change. They'll realize that it's the same thing — that we too are able to benefit from projects using our own organization. . . . Our message, our idea is so strong, that if people still prefer to stay affiliated with the syndicate it's because of that doubt, the fact that they doubt our ability to find projects and benefit from them. The other side proposes projects and that's how they win them over.[14]

The notion of 'territory', as advanced by members of the ayllu communities, denotes a productive relationship with the land that is embedded within wider social and political practices (rotation of social duties and justice in exchange for access to land), where the 'territory-land' lies at the heart of an 'economic ethos' (Weber, 1971). The notion of a primordial connection to territory is placed in direct opposition to the commercial conception of land. It is also opposed to the territorial logic of the rural syndicate community, which can be transgressed or fragmented in the name of land redistribution and the creation of new communities (Cavalcanti-Schiel, 2013: 78).

---

13. Interview (8 April 2013) with the host of a canteen in Tarabuco town, affiliated with the Peasants' Syndical Association and the women's syndicate Bartolina Sisa.
14. Interview with the Pisili Kuraka, 12 April 2013.

At the annual congress of the National Native Council of Ayllus and Markas of Qullasuyu[15] (CONAMAQ), where the Yampara Nation ayllus of Tarabuco are represented, a local representative expressed clear opposition to a market economy in the name of the idea of territory. He stated, 'We have suffered the expropriation of our territories because of business interests. The government says that we are engaging in blackmail, that we represent a risk for businesses. They want to commercialize our resources'.[16]

Individual property is seen as a kind of depravity, an attack on the idea of territory, which is the basis of the values and principles of the good life. 'Individual titles lead to individualism!', proclaimed one member of the land and territory commission at the CONAMAQ congress. This organization and its satellite NGOs have been arguing in favour of this conception of territory since the 1990s. Throughout the country, leaders of native communities that are affiliated with CONAMAQ have been socialized into using this terminology, which is now widespread and features in the principal legislative texts affirming the rights of the indigenous people and nations of Bolivia. This conception of land, which is first and foremost a 'territory-land', a place in which the family, community and a particular type of social organization are physically embedded, goes hand in hand with the desire to be a community united by reciprocity and solidarity. Wearing traditional clothing and organizing mink'a can be regarded as technologies of the self, and they are accompanied by norms that dictate renouncing individual property titles. The following interview extracts attest to this:

> Identity is the basis of the individual and identity means the principles and values that each person possesses, in this case the values of communal living, which mainly consists of thinking of others rather than merely yourself. Having a rotating system of government, practising mink'a and ayni as directed by the authorities, because you need communal work; practising mink'a so that I can get help with the sowing. But we need recognition, we need these values and principles to be institutionalized.[17]

> *Aynis, mink'as, fainas* are collective endeavours by which people support one another, but now they are disappearing because everything has become very individualized.[18]

'Good practices' such as the mink'a and ayni, mentioned by the Kuraka of the Pisili ayllu, have a long history and are still followed by the inhabitants of Tarabuco, as we have seen. However, they are in no sense exclusive to the native communities. Despite the fact that such practices have been widespread in both space and time in the Tarabuco region (see above), the ayllu members claim them as part of a unique, communal ethos. The meaning

---

15. The goal of this organization is to defend, at national level, the recuperation of territories corresponding to the geographical position of the former indigenous nations before the arrival of the Spanish.
16. Speech by CONAMAQ member, 7th CONAMAQ congress, Sucre, 28 January 2013.
17. Interview with Pisili Kuraka, 3 March 2013.
18. Interview with Yampara Nation Kuraka Mayor, 21 March 2013.

of these practices is reappropriated by a communal discourse that frequently lays exclusive claim to their use and meaning. It is presented as part of a specific value system in opposition to that of the syndicate members, who are accused of abandoning such values. The community becomes a kind of subjectivating morality, in opposition to the permeable practices of syndicate-affiliated communities. This community morality is rejected by the syndicate members, as illustrated by the following extract:

> They [members of the ayllus] call us colonized and think of themselves as decolonized [laughs]. I told them that there are no colonized people here. Yes, okay, maybe I am colonized, because I think of my own personal interest, by not thinking of others. Because before, there was the ayni, the mink'a, during which everyone worked for someone else for a day, lots of people.... But we almost never do that. Each person works for himself, we work for our own personal benefit. But it's the same with the ayllus, everyone works for himself. That's not being decolonized. They're colonized too. Anyway, we still practise the mink'a and the ayni, when we're unable to do the work on our own, and then everyone comes and brings their *yuntas*. Yes, we still do it sometimes.[19]

These reservations regarding practices such as the mink'a reveal a desire to promote a very different relationship to the land and farm work. These practices are considered to be inconsistent with the notion of 'individual interest' which, in the mind of the executive secretary, ought to prevail in Tarabuco. Like the ayllus, the agrarian syndicate lays claim to a unique ethos, based on the construction of a traditional legitimacy founded in the 1952 National Revolution, agrarian reform, the abolition of *pongueaje* (obligatory domestic service) and the redistribution of the means of production. Local leaders repeat this history at the meetings (*ampliados*) of the rural workers' syndicate sub-associations, thus reviving a historical 'regime of truth' (Foucault, 1994a). Being a member of the rural workers' syndicate involves the projection of a desire for an ideal of progress that is linked to individual ownership of the means of production. This desire for progress and development is also apparent in certain technologies of the self, involving clothing in particular, as some people refuse to wear traditional clothing in favour of 'more refined taste'.

Two opposing regimes of truth thus inform the different accounts of the 'morality' of land-related practices in Tarabuco. However, this is not a clear-cut opposition between modernity and tradition. Rather, two different contemporary institutions present themselves as either modern or traditional, but both display traces of the other in the justification of their programmes and recruitment of followers. The ayllu members' claim to practices and values that are 'ancient' is the result of their moral repositioning within this society in the face of the expansion of capitalist modes of reasoning (Roitman, 2000). The revival of ethical repertoires of action, in this case informed by

---

19. Interview with the Executive Secretary of the Tarabuco Syndical Association, Tarabuco, 12 December 2012.

ideas of reciprocity and solidarity, is an inherent part of a process of repositioning within a modern economic context (Fabricant, 2010). The following
statements illustrate this:

> Here in Pisili we have everything, what else do we need? Money? More money? We have to
> reflect and think about what we really possess, what are our products, what does *vivir bien*
> mean? It means leaving the logic of capitalist consumption behind. Lots of people still have
> a developmentalist mentality and that's not good, it won't work.[20]

> We want to recover the old ways, but the system, technology and science, prevent us from
> doing so. Technical advances make our task difficult. The ayllus are the only ones who take
> care of the land and the environment, who can really stop the development of industry.[21]

The projection of desires and the construction of subjectivity also — or
even especially — occurs in confrontation with the other, and the other's
desire. Within the spaces of this confrontation, the subject may more readily
present her/himself as a moral speaker, promoting techniques, procedures,
rules, standards and principles that constitute a space of subjective belonging.
However, these technologies of the self cannot be considered wilful actions
with the goal of attaining some form of identity (Bayart and Warnier, 2004:
24). On the contrary, they are a logical consequence of the subject being
embedded within an 'institutional genealogical space' (Legendre, 1985).
These techniques, rules and principles are elements of a subject's social life
that express her/his desire, and elements in opposition to which the subject
constructs her/himself.

The revival of ethical records connected to the land also concerns farming
tools and techniques. At the most recent *tantachawi* (meeting) of the native
authorities of the Yampara nation, great emphasis was placed on the importance of establishing an agricultural training centre where the young could
be taught respect for 'Mother Earth', agro-ecological production methods
and recovered ancestral practices and knowledge of communal organization
(Weismantel, 2006).

Tarabuco has an Institute of Agro-Industrial Training[22] where young tech-
nicians must produce an essay at the end of training in order to receive their
diploma. We interviewed one of these young people, who explained that he
wanted to write his essay on the revaluation of ancestral knowledge linked
to farm work. He wanted to conduct research on how the 'ancestors' preserved potatoes, and the tools and instruments they used to work the land.
He told us at length about the *lauk'ana*, an old type of pick made using a
solid branch that the 'ancestors' would find in the forest and choose with
care. He also told us about the old method for threshing wheat, using horses.

---

20. Interview with Pisili Kuraka, 12 April.
21. Speech by new Kuraka mayor for the Yampara Nation, at the meeting for native authorities,
    Pisili, 12 April 2013.
22. Instituto Superior Agroindustrial Carrillo Calizaya.

More generally, he was interested in the agricultural history of the region and wanted to conduct more focused research into the crops formerly grown in Tarabuco, that have disappeared due a lack of labour following the rural exodus. This young man is from Pisili, one of the seven native communities found in the Tarabuco territory. His interest in these topics, he explained, is connected to a desire to update and reclaim ancient knowledge relating to farm work. This knowledge, in his view, is closer to 'how the relationship between humans and the land should be'.[23]

We are therefore witnessing what might be called a 'war of subjectivation' (Bayart and Warnier, 2004: 12) between members of the ayllus and syndicalists, in which the subject is produced through confrontation with the other. The main concern in this confrontation is the desire to impose a particular view of what is desirable for oneself and for others as far as the relationship with the land is concerned. We are faced with two opposed regimes of truth that underpin possible narratives regarding the 'morality' of land-related practices within Tarabuco territory. The proclamation of a 'true' and 'fair' relationship to the land provided a basis for institutional methods of allocating and controlling this resource, as the process surrounding the implementation of the TIOC illustrates. This moment of rupture presents an example of very distinct cultural, institutional and socio-economic choices made by Tarabuco inhabitants.

The leaders of the ayllus, like the syndicalist leaders dealing with the hacienda regime in 1952, are seeking to position themselves as a new kind of institutional and organizational mediator in the service of the new AIOC regime that offers access to material and immaterial resources. This is possible thanks to the new constitution and the establishment of a plurinational state that enables indigenous peoples to self-govern according to their customs and traditions.

CONCLUSION

Inevitably, articulating aspirations goes hand in hand with the stipulation of moral values, norms and rules for 'good behaviour'. The land in Tarabuco can be considered a place of production of the self. This is a self that is laden with potential conflicts corresponding to the resources originating in the different organizational allegiances of those involved.

Each organization draws on its own socio-historical points of reference and interpretations of land ownership in establishing what it conceives to be the principles of a moral relationship to the land, the principles of economic life surrounding such a relationship, and consequently the values, principles and norms that are to govern society. Each organization endows its subjects

---

23. Interview, Tarabuco, 13 March 2013.

178   *Verónica Calvo*

with particular characteristics and particular capacities to engage in property relations. People accordingly have very particular rights to property,
depending on their organizational membership.

This local conflict, which involves formulating the nature of the relationship with the land, and the terms and methods of allocating it, thus generates
processes of 'autochthonization' (Bayart et al., 2001). This is a direct consequence of an 'imperative to identify' that goes hand in hand with the
establishment of this new system of autonomy. This imperative to identify,
which the inhabitants of Tarabuco must face and which is the basis for the di-
visive process of political subjectivation, leads us to conclude that the Native
Indigenous Peasant Autonomy framework functions as a system for allocating identity, resulting from the newly restructured Bolivian state since the
adoption of the new constitution in 2010. As such, the population is not governed directly, but rather by 'structuring their range of possible actions', the
'range of possible indentification' (Foucault, 1994b) — in this case, a range
of possibilities for the production of an autonomous indigenous subject, even
though conflict is the force that ultimately determines the process.

REFERENCES

Bayart, J-F. (1996) *l'illusion identitaire* [*The Illusion of Cultural Identity*]. Paris: Fayard.
Bayart, J-F. and J-P. Warnier (eds) (2004) *Matière à politique, Le pouvoir, les corps et les choses* [*Political Materials, Power, Body and Things*]. Paris: Karthala.
Bayart, J-F., P. Geschiere and F. Nyamnjoh (2001) 'Autochthonie, démocratie et citoyenneté en Afrique' ['Autochthony, Democracy and Citizenship in Africa'], *Critique Internationale* 10: 177–94.
Brubaker, R. (2001) 'Au-delà de l' "identité"' ['Beyond "Identity"'], *Actes de la recherche en sciences sociales* 139: 66–85.
Cavalcanti-Schiel, R. (2013) 'De la reluctancia salvaje del pensamiento. Memoria social en los Andes Meridionales' ['The Reluctance of the Savage Mind. Social Memory in Meridional Andes']. Unpublished manuscript.
Choque, M.E. and C. Mamani (2001) 'Reconstitución del ayllu y derechos de los pueblos indígenas: el movimiento indio en los Andes de Bolivia' ['Ayllu Reconstitution and In-digenous People Rights: Indian Movements in the Bolivian Andes'], *The Journal of Latin American and Caribbean Anthropology* 6(1): 202–24.
Fabricant, N. (2010) 'Between the Romance of Collectivism and the Reality of Individualism: Ayllu Rhetoric in Bolivia's Landless Peasant Movement', *Latin American Perspectives* 37(4): 88–107.
Fassin, D. (2009) 'Les économies morales revisitées' ['Revisiting Moral Economies'], *History Social Sciences Annals* 6: 1237–66.
Foucault, M. (1994a) 'Les techniques de soi' ['Technologies of the Self'], in M. Foucault and D. Defert (eds) *Dits et Ecrits IV* [*Writings IV*], pp. 783–813. Paris: Gallimard/Seuil.
Foucault, M. (1994b) 'Le sujet et le pouvoir' ['The Subject and the Power'], in M. Foucault and D. Defert (eds) *Dits et Ecrits IV* [*Writings IV*], pp. 222–43. Paris: Gallimard/Seuil.
Harris, O. (2010) '"Trocaban el trabajo en fiesta y regocijo" Acerca del valor del trabajo en los Andes históricos y contemporáneos' ['Bartering Work with Party and Joy: About Work Value in Historic and Contemporaneous Andes'], *Chungara, Revista de Antropología Chilena* 42(1): 221–33.

Langer, E. (1987) 'La comercialización de la cebada en los ayllus y las haciendas de Tarabuco (Chuquisaca) a comienzos del siglo XX' ['Marketing Barley in the Ayllus and Haciendas of Tarabuco at the Begining of the 20ᵗʰ Century'], in O. Harris, B. Larson and E. Tandeter (eds) *La participación indígena en los mercados surandinos. Estrategias y reproducción social. Siglos XVI a XX* [*Indigenous Participation in the South Andean Market. Strategies and Social Reproduction in the16ᵗʰ and 20ᵗʰ Centuries*], pp. 583–601. La Paz: Centro de Estudios de la Realidad Economica y Social.

Legendre, P. (1985) *Leçons IV – L'inestimable objet de la transmission. Etude sur le principe généalogique en Occident* [*The Inestimable Object of Transmission. Study on the Genealogic Aim in Occident*]. Paris: Fayart.

Murra, J. (1978) *La organización económica del estado inca* [*The Economic Organization of the Inca State*]. Mexico City: Siglo XXI Editores.

Ouweneel, A. (2003) 'The "Collapse" of the Peruvian Ayllu', in T. Salman and A. Zoomers (eds) *Imaging the Andes. Shifting Margins of a Marginal World*, pp. 81–98. Amsterdam: Aksant.

Platt, T. (1982) *Estado boliviano y ayllu andino. Tierra y tributo en el norte de Potosí* [*The Bolivian State and Andean Ayllu*]. Lima: IEP.

Platt, T. (1984) 'Liberalism and Ethnocide in the Southern Andes', *History Workshop* 17: 3–18.

Polanyi, K. (1944/1983) *La grande transformation* [*The Great Transformation*]. Paris: Gallimard.

Rivera Cusicanqui, S. (2010) *Violencias (re) encubiertas en Bolivia* [*Violence Reconcealed in Bolivia*]. La Paz: La Mirada Salviaje.

Roitman, J. (2000) 'Economie morale, subjectivité et politique' ['Moral Economy, Subjectivity and Politics'], *Critique Internationale* 6: 48–56.

Rowe, J.H. (1946) 'Inca Culture at the Time of the Spanish Conquest', in J.H. Steward (ed.) *Handbook of South American Indians, Vol. 2*, pp. 183–230. Washington, DC: Smithsonian Institute.

Scott, J.C. (1976) *The Moral Economy of the Peasant. Rebellion and Subsistence in South Asia*. New Haven, CT: Yale University Press.

Siméant, J. (2010) 'Économie morale et protestation-détours africans' ['Moral Economy and Protestation: African Detours'], *Genèses* 81: 142–60.

Strang, V. and M. Busse (eds) (2011) *Ownership and Appropriation*. Oxford: Oxford University Press.

Thompson, E.P. (1971) 'The Moral Economy of the English Crowd in the Eighteenth Century', *Past and Present* 50(1): 76–136.

Weber, M. (1971) *Economie et société, Tome 1* [*Economy and Society, Vol 1*]. Paris: Plon.

Weismantel, M. (2006) '"Ayllu": Real and Imagined Communities in the Andes', in G. Creed (ed.) *The Seductions of Community: Emancipations, Oppressions, Quandaries*, pp. 77–100. Santa Fe, NM: School of American Research Advanced Seminar Series Press.

9

The Rupture of Territoriality and the Diminishing Relevance of Cross-cutting Ties in Somalia after 1990

Markus Virgil Hoehne

INTRODUCTION

This chapter argues that the flexible attitude to territory among many Somalis in the past, which was mainly related to economic survival in a harsh environment and to limited colonial and post-colonial interference, particularly in the pastoral-nomadic sector, has been replaced with a strong vision of territoriality. In this vision, geographic space is perceived as the bounded basis of competition for power, including control of people and resources. This is part of current processes of state formation in Somalia. The changing notions of territoriality are correlated with changes in the sociality of many Somalis. The 'network logic' predominant among Somali pastoral nomads and agro-pastoralists — related to cross-cutting ties[1] transcending patrilineal descent groups and providing a basis for cooperation and integration beyond the patrilineal principle — has been replaced with a 'state logic' that focuses on fixed territories, boundaries, and social and economic exclusion.

In this contribution, I shall argue that in response to civil war, state collapse, humanitarian disaster and international interventions, spatial control has become an important parameter of political organization and the strength of a political entity. This translates into new forms of income related to humanitarian aid, trade and financial remittances. Against the backdrop of the central argument of this special issue, which establishes a strong connection between the emergence of political power and state formation through the management of property and citizenship rights (see Lund's Introduction to this special issue), and in contrast to most empirical cases in which property and citizenship are defined from the top down (such as in Ethiopia and Kenya: see Hagmann and Abbink, 2013: 583–4; Schlee, 2010: 10), the Somali case provides an example of 'bottom-up' territorialization in

I wish to thank Christian Lund and Michael Eilenberg as well as the anonymous referees of *Development and Change* for their constructive comments.

1. 'Cross-cutting ties' refer to social ties existing between individuals that cross dominant modes of belonging, e.g., those based on ethnicity, clan or class. Cross-cutting ties are established through marriage, co-residence, friendship etc., and influence the conflict behaviour of the connected persons (and, by extension, the groups to which they belong).

Rule and Rupture: State Formation through the Production of Property and Citizenship, First Edition.
Edited by Christian Lund and Michael Eilenberg.
Chapters © 2017 by The Institute of Social Studies. Book compilation © 2017 John Wiley & Sons Ltd.

the absence of an effective central government. Here, it is not the state that creates territory and spatial rights; rather, whoever can create spatial rights and defend them becomes the state. This is a process that follows local imperatives of survival in a period of extended rupture. It is, however, also a result of external agenda setting within larger policy frameworks prioritizing state building and counter-terrorism.

Territoriality, in the sense of control of geographical space including its landed resources and the local population (Sack, 1986: 19; Sikor and Lund, 2009: 14; Vandergeest and Peluso, 1995: 385), was not firmly developed in most parts of the Somali Peninsula until the mid-twentieth century. On the contrary, Somalis, whose economy was traditionally based mainly on pastoral nomadism, were considered to be a mobile people. Their boundaries were said to lie 'where the camel stops' (FitzGibbon, 1985: 20). Property relations were fluid. The main resources — pasture and water — depended on erratic rainfall and essentially had to be shared; they were considered the prerogative of Allah (Lewis, 1961: 33–6; see also Yasin Mohammed Yasin, 2010: 86). Animals were the property of individuals but usually herded within the context of (extended) families, which established usufruct rights for herders. In the pre-colonial and colonial past, some wells were considered the 'home wells' of certain lineages (Hunt, 1951), but control over these wells changed frequently with the ebbs and flows of conflict and/or migration. Only along the rivers Shabelle and Jubba in the south did an economy based on farming develop; there, farms were owned by families, while plantations were in the hands of local strongmen (some of Arabic origin) who in the nineteenth century used Bantu-speaking slave labourers imported from (today's) Tanzania.

The Somali term denoting relations between people, property and land is *degaan*. It refers to 'an area where one lives, operates a business, and feels secure enough because of the presence of a large number of one's clansmen in the wider physical area' (Farah et al., 2002: 343). *Degaan* is related to 'entitlement, security, usage and identity' (ibid.). However, it does not entail exclusive rights and often comes along with sharing one's *degaan* with other groups passing by (e.g., in the context of seasonal migration) or living nearby and (partly) using the same resources.

In the 1930s, under Italian colonial control, fertile land in southern Somalia was expropriated and given to Italian concessionaires; this disrupted local agricultural production (Besteman, 1999; Cassanelli, 1997; Menkhaus, 2003a). In the north, economic and social transformations were introduced by British 'protectors' seeking to export livestock to their garrison in Aden on the other side of the Gulf. Animal husbandry became commodified and a group of wealthy Somali merchants emerged to control the trade (Geschekter, 1985; Samatar, 1992a). Colonial policies also fostered the construction of cisterns (*berkedo*) which altered the relations of herders to the land, with implications for migration routes and the use of pastures (Korf et al., 2015: 890–1). In post-colonial Somalia, property relations changed through land reform (mainly in southern Somalia) in the 1970s; elites related to the government gained control of much of the fertile land (Menkhaus, 2003a: 147–9). Among all Somalis, political and social belonging was regulated through patrilineal group membership. In the few areas suitable for farming, a place-based identity — being born to a place — was additionally relevant. Generally, citizenship was based on *ius sanguinis*: a Somali citizen was a person born from a Somali father (or, in cases where the father was unknown, from a Somali mother).

Ruptures, understood as '"open moments" when opportunities and risks multiply . . . and when new structural scaffolding is erected' (see Lund's Introduction to this issue) had two seemingly contradictory but in many regards parallel effects on territorialization and state (de-)formation in Somalia. The first of these was that civil war and state collapse in the late 1980s and early 1990s furthered dynamics of *de*territorialization, famously described by Appadurai (1991: 193) as 'one of the central forces of the modern world'. Forced migration and subsequent diaspora formation led Gundel (2002) to characterize Somalis as a truly 'globalized nation'. The boundaries of this nation were extended even further than 'where the camel stops'. At the same time, Somalia as a state ceased to exist. Its territory was not controlled, and external (state and non-state) actors intervened at will. Only the imaginary of the state prevailed (Hansen and Stepputat, 2001). The second effect concerns *re*territorialization in the sense of spatial concentration of descent groups (in the 1990s) and 'mini-state' formation (increasingly since the 2000s), including claims to resources and populations within the territory of the former Somali Republic. The key puzzle addressed in this chapter is the shift from a borderless, non-territorially defined Somali space to a bordered, intensively territorialized Somali space that took place during this extended period of rupture which began around 1990 and is still ongoing.

'TRADITIONAL' SOMALI MODES OF POLITICS AND BELONGING

Notions of state and nation are of recent origin in the Somali setting.[2] In general, the modern state is characterized by territorial sovereignty, and by control and regulation of its resources and population. Internally, power and authority are vested in particular institutional arrangements. While power functions through coercion, authority can be legitimate or illegitimate (Weber, 1956). The state, formally, is the totality of a country's governmental institutions and officials, together with the laws and procedures that structure their activities. Democratic states seek to monopolize legal authority. This legal authority, used to issue laws and take decisions that bind its population,

2. Of course, the modern nation state is a recent feature in most parts of the world (Benjamin, 1988).

makes the state's decisions 'authoritative'.[3] Simultaneously, the ruled set out to legitimize claims (e.g., to private property) through approval by state institutions. In this way, state is characterized by dynamic relations of power and authority; it is always in the making, is always being negotiated and is part of mundane practices and embedded in concrete histories (Lund's Introduction to this issue; Hagmann and Péclard, 2010; Krohn-Hansen and Nustad, 2005; Sikor and Lund, 2009: 3). Pre-colonial Somali society was largely acephalous. Permanent positions of power and state-like structures were absent among Somalis, except for the organization of the 'sultanates' between the twelfth and the nineteenth centuries.[4] Most people lived as pastoral nomads or agro-pastoralists.

I.M. Lewis, who worked in the British Protectorate in the northwest of the Somali Peninsula, produced in his ethnography *A Pastoral Democracy* (1961) the image of a paradigmatic segmentary society. Political and social relations amongst the Somalis were regulated predominantly through solidarity within patrilineal groups (*tol*) and by customary law (*xeer*),[5] which facilitated extremely flexible group and alliance formations. In the few early urban settlements and in the areas where agriculture was practised, belonging to a place played an important additional role. Even in those settings, however, the fiction of common descent was upheld by the local communities (Barnes, 2006; Helander, 2003; Lewis, 1969; Luling, 2002). Throughout the Somali territories, alliances between groups were key in managing the risks for survival (environmental risks or conflict); besides agnatic ties, these could involve cross-clan or cross-lineage alliances based on uterine ties (through the mother's patriline), affinal ties (established through marriage), friendship, or religious orientation (Lewis, 1961).[6] Of course, belonging was related to the feeling of 'togetherness' (*asabiya*), which derives from concrete practice (arranging security through agnates or others, for example) as Jama Mohamed (2007: 239) has stressed.

State structures involving claims to exclusive territorial control and attempts to control resources and the (mobile) population were introduced only in colonial times. This project was implemented differently in the various areas in which Somalis were colonized by different powers: the British, the Italians, the French and the Ethiopians. Internal territorialization, which

---

3. Even in authoritarian or dictatorial states, the semblance of legality and legitimacy is usually sought.
4. There have been small sultanates in the north and the south of the Somali peninsula that were effectively city states. They were established at nodal points of the caravan trade between inner-Africa and the sea. Usually their power did not extend far beyond the city walls (Aregay, 1971; Cassanelli, 1982; Luling, 2002).
5. Somali place, personal and clan names in this text generally follow the Somali orthography. The Latin 'c' stands for a sound close to the Arabic 'ع' (ayn), 'x' denotes 'ح' (ha), as in, e.g., Cali or in Faarax.
6. Somalis are Sunni Muslims and traditionally belong to different Sufi *turuq*, such as Qadriya, Ahmediya and Salihiya. Since the 1950s, Salafi- and Wahabi-oriented groups have gained influence among Somalis (Abdurahman M. Abdullahi Baadiyow, 2014).

aims at 'establishing control over natural resources and the people who use them' (Vandergeest and Peluso, 1995: 385) developed furthest in the southern Somali territories under Italian rule. This was where agriculture was possible and people were partly sedentary. In the other colonial territories, indirect rule or, in the Ethiopian empire, 'garrison' rule — characterized by regular military coercion of Somali nomads — prevailed (Geshekter, 1985: 6–10; Hagmann, 2014: 14; Lewis, 2002: 41–67).

The heritage of colonial statehood was mixed. On the one hand, as elsewhere in Africa, colonialism provided a first basis for statehood within a clearly demarcated territory (although some of Somalia's borders with its neighbours, particularly with Ethiopia, remained disputed; see Drysdale, 1964). Somali nationalists took over the state system upon independence. The Somali Republic was established through the union of the British Protectorate of Somaliland and Italian Somalia in July 1960. The other Somali territories remained under the rule of the French (Djibouti), British (Kenya) and Ethiopians (Ogaden Region). Inside Somalia, the 'culture of statehood' was quite diverse: emphasis on preserving traditional forms of rule was much greater in the ex-British territory, for example, than in the part formerly under Italian dominance (Prunier, 2010). On the other hand, colonial divisions in the Horn laid the foundation for perennial inter-state conflict (Matthies, 1977). From the 1950s onward, Somalis developed a pan-Somali vision (see Map 1), which aimed at the incorporation of all ethnic Somalis and their territories into a single state (Information Service of the Somali Government, 1962). This, of course, provided serious challenges to the neighbouring states as well as to the Organization for African Unity (OAU). According to pan-Somali sentiment, clan borders did not matter, ethnic borders did. Despite the nationalist fervour, within the Somali ethnic group power was divided according to clan belonging and group size (with larger clans demanding a bigger share). Throughout the colonial and post-colonial periods, Somali and non-Somali political actors usurped and manipulated recurrent local inter- and intra-clan hostilities for their own purposes (Compagnon, 1992; Samatar, 1992b). However, the invocation of a larger Somali national identity functioned for some time as the 'glue' holding the emerging state together.

Mapping is a key technology in the process of territorialization. Vandergeest and Peluso (1995: 387) stress that 'territories are created by mapping; thus modern cartography plays a central role in the implementation and legitimation of territorial rule'. Map 1 provides a glimpse of the dominant Somali imagination related to territorial and ethnic belonging. It pictures what Somali nationalists claimed as theirs from the mid-twentieth century onward.[7] Compare Map 1 with Maps 2 and 3 below which depict more contemporary (2012 and 2016) representations of political divisions within the

---

7. In a peace treaty between Somalia and Ethiopia in 1988, claims to much of the 'western Somali lands' (known as Ogaden Region or Ethiopia's region 5 today) were officially given up by the Somali government (Zoppi, 2015).

Map 1. The Somali Peninsula: Pan-Somali Vision

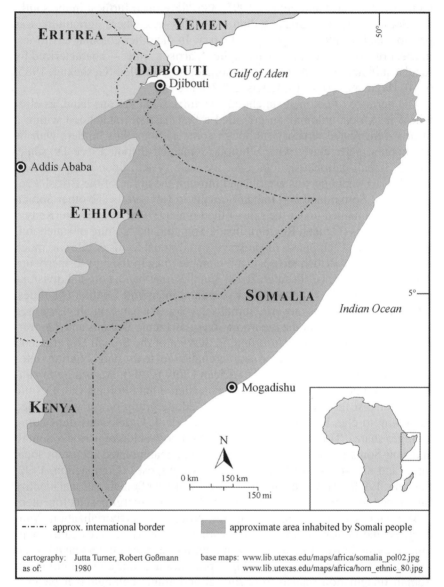

territory of the Somali Republic. One can see in Map 2 various small states or regional administrations, some of which vanished while new ones emerged (see Map 3).[8] Others, like Jubbaland, Southwest and Galmudug, developed

---

8. The area of influence of Al Shabaab is only depicted in Map 2, since Map 3 presents administrations that can claim official status (although most are still in the making). Nevertheless, Al Shabaab currently constitutes an undeniable force in the hinterland of southern Somalia.

Map 2. Political Divisions within Somalia (2012)

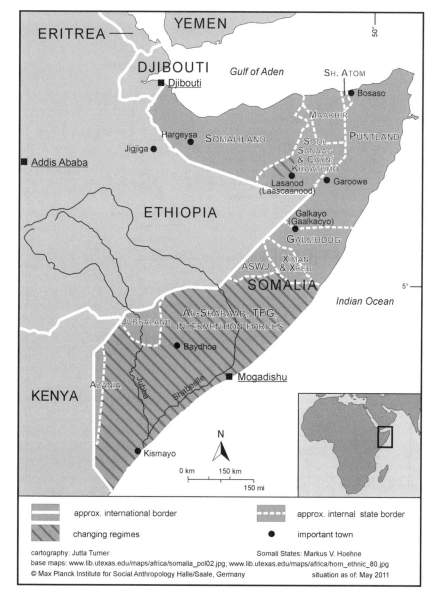

into more stable and visible ('mappable') entities between 2012 and 2016. Maps 2 and 3 exhibit various contested areas, particularly in the north where rival claims have been made by Somaliland and Puntland, and by Puntland and Galmudug. Of course, these maps are limited representations of what is actually happening on the ground, and they are shaped by particular political agendas. Nevertheless, they indicate political trends, some of which will be outlined in greater detail in the second half of this chapter.

Map 3. (Envisioned) Federal States and Contested areas (2016)

I maintain that the currently observable territorialization processes in Somalia are an expression of state re-emergence following a (modern) 'state logic', which is at odds with the 'network logic' traditionally underpinning pastoral nomadism and agro-pastoralism.[9] This state logic is centred on the control of clearly demarcated territory and exclusive claims to resources and people within it. In the long run, states increase their authority through regulating property and citizenship (Lund, Introduction). In the absence of a (modern) state, territoriality also plays a role, but is based on flexible arrangements concerning borders, resources and social and political belonging (Schlee, 2010: 6; Vandergeest and Peluso, 1995: 394). Somali political behaviour — in the absence of a state before the advent of colonialism, and in the face of a weakly administered or failing state during much of the post-colonial period — has followed a network logic. Cross-cutting ties have been an integral part of this logic.

Gluckman (1965), who is the main source in social anthropology on cross-cutting ties, stressed the importance of divided loyalties for cohesion and 'peace in the feud' in societies without central authorities. Taking Evans-Pritchard's description of the Nuer society as his example, Gluckman argues that the wide dispersal of those Nuer who by descent belong to a vengeance group, and the fact that Nuer belonging to different vengeance groups reside together (at least temporarily) in such locations as villages and water points, diminishes the probability of a conflict escalating into violence. 'Conversely, if a man of the group demanding vengeance resides among the killers, he has an interest in securing that his kin accept compensation instead of insisting on blood for blood' (ibid.: 12). In particular, the rule of exogamy and relationships established by marriage force a man to consider both loyalty to his own descent group and good relations with his in-laws (ibid.: 13, 20–1).[10]

Among Somali pastoral nomads, 'clan exogamy' was the rule at least until the outbreak of the civil war, which started in northern Somalia in the late 1980s and then moved south. The term 'clan exogamy' has to be qualified. Marriage outside of one's own group was not always marriage outside of one's own clan. Sometimes members of different lineages (within the same clan) married each other. More frequently, however, clan exogamy 'proper' was practised, such as between Isaaq/Habar Jeclo and Daarood/Dhulbahante, or between different Isaaq clans such as Habar Jeclo and Habar Yuunis

---

9. The use of the terms 'modern' and 'traditional' here does not imply 'progressive' and 'backward' or 'contemporary' and 'not contemporary'. The terms are used here as analytical constructs that refer to different representations of politics and different political legitimacies; both are current and equally relevant.

10. Schlee (1997: 578) criticizes Gluckman's functionalist focus on the maintenance of social order and cohesion. Drawing on ethnographic examples from Papua New Guinea by Hallpike and his own work in northern Kenya, Schlee stresses that cross-cutting ties established, for example, through co-residence do not necessarily cool down hostilities but sometimes lead to conflict escalation. Evidence from Somalia — not presented in this chapter for lack of space — can support either Gluckman's (functionalist) or Schlee's (processuralist) analysis.

(in the north). Location and the distribution of vital resources in a given area shaped intermarriage patterns. In the pastoral-nomadic setting, one traditionally found a marriage partner from among neighbouring clans with whom one shared the pasture and water, but with whom one also frequently fought over access to these scarce resources. Relationships and alliances beyond patrilineal descent could therefore be based on uterine, affinal and/or contractual ties, with the latter being established under customary law (*xeer*) or shari'a. In some contexts, such as religious settlements (called *jameeco*, referring to a religious 'congregation') or in towns, additional ties could be forged along lines of religious or emotional affinity. Still, in political life throughout the twentieth century, 'clan' (as shorthand for groups based on patrilineal descent) remained a key factor. President Maxamed Siyaad Barre (1969–91) provides a prominent example of the strategic use of cross-cutting ties in alliance formation. Despite the 'anti-tribalist' rhetoric of his government, which officially promoted 'scientific socialism', he carefully stabilized his rule through allying his own descent group, the Marrexaan, with his mother's clan, the Ogaden, and the Dhulbahante, which was the clan of several of his sons-in-law. This alliance became (in)famous among Somalis under the abbreviation MOD, which was used as code to hint at nepotism within the 'revolutionary' government (Lewis, 1994: 165).

During the escalating violence at the beginning of the civil war, cross-cutting ties offered protection for individuals and groups and channels for communication between enemies. This was the case, for instance, when fighting erupted in a place called Ceerigaabo in northern Somalia. There, members of various Isaaq and Daarood/Harti clans resided together and were connected through intermarriage over generations. While the local Isaaq from 1988 onwards supported the guerrillas of the Somali National Movement (SNM), the Daarood/Harti as a rule stood on the side of the government. During intense internecine fighting, in-laws sometimes assisted each other, providing safe passage through enemy lines. Also, women belonging by patriline to one side but being married to the other (and whose children belonged to the patriline of the husband) occasionally served as messengers. Given the intensity of civil war, however, the power of these ties to curtail conflict was limited. After the SNM had won in the north in 1991, it took many years to restore social relations.[11] One consequence was that clan or even lineage endogamy became more frequent in and around Ceerigaabo.[12] Only since the early 2000s have marriage ties across descent lines become more frequent again.[13]

In the agro-pastoral settings in southern Somalia, the key economic resources are farmland and plantations, where fruits (e.g., bananas, papayas,

11. Interview with Ismaaciil Xaaji Nuur, Ceerigaabo, 17 June 2004.
12. Interview with Ibraahim Xuseen Yuusuf Shiine, Ceerigaabo, 14 June 2004.
13. Interview with Qamar Taleex, Ceerigaabo, 3 May 2004.

mangos, melons, oranges), vegetables (e.g., tomatoes, onions), and cereals (e.g., sorghum) are grown. Much of the farming is rain-fed, except along the Shabelle and Jubba, which are the country's only two permanent rivers. Traditionally, the area has seen a steady flow of immigration from other Somali territories and beyond (including non-Somali immigrants). Labour, property rights and security were therefore organized locally through forms of belonging based on co-residence and adoption into composite clans. Helander (1997: 135), who did basic ethnographic research on politically marginalized Somali agro-pastoralists in the 1980s, mentions that *sheegat*,[14] which he translates as 'adoption', is based on the claim of a politically weaker group to belong to a politically stronger group — a claim which is tolerated by the latter. *Sheegat* is therefore also a strategy to secure land and rights to resources. Helander observed that among the Raxanweyn residing in the regions Baay and Bakool members belonging to the same lineages or clans were integrated into different clans (ibid.: 134–5, 139). This created a network of relationships in which patrilineal descent cross-cut with *sheegat* relationships, both of which created demands for loyalty. In Helander's view (ibid.: 140–2), adoption and co-residence were factors diminishing the prevalence of violent conflict among the Raxanweyn (before, but also after the state collapse in 1991).

In the Somali case, cross-cutting ties may not prevent fighting. However, they offer starting points for peaceful conflict settlement during or after episodes of violence. Sometimes, this is also when new cross-cutting ties are established. In the case of a particular 'bad' killing (which contravenes customary 'humanitarian law' among Somalis),[15] an unmarried girl (or even several girls) from the family of the killer(s) can be given by the elders for marriage to the injured group, on top of the compensation in livestock or the equivalent in money. This tradition is called *godob reeb*, which translates as 'extinguishing hatred/resentment'. Thus, affinal ties between former enemies are forged, and the loss of life of the one group is 'replaced' by the child/children born to the girl(s) from the other group.[16]

In sum, concerning modes of politics and belonging, it is clear that stable state structures were the exception, not the rule, in the Somali territories until the mid-twentieth century. Even after the establishment of the Somali Republic, state administration remained weak in many parts of the country (except for the first decade or so of the socialist dictatorship from 1969

---

14. *Sheegat* comes from the Somali verb *sheegasho*: 'claiming, recounting one's ancestry'.
15. Aspects of customary 'humanitarian law' among Somalis are captured by the expression *bir ma geydo*, which literally means 'not hurt by iron' but can more loosely be translated as 'spared from the spear'. According to these norms, women, children, the elderly, traditional authorities and messengers between parties in conflict would be exempt from violence. Activities like rape or the mutilation of the dead body would be considered improper.
16. It is noteworthy that this tradition is practised with the consent of the girl(s) 'presented' as *godob reeb*. A young woman can also refuse this kind of arrangement.

to around 1980). Politics in the centre as well as at the peripheries was strongly influenced by the network logic existing among Somali pastoral nomads and agro-pastoralists. Among most Somalis, belonging was not constituted through land, but through patrilineal descent.[17] Clan identity in combination with cross-cutting ties provided for physical security and political and military mobilization. Conceptions of fixed and bounded territory were, if relevant at all, only of secondary importance in this context.

CHANGING NOTIONS OF TERRITORIALITY AND RELEVANCE OF CLAN BOUNDARIES

Before the Civil War (Pre-1988)

The dynamics of deterritorialization and reterritorialization discussed in this chapter became most pronounced in the wake of civil war from the late 1980s onward. Yet it is important to clarify that, even before that time, changes in the resource base of the society led to transformations concerning territoriality, including property rights and citizenship. I have mentioned above that during the colonial period the Somali economy was transformed from serving mainly subsistence ends to also producing for the market, including exports, involving the livestock sector in the north as well as the plantations in the south. This transformation continued in the 1970s and 1980s. De Waal (1996: n.p.) found that '[i]n the early 1980s, livestock exports through Berbera [the main port in the north] provided over 75 per cent of Somalia's recorded foreign currency income' and that '[t]he export-orientation of the trade entailed very careful management of herds as they moved north towards Berbera. An important result of this was the creation of pastoral enclosures to provide feed for the herds. In many areas, most of the best pastureland is now privately owned' (ibid.).

However, it was not only export trade that resulted in claims to land and the establishment of property regimes in an area that previously was public freehold and characterized by ad hoc arrangements for use between lo-cal groups. Inter-clan competition and nepotism, unfolding in post-colonial Somalia particularly in the later years of the Barre dictatorship, led to the es-tablishment of grazing enclosures and exclusive land claims (around newly built wells, for example) by groups in favour with the regime. This dimin-ished the viability of pastoral nomadism for many, who then became paid

---

17. While belonging to a family (*u dhashay*) is the dominant mode of belonging, the concept of belonging to a place (*ku dhashay*) also exists. Barnes (2006) emphasizes that the two concepts can be seen as complementary rather than exclusive modes of belonging. In the context of (forced) migration within Somalia but also abroad (mainly from 1988 onwards), the concept of *ku dhaqmay* ('getting used to') gained significance, capturing the adjustment to a new place of (mainly urban) settlement.

herders, moved to the cities, or ended up in refugee camps. These socio-economic transformations were fostered also by the disastrous drought that hit mainly northern and central Somalia in 1974–5. Towards the end of it, more than half a million nomads from within the Somali Republic, but also from the neighbouring Somali territories in Ethiopia, had taken shelter in refugee camps in the country. The Somali government took the opportunity to combine drought relief with a sedentarization campaign. Thousands of nomads were settled in newly established agricultural and fishery coopera-tives in the south and along the Somali coast.[18] Finally, when the Ogaden war (1977–8) between Somalia and Ethiopia ended in Somali defeat, hun-dreds of thousands of Somalis from Ethiopia fled to Somalia. Again, the state had to appropriate land, particularly in the fertile areas in the south and around urban settlements and some farming areas in the north, to resettle these refugees (Cassanelli, 1997: 71).

A further decisive development was the land reform initiated by the Somali government in 1975. The land tenure law coming into force that year declared that 'all land was state property, in effect nationalizing all holdings. This concept, that the land belonged to the state, was later incorpo-rated in the 1979 Constitution' (Whitaker, 1982: 143). Accordingly, arable land could be possessed only through holding concessions issued by the Ministry of Agriculture, which imposed statutory limits on the size and the transfer of holdings. Officially, 'the law's basic intent ... was to change tra-ditional landholdings into a system of leaseholds' (ibid.). In fact, however, it served to further marginalize already underprivileged agro-pastoralists and farmers while providing elites close to the government with a chance to register land titles and to gain control (at least nominally) over much of Somalia's fertile land (Cassanelli, 1997: 72). Menkhaus (2003a: 147) stressed that '[i]n many instances, villagers were transformed from indepen-dent smallholders to sharecroppers or landless wage labourers for absentee landlords in Mogadishu, some of whom arrived to survey their new holdings with the backing of armed police or soldiers'. Creating property rights for supporters of the regime in the arable south, but also with regard to pastures, wells and farmlands in parts of the north, was a central means of staying in power for President Siyaad Barre for more than 20 years (Cassanelli, 2003: 22). The 1980s saw hyperinflation, the decline in overseas markets for Somali livestock, the return of thousands of Somali oil workers from the Gulf states and — related to that and to the changes in the pastoral-nomadic economy — massive urbanization (the population of Mogadishu rose from 50,000 in 1960 to half a million in the mid-1980s). Urbanization created an increased demand for food, including vegetables and fruit. In combination, these factors prompted an unprecedented land rush toward the end of the Barre regime (Cassanelli, 1997: 71–2).

---

18. The Ethiopian government at that time reacted in a similar way, seeking to settle and therefore control Somalis in the Ogaden region (Korf et al., 2015: 892).

During the Period of Rupture (from 1988 onwards)

In the late 1980s, the Somali state descended into chaos. President Barre lost his grip on power until, shortly before his fall in January 1991, he was being mocked as 'mayor of Mogadishu'. Several clan-based guerrilla movements sprang up under the leadership of warlords, all of whom were members of the military, political and business elite. Initially, they were united in their aim to topple the dictator. But once Barre had fled the capital,[19] these movements and their leaders started to fight each other, competing over power and resources. In southern Somalia, the struggle for land that had begun in the 1970s continued. The guerrillas, particularly the Hawiye-dominated United Somali Congress (USC), chased out members of the former state elite close to Barre, most of whom were Daarood (Kapteijns, 2013). They took over the land that the latter had secured through the land reform. The USC fighters presented themselves as liberators, but for local farmers and agro-pastoralists, the guerrillas were just a new group of oppressors. The situation worsened when periodic drought, in combination with the devastation caused by multiple armed bands who repeatedly plundered the farmland and local storage facilities as they passed through, led to famine in southern Somalia. Between the end of 1991 and early 1993, some 300,000 Somalis died from hunger and related diseases. The bulk of the victims were farmers and agro-pastoralists inhabiting the most fertile zone of the country. Humanitarian aid was hijacked by the militias from the pastoral-nomadic groups and international NGOs were forced to pay 'protectors' (Cassanelli, 1997: 68; De Waal, 1997: 163–73).

This humanitarian disaster prompted an international military intervention led by the United Nations (UN) and the USA in Somalia at the end of 1992, but this intervention did not stop the fight for power and resources. It actually fuelled it. It established warlord militias as security providers and awarded warlords additional political capital as the main discussion partners at the various Somali 'peace conferences'. Moreover, in some areas, the 'liberators' sought to legitimate their claims to land and control over local people by marrying into local communities and gaining central positions in district councils (Cassanelli, 1997: 73; De Waal, 1996). These councils were established by the UN to foster 'bottom-up' reconstruction, which, however, faltered with the withdrawal of the UN forces in 1995.[20]

---

19. Barre formed his own militia, called the Somali National Front, which fought for his return to power until he finally left Somalia for Nigerian exile, where he died in 1994.
20. The 'peacekeepers' under US command had withdrawn in 1994, after 18 American soldiers were killed in Mogadishu while pursuing the warlord Maxamed Faarax Caydiid in October 1993. In the same operation, hundreds of Somalis — mostly civilians — were killed by the indiscriminate use of force on all sides. The UN 'blue helmets' took many more casualties in 1993–4 and eventually gave up on Somalia.

In the 1990s, control over internal resources (farmland and its products, and slave-like workers belonging to marginalized populations)[21] and economic nodal points (harbours, airports and roads) — in combination with access (as strongmen or gatekeepers) to external resources like aid and political recognition — drove the war economy of Somalia (Bakonyi, 2011; Besteman and Cassanelli, 2003).[22] Generally, violence and state weakness heighten territorial politics (Sjögren, 2015). In Somalia, fighting continued the process by which members of dominant descent groups (some of which, like Hawiye, had been marginalized themselves by the previous dictatorship) sought to gain power and resources, expanding their areas of influence. Cassanelli (1997: 74) underlines that '[t]he process of "pastoral" expansion is a deeply rooted pattern in Somali history, and . . . the events of the recent war are only the latest manifestation of this territorial imperative'. In my view, the dynamics of deterritorialization and reterritorialization in Somalia from 1991 onwards go much beyond the historically established pattern. Many more people had to flee and the re-definition of territory was much more comprehensive and lasting than had been the case in the past. Traditional coping mechanisms collapsed in the face of this enormous violence and disaster.

Territory always has identity-related dimensions (Verweijen and Vlassenroot, 2015: 193). All over Somalia in the course of the civil war, the convergence between descent groups and territory grew stronger. People had to flee their 'clan home' areas (*degaan*) which provided physical security. Many urban dwellers ended up in the countryside, in places they had never seen before. They had to adapt and, eventually, they and their relatives who had fled abroad started to invest in these places. For militias and warlords, too, controlling strategically important locations was a prerequisite for gaining political recognition as important players by outsiders and profiting from the war economy. The relationship between patrilineal descent groups and territories became more permanent, stable and exclusive during the protracted and intense Somali conflict, also as a result of the external approaches to stabilize the country, as will be outlined below. This new territorial impetus manifested itself in numerous 'mini states' and regional administrations that have emerged within collapsed Somalia since 1991.

NEW STATE FORMATIONS WITHIN COLLAPSED SOMALIA

The new political entities discussed in this section exhibit a minimum of territorial control and internal administration based on local or regional

---

21. Schlee (2008: 113) correctly points out that not only land but also the underprivileged farmers working on it were part of the resources fought over between various militias.
22. A report published by UN-Habitat (2008: 26–7), for instance, claimed that Kismaayo seaport yielded an income of over US$ 400,000 per month, and checkpoints in Afgooye produced some US$ 4.3 million per year as income for local militias.

government institutions and security forces. The first state-like entity that was set up in collapsed Somalia was the Republic of Somaliland in north-western Somalia in 1991. It has declared itself an independent state, but lacks international recognition. Its territory is the land that had been demar-cated and governed as a protectorate by the British until 1960. Its inhabitants belonged to different clan families, but were bound together by a common history, common experiences, friendship and intermarriage. These factors provided a huge potential for cross-cutting ties among the different clans in the region. However, Somaliland's political formation from 1991 onward was driven in the main by members of the Isaaq clan family (consisting of various clans),[23] who constituted the majority of the population in the region. Members of other descent groups, such as the Gadabuursi and Ciise in the west or the Warsangeli and Dhulbahante in the east of Somaliland, were the numerical minority in the northwest, but they belonged to clan families — Dir and Daarood — that were widely connected throughout Somalia (and beyond). They partly opposed the secession of Somaliland from Somalia in 1991, but finally accepted it for the sake of peace. To date, Somaliland does not enjoy international recognition, and political ten-sions still exist, particularly in the east of the secessionist republic (Hoehne, 2015).

Puntland was set up in northeastern Somalia in 1998. It mimicked So-maliland's state-formation process in many regards (Hoehne, 2009). The decisive difference between the two state-like entities, however, was that from the beginning Puntland was meant to be a descent-based entity. Its con-stituency was defined as descendants of a common ancestor named Harti. Majeerteen, Dhulbahante and Warsangeli were the biggest and therefore po-litically most influential groups within the Harti clan coalition.[24] Power in the government, with its seat in Garoowe, was divided to reflect proportional clan size/strength. The Harti clans are to some degree related through in-termarriage. However, the different colonial heritages (the Dhulbahante and Warsangeli were part of the British protectorate, whereas the Majeerteen were under Italian suzerainty) created some 'cultural' distance between these groups; additionally, rivalry between the 'brothers', with Majeerteen as the 'eldest' (according to genealogical 'fiction') demanding most power and in-fluence in the new administration, created occasional rifts among Puntland's constituencies. Still, a strong basis for political cohesion in Puntland after 1998 was common political orientation. The Harti had established an au-tonomous regional administration, but their final aim was the establishment

---

23. Members of other clans were of course involved and at times played important roles. Between 2002 and 2010, the President of Somaliland was a member of the Dir/Gadabuursi group. However, he and other non-Isaaq in Somaliland politics were always surrounded by powerful Isaaq actors.

24. Power in the Somali setting is first a function of man-power (how many armed men can a group mobilize) and, second, a function of economic and other resources.

of a united Somalia. This brought them into conflict with Somaliland over its secession and led to the contestation of the Dhulbahante and Warsangeli territories between Somaliland and Puntland.

New political entities also came into existence in central and southern Somalia. The Raxanweyn Resistance Army (RRA) was founded in the mid-1990s as an armed movement of the previously underprivileged and oppressed agro-pastoralists in the regions Baay and Bakool. The RRA's main campaign was directed against the Hawiye warlord militias who had plundered their fertile lands from 1991 onwards. The RRA gained control over the regions Baay and Bakool and, backed by Ethiopia, established its own regional administration there in 1998. In the context of its programme to foster district administrations, the UN was sympathetic towards the RRA's emergent authority. In Baay and Bakool, the mode of belonging to a territory prevalent among Somali agro-pastoralists had been translated into a new political structure. People who had cooperated as farmers in these regions now worked together in their own state-like administration in self-defence against militias from other clan families. But when the RRA leadership disagreed about supporting or opposing the Transitional National Government (TNG) that was set up in Djibouti in 2000, fighting broke out in the Baay and Bakool regions, and the regional administration fell apart (Bakonyi, 2013). The cross-cutting ties existing among the various members of the Raxanweyn clan family (mentioned above with reference to Helander) did not prevent the fighting. In 2014, the Southwest State of Somalia was established as a regional administration whose core is the Raxanweyn clan plus some others, and which covers the regions Baay, Bakool and Lower Shabelle (Mosley, 2015: 10).

Two other state-like entities that claim territorial control and exhibit some (rudimentary) administration are Galmudug and Jubbaland. Galmudug was created in 2006; in the north it borders Puntland, and it is dominated by various Hawiye clans. Jubbaland is in the far south of Somalia, bordering Kenya. It existed as a warlord fiefdom between 1998 and 1999, was partly reestablished as Azania in 2010, but then reassumed the name of Jubbaland. Its political centre is the port town of Kismaayo, and its core constituency is made up of Hawiye, Dir and Daarood clans (see Map 3 above).

Within several of these entities, new fissions or attempts to 'secede' have occurred in recent years. The Warsangeli in the borderlands between Somaliland and Puntland established the short-lived Maakhir state between 2007 and 2009. Just south of the Warsangeli, the Dhulbahante set up the Sool, Sanaag and Cayn (SSC) administration in 2009. This was succeeded by the Khaatumo State of Somalia, founded in the Dhulbahante territories in January 2012. Some diaspora hardliners belonging to the Gadabuursi clan declared the 'Awdal Republic' in the far west of Somaliland in 2009. Also in Puntland, east of Bosaso, the Siwaqroon lineage of the Majeerteen clan sought briefly to create its own fiefdom called Ras Caseyr state (Mohamed Beerdhige, 2012). Finally, the 'state' called Ximan iyo Xeeb was carved out of southern Galmudug around the coastal town Hobiyo, dominated by Hawiye/Habar Gedir/Saleebaan (see Map 2 above).

It is notable that most of these political projects are driven by a dominant agnatic group. Thus, in a simple way one could speak of processes of segmentary mini-state formation, which of course involved a significant transnational aspect, since often diasporic actors of a particular patrilineal descent group lobbied for and financially supported the emerging politico-territorial entities.[25] However, some of these entities were officially based on political visions beyond clan interest. Somaliland entertained the vision of becoming an independent state within the borders of the former British Protectorate. This included non-Isaaq. Puntland was a clan-based state but its supporters had the vision of re-establishing Somalia as a federal state. The polity is therefore — at least theoretically — inclusive in orientation. Still, in general, 'clan citizenship' is a key factor defining these administrations.[26]

Their economies are based on three pillars: trade, aid and remittances. Somaliland and Puntland export considerable numbers of livestock from the wider region through their ports of Berbera and Bosaso, respectively, to the Arab Peninsula. They import goods (mainly from Asia and Arabia) for local consumption, but also for markets in southern Somalia and Ethiopia. Jubbaland and Southwest State in southern Somalia also rely heavily on trade. Additionally, all mini-states and regional administrations are very dependent on humanitarian aid and investments from the diaspora. The total volume of humanitarian aid provided to Somalia in 2015 was US\$ 611,067,176.[27] The estimated annual total of remittances to Somalia is US\$ 1.3 billion.[28] Different regions profit differently from aid and remittances, and as a rule these resources concentrate in urban settings rather than the countryside. Remittance money is sent, mostly in small amounts of US\$ 50–200, by members of the Somali diaspora. It supports family survival and the education of children, but also helps to establish hotels, restaurants, shopping malls, universities and commercial companies (Lindley, 2010). It therefore creates property, legitimated by local clan and/or state-like authorities. Related to that, real estate prices went up steeply over the past few years in booming places like Hargeysa, Garoowe and Mogadishu, but also in the more peripheral outliers like Laascaanood, Gaalkacyo or Baydhabo (UN

---

25. Drawing on the concept of 'long-distance nationalism' (Glick Schiller, 2005) one could speak of 'long-distance clannism' here.
26. Interestingly, the Islamist forces in Somalia that engaged in the civil war only once set up a lasting regional administration, which centred on the town of Luuq in southwestern Somalia, around 1994. It was bombarded by the Ethiopian air force in 1996. Al Shabaab set up many local administrations but never aimed at establishing 'clan state borders' within Somalia. On the contrary, it rejected clannism, federalism and any of the above mentioned 'mini states'. Its vision was based on Somali nationalism and the community of Muslims (Arabic: umma).
27. https://fts.unocha.org/reports/daily/ocha_R10c_C193_Y2015_asof___1603130231.pdf
28. https://www.gov.uk/government/uploads/system/uploads/attachment_data/file/418690/15-03-11_UK-Somalia_Remittance_Factsheet.pdf

Habitat, 2008: 114). In Somali, this new phenomenon of diaspora cum local investment can be captured by the term *dhis degaankaaga* ('build your clan homeland') (Hoehne and Ibrahim, 2014: 73) and it of course also changes general notions of territoriality. The clan-based citizens of the mini-states and their diasporas invest locally and make land valuable. Territorial control over people and resources has therefore become very relevant for the political entities which have popped up all over collapsed Somalia in the past two decades. Many locals across the country (and their relatives abroad) now have a much greater stake in non-movable property and in land than was the case before 1990, when most private property was concentrated in the hands of elites based in the few urban centres like Mogadishu or Hargeysa.[29]

In the formation of these state-like entities, factors which went beyond local considerations of survival and security were also important, notably various international policies toward stateless Somalia. After the humanitarian intervention in Somalia by UN and US forces in the early 1990s had failed to bring about a new central state, the international community abandoned Somalia for a while. Subsequently, the so-called building-block approach was advocated, which involved fostering the establishment of regional administrations such as Somaliland and Puntland as a way to stabilize collapsed Somalia. This approach was under discussion around the time that Puntland was created (August 1998) and also informed the establishment of the RRA administration in the regions Baay and Bakool, and the formation of Jubbaland in southern Somalia in the late 1990s. It was submitted by Ethiopia to the Intergovernmental Authority on Development (IGAD) in late 1998 (Bryden, 1999: 134).

At a peace conference for Somalia in Kenya (2002–5), the delegates agreed on a federal structure for the Somali state. The outcome was the establishment of the Transitional Federal Government (TFG). Puntland and — in the view of the conference participants — Somaliland qualified as first federal states, which could be followed by others.[30] The federal arrangement for Somalia was developed further by the provisional constitution of Somalia that came into force in 2012. However, its provisions (particularly Article 49) concerning the formation of federal states are ambiguous, which has led to political conflict between the central government and various (emerging) regional administrations in recent years (Mosley, 2015: 9). Some years ago, Menkhaus cautioned that 'in the building-block scenario each federal state will be viewed locally as the "seat" for a particular clan; in the zero-sum

---

29. Ibrahim (2010) presents a very insightful study on the relationship between economic investments and peace and state building in Hargeysa.

30. Needless to say, the supporters of Somaliland saw this differently. The government in Hargeysa refused to participate in the conference and did not recognize the TFG as having any authority over the 'independent state' of Somaliland. In 2012, a dialogue between representatives of Somalia and Somaliland was agreed upon at a donor meeting in London. So far, this dialogue has not yet brought the two sides closer together.

game of political representation, there will be little tolerance for competing claims of other clans resident in the region' (Menkhaus, 2003b quoted in UN Habitat, 2008: 29). He predicted that this would lead to armed conflict and splintering of groups along patrilineal descent lines, and the multiplication of new states (ibid.).

Another boost to territorial politics, including conflict over territory, was given by the US administration in September 2010, when Jonny Carson, then the Assistant Secretary for African Affairs in Washington, excited many Somalis with his statement that the US would follow a 'two-track approach' to Somalia in the future to help the country and to combat terrorism. The first track involved supporting the TFG, which had been reformed at a conference in Djibouti in 2009 and now also included 'moderate' Islamists. The second track entailed engagement with Somaliland and Puntland, but also with local authorities in South-Central in order to end two decades of instability and violence in Somalia (Mwaura, 2010).[31] This spurred the establishment of administrations like the SSC, followed by the Khaatumo State of Somalia, as outlined in the following section. The gestation of these entities provides an ethnographic example of the dynamics of territorialization on the ground. It also illustrates what the emergence of mini-states and regional administrations in Somalia means for the time-honoured social institution of cross-cutting ties among Somalis.

THE STATE LOGIC AT WORK: DEFENDING LAND AND RESOURCES, AND FORGING EXCLUSIVE IDENTITIES

The Dhulbahante and their clan homeland (today's regions of Sool, Sanaag and Cayn or southern Togdheer) are split between Somaliland and Puntland (see Map 2 above). They were part of the British Protectorate from which Somaliland 'inherited' its borders in 1991. They are also part of the Harti clan coalition, which provides the genealogical basis of Puntland. Until the early 2000s, however, the Dhulbahante territory was not controlled by any of the 'state-like' powers in the region. Local governance was exercised mainly by traditional authorities. Things changed when the armies of Somaliland and Puntland began to fight over control of the Dhulbahante territory from early 2004 onward. In October 2007, Somaliland ousted the army of Puntland from Laascaanood, the capital of Sool region and the most important town of the clan. Since then it has controlled much of the Dhulbahante homeland (Hoehne, 2009, 2015).

---

31. This formalized an already existing 'twin-track' approach that members of the international community had followed earlier, engaging with various regional administrations and governments 'as they come along and go', while still trying to push for a central-state solution (UN Habitat, 2008: 22).

In reaction to the occupation of their territory by the Somaliland army, 14 of the 15 highest-ranking traditional authorities of the Dhulbahante clan at that time held a meeting (*shir*) in Boocame, a small town in the southeast of the Sool region. They released a declaration on 22 November 2007, which stated, among other things:

> 2. We warn that administration ['Somaliland'] against aggression, the presence [of its troops] and the capture of our territory.
> 3. We only recognize clan borders that have always existed and the regional jurisdictions of the last Somali Government [1969–91].
> 4. We warn about war and more bloodshed among neighbours that will lead to long-lasting conflict.
> 5. *There were links among these people* [meaning Isaaq and Dhulbahante] *in terms of culture, shared territory and blood, which should have been respected but such ties were broken by the invasion of the Hargeisa administration.*
> (italics added)[32]

On a visit in Buuhoodle in 2004, I heard Dhulbahante elders — who politically were strongly pro-Puntland — describe their Isaaq neighbours thus: '*Waa isku degaan, waa isku dhaqan; waanu is dhalnay*' ('We live in the same (shared) clan homeland, we have the same culture; we gave birth to each other').[33] They recognized the social and cultural affinity between themselves and the Isaaq. But they also stressed that, politically, the Dhulbahante reject the break-up of Somalia and even more, perhaps, the establishment of Isaaq hegemony over them and their territory. Later, the chairman of the elders mentioned: 'If the people in Hargeysa [meaning the Isaaq] would drop the issue of secession, the Dhulbahante and Isaaq would be brothers'.[34] This showed a recognition of the importance of cross-cutting ties. It also showed, however, their sensitivity towards territorial control (as did the Boocame declaration cited above). The Dhulbahante were increasingly worried about Isaaq wanting their land and resources.

The relevance of cross-cutting ties decreased as tensions between Isaaq and Dhulbahante increased from the mid-2000s onward. In 2009, Dhulbahante activists supported by the diaspora established the SSC, the main aim of which was to 'liberate' their clan homeland from what they saw as Somaliland (meaning: Isaaq) military occupation. They were disappointed by the lack of military engagement on the side of the Puntland administration to re-conquer Laascaanood after Somaliland's army had taken it in October 2007. They saw this as a betrayal of *Hartiniimo* (Harti-solidarity). One of the leading figures within the SSC explained: 'Somaliland wants the land,

---

32. Online: http://markacadey.banadir24.com/main/news.php?readmore=2405 (accessed 18 January 2011). Note that this declaration was originally written in Somali. It was translated by the staff of GaroweOnline.com. The English transliteration is theirs.
33. Interview with Maxamuud Xaaji Cumar Camey and some others, Buuhoodle, 12 March 2004.
34. Ibid.

not the people; Puntland wants the people, not the land. We [the SSC] want to work for the development of our people and our land'.[35] This statement indicates a fundamental shift in the structure of political organization. It outlines the motivation of the local actors to establish territorial control in order to manage local citizens and the resources available, including humanitarian aid.[36] It also makes it quite obvious that some changes have been happening regarding the Dhulbahante's conception of their clan and the social ties between them and the others, particularly the Isaaq to the west and the Majeerteen to the east. In 2009 they saw themselves increasingly unrelated to Isaaq, with whom in earlier times they had been intensively connected through marriage, neighbourhood and personal friendships. They simultaneously distanced themselves from Puntland, particularly from the Majeerteen leadership (despite common ancestry and the joint political project to rebuild Somalia), because the latter did not organize the recapture of Laascaanood, and seemed to be indifferent to *Hartiniimo*.

The change of perspective of many Dhulbahante regarding territory and cross-cutting ties in the region was buttressed by military confrontations and experiences of violence in the region (mini-ruptures, so to speak). Between the end of 2009 and mid-2010, SSC militias and Somaliland forces engaged in skirmishes in the area southeast of Burco and around Buuhoodle, which was the SSC's core territory. Then a decisive conflict escalated over the control of a grazing reserve in Kalshaale (see Map 4). Kalshaale serves as a buffer zone between Dhulbahante and Isaaq/Habar Jeclo. In mid-October 2010 tensions between the groups arose when Habar Jeclo men started building some cisterns (*berkedo*) in the area. This was not the first time Habar Jeclo had engaged in building something there. Previously the Dhulbahante, too, had engaged in the construction of a mosque in another part of these contested clan borderlands.[37] The problem was that, in the pastoral-nomadic setting in which resources usually have to be shared among locals including neighbours from different clans, building a house, a mosque or a cistern in a previously uninhabited place stakes a claim to that place. In this way, descent groups can expand and secure important resources (grazing and wells) for themselves. In other areas of (northern) Somalia, this *berked*-driven villagization has been identified as a problem, as it 'continues to absorb sizable portions of the land at the expense of the communal grazing fields' (UN Habitat, 2008: 115). An additional factor in the Kalshaale incident was that the establishment of cisterns by Habar Jeclo carried the connotation of 'state

---

35. Telephone interview with Saleebaan Ciise Axmed Xagla Toosiye, 27 January 2011.
36. There are speculations that oil can be found in Dhulbahante territory, near Xudun. Explorations are ongoing, but are frequently interrupted by armed clashes between Somaliland troops and local militias. The government in Hargeysa issues concessions to foreign companies and hopes to profit from these if oil is found. Locals sabotage these efforts and claim potential oil resources as theirs.
37. Interview with Axmed Ciige, Burco, 19 March 2012.

Map 4. Area of SSC Operations 2010–11, including Kalshaale

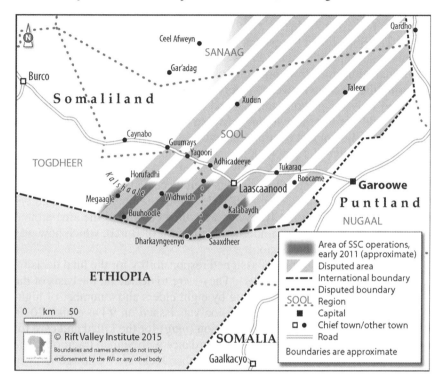

control'. In June 2010, Axmed Siilaanyo, a Habar Jeclo man, had been elected president of Somaliland. Subsequently, many Dhulbahante became concerned about the potential overlap between clan and state expansion at their expense. In order to prevent further conflict, Dhulbahante from Buu-hoodle asked the Habar Jeclo groups involved to stop building cisterns in Kalshaale in mid-October 2010. The Habar Jeclo refused.

The elders of both sides, however, agreed to talk about the issue after Ramadan. The period of Ramadan was a busy time, as people went on Hajj and herders and traders were involved in selling and shipping goats to Saudi Arabia for the celebrations after the fasting month. Shortly before the end of Ramadan, one elderly man from Dhulbahante, who was passing by Kalshaale with his animals on his way to the port of Berbera, was shot dead by Habar Jeclo. The local nomads allegedly accused him of being one of those Dhulbahante who wanted to prevent them from building their cisterns.[38] On 15 November 2010, a group of Dhulbahante fired on a group

---

38. Interview with Axmed Daakir, Laascaanood, 11 December 2010; interview with Siciid Xaaji Nuur, Hargeysa, 27 February 2011.

of Habar Jeclo — who were praying the Eid prayer after Ramadan when the attack took place — in the area of Kalshaale, killing seven and wounding six men. Three Dhulbahante were killed and three others wounded in the attack. The Somaliland troops that were already in the vicinity went straight to Kalshaale to position themselves between the two warring factions. The traditional authorities from both groups rushed to the conflict site.

During the meeting between elders the Dhulbahante argued that the place was used only for grazing animals and should not become a place where people build permanent dwellings. Moreover, after the heavy fighting the Dhulbahante did not feel comfortable living with the Habar Jeclo in the area. They also felt that the Habar Jeclo, who could rely on support from the Somaliland army and were 'close to President Siilaanyo', were in a stronger position and would, once their cisterns were accepted, expand further; this had happened in the past. The Kalshaale conflict reminded many Dhulbahante of the fact that some 100 years ago, they controlled the area around Caynabo with its numerous important wells, east of Burco, which now was in the hands of the Habar Jeclo.

The Somaliland government assigned responsibility for the final decision to a group of nine religious leaders. They were to decide on the basis of the shari'a. The sheikhs were supported by eight elders and a number of high-ranking traditional leaders. The decision was issued on 9 December 2010. It ordered both sides to pay compensation (*mag*) for the killed and care for the wounded until they recovered, in accordance with Somali traditions. The core of the decision, however, was that Habar Jeclo were allowed to keep their three cisterns in the Kalshaale area, while Dhulbahante were allowed to build three cisterns too. Beyond that, further constructions in the area were declared illegal and both sides should jointly use the place. This decision was accepted by the Habar Jeclo and rejected by the Dhulbahante.[39] The members of the Dhulbahante delegation from Buuhoodle and from other parts of the clan territory retreated in anger.[40] The mediation had failed; tensions in the area remained very high.

On 9 January 2011, President Axmed Siilaanyo declared that the mediators had done good work, all clan militias should leave the area, and Kalshaale was for the time being a military zone controlled by the Somaliland national army.[41] This decision was seen by Dhulbahante as a further step in the wrong direction, potentially cementing Somaliland state control, which converged with Habar Jeclo control over the land and its resources. They mobilized against what they now perceived as illegal occupation of their territory,

39. Interview with Maxamed Qoryooley, Laascaanood, 12 December 2010; Maakhir.net, 9 December 2010: Go'aan Laga Soo Saaray Nabadayntii Kalshaale Online: http://maakhir. net/2010/wararka/3203-goaan-laga-soo-saaray-nabadayntii-kalshaale.html
40. Interview with Maxamed Qoryooley, Laascaanood, 12 December 2010.
41. Boocame Media, 9 January 2011: Axmed Maxamed Siilaanyo oo Go'aan Ka soo saaray Arinta Kalshaale. Online: http://www.boocame.com/?p=8578

similar to the situation in Laascaanood from 2007 onward. Many ordinary Dhulbahante saw themselves as having nowhere to go, squeezed between the powerful Isaaq, supported by the Somaliland army, to the west and the north, and the Ethiopian border to the south.[42] Here it is important to note that in the wake of the reignited insurgency of the Ogaden National Liberation Movement (ONLF) in eastern Ethiopia in 2007, the government in Addis Ababa had tightened control of the border between Ethiopia and Somaliland, which runs south of Laascaanood and exactly through Buuhoodle, a town divided into Ethiopian and Somali sections (Hagmann, 2014).

In this situation, the SSC, which up to this point had avoided open involvement, took over the coordination of the Dhulbahante armed resistance. On 30 January 2011, the first clashes between Dhulabahante/SSC units and Somaliland troops happened around Hagoogane, a village near Kalshaale. On 31 January there were anti-Somaliland demonstrations in Laascaanood. On 7 February, SSC and Somaliland troops engaged in a battle in the Kalshaale area that left several dozen people dead and up to 100 wounded on all sides.[43] The intensity and length of this fighting indicated, first, that the Dhulbahante diaspora may have systematically invested in upgrading the military capacity of the SSC; and, second, that Dhulbahante lineages from the area of Buuhoodle had integrated the heavy weapons under their control into the SSC arsenal, at least temporarily, and sent their men to fight with the SSC. In the following weeks, more fighting occurred around Buuhoodle. In total, more than 100 people died.[44] An economic effect of the fighting was that the routes of livestock trade changed and animals owned by Daarood from Region 5 in Ethiopia and the Buuhoodle area were no longer brought to the port of Berbera in Somaliland (which had better facilities), but to the port of Bosaso in Puntland to be exported.

The situation in the Kalshaale area has calmed down since mid-2012. A local politician eventually brokered a separate peace between the Dhulbahante in the area and the administration in Hargeysa, and the Somaliland forces left the Dhulbahante land between Buuhoodle and Kalshaale. Simultaneously, however, Dhulbahante set up a new regional administration called Khaatumo State of Somalia. It was founded in Taleex in January 2012 and claimed to represent the Dhulbahante in addressing the government in Mogadishu and the international community. For two years Khatuumo forces, equipped with diaspora money, fought Somaliland and Puntland forces in the region and established a rudimentary administration in the Dhulbahante territories except Laascaanood and other places along the tarmac road to Burco that were

---

42. Informal talks with various people in Laascaanood in December 2010.
43. SRCS Lasanod Branch, 9 February 2011: Situational analysis report on the Kalshaale hostilities; SomalilandPress, Somaliland: Fighting erupts in Kalshale between troops and clan militia. Online: http://somalilandpress.com/somaliland-fighting-erupts-in-kalshale-between-troops-and-clan-militia-20008
44. Exact numbers are difficult to establish in this case.

under the control of the Somaliland army (see Map 4 above). In Taleex, and later in Buuhoodle, the Khaatumo administration built provisional airports that were supposed to facilitate political contact with Mogadishu and diplomatic relations abroad, as well as the direct delivery of aid. But the administration did not succeed in 'liberating' the Dhulbahante clan homeland. Additionally, it was weakened by internal power struggles toward the end of 2014. In 2016, the Khaatumo state was largely reduced to a nominal existence: much diaspora support was withdrawn and there were scarcely any resources to build the mini-state.

Still, when visiting Buuhoodle in February 2015, I passed an official checkpoint with a signboard announcing my entry into the Khaatumo State of Somalia. This was a clear territorial marker, which, like flags or murals elsewhere, establishes political identity and underlines (often contested) claims to territorial control (Sikor and Lund, 2009: 14). In Buuhoodle I met numerous 'state officials' who sought to convince me that when planning my next visit I should apply for a visa with the Khaatumo representative in Nairobi and then fly in directly from there. Again, this is a clear strategy of establishing claims over people and resources, in line with forming a (regional) state. Shortly after I had spoken to Khaatumo officials in town, I was approached by members of the Puntland armed forces: they insisted that Buuhoodle was under their control and I was supposed to contact Garoowe if I wished to come again. All of these actors were locals from various closely related Dhulbahante lineages. Despite their internal political differences, they were united in their rejection of any influence from the Somaliland side.

In this way, inter-clan conflict became politicized and led to the rejection of any official contact with the government in Hargeysa. Yet, one has to consider the dialectical aspects of this matter. It was the hegemonic claim of the Somaliland government (that the Dhulbahante lands were part of Somaliland) that charged the inter-clan relations in the area (between Dhulbahante and Isaaq) with huge political significance. Both factors influenced locally existing cross-cutting ties and strained them, exemplified by the rise in the divorce rate between Dhulbahante around Buuhoodle and Isaaq from south of Burco (who traditionally inter-marry) during the conflict. The following two anecdotes from Laascaanood confirm the same point of changes in sociality. In December 2010, one Dhulbahante woman whose sister was married to an Isaaq man and who was living with her children in Burco, in central Somaliland, told me: 'I do not want to visit my sister. She lives among the Isaaq. I do not like Isaaq'. I asked her if she would, at least, go to Burco and seek refuge with her sister if the security situation in Laascaanood deteriorated due to armed conflict (which at that moment was a real danger). She rejected the idea out of hand.

On another occasion, in March 2012, I gave a talk on 'Different views on trauma and transitional justice and their implications for state formation and development in northern Somalia' at the Nugaal University in Laascaanood.

In the discussion afterwards, some students and lecturers challenged some of my propositions. They demonstrated what I perceived to be exclusionist 'hardliner arguments', stressing the historical and political differences between Dhulbahante and Isaaq, and the readiness to fight for their convictions. This was fully in line with the claim of the then newly established Khaatumo administration to exclusive representation of the locals and control of the resources in the area; all people present during the discussion were strong Khaatumo supporters. My central argument in the discussion was that as long as both the supporters of Somaliland (mainly Isaaq) and their opponents (in this case, Dhulbahante) adhered to a narrow-minded vision of history and politics, no compromise was possible. This would lead to more conflict and potentially to a new civil war, which would have its epicentre in the Dhulbahante lands. I also suggested that the opinions of the youth on both sides were decisive, since young people were the demographic majority and the future leaders of their communities. Eventually, I suggested a youth exchange between students in Hargeysa and those in Laascaanood to learn more about each other's daily realities and political visions. In response to my suggestion, an elderly female student who was a mother rose to reject this idea because 'if our children go to Hargeysa, they will be massacred by Isaaq'. Most of the young people in the lecture hall supported this statement. They interpreted the relationship between them and the Isaaq in the light of the recent fighting around Kalshaale and Buuhoodle, in which many Isaaq soldiers had died or been wounded. This, in their view, would trigger revenge killings. The fact that many (older) Dhulbahante were married to Isaaq and that at the time, despite the conflict that had escalated between local militias and the Somaliland forces, Dhulbahante could reside peacefully in Hargeysa (from where I had come to give my lecture), was completely ignored. Among the locals of Laascaanood, the idea of cross-cutting ties had lost its appeal in the face of conflict over state formation in this part of Somaliland/Somalia, with potentially long-term consequences (if, for example, the younger generation would avoid going to Burco or Hargeysa for higher education or work, and rather orient itself further east or south).

CONCLUSION

Many places in Africa are 'seeing the emergence of new regimes of territorialization, including reordered states, complex transnational regimes, subnational entities, new localities and transborder formations' (Engel and Olsen, 2012: 51). The Somali case outlined in this chapter may seem just another case in point, but a number of factors make territorialization processes within Somalia stand out. First, they take place in the absence of an effective central power. This makes them somewhat more volatile than most other cases but similar, in this regard at least, to the dynamics of territorialization in parts of the Democratic Republic of Congo (DRC) (see Hoffmann, Vlassenroot and

Marchais, this issue; Raeymaekers, 2010: 576–9). A second distinguishing feature is that these processes are running counter to the 'network logic' underpinning Somali sociality, a cohesive force that until recently prevailed largely in disregard of territoriality. In contrast, the emergence of mini-states and regional administrations outlined in this chapter follows a 'state logic' that is concentrated on a strong vision of territoriality and, related to that, control over people and resources in geographically bounded space. In this regard, the current process is not simply an indicator, as Leonard and Samatar (2011: 567) have claimed, of the re-emergence of clan governance 'as one of the fundamental organizing principles for attempts at civil order'. Clan governance in the past always involved cross-cutting ties (e.g., for establishing inter-clan alliances) and was not based on firm territorial control. Nor does it demonstrate, as Cassanelli suggested (1997: 74), the usual pattern of pastoral expansion (the latter may have been true of the movements of Hawiye into southern Somalia in the 1990s, but the more recent territorialization does not fit this pattern).

What has emerged in Somalia during the extended period of rupture, particularly after 1990, is a new form of territoriality that binds descent groups more strongly to certain locations and landed resources than was previously the case in known Somali history. This is also generating a new form of belonging among many Somalis. This echoes a concern voiced by Mohamed Haji Ingiriis (2015: 70) when he mentioned that territorial rearrangements currently underway in the country may 'turn "Somali society" into a collection of mini Somali societies without any national identity [or, in my view: any idea of a "common good"].'

The dynamics outlined in this chapter contradict, to some degree, earlier ideas about Somalis as a mobile and even 'globalized nation' (preserving their national identity across state borders; see, e.g., Laitin and Samatar, 1987). Or — to describe this complex juncture more succinctly — the fact that Somalis are globalized (and involved in processes of deterritorialization characteristic of contemporary modernity) does not prevent the same Somalis from advancing on a path toward reterritorialization (and 'long distance clannism', as mentioned above, is important in this regard).

This chapter identified the following three factors as drivers of the territorialization processes: first, violence and state collapse, which triggered internal flight into previously sparsely populated clan homelands and abroad; second, diaspora formation, which is a long-term process and eventually facilitated transnational investments in clan homelands; and third, the presence of external agendas to rebuild the state and fight (or at least contain) terrorism, together with a strong dependence on humanitarian aid that was distributed according to localities and not assigned to descent groups (as some Somalis would probably have preferred).

Thus, I have shown that 'territorial sovereignty' is on the rise (Vandergeest and Peluso, 1995: 385). Friction emanates, however, from the fact that in the Somali case belonging is still predominantly defined through patrilineal descent. In segmentary lineage societies, descent does not provide for stability. Groups unite and separate according to situation and interest and, therefore, no clear-cut 'borders' between groups can be established based on descent alone. Traditions of clan exogamy, which prevailed until recently (and are still relevant, although less than in the past) also make it very difficult to delineate the borders of separate clans. It is telling, in this regard, that officials of Khaatumo state (upon my request) never could clarify where the boundaries of their state lay.

Ongoing conflicts in parts of Somalia can be interpreted as vernacular attempts to define a new political order that allows for territorial sovereignty and is therefore more absolute and stable than an order based on social networks. In the process, Somali society is becoming more sedentary. But this is a process rife with conflicts over boundary making, which is observable with regard to recent fighting in northern Somalia (between Somaliland and Puntland, and between Khaatumo state and Somaliland) and the setting up of federal states in southern Somalia. Still, I must disagree with Mosley's conclusion (2015: 17) that '[t]he political processes and state formation projects currently under way do not represent bottom-up approaches. Rather these are decentralized approaches for managing a larger group of elite interests'. In my view, while elite interests are certainly involved, this chapter has shown that dynamics of *de*territorialization and *re*territorialization have been characteristic for Somalia for a long time, starting before the beginning of the rupture in the late 1980s. The current process of state formation is a complex mixture of internal bottom-up processes and external, partly structural factors. Its analysis must take into account interferences in the name of state building (in the 1990s) and counter-terrorism (in the 2000s), and the creative reactions of Somali actors to these, as well as the 'hardening' of state borders in the region in general, particularly between Ethiopia and Somalia (and possibly also between Kenya and Somalia) in response to protracted conflict in the Somali territories.

REFERENCES

Abdurahman, M. Abdullahi Baadiyow (2014) *The Islamic Movement in Somalia: A Study of the Islah Movement, 1950–2000*. London: Adonis and Abbey.
Appadurai, A. (1991) 'Global Ethnoscapes: Notes and Queries for a Transnational Anthropology', in Richard G. Fox (ed.) *Recapturing Anthropology: Working in the Present*, pp. 191–210. Santa Fe, NM: School of American Research Press.
Aregay, M.W. (1971) 'Southern Ethiopia and the Christian Kingdom 1508–1708, with Special Reference to the Galla Migrations and their Consequences'. Unpublished PhD thesis, SOAS, University of London.
Bakonyi, J. (2011) *Land ohne Staat: Wirtschaft und Gesellschaft im Krieg am Beispiel Somalias* [*Country without State. Economy and Society in Times of War: The Example of Somalia*]. Frankfurt am Main: Campus.
Bakonyi, J. (2013) 'Authority and Administration beyond the State: Local Governance in Southern Somalia, 1995–2006', *Journal of Eastern African Studies* 7(2): 272–90.

Barnes, C. (2006) '*U dhashay – ku dhashay* [Born to – Born in]: Genealogical and Territorial Discourse in Somali History', *Social Identities* 12(4): 487–98.

Benjamin, G. (1988) 'The Unseen Presence: A Theory of the Nation-State and its Mystifications'. Working Paper No. 91. Singapore: National University of Singapore, Department of Sociology.

Besteman, C. (1999) *Unraveling Somalia: Race, Violence and the Legacy of Slavery*. Philadelphia, PA: University of Pennsylvania Press.

Besteman, C. and L. Cassanelli (2003) 'Introduction: Politics and Production in Southern Somalia', in C. Besteman and L. Cassanelli (eds) *The Struggle for Land in Southern Somalia: The War behind the War* (2nd edn), pp. 3–12. London: HAAN.

Bryden, M. (1999) 'New Hope for Somalia? The Building Block Approach', *Review of African Political Economy* 26(79): 134–40.

Cassanelli, L.V. (1982) *The Shaping of Somali Society. Reconstructing the History of a Pastoral People, 1600–1900*. Philadelphia, PA: University of Pennsylvania Press.

Cassanelli, L. (1997) 'Somali Land Resource Issues in Historical Perspective', in W. Clarke and J. Herbst (eds) *Learning from Somalia: The Lessons of Armed Humanitarian Intervention*, pp. 67–76. Boulder, CO: Westview Press.

Cassanelli, L. (2003) 'Explaining the Somali Crisis', in C. Besteman and L. Cassanelli (eds) *The Struggle for Land in Southern Somalia: The War behind the War* (2nd edn), pp. 13–28. London: HAAN.

Compagnon, D. (1992) 'Political Decay in Somalia: From Personal Rule to Warlordism', *Refuge* 12(5): 8–13.

De Waal, A. (1996) 'Class and Power in a Stateless Somalia. A Discussion Paper'. http://justiceafrica.org/wp-content/uploads/2016/07/DeWaal_ClassandPowerinSomalia.pdf (accessed 29 March 2016).

De Waal, A. (1997) *Famine Crimes. Politics and the Disaster Relief Industry in Africa*. Oxford: James Currey.

Drysdale, J. (1964) *The Somali Dispute*. London: Pall Mall Press.

Engel, U. and G.R. Olsen (2012) 'Authority, Sovereignty and Africa's Changing Regimes of Territorialization', in S. Cornelissen and F. Cheru (eds) *Africa and International Relations in the 21st Century*, pp. 51–65. New York: Palgrave.

Farah, I., A. Hussein and J. Lind (2002) 'Degaan, Politics and War in Somalia', in J. Lind and K. Sturman (eds) *Scarcity and Surfeit: The Ecology of Africa's Conflicts*, pp. 321–56. Pretoria: Institute for Security Studies.

FitzGibbon, L. (1985) *The Evaded Duty*. London: Rex Collins.

Geshekter, C.L. (1985) 'Anti-Colonialism and Class Formation: The Eastern Horn of Africa before 1950', *International Affairs* 18(1): 1–32.

Glick Schiller, N. (2005) 'Long-Distance Nationalism', in M. Ember, C.R. Ember and I. Skoggard (eds) *Encyclopedia of Diasporas*, pp. 570–80. New York: Springer.

Gluckman, M. (1965) *Custom and Conflict in Africa* (2nd edn). Oxford: Basil Blackwell.

Gundel, J. (2002) 'The Migration–Development Nexus: Somalia Case Study', *International Migration* 40(5): 255–81.

Hagmann, T. (2014) *Talking Peace in the Ogaden: The Search for an End to Conflict in the Somali Regional State in Ethiopia*. Nairobi: Rift Valley Institute.

Hagmann, T. and J. Abbink (2013) 'Twenty Years of Revolutionary Democratic Ethiopia, 1991 to 2011', *Journal of Eastern African Studies* 5(4): 579–95.

Hagmann, T. and D. Péclard (2010) 'Negotiating Statehood: Dynamics of Power and Domination in Africa', *Development and Change* 41(4): 539–62.

Hansen, T.B. and F. Stepputat (2001) 'Introduction: States of Imagination', in T.B. Hansen and F. Stepputat (eds) *States of Imagination. Ethnographic Explorations of the Postcolonial State*, pp. 1–40. Durham, NC: Duke University Press.

Helander, B. (1997) 'Clanship, Kinship and Community among the Raxanweyn: A Model for Other Somalis?', in H.M. Adam and R. Ford (eds) *Mending Rips in the Sky: Options for Somali Communities in the 21st Century*, pp. 131–43. Lawrenceville, NJ: Red Sea Press.

Helander, B. (2003) *The Slaughtered Camel: Coping with Fictitious Descent among the Hubeer of Southern Somalia*. Uppsala: University of Uppsala Press.

Hoehne, M.V. (2009) 'Mimesis and Mimicry in Dynamics of State and Identity Formation in Northern Somalia', *Africa* 79(2): 252–81.

Hoehne, M.V. (2015) *Between Somaliland and Puntland: Marginalization, Militarization and Conflicting Political Visions*. Nairobi: Rift Valley Institute.

Hoehne, M.V. and M.H. Ibrahim (2014) 'Rebuilding Somaliland through Economic and Educational Engagement', in L. Laakso and P. Hautaniemi (eds) *Diasporas, Development and Peacemaking in the Horn of Africa*, pp. 53–76. London: Zed Books.

Hunt, J.A. (1951) *A General Survey of the Somaliland Protectorate 1944–1950*. Hargeisa: Somaliland Protectorate.

Ibrahim, M.H. (2010) 'Somaliland's Investment in Peace: Analysing the Diaspora's Economic Engagement in Peace Building'. Diaspeace Working Paper No. 4. https://jyx.jyu.fi/dspace/bitstream/handle/123456789/36878/DIASPEACE_WP4.pdf?sequence=1 (accessed 29 March 2016).

Information Service of the Somali Government (1962) *The Somali Peninsula. New Light on Imperial Motives*. Mogadishu: Information Services of the Somali Government.

Jama Mohamed (2007) 'Kinship and Contract in Somali Politics', *Africa* 77(2): 226–49.

Kapteijns, L. (2013) *Clan Cleansing in Somalia. The Ruinous Legacy of 1991*. Philadelphia, PA: University of Pennsylvania Press.

Korf, B., T. Hagmann and R. Emmenegger (2015) 'Re-spacing African Drylands: Territorialization, Sedentarization and Indigenous Commodification in the Ethiopian Pastoral Frontier', *The Journal of Peasant Studies* 42(5): 881–901.

Krohn-Hansen, C. and K.G. Nustad (2005) 'Introduction', in C. Krohn-Hansen and K.G. Nustad (eds) *State Formation: Anthropological Perspectives*, pp. 3–26. London: Pluto Press.

Laitin, D.D. and S.S. Samatar (1987) *Somalia. Nation in Search of a State*. Boulder, CO: Westview Press.

Leonard, D.K. and M.S. Samatar (2011) 'What Does the Somali Experience Teach Us about the Social Contract and the State?', *Development and Change* 42(2): 559–84.

Lewis, I.M. (1961) *A Pastoral Democracy. A Study of Pastoralism and Politics among the Northern Somali of the Horn of Africa*. Oxford: Oxford University Press.

Lewis, I.M. (1969) 'From Nomadism to Cultivation. The Expansion of Political Solidarity in Southern Somalia', in M. Douglas and P. Kaberry (eds) *Man in Africa*, pp. 59–78. London: Tavistock.

Lewis, I.M. (1994) *Blood and Bone. The Call of Kinship in Somali Society*. Lawrenceville, NJ: Red Sea Press.

Lewis, I.M. (2002) *A Modern History of the Somali: Nation and State in the Horn of Africa*. Athens, OH: Ohio University Press.

Lindley, A. (2010) *The Early Morning Phone Call. Somali Refugees' Remittances*. Oxford: Berghahn Books.

Luling, V. (2002) *Somali Sultanate. The Geledi City-State over 150 Years*. London: HAAN.

Matthies, V. (1977) *Der Grenzkonflikt Somalias mit Äthiopien und Kenia.Analyse eines zwischenstaatlichen Konflikts in der Dritten Welt* [*Somalia's Border Conflict with Ethiopia and Kenya: Analysis of an Inter-state Conflict in the Third World*]. Hamburg: Institut für Afrika-Kunde.

Menkhaus, K. (2003a) 'From Feast to Famine: Land and the State in Somalia's Lower Jubba Valley'. In C. Besteman and L. Cassanelli (eds) *The Struggle for Land in Southern Somalia: The War Behind the War*, pp. 133–53. London: HAAN.

Menkhaus, K. (2003b) 'Warlords and Landlords: Non-state Actors and Humanitarian Norms in Somalia'. Paper presented at the Conference Curbing Human Rights Violations by Armed Groups, Canada (November).

Mohamed Beerdhige (2012) 'Politics of Ethnicity and Resources in Puntland'. SomaliReport.www.somaliareport.com/index.php/post/2737/Politics_of_Ethnicity_and_Resources_in_Puntland (accessed 29 March 2016).

Mohamed Haji Ingiriis (2015) 'Politics as a Profitable Business: Patronage, Patrimony, Predata-
tion, and Primordial Power in Contemporary Somalia', *Journal of Somali Studies* 2(1–2):
67–97.

Mosley, J. (2015) 'Somalia's Federal Future: Layered Agendas, Risks and Opportunities'. London: Chatham House. Online: www.chathamhouse.org/publication/somalias-federal-future-
layered-agendas-risks-and-opportunities#sthash.m5h5bFjw.dpuf (accessed 29 March 2016).

Mwaura, P. (2010) 'U.S. Top Official Hopeful in New "Dual-track" Somalia Policy'. http://www.
garoweonline.com/english/index.php?option=com_content&view=article&id=330:us-top-
africa-diplomat-hopeful-in-new-qdual-trackq-somalia-policy&catid=55:somalia&Itemid=
79 (accessed 11 March 2011).

Prunier, G. (2010) 'Benign Neglect Versus la Grande Somalia: The Colonial Legacy and the
Post-Colonial Somali State', in M.V. Hoehne and V. Luling (eds) *Milk and Peace, Drought
and War: Somali Culture, Society and Politics*, pp. 35–49. London: Hurst.

Raeymaekers, T. (2010) 'Protection for Sale? War and the Transformation of Regulation on the
Congo–Ugandan Border', *Development and Change* 41(4): 563–87.

Sack, R.D. (1986) *Human Territoriality. Its Theory and History*. Cambridge: Cambridge University Press.

Samatar, A.I. (1992a) 'Social Classes and Economic Restructuring in Pastoral Africa: Somali
Notes', *African Studies Review* 35(1): 101–27.

Samatar, A.I. (1992b) 'Destruction of State and Society in Somalia: Beyond the Tribal Conven-
tion', *Journal of Modern African Studies* 30(4): 625–41.

Schlee, G. (1997) 'Cross-Cutting Ties and Interethnic Conflict: The Example of Gabbra Oromo
and Rendille', in K. Fukui, E. Kurimoto and M. Shigeta (eds) *Ethiopia in Broader Perspective.
Papers of the XIIIth International Conference on Ethiopian Studies*, pp. 577–96. Kyoto:
Shokado Book Sellers.

Schlee, G. (2008) *How Enemies Are Made: Towards a Theory of Ethnic and Religious Conflicts*.
New York: Berghahn.

Schlee, G. (2010) 'Territorialising Ethnicity: The Political Ecology of Pastoralism in Northern
Kenya and Southern Ethiopia'. Working Paper No. 121. Munich: Max Planck Institute for
Social Anthropology.

Sikor, T. and C. Lund (2009) 'Access and Property: A Question of Power and Authority',
Development and Change 40(1): 1–22.

Sjögren, A. (2015) 'Territorialising Identity, Authority and Conflict in Africa: An Introduction',
Journal of Contemporary African Studies 33(2): 163–70.

UN Habitat (2008) 'Land, Property and Housing in Somalia'. http://www.nrc.no/arch/_img/
9195234.pdf (accessed 29 March 2016).

Vandergeest, P. and N. Lee Peluso (1995) 'Territorialization and State Power in Thailand', *Theory
and Society* 24(3): 385–426.

Verweijen, J. and K. Vlassenroot (2015) 'Armed Mobilisation and the Nexus of Territory, Identity,
and Authority: The Contested Territorial Aspirations of the Banyamulenge in Eastern DR
Congo', *Journal of Contemporary African Studies* 33(2): 191–212.

Weber, M. (1956) *Wirtschaft und Gesellschaft, Bd. II* [*Economy and Society, Vol II*]. Cologne
and Berlin: Kiepenheuer and Witsch.

Whitaker, D.P. (1982) 'The Economy', in H.D. Nelson (ed.) *Somalia: A Country Study*, pp. 133–
78. Washington, DC: US Government Printing Office.

Yasin Mohammed Yasin (2010) 'Trans-border Political Alliance in the Horn of Africa: The Case
of the Afar-Issa Conflict', in D. Feyissa and M.V. Hoehne (eds) *Borders and Borderlands as
Resources in the Horn of Africa*, pp. 85–96. Woodbridge: James Currey.

Zoppi, M. (2015) 'Greater Somalia, the Never-ending Dream? Contested Somali Borders: The
Power of Tradition vs. the Tradition of Power', *Journal of African History, Politics and
Society* 1(1): 43–64.

10

Legal Rule and Tribal Politics: The US Army and the Taliban in Afghanistan (2001–13)

Adam Baczko

INTRODUCTION

By comparing the approaches of the US Army and the Taliban in Kunar, Afghanistan, this chapter looks at how militarized groups compete for authority by ruling over property and citizenship. After the American-led intervention in Afghanistan in 2001, entire regions remained beyond the reach of the newly installed regime and came progressively under the rule of the Taliban. The Western intervention primarily affected the cities, where society had been deeply transformed. Just as in the 1980s, the countryside became the theatre of intense fighting and political struggle, which translated into private conflicts, generally crystallizing over land issues. The province of Kunar, in the east of the country at the border with Pakistan, witnessed some of the fiercest fighting of the war, in addition to a rise in land conflicts. By 2013, despite a large investment of resources by the United States, the US Army was forced to withdraw, the Kabul regime had lost control of the province, and the Taliban had taken over most of the countryside.

Armed violence alone does not account for the failure of the US intervention and the taking over of most of the countryside by the Taliban. Rather than the insurgency/counter-insurgency frame which is regularly applied in academia and beyond to characterize the war (e.g. Giustozzi, 2012), by focusing on the ruling of land and space, I look at 2001–13 in the perspective of the longer history of the formation of the Afghan state, 'a historical process of conflicts, negotiations and compromises between different groups' (Berman and Lonsdale, 1992: 5; see also Bayart, 2009). Historically, Kunar has been a typical case of a province defined by the state as a margin,

The fieldwork and research for this chapter were made possible by the European Research Council (ERC) funded programme 'Social Dynamics of Civil Wars' and the ANR project 'Ni guerre, ni paix'. I would like to thank Gilles Dorronsoro, Christian Lund, Michael Eilenberg, Adele Blazquez and two anonymous reviewers for their comments on the text. All my gratitude goes to the Kunari people with whom I spent time in my successive trips, and whose trust allowed me to stay with them and to interview them. As the war is still raging on, I have kept the quoted interviews anonymous. This chapter is dedicated to Alain de Bures, who first introduced me to Kunar, where he had worked for more than 30 years.

a borderland, in which authority was exercised through various direct and indirect means (Barkey, 1994; Das and Poole, 2004; Korf and Raeymaekers, 2013). Defining who is part of the polity, the rights accompanying political belonging, and how the land may be appropriated have been central features of the implementation of authority. Conversely, it is in such margins that the central authority and its regimes of property and citizenship were repeatedly questioned and reconfigured (Ramirez, 2011; Roitman, 2005; Trejo, 2012). After 2001, Kunar experienced a particularly brutal version of the US Army strategy in Afghanistan, focused on hunting 'terrorists' and strengthening local institutions at the expense of the central authority in Kabul, which other US agencies were supporting as part of a project of 'state building'. It was also one of the provinces — with neighbouring Nuristan — in which the Taliban quickly took control of a large part of the territory and imposed its rule. Cross-cut by the US Army and opposed by the Taliban, Hamid Karzai's regime in Kabul never managed to apply its authority beyond the provincial capital.

To account for the US Army and the Taliban modes of governance in Kunar, I distinguish between two ideal types, a political model of governance and a legal one, the former based on conciliation and negotiation, the latter on the strict application of procedures and decisions. Both modes of governance require armed force to uphold authority, especially in a context of civil war where the monopoly of violence is questioned. Yet they also rely on conflict resolution and the capacity to define criteria of belonging to the political community and rights deriving from it. It is on the latter issues that the political and legal modes of governance differ: they correspond to two visions of the relations between political authority, citizenship and property.

On the one hand, the political mode of governance depends on the ability of leaders to settle deals, which requires them to be non-partisan, and implies a collective definition of ownership and a mediated definition of citizenship. Since the middle of the nineteenth century, the political mode of governance has been upheld by tribal elites. When the US Army entered Kunar, they attempted to buy the support of the tribal elites by funding and implementing programmes supporting a revival — in fact a reinvention — of tribal institutions. Yet they engaged in tribal politics without understanding its principles (in particular the need to remain non-partisan) or its effect (collective interpretations of the disputes), with the consequences of aggravating violence.

On the other hand, the judicial model requires a monopolistic leadership whose orders and judgments are enforced, and corresponds to an individual definition of possession and a direct relation between the citizen and the state. The Afghan kings, and a growing civil service over which they presided, were the main promoters of this rule. If in the middle of the nineteenth century the tribal and state elites were indeed competing for authority in Kunar, this opposition had become more conceptual a century later. The state's judicial mode of governance had definitively asserted itself over the tribes, whose political mode of governance had become increasingly dependent on the state's strategy and resources. In an apparent paradox, it is the Taliban that has acted in continuity with the Afghan state, perceiving itself as such. It emphasized the construction of a judicial system, with predictable procedures and systematic enforcement of verdicts. In a context where disputes had familial, tribal and ethnic dimensions, the Taliban mode of governance appeased social relations, reducing conflicts to judicial affairs, for which the verdict was to be considered final.

Why did the United States circumvent the state and support tribal politics? Why, conversely, did the Taliban act as a state? Within the intervention in Afghanistan, the diversity of agencies (international, American, Afghan, military, civilian, private, public–private, public, etc.) led to various and often contradictory priorities and strategies, from 'state building' to 'grassroots democracy', from a focus on development to women's rights, counter-narcotics, or terrorism. Yet, despite these numerous differences, the actors of the US intervention shared a common (mis)understanding of Afghanistan. Hilly topography and orientalist romanticism both participated in the formation of an 'imaginary anthropology' of Kunar, and of Afghanistan more generally (Dorronsoro, 2014; Monsutti, 2013). The American (or Western) military and civilian experts focused on the tribal nature of social relations in Afghanistan, interpreted through Geertz's primordial lens (Akram-Lodhi, 2016; Braithwaite and Wardak, 2013; Gant, 2009; Geertz, 1973; Martin, 2015; Ronfeldt, 2007; Wardak and Braithwaite, 2013). They reinterpreted modern Afghan history, using Ibn Khaldun's classical cycles of centralization by the state versus rebellion by the tribes to account for the Taliban resurgence, reduced to a congruence of various segmentary and local interests (Barfield, 2010; Johnson and Zellen, 2014; Rothstein and Arquilla, 2012). Afghanistan was described as an 'ungoverned space' (Clunan and Trinkunas, 2010) or an unruly 'graveyard of empires' (Jones, 2009), and always deemed fundamentally different (Mason, 2011). Local society was thus accounted for in a straightforward manner: independently-minded tribal Afghans resisted modernization and state penetration, a narrative to which was often added that of religious extremism (Barfield, 2010; Junger, 2010; Williams, 2008).

This interpretation of Kunar's social dynamics could rely on the anthropological studies of the border areas in eastern Afghanistan and Pakistan from the 1950s to the late 1970s. In their writings, Frederic Barth (1959), Akbar Ahmed (1976), Charles Lindholm (1981) and Louis Duprée (1984) had all described a self-governed region without much presence of the state — an 'ordered anarchy', in Lindholm's words. Between ideal grassroots democracy and Hobbesian dystopia, these apolitical interpretations missed the historical role of the state since the nineteenth century (Dorronsoro, 2005; Gregorian, 1969). On the eve of the civil war, tribe elites in Kunar, as in the rest of Afghanistan, had been severely weakened by a century of economic and social transformations (Anderson, 1975, 1978; Tapper, 1983). The

Taliban, on the other hand, were born out of the civil war in the 1990s and developed by mobilizing over the demand for law and order. In the 2000s, the same claims — unanswered by the Western intervention and the new regime in Kabul — allowed them to implant themselves again in Kunar, and more generally in Afghanistan. The Taliban emphasized the construction of a centralized parallel administration with shadow governors, judges and health and security officers at the district, provincial and national levels. They provided judicial services and taxed the most lucrative economic activities — opium cultivation and international development projects in particular (Baczko, 2013; Giustozzi, 2009).

This chapter is based on fieldwork carried out in Afghanistan from 2010 to 2015. During those six years, I went to Afghanistan once or twice a year, staying between one and three months each time. Because of the precarious security situation in Kunar, I favoured repeated short stays of several days, conducting non- and semi-structured interviews primarily with people involved in interpersonal conflicts over land and family issues, in particular those who had been involved with the Taliban courts. Presence in Kunar also allowed some direct observations and informal talks, and sometimes interviews with members of militarized groups (the Asadabad Provincial Reconstruction Team, Afghan auxiliaries to the US Army, US Army personnel, Taliban judges, Taliban fighters). I conducted additional interviews in the cities of Kabul and Jalalabad, where it was easier for some people to meet me and discuss their experiences. During my visits, I worked and stayed with several privileged informants who introduced me to people, translated during the interviews, and encouraged in my interviewees the trust they showed when speaking to me in such a complex environment. All my privileged informants exhibited some degree of ambiguity in their social and political positions — Alain de Bures for being a foreigner who had lived for 30 years in the region, including under Taliban rule; the others, Afghans, for being connected to both sides of the war because of their family networks and personal trajectories. This provided me, and them, with relative security, especially with regard to insurgency, which by that time controlled most of the countryside. Further fieldwork in Ghazni, Nangarhar, Laghman, Kandahar and Kunduz provinces, and a research project with Antonio Giustozzi and Claudio Franco for Integrity Watch Afghanistan on the Taliban judicial system — based on interviews with tens of Taliban fighters, commanders, judges and court users (see Giustozzi et al., 2012) — have on the whole confirmed, despite local specificities, the general patterns that I observed in Kunar over land issues and Taliban courts.

In the following pages, I contextualize the confrontation between the US Army and the Taliban in Kunar in a longer historical perspective. I begin with tribal politics before the civil war, and reflect on how the US Army managed social relations in this context after 2001. I then examine the formation of the state in Kunar and how the Taliban insurgency remobilized the same mode of governance in their own administration of the province.

THE DECLINE AND REINVENTION OF TRIBAL POLITICS

The US Army, and in particular the Special Forces, managed social relations in Kunar via a mode of governance based on negotiations and settlements. Because it was the most powerful actor in the region from 2002 until its withdrawal in 2013, people would turn to the American military to solve collective and individual disputes. Soldiers participated in the management of local conflicts, cross-cutting the regime's administration. They considered they were adapting to the 'local' ways of the region, and indeed they were alluding to patterns and practices that echoed the methods used by tribal elites to maintain some authority until the 1978 insurrection. Jihadi commanders, who emerged in the struggle against the invasion by the Soviet Union and had become local strongmen in the 1990s and 2000s, had also employed similar forms of governance. This political mode of management of social relations was based on the principle that a political actor could locally impose a deal between contenders by adopting a non-partisan position. Yet, when the American military applied a similar type of rule in Kunar, they got involved in local politics, looking for allies in their 'war against terror'. Eager for intelligence, they overlooked the importance of not having stakes in private and collective conflicts.

The Tribes: Conciliation, Negotiation and Arbitration

The political mode of governance was applied in Kunar by the tribal elites to deal with numerous conflicts relating mostly to land, but also to matrimonial, tribal and ethnic questions. The origin of this model lies in the local socio-economic structure: Kunar is a province of small owners, in which land ownership is the main resource. Arable lands are scarce in mountainous terrain, representing less than a tenth of the province's 4,000 km². In addition, cultivable land is scattered and poor, with a yield significantly worse than the national average (Ghani, 1984: 152). The population is almost entirely rural, with the exception of the inhabitants of the provincial capital of Asadabad. The latter remains a rural town, organized around one street which serves as the commercial interface for the products of the surrounding countryside and the manufactured goods from outside. The population of Kunar thus lives, directly or indirectly, from the 32,000 hectares of arable land. Unlike Kandahar, Mazar-e Sharif or Ghazni provinces, large domains are rare, with the exception of the high forestlands, which yield little revenue and are mostly used as seasonal pasture for the sheep. The poor quality of the land, its limited size and its dispersion restricted capitalist accumulation. In addition, the fragmentation of plots was encouraged by Afghan legislation, inspired by Islamic Law. Each time someone managed, despite the topography, to create a domain of some size in Kunar, their death would terminate the accumulation via an imposed division of the goods amongst the descendants

(Ghani, 1984: 95–102). The land remained somewhat evenly distributed, therefore, with an average of 1 ha for a family of 10, fostering a relatively egalitarian social structure.

In such conditions, cultivable land was both a private good and a private stake, at the core of neighbourhood and family relations. Plots were bought and sold, and circulated among individuals. In the archives of the Islamic court of Asadabad, Ashraf Ghani found no fewer than 236 cases of land transactions between 1885 and 1890. His investigations show an open and dynamic market, with Hindu traders in Asadabad playing a central role, buying and selling properties (ibid.: 98–9). Cultivable land in Kunar has been used as a stock of capital, easily changeable into liquidities. It allowed families to face difficult times and to afford significant expenditures, in particular those conferring social status, such as the payment of a dowry. Collective conflicts — between villages, tribes or ethnic groups — were generally about non-arable lands, such as forests and pastures.[1]

If arable land remained a private issue in Kunar until the war, the fragility of its possession turned it into a recurrent cause of conflict. Few owners had titles attesting judicially to the possession of their good and its precise boundaries. In addition, the setting of boundaries was not visible in the landscape and depended exclusively on the memory of each of the proprietors. Similarly, no cadastre and very few recordings of the limits of specific fields had been collected. Ultimately, the system of demarcation of the plots functioned through the defence of one's property against neighbours who might be tempted to grab some or all of it. In other words, defence and deterrence were integral to land ownership. The mutual nature of this deterrence meant that it defined effectively the boundaries between the plots. Yet this mechanism implied constant tension between neighbours. In the 1970s, the anthropologist Whitney Azoy described this dynamic, which affected peasants in Kunar:

> Everyone in a local community has some sense of whose land is whose. The absence, however, of precise survey and standardized documentation leads to disputes that are pursued through self-help. For all landholders, large and small alike, there is a constant need for vigilance against encroachment. Only such watchfulness and forceful appearance of potential response can prevent predation. . . .

> Boundary lines are vague, irrigation barrages are flimsy, sheep are easily led away, and women are considered wild cards because of their innate sexuality. Virtually everyone, even more to the point, is a potential predator. Obviously some sort of deterrent is necessary (Azoy, 2003: 31–2).

---

1. In 1896, during the conquest and conversion to Islam of Nuristan by King Abdul-Rahman Khan, Pashtun and Safi tribes of Kunar took possession of the non-cultivable high lands at the expense of Dardic-speaking, non-Islamic minorities. Since then, tensions between the communities of the province have often crystallized around those lands.

For the people involved, the handling of a dispute about land was critical. Whosoever allowed himself to look weak, while a neighbour or a kinsman was trying to appropriate his lands, increased the risk of attacks in the future. To fight back became necessary, both to protect one's property and to deter further attempts. Land disputes, even benign, could rapidly escalate and turn into cycles of reprisals.

The violence related to land took place in an environment characterized by extremely dense social networks. Any individual action lived on in an ethic of honour (*namus*), incarnated in the name (*nam*) which was passed on from father to son (Edwards, 1996: 41). Personal reputation played a fundamental role in people's place within the community, which was an amalgamation of various identities — tribal, ethnic or village-based. It was those social networks that could be mobilized to face rival claims, but they simultaneously created an omnipresent risk of escalation of the conflict from a private to a collective one. Against such a threat of exacerbated violence, extremely strict regulation over the use of force accompanied the insertion in social networks. As Pierre Centlivres (1997: 51) explained:

> Violence in Afghanistan is part of culture; it is not in rupture with it. It is therefore an event, a daily presence, 'traditional' in a sense, and recurring. Maybe, here and there, it reaches an extreme degree, yet in no way out of normality. One can even speak of a valorization of violence, to the extent that it is, with the strict rules that Afghan society shares with other types of societies, inseparable from honour, from the ideal of the free man, from the correct management of its affairs, from an ethic of conflict (Jamous, 1981; Pitt-Rivers, 1977). 'It has been said of those societies' Pitt-Rivers points out, 'that they were without law or anarchical and it is true that they are prone to intestine violence, but this very violence obeys rules as strict as those of a sacred game'.

Violence was part of daily life long before the war. Because it was considered normal, it was also normalized. The same ethic of honour that encourages a person to avenge spilled blood specified the acceptable forms and correct conditions of retaliation. To describe those social relations in the neighbouring valley of Swat in Pakistan, the anthropologist Charles Lindholm uses the expression quoted earlier, 'ordered anarchy' (Lindholm, 1981: 148). Individuals were sovereign, with no institution capable of preventing them from using force, but strict rules imposed the form that their action should take. Akbar Ahmed argues in the same vein that weak social stratification, fuelled by the parcelling up of land, preserves the values of independence and reciprocity between people, providing a solid basis for tribal structures (Ahmed, 1976).

These tribal institutions, composed of an elite of notables (*khan*) and village heads (*malek*), regulated rivalry and violence through conciliation, negotiation and sometimes arbitration. Such settlements were delivered in various ways — for instance, by convening a *jirga* or *shura*, a gathering of local elites — but all followed the same principle of non-partisan position-ing. This was achieved either by inviting people considered external to the dispute, or by bringing in people considered close to each of the conflicting parties. Despite having personal interests, tribal leaders might attain a non-partisan position by having large networks of patronage, obvious charisma, or recognized traditional or religious knowledge. A classical figure in Kunar with a major role in dispute conciliation was the *sadat*, a saint who claimed descent from the Prophet Mahomet (Ghani, 1978: 269; Lindholm, 1979: 489). The *sadats'* positioning outside the social networks, the respect they commanded, and sometimes their charisma all gave weight to their judgments. Traditionally, the *sadat* would receive land at the border of regions owned by rival lineages, tribes or ethnic groups: his role was to separate the rivals and avoid further conflict (Ghani, 1978: 269).

The disaggregation of the traditional elites during the conflict with the Soviet Union led to the dislocation of this tribal mode of governance in the 1980s, and its replacement by a new social group, the commanders, whose legitimacy was built by leading fighters (Edwards, 2002; Rubin, 2002). Their profiles varied, with different religious, tribal or higher education backgrounds, and they imposed their rule on Kunar using the features of existing rule (Dorronsoro, 2005). Until the Taliban takeover of the province in 1996, they settled disputes and struck deals, but in an arbitrary way, in line with their own interests and those of their supporters. In order to impose themselves they mobilized along family, tribal and ethnic lines, often transforming private disputes into collective conflicts. When the United States chased the Taliban from Afghanistan, these commanders, many of whom had taken refuge with the Northern Alliance, returned and monopolized local positions and resources.

The US Army: Imaginary Afghanistan and the Instrumentalization of Social Relations

When the US Army entered Kunar in 2002, the soldiers attempted to engage with existing social relations, mobilizing patterns from the tribal mode of governance but without following its core principle of non-partisan positioning. Indeed, the American military imagined Afghanistan as a tribal country that had always resisted any centralized rule. They based their interpretations on the nineteenth and twentieth century anthropology of Pashtun societies, within an overview similar to Lindholm's 'ordered anarchy', and on the orientalist literature. Ibn Khaldun and his book on the fourteenth-century Arab Maghreb is regularly quoted, often without having been read. The Special Forces — the only troops to be deployed in Kunar during the early years — were especially subjected to this imaginary anthropology of Afghanistan. This orientalism was tainted with racism, obvious in the comparison between Afghans and Native Americans. One unit named its military post Fort Navajo, while Major Jim Gant, who commanded the Special Forces detachment in 2003–4, nicknamed a village leader Sitting Bull (Gant, 2009: 16).

A few years after his deployment, Gant wrote 'One Tribe at a Time', a pamphlet reflecting on his experience in Kunar. With the words of Major Gant, an imaginary Afghanistan swam into view, a country of clans, unaffected by history, from which the state had always been absent. Throughout, the essay develops the same essentialist idea:

> The central cultural fact about Afghanistan is that it is constituted of tribes. Not individuals, not Western-style citizens — but tribes and tribesmen. It is my deep belief — and the thesis of this paper — that the answer to the problems that face the Afghan people, as well as other future threats to US security in the region, will be found in understanding and then helping the tribal system of Afghanistan to flourish. (ibid.: 9)

> When one says 'Afghan people' what I believe they are really saying is 'tribal member'. (ibid.: 11)

> Their tribal systems have been there for centuries and will be there for many more. (ibid.: 12)

> Afghanistan has never had a strong central government and never will. That is a fact that we need to accept, sooner rather than later. (ibid.: 13)

The pamphlet had considerable resonance. It was recommended reading for the American soldiers before their deployment in Afghanistan. General McCrystal, head of the military coalition between 2009 and 2010, distributed 'One Tribe at a Time' to all his commanding officers. His successor, General Petraeus, praised the text repeatedly. Similarly, David Kilcullen, an Australian officer who became a very close adviser to Petraeus, described Afghanistan and Kunar as an area where tribes rule without central authority (Kilcullen, 2009: 77). The American military was wrong about Kunar, and more generally about Afghanistan; it missed both the dislocation of traditional institutions in the 1980s and the demand for the state, one of the drivers for the rapid rise of the Taliban in the 1990s and 2000s.

The tribal vision of the US Army led it to cross-cut the new regime of Hamid Karzai, undermining its fragile legitimacy. It implemented its rule by defining the village as the scale of political action and the tribe as the political community. Special Force units organized their own gatherings of selected leaders that they named *shura* or *jirga* and that they convened on a regular basis. People went directly to the officers in order to obtain development projects for their village and to solve disputes, undercutting the renascent administration. In 2005, the governor of Kunar, Sayed Faizal Akbar, resigned from his position, explaining that the involvement of the American military in local politics was hindering his management of the province.

The bypassing of the state became significant once foreign intervention expanded, with regular troops being deployed in Kunar. Every US Army officer received US$ 1 million that could be spent freely in his area to buy intelligence or fund projects. A dedicated unit, the Provincial Reconstruction Team (PRT), was created to fund civilian projects aimed at 'winning hearts and minds'. The highly paid consultants I met in 2010 at the Asadabad base — a Texan rancher, a crop specialist from Michigan University and a young graduate from a top US university — were all ignorant of Afghanistan, not to speak of Kunar. They had a budget of more than US$ 80 million, equivalent to between a quarter and a half of the total economy of the province, which they did not know how to spend. While the PRT would almost never leave the Asadabad military base and lacked translators, those who had access to the restricted area — the entrepreneurs who fed the US Army with auxiliaries and intelligence — quickly monopolized the contracts and the distribution of money. In keeping with the global trend of the privatization of development in relation to military interventions (Nagaraj, 2015), for-profit and non-profit organizations were directly contracted to provide services, ranging from supply to governance. Development Alternatives Incorporated, a US company, managed three districts of Kunar directly for several years. It made deals with tribal leaders and offered projects to those who would accept the exclusion of the Taliban from their region.

The cross-cutting of the Afghan state also affected the security sector, through the formation of militias. The Special Forces detachment in Asadabad set up a force of 800 fighters, well-paid volunteers outside of the state payroll and authority. The US Army also armed ethnic minorities, such as the Pashai fighters of the former jihad commander Hazrat Ali, and used his men to secure segments of the road between Jalalabad and Asadabad. More generally, weapons and money were distributed to build 'tribal militias' (Kilcullen, 2009). Yet, by arming groups they perceived to be tribes or minorities, hastily mapped, and giving them legitimacy by calling them Afghan Local Police, the Americans were effectively supporting warlords (Hakimi, 2013). In order to pacify Kunar, they gave commanders and the population the means to bypass the state, and to solve their conflicts independently through the use of force.

Naively, without any serious understanding of the dynamics in the province, the US Army thus became involved in local conflicts. Major Jim Gant explains in detail how he obtained the favour of a tribal leader:

> The highland people had taken and were using some land that belonged to the lowland people. The Malik told me the land had been given to his tribe by the 'King of Afghanistan' many, many years ago and that he would show me the papers. I told him he didn't need to show me any papers. His word was enough. ... I made the decision to support him. 'Malik, I am with you. My men and I will go with you and speak with the highlanders again. If they do not turn the land back over to you, we will fight with you against them'. (Gant, 2009: 18)

Major Gant suggests — a laconic 'suffice it to say that the dispute with the highlanders was resolved' — that he helped his 'friend' to grab the contested land (ibid.: 19). The US military indeed followed patterns of the tribal mode of managing social relations, but without taking a non-partisan stance. Their strategy of local co-optation and deals upset social relations and existing settlements, and the partisan logic of the Special Forces turned them into the blind arm of private vengeances.

To fight its 'war on terror', the US Army instrumentalized social relations; at the same time it became an instrument of local revenge (Baczko, 2012; Martin, 2015). The mission of the Special Forces detachments was to track and eliminate Al Qaeda and Taliban militants, without distinctions (Strick van Linschoten and Kuehn, 2012). Their activities remained separated from the rest of the foreign intervention, outside of NATO command, under the exclusively American 'Enduring Freedom' command. Deployed for six months to one year, these elite troops operated in Kunar without practical supervision, following informal channels. As a former Afghan translator with the American Special Forces in Kunar in the first years of the intervention explained:

> ODB [Operation Detachment Battle, the name used by the Special Forces detachment in the provinces] carried out its operation without supervision; we would never write reports; we were totally independent. We would shoot first, ask questions later. In Kunar, a lot of the arrested people were not Taliban.
>
> [Me: How did you know?]
>
> I was translating during the interrogation, it was obvious during the interrogation.

Ignorant of the local dynamics, the Special Forces favoured any person who would provide them with information (Akbar, 2005). In this way, Malek Zarin, a former commander from the jihad against the Soviet, known as a wood trafficker, won the trust of the soldiers. In addition to providing intelligence, he supplied the bases and also proposed his son as a translator. Until his death in a suicide bombing in 2011, he used the American support to fight his former rival commanders in the high Kunar valley. Furthermore, 'targeted killings' operations, often conducted at night, exacerbated conflicts (Gopal, 2014). The intelligence used was often based on denunciation, much of which was calumny. Accusing a rival of being Taliban, in a context in which the Special Forces had an elastic licence to kill, was an easy way to get rid of an annoying neighbour or kinsman. The US Army thus transformed private disputes and old rivalries into collective conflicts between tribes and ethnic groups, and politicized them.

LEGAL RULE AND THE STATE

In the territory that they control in Kunar, the Taliban operate a law-based mode of governance, based on procedural decision making and enforcement. Court verdicts and edicts are the components of a largely monopolistic management of social relations. In the 1990s, when they took power, and since the 2000s, in the territory they governed as an insurgency, the Taliban imposed themselves, building hierarchical institutions which applied procedures taken from a combination of positive and religious law. This mode of governance was largely in keeping with the process of socio-genesis of the state that had started at the end of the nineteenth century. Far from the orientalist vision of a country without a state, Afghanistan, with borders that remained stable for more than a century, was a country in which the state asserted itself in a continuous manner. The Taliban courts, like those of the Afghan state, promoted a vision of authority directly exerted between the state and its subjects, and of property as the possession of an individual. This rule extended beyond the limited resources of the judicial institutions by delegating to the tribes the power to rule on a steadily declining range of issues requiring judgment. What the anthropologists studying Pashtun tribes had overlooked, is that they were not so much an alternative source of authority as part of a continuing process in which the growing influence of a central state was slowly asserting its monopoly of violence.

The Forgotten State

From its formation at the end of the nineteenth century, the Afghan state has been a determinant actor in Kunar. The structure of land ownership and identities has evolved through the various policies and guarantees put forward by the state in steering a fragile balance between an imprecise demarcation of plots of land and the traditional regulation of violence. The monopoly of the state in Kunar thus followed an Eliasian process of autonomization of the political authority from its tribal legitimacy (Elias, 1982). In the nineteenth century, the King of Afghanistan was a *primus inter pares*, a tribal leader above the other tribal leaders, who constantly had to demonstrate his superiority. He arbitrated conflicts and negotiated settlements, based on relations of patronage typical of tribal rule. With the reign of Abdul-Rahman Khan (1880–1901), the King started to derive his authority from alternative sources, both religious and political. Abdul-Rahman Khan was proclaimed Emir al-Mumenin, Commander of the Believers, by the religious savants, the *ulema*, and engaged in several military campaigns. Through two military campaigns, he unified the two territories of Hazarajat and Kafiristan (the country of the unbelievers), renamed Nuristan (the country of the light). This process of conquest followed both a political rationale — the two mountainous regions refused to recognize the authority of the King — and a religious one, since they were populated respectively by Shias and non-Muslims (Kakar, 1979). His successors continued his work by modernizing the bureaucracy and by implementing a series of reforms. Revealingly, the term 'Afghan' progressively turned from an ethnonym describing the Pashtun into a demonym describing all the citizens of the internationally recognized country of Afghanistan. The assertion of the state was regularly contested by traditional elites, especially in the 1920s, when the eastern tribes rebelled, taking Kabul and overthrowing the King. Yet by the 1940s, with the mechanization of the army, the state had imposed its rule and the tribes had lost the ability to challenge it (Gregorian, 1969).

The contentious formation of the Afghan state was particularly visible in Kunar when the tribes rose again in 1947. The conflict started over two issues that directly concerned both the monopoly of violence and the definition of citizenship. Until the 1940s, the tribes had regularly provided a discretionary quota of men and money. These men were grouped in the same regiments and positioned in the province, or in the neighbouring city of Jalalabad. Recruitment and imposition therefore followed a logic of tribute and reflected a vision of citizenship that was mediated by membership of the tribe. In 1947, King Zaher Shah decreed that recruitment and tax collection would be direct. The recruits would be scattered across the country, and people would be taxed as citizens, without any form of mediation. This display of the shift from the ethnic-tribal definition to a national one triggered the revolt of the tribes of Kunar. The troops of the monarchy curbed the uprising and its leaders were exiled to the north of the country. The repression of Kunar's revolt was a moment of simultaneous affirmation of the state's monopoly of violence and the supremacy of individual citizenship over lineage. In the following decades, dedicated high schools were opened in Kabul to which the tribal elites sent their sons to become part of the state's bureaucracy (Edwards, 2002).

When anthropologists observed provinces such as Kunar, they did not see the state and therefore deemed it absent.[2] Yet the state was everywhere. The court of Asadabad dated from the end of the nineteenth century. It ruled continuously until the 1978 insurgency, basing its authority on Islamic Law, a religious legitimacy and an alternative to the traditional tribal one. As Ghani (1983: 353) explains:

> Whereas the 79,000-strong army provided the state with the power to sanction the suppression of local customs, the prevalence of significant divisions within the rural area turned courts into major centers of recourse for dispute-settlement. The imposition of sharia not only changed the symbolic system of reference of the disputants but it also opened the disputing arena to new actors, the most significant of whom were women. The form of the law was defined by the state while its content was determined by patterns of conflict at the local level. The existence of appeal, however, gave the state an important role in the arbitration of social relations within the civil society. The entry of the state as arbitrator of social cleavages allowed it to consolidate its role in the management of the flow of material and human resources in and out of the local community.

---

2. Anthropologists were largely influenced by the situation on the other side of the border, in the tribal areas of Pakistan. British imperial rule had led to the promulgation in the 1870s of dedicated crime regulations based on reinvented customs and traditions (Hopkins, 2011). Although, until the drawing of the Durand line in 1893, this imperial governmentality could be applied in Kunar, the British administration in Peshawar had little influence in territories so far from its bases. Kunar (and Afghanistan more generally) did not experience prolonged colonial rule, only limited influence from the bordering British dominion over India (Hanifi, 2011).

In the twentieth century, the tribal institutions continued with their dispute-resolution mechanisms, but did so within a state frame (Tapper, 1983). The characterization of an 'ordered anarchy' and the vision of self-governance through tribal institutions overlooked the role of 'last resort' of Kabul, which had become necessary to the authority of the traditional elite. When violence escalated to a degree that the tribes could no longer contain, the affair was taken over by the state, whose authority was guaranteed by coercion. The judicial mode of state governance was therefore not asserted in contradiction to the political mode of tribal governance, although in the long term it did undermine it and impose itself as the dominant form of rule. The state court solved conflicts that the tribes were unable to regulate and resolve, producing a frame within which the authority of the notables was expressed, at the same time that the presence of the state was strengthening. In fact, the tribal governance as it survived through the twentieth century can be compared to a particular form of delegation (Hibou, 1998). The tribal reading of social life in Afghanistan is reminiscent, though beyond the colonial framework, of the confusion that Mahmood Mamdani denounces when he explains that British indirect rule hides a specific form of decentralized despotism, which is in a sense another particular form of delegation (Mamdani, 1996). The civil war, which started in 1978, demonstrated the dependence of the tribes on the state. Indeed, with the exception of the town of Asadabad, the bulk of Kunar remained outside the reach of Kabul until the coming of the Taliban in 1996. The tribal elite, which tried to rule the province, lost the ability to regulate violence and to solve disputes, showing how much they depended on the state through the effects of its absence.

The Taliban: The Judicial Management of Collective Conflicts

The governance of the Taliban in the 1990s and 2000s shared a strong insistence on justice and procedure, from a state perspective. The armed movement emerged in the mid-1990s in the south of Afghanistan, in opposition to the strife and disorder resulting from the rivalries between commanders, hence the 'justice and order' inscription on their white flags (Davis, 1998). Kunar had suffered under such conflicts and the Taliban were welcomed when they entered the province, almost without resistance, in 1996. The court of Asadabad was among the first institutions they set up in the province. The Taliban judicial system took advantage of their exteriority — the movement as such was not involved in the various feuds that existed in the province. A general amnesty was declared for the period of the civil war. Added to harsh punishments cast by the judges for any subsequent private use of force, the amnesty stopped the revenge cycles that had been running for more than 15 years. People who lived in Kunar between 1996 and 2001 recurrently referred in interviews to this period as one of relative appeasement, especially regarding land issues.

From 2003, when Taliban militants started to come back to the province, they positioned themselves in opposition to the extreme corruption that characterized the administration of the province and the disorder related to the return of the Jihadi commanders, and also to the strategy of the US Special Forces. Against the instrumentalization of social relations by the US Army they brought a moralistic rhetoric, supported by a claim to religious legitimacy. Rejecting any ethnic, tribal or partisan claim in Kunar, they depoliticized conflicts into judicial affairs by positioning themselves as impartial judges.

Compared to the limited resources of the insurgency, the Taliban mode of governance over-emphasized institutions and formalism. While fighting the US Army, the Taliban invested time and resources in organizing a proto-state structure with procedures, official documents and internal regulations. This parallel administration was hierarchical and centralized. In every district, a governor was nominated and was responsible to the Taliban governor of the province. The latter was then responsible to a committee in charge of eastern Afghanistan and to the executive body of the Taliban in Quetta, Pakistan (Giustozzi and Baczko, 2014). That such a hierarchized system remained functional despite the daily killings of cadres by the US Special Forces is suggestive of its degree of organization. In addition, the insurgency managed to take over the public services that the local administration of Karzai's regime, undermined by corruption and nepotism, had neglected, and became effectively *the* authority. The movement asserted its authority over the everyday life of the inhabitants of the rural areas of Kunar. The Taliban collected taxes from people and from national and foreign organizations working in the province. It controlled prices in the markets and delivered authorization to work in its areas — including to international NGOs, as long as their work had been praised by the villagers and they had no ties to the Western military coalition. They even organized their own school system (Giustozzi and Franco, 2011). Any official document was stamped with the official designation of the Taliban regime, 'Islamic Emirate of Afghanistan', a way to reassert their interpretation of history, that of a government in exile facing a foreign occupation.

The judicial system was the core institution of the Taliban governance apparatus. Judges were appointed in each district to resolve disputes and manage social relations. As in the 1990s, the judge was the central figure of a moralistic rule that emphasized order. Islamic Law, and more specifically the Koran and collections of Hadiths, constituted the main jurisprudential references. The implementation of justice remained the exclusive domain of clerics, trained in religious schools and socially recognized as competent to administer Islamic Law. Like other Taliban institutions, the courts were centralized, with appeal and supervision systems at the district, province and national levels. Altogether, the Taliban system of justice managed hundreds of judges all over Afghanistan — far more than the foreign-supported official justice system (Baczko, 2013).

Judges used practices that in part resembled those of a formal procedural justice system, though a summary one. To lodge a complaint, one had to fill in an application for the judge. An investigation was set up by the judge and his assistants — this generally took anything from a few days to several weeks — and a hearing was organized with both disputing parties, in the common room of a house, set as the court for the occasion. The hearing generally lasted from a few hours to a whole day. The judge, supported by assistants, looked into the documents and listened to the witnesses brought by the parties. He would then make his determination or, if necessary, devote some time to further investigation. The speed of the judgment was particularly appreciated, especially in comparison with the slowness of the incumbent court in Asadabad, in which cases could take years, depending on the levels of corruption. Witnesses were central to the judicial process in Kunar. While Islamic Law legitimated a focus on testimonies, an even more decisive factor was the lack of documents or material proofs, especially in relation to land issues. The sentence of the judge was written on a piece of paper, stamped with the seal of the Islamic Emirate of Afghanistan, the name of the Taliban state. The paper was presented as an official document, which the Taliban judge kept as a record of the judgment, with a serial number.

In practice, the sentences of the Taliban judges included a degree of ad hoc deliberation. For instance, a notable from Shal Valley explained to me how, in a dispute relating to demarcation between two plots examined in 2012, the Taliban judge questioned him and the other elders of the village, one by one. He followed the majority opinion, but presented his verdict as if it were an application of Islamic law. As he was close to the Taliban, he knew how the verdict had been reached, but the other elders did not. The Taliban had no dedicated police force and the courts' verdicts were enforced by the fighters, making it very difficult to oppose a sentence outside of their own system of appeal. This contrasted again with the incumbent system of justice, in which the judges would not go out of Asadabad due to the security situation, and the verdicts were often negotiable if the losing party was willing to pay the judge or the police. As an inhabitant from Shal Valley put it to me in 2010: 'The Taliban judges say what they will do and they do what they have said'. Another inhabitant from Asmar contrasted it with the incumbent system of justice: 'What is the difference between the government judges and Taliban ones? When the Taliban judge pronounces a sentence, they implement the decision. When they say something, they mean it'.

The Taliban explicitly organized their system in a non-partisan manner. Judges were prevented from forming ties with the population and becoming biased through nominations from outside the province or district, and by regular rotation. Judges were deemed impartial and their actions perceived as unbiased and not inclined towards any particular community or social group. The ethnic minorities, Gujars or Nuristanis, who had often held grudges relating to the use of pasture lands or forest high in the mountains, repeatedly won cases against Pashtuns, who constituted the majority of the insurgency. The judges were closely monitored by the Taliban provincial administration, to whom judges were required to send a copy of each of their verdicts, and who regularly checked among the population how the work of the judge was perceived. This system of justice allowed the Taliban to solve numerous private conflicts, some of which had been going on for years. In cases of land conflict, the Taliban courts issued property titles that were accepted by the incumbent administration. By doing so, they were creating, in the uncertain context of the civil war, an environment with norms, in which property was recognized and guaranteed by a political authority.

By rebuilding a balance between political order and property, the Taliban produced norms of justice, and came to be recognized as the effective authority in Kunar. In continuity with the formation of the state in Afghanistan, the Taliban reduced the space available to a mode of governance based on deals, settlements and arbitration. The Taliban still let the villagers attempt to solve their problems, as long as no crime had been committed or no one filed a complaint. It was also careful not to antagonize the population — for instance, it avoided implementing in Kunar the half-share of inheritance to which unmarried and widowed women are entitled under Islamic Law. Judges could be contacted by mobile phone and made regular rounds to villages, asking the population if they wanted to report any issue.

CONCLUSION

This chapter has argued that armed assertion of power alone does not account for the defeat of the US Army and the taking over of the countryside by the Taliban. Both armed actors involved themselves in land issues, but through very different governance practices. On the one hand, the US Army, and in particular the Special Forces, circumvented the nascent regime in Kabul, thus contradicting the approach of other US agencies which were supporting the regime in a process of 'state building'. The American soldiers negotiated directly with people who provided them with information and with auxiliaries — defined by the military as 'tribal elites' — and in return offered these 'friends' support and resources. Thus, the US Army became involved in local land conflicts, defining ownership as a collective issue and turning to these 'tribal elites' as representatives and arbiters. Conversely, the Taliban progressively built a centralized parallel administration, based on courts, in which they implemented mechanisms to avoid corruption and partisanship. When possible, the Taliban courts individualized land conflict, reducing the stakes.

To understand the effects of the US Army and Taliban rule in Kunar, this chapter compared two ideal-typical models of governance, a legal and a political one, which differ in how they define the regime of property and citizenship, with direct implications for violence and authority. The differentiated effects of these two rules also derived from their inscription in the political history of Afghanistan, in particular the formation of the Afghan state as the slow imposition of a legal rule over tribal politics. As the American military was inspired by an imaginary anthropology of Afghanistan as a stateless country ruled by tribes, it missed a central point: tribal institutions had been dependent on the Afghan state during the twentieth century. The Taliban, on the other hand, perceived itself to be the Islamic Emirate of Afghanistan, a legitimate authority faced with a foreign invasion. It therefore strove to rebuild its administration, performing the state. Its court system allowed it to position itself as the guarantor of property rights, and therefore make its rule serve the interests of many small owners in Kunar.

The competition between the US Army and the Taliban is a case of armed confrontation in which different militarized groups compete to impose rule by controlling access to citizenship and landed property. In Kunar, citizenship proved less of an issue than property, but contemporary civil wars provide numerous examples in which both become stakes. Such a perspective builds on the recent calls to revisit legitimacy and sovereignty (Hansen and Stepputat, 2006; Lund, 2013; Monsutti, 2012; Randeria, 2007). Armed actors position themselves as the authority by providing access to rights and by arbitrating related conflicts. In Syria, for instance, the rebels, the Kurdish Democratic Union Party (PYD) and the Islamic State each created judiciary systems, which compete with the incumbent one. These courts play a central role in defining who is part of the polity and with what rights (Baczko et al., 2016). Similarly, in the eastern regions of the Democratic Republic of Congo, militarized groups participated in the construction of ethnic categories, in particular by drawing exclusionary lines that closely reflected land ownership (Vlassenroot, 2002). In Colombia, the Revolutionary Armed Forces (FARC) contested the state by implementing its own administration, in a close relationship with local rural communities (Esposina, 2009). These various configurations suggest that defining the regimes of property and citizenship will determine whether a militarized actor is able to impose its authority effectively and assert some degree of sovereignty.

REFERENCES

Ahmed, A. (1976) *Millennium and Charisma among Pathans: A Critical Essay in Social Anthropology.* London: Routledge and Kegan Paul.
Akbar, H. (2005) *Come Back to Afghanistan: A California Teenager's Story.* London: Bloomsbury.
Akram-Lodhi, H.A. (2016) '"One Stone Is Enough to Drive Away a Hundred Birds": Peasants, Land and Resistance in Contemporary Afghanistan', *Journal of Agrarian Change* 16(1): 168–79.
Anderson, J. (1975) 'Tribe and Community among the Ghilzay Pashtun: Preliminary Notes on Ethnographic Distribution and Variation in Eastern Afghanistan', *Anthropos* 70: 575–601.
Anderson, J. (1978) 'There are no Khans Anymore: Economic Development and Social Change in Tribal Afghanistan', *Middle East Journal* 32: 167–83.

Azoy, W. (2003) *Buzkashi: Game and Power in Afghanistan*. Long Grove, IL: Waveland Press Inc.

Baczko, A. (2012) 'Les Revers de l'Armée Américaine dans la Guerre d'Afghanistan: Le Cas de la Kounar' ['The US Army's Setbacks in the Afghanistan War: The Case of Kunar'], *Politique Américaine* 19: 11–26.

Baczko, A. (2013) 'Judging in the Midst of Civil War: The Taliban Courts in Afghanistan (2001–2013)', *Politix* 104(4): 25–46.

Baczko, A., G. Dorronsoro and A. Quesnay (2016) *Syrie: De la Révolution à la Guerre Civile* [*Syria: From Revolution to Civil War*]. Paris: CNRS Editions.

Barfield, T. (2010) *Afghanistan: A Cultural and Political History*. Princeton, NJ: Princeton University Press.

Barkey, K. (1994) *Bandits and Bureaucrats: The Ottoman Route to State Centralization*. Ithaca, NY: Cornell University Press.

Barth, F. (1959) *Political Leadership among Swat Pathans*. London: The Athlone Press.

Bayart, J.-F. (2009) *The State in Africa: The Politics of the Belly*. Oxford: Polity Press.

Berman, B. and J. Lonsdale (1992) *Unhappy Valley: Conflict in Kenya and in Africa*. Athens, OH: Ohio University Press.

Braithwaite, J. and A. Wardak (2013) 'Crime and War in Afghanistan Part I: The Hobbesian Solution', *British Journal of Criminology* 53(2): 179–96.

Centlivres, P. (1997) 'Violence Légitime et Violence Illégitime: À Propos des Pratiques et des Représentations dans la Crise Afghane' ['Legitimate Violence and Illegitimate Violence: On the Practices and Representations in the Afghan Crisis'], *L'Homme* 37(144): 51–67.

Clunan, A. and H. Trinkunas (eds) (2010) *Ungoverned Spaces: Alternatives to State Authority in an Era of Softened Sovereignty*. Stanford, CA: Stanford Jones.

Das, C. and D. Poole (eds) (2004) *Anthropology in the Margins of the State*. Santa Fe, NM: School for Advanced Research Press.

Davis, M. (1998) 'How the Taliban Became a Military Force', in W. Maley (ed.) *Fundamentalism Reborn? Afghanistan and the Taliban*, pp. 43–72. New York: New York University Press.

Dorronsoro, G. (2005) *Revolution Unending: Afghanistan, 1979 to the Present*. New York: Columbia University Press.

Dorronsoro, G. (2014) 'Le Déclin de l'Institution Tribale en Afghanistan' ['The Decline of the Tribal Institution in Afghanistan'], in H. Dawod (ed.) *La Constante 'Tribu', Variations Arabo-Musulmanes* [*The Constant 'Tribe', Arab-Muslim Variations*], pp. 93–117. Paris: Demopolis.

Duprée, L. (1984) 'Tribal Warfare in Afghanistan and Pakistan: A Reflection of the Segmentary Lineage System', in A.S. Ahmed and D. Hart (eds) *Islam in Tribal Societies*, pp. 266–86. London: Routledge and Kegan Paul.

Edwards, D. (1996) *Heroes of the Age: Moral Fault Line on the Afghan Frontier*. Berkeley, CA: University of California Press.

Edwards, D. (2002) *Before Taliban: Genealogies of the Afghan Jihad*. Berkeley, CA: University of California Press.

Elias, N. (1982) *The Civilizing Process, Vol. II: State Formation and Civilization*. Oxford: Blackwell.

Esposina, N. (2009) 'El Campo Jurídico del "Otro Derecho" en la Sierra de La Macarena. Elementos para un Análisis Crítico de la Justicia Alternativa en una Zona de Fuerte Conflicto Armado' ['The Judicial Field of the "Other Law" in the Macarena Sierra. Elements for a Critical Analysis of Alternative Justice in a Zone of Strong Armed Conflict'], *Revista Colombiana de Sociología* 32(2): 133–55.

Gant, J. (2009) 'One Tribe at a Time: A Strategy for Success in Afghanistan'. Los Angeles, CA: Nine Sisters Imports. http://www.operationspaix.net/DATA/DOCUMENT/5042⌐v⌐One_ Tribe_at_a_Time___A_Strategy_for_Success_in_Afghanistan.pdf

Geertz, C. (1973) *The Interpretation of Cultures*. New York: Basic Books.

Ghani, A. (1978) 'Islam and State-building in a Tribal Society: Afghanistan 1880–1901', *Modern Asian Studies* 12(2): 269–84.

Ghani, A. (1983) 'Disputes in a Court of Sharia, Kunar Valley, Afghanistan', *International Journal of Middle Eastern Studies* 15(3): 353–67.

Ghani, A. (1984) *Production and Domination: Afghanistan, 1747–1901*. New York: Columbia University Press.

Giustiozzi, A. (2009) *Koran, Kalashnikov, and Laptop: The Neo-Taliban Insurgency in Afghanistan*. New York: Columbia University Press.

Giustozzi, A. (ed.) (2012) *Decoding the New Taliban: Insights from the Afghan Field*. Oxford: Oxford University Press.

Giustozzi, A. and A. Baczko (2014) 'The Politics of the Taliban's Shadow Judiciary, 2003–2013', *Central Asian Affairs* 1(2): 199–224.

Giustozzi, A. and C. Franco (2011) *The Battle for Schools: The Taleban and State Education*. Kabul: Afghan Analysts Network.

Giustozzi, A., C. Franco and A. Baczko (2012) 'Shadow Justice: How the Taliban Run their Judiciary'. Kabul: Integrity Watch Afghanistan.

Gopal, A. (2014) *No Good Men among the Living: America, the Taliban, and the War through Afghan Eyes*. New York: Metropolitan Books.

Gregorian, V. (1969) *The Emergence of Modern Afghanistan*. Stanford, CA: Stanford University Press.

Hakimi, A. (2013) 'Getting Savages to Fight Barbarians: Counterinsurgency and the Remaking of Afghanistan', *Central Asian Survey* 32(3): 388–405.

Hanifi, S.M. (2011) *Connecting Histories in Afghanistan: Market Relations and State Formation on a Colonial Frontier*. Stanford, CA: Stanford University Press.

Hansen, T. and F. Stepputat (2006) 'Sovereignty Revisited', *Annual Review of Anthropology* 35: 295–315.

Hibou, B. (1998) 'Retrait ou Redéploiement de l'Etat?' ['Retreat or Redeployment of the State?'], *Critique internationale* 1(1): 151–68.

Hopkins, B. (2011) 'The Frontier Crimes Regulation and Frontier Governmentality', *The Journal of Asian Studies* 74: 369–89.

Jamous, R. (1981) *Honneur et Baraka: Les Structures Sociales Traditionnelles dans le Rif* [*Honour and Baraka: Traditional Social Structures in the Rif*]. Cambridge: Cambridge University Press.

Johnson, T. and B. Zellen (eds) (2014) *Culture, Conflict, and Counterinsurgency*. Stanford, CA: Stanford University Press.

Jones, S. (2009) *In the Graveyard of Empires: America's War in Afghanistan*. New York: W.W. Norton and Company.

Junger, S. (2010) *War*. New York: Twelve.

Kakar, H. (1979) *Government and Society in Afghanistan: The Reign of Amir Abddur Rahman Khan*. Austin, TX: University of Texas Press.

Kilcullen, D. (2009) *The Accidental Guerrilla: Fighting Small Wars in the Midst of a Big One*. Oxford: Oxford University Press.

Korf, B. and T. Raeymaekers (eds) (2013) *Violence on the Margins: States, Conflict, and Borderlands*. London: Palgrave Macmillan.

Lindholm, C. (1979) 'Contemporary Politics in a Tribal Society: Swat District, NWFP, Pakistan', *Asian Survey* 19(5): 485–505.

Lindholm, C. (1981) 'The Structure of Violence among the Swat Pukhtun', *Ethnology* 20(2): 147–56.

Lund, C. (2013) 'Fragmented Sovereignty: Land Reform and Dispossession in Laos', *The Journal of Peasant Studies* 38(4): 885–905.

Mamdani, M. (1996) *Citizen and Subject: Contemporary Africa and the Legacy of Late Colonialism*. Princeton, NJ: Princeton University Press.

Martin, M. (2015) *An Intimate War: An Oral History of the Helmand Conflict*. London: Hurst.

Mason, W. (2011) *The Rule of Law in Afghanistan: Missing in Action*. Cambridge: Cambridge University Press.

Monsutti, A. (2012) 'Fuzzy Sovereignty: Rural Reconstruction in Afghanistan, between Democracy Promotion and Power Games', *Comparative Studies in Society and History* 54(3): 563–91.

Monsutti, A. (2013) 'Anthropologizing Afghanistan: Colonial and Postcolonial Encounters', *The Annual Review of Anthropology* 42: 269–85.

Nagaraj, V. (2015) '"Beltway Bandits" and "Poverty Barons": For-Profit International Development Contracting and the Military-Development Assemblage', *Development and Change* 46(4): 585–617.

Pitt-Rivers, J. (1977) *The Fate of Shechem or the Politics of Sex. Essays in the Anthropology of the Mediterranean*. Cambridge: Cambridge University Press.

Ramirez, M. (2011) *Between the Guerrilla and the State: The Cocalero Movement, Citizenship, and Identity in the Colombian Amazon*. Durham, NC: Duke University Press.

Randeria, S. (2007) 'The State of Globalization: Legal Plurality, Overlapping Sovereignties and Ambiguous Alliances between Civil Society and the Cunning State in India', *Theory, Culture & Society* 24(1): 1–33.

Roitman, J. (2005) *Fiscal Disobedience: An Anthropology of Economic Regulation in Central Africa*. Princeton, NJ: Princeton University Press.

Ronfeldt, D. (2007) 'In Search of How Society Works: Tribes — The First and Forever Form'. Rand Working Paper No. 433. Santa Monica, CA: Rand Corporation.

Rothstein, H. and J. Arquilla (eds) (2012) *Afghan Endgames: Strategy and Policy Choices for America's Longest War*. Washington, DC: Georgetown University Press.

Rubin, B. (2002) *The Fragmentation of Afghanistan: State Formation and Collapse in the International System*. New Haven, CT: Yale University Press.

Strick van Linschoten, A. and F. Kuehn (2012) *An Enemy We Created: The Myth of the Taliban/Al Qaeda Merger in Afghanistan, 1970–2010*. London: Hurst.

Tapper, R. (ed.) (1983) *The Conflict of Tribe and State in Iran and Afghanistan*. London: Croom Helm.

Trejo, G. (2012) *Popular Movements in Autocracies: Religious Repression, and Indigenous Collective Action in Mexico*. Cambridge: Cambridge University Press.

Vlassenroot, K. (2002) 'Citizenship, Identity Formation & Conflict in South Kivu: The Case of the Banyamulenge', *Review of African Political Economy* 29(93–4): 499–516.

Wardak, A. and J. Braithwaite (2013) 'Crime and War in Afghanistan Part II: A Jeffersonian Alternative?', *British Journal of Criminology* 53(2): 197–214.

Williams, B. (2008) 'Afghanistan's Heart of Darkness: Fighting the Taliban in Kunar', *CTC Sentinel* 1(12): 1–4.

11

Taxation, Stateness and Armed Groups: Public Authority and Resource Extraction in Eastern Congo

Kasper Hoffmann, Koen Vlassenroot and Gauthier Marchais

INTRODUCTION

State collapse, followed by two decades of trans-scalar armed conflict, has turned the eastern regions of the Democratic Republic of the Congo (henceforth: the Congo) into a deeply fragmented political space in which a wide range of actors including state officials, armed groups, customary chiefs, church leaders, civil society members and international organizations compete to assume public authority over people and resources. Authority mirrors the ebbs and flows of these power struggles as different actors gain and lose the capacity to institute order.

Taxation is a pivotal part of these struggles to assume public authority. Until recently the view on taxation in the Congo was dominated by the 'greed' literature of the early 2000s, which largely framed taxation during conflict as predatory and violent.[1] However, more recent ethnographic studies which focus on how authority and order are produced in conflict zones have shown that the social relations of taxation are far more complex, ambiguous, ordered and reciprocal than the 'greed' literature claims (Garrett et al., 2009; Laudati, 2013; Raeymaekers, 2010; Sanchez de la Sierra, 2015; Schouten, 2013; Titeca, 2011; Verweijen, 2013). Most often, these relations involve the provision of goods in exchange for resource extraction. These fiscal bargains are predominantly, though not exclusively, centred around the provision of protection, security and justice, particularly when armed actors are involved. These taxation-for-protection arrangements may involve the

The authors would like to thank the editors of the Rule and Rupture special issue, as well as Judith Verweijen, David Newbury and two anonymous referees for their comments on earlier drafts of this chapter. This research was funded by the Justice and Security Research Programme, a DfID-supported international research consortium (http://blogs.lse.ac.uk/jsrp/); a PhD scholarship from the Institute of Society and Globalization, Roskilde University and the Danish Institute for International Studies; and a PhD studentship from the Department of International Development of the London School of Economics and Political Science.

1. According to this theory it is 'easy' for 'greedy' armed groups to impose predatory taxation on primary commodities during 'civil war' (e.g. Berdal and Malone, 2000; Collier and Hoeffler, 2004; de Soysa, 2000).

Rule and Rupture: State Formation through the Production of Property and Citizenship, First Edition.
Edited by Christian Lund and Michael Eilenberg.
Chapters © 2017 by The Institute of Social Studies. Book compilation © 2017 John Wiley & Sons Ltd.

protection of individuals, of property, of infrastructure and of economic activity and production, with security provided either on an individual basis as 'private protection' or as a more public good.

While this recent literature has offered rich insights into the novel forms of taxation and order making that emerge in conflict zones, it has rarely focused on how long-term historical processes shape contemporary practices.[2] In this contribution, we attempt to fill this gap by tracing the historical antecedents of the modes of taxation that armed groups deploy in eastern Congo. Drawing on both historical material and field research in the neighbouring territories of Kalehe (South Kivu) and Walikale (North Kivu) we argue, first, that taxation is at the core of armed groups' production of public authority and citizenship and, second, that taxation practices are strongly conditioned by institutionalized registers of authority and practices of order making. To acknowledge the complex relations of authority of which taxation is a part, we define taxation broadly as the obligation to contribute resources (money, goods or labour) to a public authority in return for services and goods. By 'public authority' we mean a form of authority which is built on a modicum of mutual recognition between rulers and ruled, and distinct from purely personal relations (Lund, 2006: 678).

Contrary to pillaged resources, taxes not only constitute resources for power holders; they also entail processes of recognition of the authority of those power holders, as well as the citizenship (or membership) of the populace in a political community (ibid.: 696; see also Lund's Introduction to this issue). Taxation thus enmeshes people in a web of generalized reciprocity based on mutual obligations and rights. In this sense, taxation epitomizes the social contract between authorities and citizens of a given 'imagined community' (Anderson, 1983; Martin et al., 2009). It is important to emphasize, however, that taxation establishes unequal relations of power and exchange between people. These are based on certain normalized understandings of community, order, duty and citizenship, which, if necessary, are secured by force. As we show, taxation in eastern Congo is embedded in historically contingent practices and discourses of authority, and in particular in a 'language of stateness' (Hansen and Stepputat, 2001: 8). This 'language of stateness' was introduced through colonization and includes the principle of territorial sovereignty, often articulated in nationalist and legal discourse; the production of knowledge about the people living on this territory through censuses and other bureaucratic instruments; and the accumulation of resources through taxation and various forms of dispossession. Importantly, public signs, rituals and spectacles connect all of these operations to the very idea of the state.

---

2. But see the literature on vigilantism (Heald, 2006; Meagher, 2007; Pratten, 2008; Pratten and Sen, 2007), which pays particular attention to tracing the organizational and institutional histories of contemporary forms of non-state security provision. See also Raeymaekers (2014).

In spite of the current fragmentation of authority in eastern Congo, the political order remains deeply anchored in a 'language of stateness'. It continues to resonate with the social imaginaries of public order and is reinvented by state as well as non-state actors (Hoffmann and Vlassenroot, 2014; Titeca and De Herdt, 2011). We suggest that the taxation practices of armed groups in eastern Congo draw on this language of stateness. In particular, we suggest that they evoke local customary and national territorial understandings of citizenship and political community, in order to assume public authority and to tax populations. This is not to say that taxation practices have remained the same since colonialism. Rather it is argued that taxation practices of armed groups — consciously or unconsciously — draw upon, mobilize, evoke and perform the language of stateness when they tax people.

The chapter focuses on the territories of Kalehe and Walikale.[3] Both territories have witnessed two decades of armed group proliferation and increased competition over local power, leading to a deeply fragmented political space and constant competition over public authority. Our analysis is based on long-term fieldwork in the area (1997–2015) where we have carried out numerous interviews with a wide range of respondents, including customary authorities; juridical and security authorities such as police agents, territorial administrators, soldiers, intelligence agents and court clerks; but also representatives of armed groups, petty traders, farmers, civil society representatives, NGO workers, priests, health workers, miners, journalists, craftsmen, educators, students and peddlers.

The chapter starts by analysing colonial practices of taxation, outlining the taxation regime of the Congo Free State (CFS). Attention then turns to the period since the take-over of the Belgian state, with a focus on the Kalehe and Walikale area, including an examination of taxation practices during the Mobutu era. The following section focuses on the taxation practices that emerged during the Congolese Wars through the study of two Mai-Mai groups from Kalehe: the Mai-Mai of General Padiri and the Mai-Mai Kalehe. The final section looks at today's taxation practices based on a study of the Mai-Mai Kifuafua from Walowa-Loanda in Walikale.

COLONIALISM AND THE TRANSFORMATION OF ECONOMIC AND POWER RELATIONS

Prior to colonial penetration, the social landscape in Kalehe and Walikale consisted of an assortment of interconnected polities, which straddled two

---

3. While our findings are obviously empirically circumscribed, our conceptual contribution has a wider reach. We focus on the Batembo and Bahavu areas of Kalehe and Walikale. In Kalehe we draw on field research in the mainly Batembo areas of Kalima, Mubuku, and Buloho, and the mainly Bahavu area of Mbinga-Sud. In Walikale we draw on fieldwork carried out in the mainly Batembo area of Walowa-Loanda.

vast cultural areas. To the west were the forest cultures of the Congo Basin, such as the Batembo and the Banyanga, where people lived in small, independent but highly interactive polities, and to the east, the more centralized highland states of the inter-lacustrine cultures, such as the Bahavu (Biebuyck, 1957; Newbury, 1991: 43–7; Newbury, 2009: 2–3).[4] In the polities of the forest cultures a high degree of individual mobility meant that contacts among different groups were frequent, but not enduring. Therefore, ideas and material items diffused extensively and political entities were never territorially bound. Executive power was dispersed among many groups, individuals and families. Although internally differentiated, these groups acted together. They arrived at decisions communally and performed their functions communally. Importantly, therefore, status was defined more by ritual function and proximity to royal status than by descent. This meant that a very high proportion of families were directly tied to the ritual or executive complex of a given polity (Newbury, 1991: 51–2). In both of these cultural areas, tributes were part of a complex system of social exchange and mutual responsibility between chiefs and ordinary people. These tributes were integral to the recognition of the legitimacy of royal authority and vital for establishing social cohesion and political order.[5]

The colonial language of stateness and logic of state making brought a wholly different understanding of political space, order and methods of rule to the Congo. Science, modern technology, bureaucracy, law, coercion and Christian morality were deployed to bring order and certainty to what was described as a dark and wild place (Hoffmann, 2014: 63). Violence and resource extraction marked the colonial state during the CFS period under Leopoldian rule (1885–1908). To ensure its fiscal viability, this vast colony was divided into the distinct categories of *terres indigènes* (native land) and *terres vacantes* (vacant land), and all vacant land was assigned to the state for exploitation.[6]

This scission of the colonial territory also inaugurated two distinct politico-legal spheres: the civil society of the white citizenry and the tribe of the native subjects (cf. Mamdani, 1996). The natives were subjected to indirect rule through so-called *chefs coutumiers* (customary chiefs), who were embedded into the colonial administration as early as 1886 (Hoffmann, 2014: 121).

---

4. This term denotes an ensemble of similar cultures stretching from Lake Albert, the Victoria Nile and Lake Victoria, in the north and east, to Lake Edward and the Mitumba Mountains (west of Lake Kivu) in the west, and to Burundi and Buha (in Tanzania, just south of Burundi) in the south. Though heterogeneous, these cultures were characterized by highly centralized political organizations, a high degree of social differentiation within individual polities, and mixed economies based on cattle keeping and seed agriculture (Newbury, 1991: 330–1).
5. For more details, see Biebuyck (1966) and Newbury (1991).
6. The delimitation of the native lands severely underestimated the land actually in use by the natives. After vigorous protests in Europe the vacant land was subdivided into three different zones in 1892: one free zone open to commercial exploitation, one zone to ensure the economic viability of the state, and a *Domain privé* reserved for the state (De Clerck, 2004: 255).

However, during the CFS period many of these chiefs were former soldiers of the colonial army or freed slaves, rather than customary authorities which had existed previously (Northrup, 1988: 40). In 1891 these chiefs became even further integrated in the colonial government apparatus with the creation of the institution of the *chefferie* (chiefdom), which ostensibly regrouped natives belonging to the same 'ethnic type' within the 'traditional' boundaries of their tribal homelands. In reality, however, their populations remained highly heterogeneous. In this way, the notion of an ethnic territory (chiefdom) became embedded in a language of stateness.

The violent inclusion of the natives into the new state and the global economy profoundly disturbed the old system of tributes. The entire state-making project rested on the principle that the colonized should bear the cost of their own government and the mission to civilize them. The CFS imposed a regime of taxes on the natives to be paid either in natural commodities, notably ivory and rubber, or in corvées (labour services). Lacking manpower, resources, infrastructure and legitimacy, the CFS to a large extent outsourced the extraction of resources to the 'customary chiefs'. Thus, a law of 1891 defining the role of native chiefs required that at the certification and investiture of each African chief a list would be made of these *prestations* (services) to be furnished to the state.[7] These were in addition to the tributes natives already paid to chiefs. While the *prestations* were framed as taxation by the colonizers,[8] there was no social contract between the colonizers and natives — except between the colonizers and their local allies. This form of sedentary plunder was particularly widespread in the western parts of the territory, where the colonizers had first penetrated and created a vast plantation economy based on rubber exploitation. The extent to which the CFS depended on pillaged resources acquired through forced labour is expressed in the export value of rubber compared to other products. Between 1896 and 1901 its relative value rose from 53 per cent to 87 per cent of the total value of exports (Ndaywel è Nziem, 1998: 332).

Violence was an omnipresent companion of colonial resource extraction in the CFS.[9] Rape, torture, whipping, hostage taking, mutilation, surprise raids and summary executions underpinned the *prestations* system (Harms, 1983; Ngbwapkwa, 1993; Roes, 2010; Vellut, 1984). On the lands owned by the state this was approved by an unpublished decree from 1892 that authorized the secretary of the state 'to take whatever measures he regards useful or necessary to ensure the exploitation' (Northrup, 1988: 41).

---

7. Decree: 'Chefs indigènes – Investiture', Art. 4. *Bulletin Officielle de l'État Indépendant du Congo,* 7th year, Nr. 10, October 1891: 259–61.
8. In the official *Encyclopédie du Congo Belge*, native taxes were framed as a contribution to the common expenses and a gesture of allegiance to the government (Gille, 1951: 737).
9. While this could be said of all the colonial states in Africa (Mbembe, 2001), the CFS became notorious for it.

In the eastern part of the CFS, where Kalehe and Walikale are situated, a different form of resource plunder was predominant. The area corresponded to the zone of influence of Zanzibari slave traders, the major adversaries of the CFS. During the war against the Zanzibari (1892–5), colonial forces lived mainly off the land, carrying out raids for food, slaves and war booty wherever they passed (Ndaywel è Nziem, 1998: 284–5; Roes, 2010: 635; Vellut, 1984). Following the defeat of the Zanzibari, the Europeans took over the institutions, personnel and policies left behind by the Zanzibari traders.[10] The local intermediaries of the Zanzibari became vital allies of the CFS: they provided food provisions and porters, much as they had done for their former Zanzibari masters. In 1893, a special 'taxation' regime, which made more extensive demands for porterage, ivory and rubber on natives, was put in place in eastern Congo to cover the expenses of the war against the Zanzibari. The obligations under this heading exceeded all others in their magnitude and onerousness (Northrup, 1988: 42).

During these tumultuous times, African political institutions struggled to adapt. Chiefs were caught in a cruel dilemma. They had to protect their peoples as much as possible but at the same time they also had to satisfy the state's demands for labour and contributions, or run the risk of being replaced by chiefs picked by the government, who were more willing to do the bidding of the colonial masters.

TAXATION, COERCION AND THE INSTITUTIONALIZATION OF ETHNO-TERRITORIAL CITIZENSHIP

The Belgian colonial state (1908–60) has often been portrayed as a hege-monic Behemoth, which, supported by the moral authority of the Church and the capital of large enterprises, imposed a new ruling structure (e.g. Young, 1965). However, natives did play significant roles in the profound transformation of local societies that resulted from European penetration. In the Kivu region, for example, circumstances meant that there was scope for natives to shape the situation to their advantage. First, the colonizers were mainly preoccupied with defending the state's border to the east against German and British imperial interests.[11] As a result, colonial presence was limited to a series of forts erected on the border to defend it. Second, due to a lack of transport infrastructure, resources and personnel, the colonizers

---

10. In 1893, Governor General Théophile Wahis described the regime in eastern Congo as follows: '[it is] in short just about what had been created by the Arabs. The division of territory is what they had established. The personnel, who occupy the regions here and there, are those whom they sent here' (quoted in Northrup, 1988: 43).
11. For more details on this imperial controversy, which nearly triggered a new scramble for Africa in 1894, see Louis (1963).

were dependent on native chiefs to provide food supplies,[12] labour and building materials. Third, because army mutineers held out in the area (Njangu, 1973), Kivu was the last region to be explored and 'pacified'.[13]

Certain local elites seized the opportunity to strengthen their position in local power struggles by collaborating with the new colonial actors. By mobilizing the labour of their subjects these local elites provided the colonizers with the resources they needed, and in return received protection and recognition from the colonial government. However, if the tenuous position of the state implied increased scope for local resistance and room for manoeuvre for native elites, it also meant that the colonizers had to rely on coercion, which remained integral to 'taxation'. Chiefs and communities who refused to provide the demanded contributions and corvée labour found themselves targeted by police and military operations (Bishikwabo, 1984). Under these conditions one of the most important benefits of collaboration for local elites and their populations was simply to avoid being subjected to the repressive measures of the colonial authorities. In this respect, colonial taxation practices ushered in new taxation-for-protection arrangements.

This dynamic was also at play in Kalehe, where two Bahavu chiefs who ruled the lakeside area (Lushombo and Biglimani) collaborated with the colonial authorities. Both chiefs provided much-needed supplies and achieved official recognition from the colonial authorities (Hoffmann, 2014: 159; Shanyungu, 1976: 51–2). By contrast, in the forested regions, reported to be rich in ivory and rubber, the colonizers met armed resistance from local chiefs and populations who refused to provide contributions to the Europeans. To subdue these areas, military expeditions were carried out against insurgent chiefs and their followers in 1911–12, resulting in the deaths of more than 250 natives. However, these campaigns failed to bring these regions fully under colonial control (Hoffmann, 2014: 161–6). The outbreak of World War I further reinforced the coercive aspect of resource extraction in the region. During the war, the colonial army of Belgian Congo invaded German-held Ruanda-Urundi. Scores of people from Kalehe and Walikale died from disease and exhaustion while carrying supplies and munitions to the front (ibid.).

The end of World War I signalled the replacement of public authority and resource extraction carried out primarily through force, by authority of an increasingly technocratic and bureaucratic nature aiming to develop (*mettre en valeur*) the colony in eastern Congo. However, the changes were not immediately felt in most Batembo areas, where the population refused to

---

12. The Europeans relied on native food supplies to sustain the colonial project across the colony since they did not produce food themselves (Ndaywel è Nziem, 1998: 339).
13. Lake Kivu itself was not 'discovered' until 16 June 1894 by the expedition of the German explorer Count von Götzen.

accept colonial sovereignty. As a result, certain parts remained subject to military rule until 1919–20 (ibid.).

In the long run, the transition to a more technocratic native policy involved momentous changes. The introduction of a head tax, the amalgamation of smaller chieftaincies, the creation of native courts, and the relocation of different populations served to create more hierarchical systems of rule revolving around the control of territory and population. This led to the concentration of authority and resources in the hands of the chiefs and their supporters at the local level. This, in turn, allowed for a more efficient imposition of order and resource extraction (Newbury and Newbury, 1982). The measures were introduced over time and met with different kinds of obstacles.

For example, when the amalgamation of small, so-called unsustainable chieftaincies into bigger ones was implemented in the 1920s,[14] it led to the creation of a new and large Buhavu chiefdom in Kalehe and the incorporation of several previously independent chiefdoms. The chiefdom was ruled by a new figure of authority: the *grand chef* of the Bahavu, Bahole, who was the successor of Lushombo. Bahole thus became the ruler over a new territorial entity, which stretched into the eastern edge of the equatorial rainforest. Moreover, he was supposed to work according to one set of customary rules, to be enforced by the newly created native courts. While the new territory was defined mono-ethnically by the colonial authorities, in reality its populations were highly heterogeneous.

The creation of the Buhavu chiefdom caused resentment and resistance among the Batembo who refused to respect the *grand chef* as a public authority. Taxation was a major bone of contention and several Batembo chiefs refused to pay taxes to Bahole (Hoffmann, 2014: 186). As the territorial administrator noted:

> The populations [of Kalima] do not accept any other authority than the mubutetu chief. The influence and prestige of the chief of the musibura [Bahole] is almost nil; tribute was brought to him for the first time in 1934, after an energetic and direct pressure by the European administration. The emissaries that the Mwami have sent to this province have been very badly received.[15]

In 1934, in order to better estimate the number of taxable subjects among the Batembo, the colonial authorities attempted to regroup the populations in villages along roads. This proved equally difficult, as the Batembo continuously evaded and deceived colonial agents.[16] As the annual report of

---

14. Ministère des Colonies, Section d'Affaires Indigènes et Main d'Oeuvre. Folder: 1640-9205. Circular Nr. 505, signed by Minister of Colonies Louis Franck. Retrieved from the archive of the Belgian Ministry of Foreign Affairs.
15. J.M. Derscheid Collection, University of Florida Digital Collections: 'Bahavu. Province du Karima (Kalima des documents administratifs). Notes A. Braun. January 1935'. http://ufdc.ufl.edu/AA00002627/00001?search=karima
16. Ministère des Colonies. Section d'Affaires Indigènes et Main d'Oeuvre. Folder: 82. 'Commentaires du Commissaire de District du Kivu sur le rapport annuel de 1934 du territoire des Bahavu'. Retrieved from the archive of the Belgian Ministry of Foreign Affairs.

the Bahavu chiefdom recorded in 1932: '[t]he desire to evade any authority has pushed these natives to construct huts beyond any reach. If a path leads to a village it will be moved to a neighbouring mountain. If we arrive in this village, only two or three old women are left'.[17] Throughout the colonial era, the colonial authorities were frustrated by what they saw as the unfavourable attitude of the Batembo towards civilization, earning them a reputation as exceptionally savage. This prejudice denied the Batembo the right to an independent chiefdom, and thus independent ethnic citizenship, with the exception of the small chiefdom of Buloho, which was recognized in 1945.

While the taxation regime was met with resistance, it also created a new kind of social contract revolving around the 'imagined community' of the ethnic group. In 1933, the colonial authorities introduced a *caisse* (treasury) in the chieftaincies. The *caisse* was a public fund which centralized the resources of the chiefdom. These resources were earmarked to contribute to covering the administration of the chiefdom. In this way a new kind of fiscal bargain emerged whereby members of the chiefdom received something in return for the resources they paid to the chief. These resources were neither a tribute to the 'chief' nor an obligatory contribution imposed by a violent external force. Instead they were a contribution to the 'ethnic community', as a territorially bounded imagined community. In this way taxation helped to create ethnic forms of citizenship.

Ultimately, the subjugation of the Batembo to the Bahavu chief contributed to the growth of a Batembo political identity and community. Colonial reports indicate that in the Batembo areas, from the mid-1930s onwards, censuses were conducted, taxes paid, budgets made, labour conscripted, native courts created, money introduced, villages regrouped, and roads and buildings constructed. In short, even in Batembo areas a more bureaucratic language of stateness gradually took hold (cf. Hoffmann, 2014). In 1945, Batembo leaders started formulating claims for a separate Batembo territory[18] and by 1956 Batembo leaders had created the 'ethnic' associations — the Union d'Entreaide Batembo — all signs that a new kind of Batembo territorial political identity was emerging.

SCARCITY, EXTORTION AND THE RUPTURE OF THE FISCAL BARGAIN

Independence brought sudden and dramatic changes to eastern Congo even if the nature of the state and its forms of taxation were only partially reformed during decolonization. Certain core features of the colonial taxation regime remained. The chiefs continued to collect the head tax, for which the vast

---

17. Ministère des Colonies. Section d'Affaires Indigènes et Main d'Oeuvre. Folder: 82. 'Rapport annuel. Territoire des Bahavu de 1932'. Retrieved from the archive of the Belgian Ministry of Foreign Affairs.
18. Interview, village chief, 28 September 2011, Bulambika; Interview, Councillor to the Provincial Assembly of South Kivu, ca. November 2012, Bukavu.

majority of the population in the rural areas was liable.[19] Rural residents also still paid taxes both to the central state and to the chiefdoms, although they received few public services and goods in return. Furthermore, coercion remained integral to taxation.

However, under Mobutu, there was an important change in the language of stateness. The Mobutu regime consciously set out to turn the colonial state into a nation state, rather than a collection of tribes haphazardly brought together by colonial intervention. Taxes paid to the state were now framed as a contribution to the imagined community of the Zairian nation state rather than to an externally imposed colonial state. The state- and nation-building project of the Mobutu regime combined the colonial model of authoritarianism and centralized control with unitary nationalist discourse, articulated in the successive doctrines of 'authentic Zairian nationalism', 'authenticity' and 'Mobutism'. It stressed order, control, discipline and work, in particular, as a move away from the disorder of the tumultuous first five years of independence, which were marked by war and political uncertainty. The duty of the citizens was to obey and support the new ruler, who was presented as the embodiment of the nation. Paying taxes and working conscientiously were framed as the primary duties of the citizenry *vis-à-vis* the sovereign (Callaghy, 1984: 322–3).

The regime's legitimacy began to crumble when its provision of public goods declined drastically following the virtual collapse of the state economy in the mid-1970s, in the wake of the sharp drop in copper prices of 1973 and the effects of patrimonial rule.[20] While the regime's provision of public goods and the economic conditions of most *Zaïrois* declined, the official and unofficial fiscal burden increased,[21] and compulsory unpaid civic work called *salongo* was introduced to instil a sense of civic education and to compensate for dwindling government resources (Callaghy 1984: 299–303). Even if this was unevenly imposed — and sometimes hardly imposed at all — it still echoed the despised colonial practice of corvée labour. In practice, *salongo* was often used for private purposes by authorities. Fairhead (1992) provides an illustrative example from the chieftaincy of Bwisha in North Kivu from the late 1980s. *Salongo* was organized by the customary authorities, usually the village chief and the president of the state party's so-called *comité de base* (grassroots committee). Common tasks included cultivating the fields of customary authorities, and building and maintaining their houses. On rare

---

19. The head tax also constituted the main source of revenue for the chieftaincies, usually around 50 per cent. The chieftaincies were allowed to keep 50 per cent of those taxes: the rest were sent to the zone and to the central state (Callaghy, 1984: 370).
20. For instance, the Mobutu regime's allocation of resources to health and education dropped from 17.5 per cent in 1972 to 2.1 per cent in 1992.
21. Although such numbers should be taken with extreme caution, scholars estimated the fiscal burden on rural populations to have been as high as 50 per cent, not including bribes and other illegal forms of extortion (Callaghy, 1984: 370; Young and Turner, 1985: 96)

occasions, the work went towards constructing roads or to social infrastructure such as schools and clinics. Superiors justified their private use of community labour by claiming that it was compensation for unpaid posts.

With the deepening economic decline, which had a dramatic effect on the core foundations of patrimonial rule, taxation became further informalized, privatized and decentred. As Schatzberg has shown, the combination of rampant insecurity among state agents, who never knew how long they would be able to keep their positions, and the 'overwhelming condition of economic scarcity', led them to accumulate as many resources as rapidly as they could by extracting them from those in inferior positions (Schatzberg, 1980: 184). The effect of these developments was increased scarcity and insecurity among 'tax-payers'. The security forces in particular became a 'free-floating source of insecurity' (Schatzberg, 1988: 70).[22] Roads throughout the country were peppered with roadblocks erected by army units, state party youth groups, or local police conducting *opérations de rattisage* (search and sweep operations), which were supposedly intended to haul in illegals but were yet another form of extraction (Callaghy, 1984: 288–90; Fairhead, 1992: 22–3). These practices of extortive resource extraction undermined the legitimacy of local authorities, including those in the Kivu region (Callaghy, 1984; Newbury, 1984). As taxation became little more than thinly-disguised predation, people were mobilized to protest this breach of the social contract with authorities. Catharine Newbury provides a striking example from Buloho chiefdom in Kalehe. Here, in 1982, a group of cassava-producing women protested against the multiplication of irregular taxes by state and customary officials: over the 10 km to the market, three different levies were imposed at stream crossings where barriers could not be evaded. The women were driven to their unprecedented act of protest because of the declining terms of the cassava trade and because the new taxes provided nothing in return (Newbury, 1984: 48). By claiming the right to something in return for payment, they maintained that what they paid was tax rather than extortion money. One woman expressed her dissatisfaction as follows:

> We would like to know what is being done with the money collected for this tax. ... In this region there is no road, no bridge, nor even a market like that at Bulambika. So what projects are being financed by this money? These thirty *makuta* which [the chieftdom] has added to the twenty *makuta* — what do they do with this profit? (quoted in Newbury, 1984: 41)

In addition to this informalization and privatization of taxation, the socio-economic protection provided by the customary chiefs came under stress in 1973, when previously protected customary lands were nationalized and made available on the market. In much of the Kivus, customary chiefs

---

22. Also increasing the total fiscal burden on Congolese citizens was the fact that it was common practice for tax collectors and other officials to simply keep a portion for themselves (Schatzberg, 1988: 195).

exploited these new opportunities by selling off large tracts of customary land to the wealthy politico-commercial, largely urban elite, of which many were connected to the regime. This process profoundly shook the authority of the chiefs as an increasing number of peasants — youths in particular — found themselves excluded from its systems of socio-economic protection (Vlassenroot and Van Acker, 2001).

In Kalehe, the increased competition for resources also had ethnic connotations. For instance, Batembo leaders continued the struggle begun during the colonial period by repeatedly seeking recognition as an independent chiefdom (Hoffmann, 2014; Pindo, 1977). The right to taxation was integral to these claims because, just as during the colonial era, chiefdom revenues continued to be generated locally through fees and taxes (Callaghy, 1984: 368–9). These recurrent claims were not merely symbolic; they constituted politico-economic claims to self-government over pivotal resources, including taxes. As one prominent leader in Kalima expressed it:

> We [did] not have chiefdom or a customary legislation which is recognized in Kinshasa — and these Bahavu — all they did was to dominate us. They had their hands on the market of Bunyakiri, that is, all the taxes were used in their favour, they could do that because of our non-recognition from Kinshasa ... that is to say that if you are recognized by Kinshasa then you can develop because there is going to be a fund which is destined for your chiefdom.[23]

WAR, TAXATION AND THE RECONFIGURATION OF PUBLIC AUTHORITY

The failed democratization process (1990–6) and the First and Second Congo Wars (1996–7 and 1998–2003) constituted a series of interconnected ruptures, which brought profound social and political changes to eastern Congo (Tull, 2003; Vlassenroot and Raeymaekers, 2004). During the Congo Wars, armed groups started proliferating and a new class of politico-military rulers with ties to Kinshasa or to foreign regimes rose to prominence. They fought to assume public authority over territory and populations and engaged in complex and fluid alliances with local authorities and with international political and business interests. New networks of 'profit, power and protection' (Vlassenroot and Raeymaekers, 2004: 21) were constituted which initiated new fiscal bargains and experimented with different forms of taxation that often revolved around the provision of protection. These taxes-for-protection arrangements again were largely framed in a language of stateness, with taxes being presented as obligatory contributions to the defence of local ethnic communities and the nation state — the two constitutive imagined political communities in the Congo. Furthermore, rather than introduce new forms of taxation, the actual operation of taxation resembled forms associated with the Congolese state. As taxation was now part of open armed

---

23. Interview, ex-Mai-Mai administrator and schoolteacher, Bukavu, 27 November 2005.

struggles for control over territory, people and resources, the coercive aspect became more prominent, as it had been in earlier periods. As taxation became part of the logic of war, it also became more militarized (cf. Verweijen, 2013).

These dynamics could also be observed in Walikale and Kalehe. During the Second Congo War, these territories were part of the battleground between the Rwandan-backed Rassemblement Congolais pour la Démocratie-Goma (Congolese Rally for Democracy-Goma, RCD-G), which controlled the main towns and certain strategic economic areas including mining centres, and a constellation of Rwandan Hutu insurgents and local Mai-Mai groups that held sway in the hinterlands and eventually received support from the Congolese government. The most powerful of these Mai-Mai groups was led by Padiri Bulenda, and was dominated by Batembo from Kalima, Mubuku, Buloho and Waloa-Loanda. The group claimed to be an autochthonous resistance movement defending the Congolese native 'Bantus' from foreign invaders seeking to create a 'Tutsi-Hima empire' in central Africa. It was a narrative which resonated among the 'autochthonous' populations across the Kivus, not only because the racial categories which were evoked by it had been part of the language of stateness for generations (Newbury, 1978), but also because the same population had been exposed to brutal treatment by the RCD-G (Hoffmann, 2015; Jackson, 2006). At its peak, the group controlled large swathes of territory in the rural Kivus. By invoking the principle of national sovereignty, it was able to mobilize large segments of the population to contribute monetary and in-kind taxes. Echoing practices of the Mobutu state, Mai-Mai authorities created *comités de soutien* (support committees). These committees were organized at the village level by customary chiefs and Mai-Mai elements to mobilize local residents to provide food, money, labour and recruits to the Mai-Mai (Hoffmann, 2015). Special taxation practices were developed for lucrative economic activities, in particular mining, which came under centralized control by the group's military headquarters.[24]

Taxation was framed as a key contribution to the restoration of the 'authority of the state'.[25] It was also an important element in the creation of an elaborate administrative framework built on the model of the defunct Congolese state. Even in its routine exercise of public authority, the group enacted a language of stateness. Communications, regulations, licences, travel permits, arrest orders, memos, etc. were framed in legal-bureaucratic language and made to look as official as possible. Yet, the group also enacted customary registers of authority, for instance by their extensive use of ancient healing techniques and purification rituals known as *dawa*. In their local

---

24. Interview with Major Muhindo Changoco, former adjunct of General Padiri, Bagira, 14 June 2013.
25. Memorandum: 'Mémorandum sur la participation de l'entité Mai-Mai à la gestion de la transition adressé à son Excellence le général major Joseph Kabila, Président de la République', 27 September 2004. Entité Mai-Mai/EST. Coordination des Affaires Intérieures. Bukavu.

stronghold, the use of *dawa* techniques provided another layer of legitimacy as it bore witness to their claim that they embodied the authentic culture of the Batembo (for further details, see Hoffmann, 2015). The group also cultivated support among the Batembo by claiming to fight for the old dream of creating a Batembo territory.

While the group often resorted to violence and intimidation to obtain compliance with its fiscal bargain, it also attempted to develop the areas it ruled. It encouraged health services, schools and various other institutions to continue their activities under the group's protection. The heavy fiscal burden imposed on local populations was justified by the assertion that everybody had to contribute what they could. The war, it was argued, threatened the very survival of the Congolese nation and taxation was framed as an obligatory contribution to its defence, an *effort de guerre* (war effort). Despite the group's deep roots in local society, the pressure to provide food, money and porterage of munitions, as well as the forced recruitment of youth and children, strained the social contract between Padiri's Mai-Mai and the civilian population. There was a certain room for manoeuvre, however: the close personal relations between Mai-Mai soldiers and local residents occasionally enabled the latter to persuade the Mai-Mai authorities to improve the terms of the fiscal bargain by, for instance, lightening the tax burden imposed on them, disciplining misbehaving combatants, or taking steps to improve the security situation (Morvan, 2005).

Nevertheless, Padiri's group had difficulties imposing its authoritarian and centralized regime beyond its stronghold. Local branches of the group were unhappy with the predominance of the Batembo from Kalima, Mubuku and Buloho in the Mai-Mai movement. This led to repeated splintering of the group, and even to confrontations between factions (Morvan, 2005). A case in point is the Mai-Mai Kalehe.[26] This group was active between 1998 and 2004 in the highlands and midlands of the Mbinga-Sud *groupement* (grouping),[27] in the Bahavu areas of Kalehe territory, and counted several Bahavu among its leaders.[28] Like other security forces before it, including Mobutu's army and other rebel groups, the group set up roadblocks, made access to the local market subject to the payment of entry fees, and positioned soldiers at strategic sites to tax agricultural products and forest products and resources.[29] Furthermore, in order to tax households, the group registered

---

26. The Mai-Mai Kalehe was formed by Major Muhindo Changoco, a former adjunct of Padiri in Bunyakiri who had broken away from Padiri's group to form his own, basing itself in the Southern Highlands of Kalehe around the town of Katasomwa. From 1997 to 1998, the group created strong ties with the Local Defence Forces of Lemera and Kasheke under the leadership of Cisayura, eventually merging forces to form the Mai-Mai Kalehe.
27. In Congolese legislation, a *groupement* is a sub-division of a chiefdom or a sector. The *groupement* is in turn sub-divided into *localités* (localities, which are sometimes referred to as *villages* [villages]).
28. Jean Paul Eneondo Sido and Cisayura Bienvenue were natives of the *localité* of Kasheke in Mbinga Sud; Major Muhindo Changoco had both Havu and Tembo origins.
29. Interview, Lieutenant Colonel Cisayura, Kavumu, June 2013.

the population and monitored its contributions.[30] The Mai-Mai Kalehe tried to legitimize its right to levy war taxes on the population in two ways. Firstly, like Padiri's Mai-Mai, it framed its combat as a defence of the nation against foreign invaders. This security discourse found a receptive ear, not only among the Bahavu, but also among certain Bahutu in the highlands and midlands, who were also frustrated with RCD-G rule. Secondly, it framed itself as a Bahavu defence force locally, which enabled it to obtain support from a wide spectrum of influential Bahavu notables, ranging from business operatives to customary and civil authorities and religious leaders. In this sense, the fiscal bargain proposed by the group evoked both local and national forms of citizenship.

Nevertheless, the group faced severe difficulties in constituting itself as a legitimate taxing authority, for several reasons. First, the group relied extensively on coercion of local authorities and populations to impose its rule and levy taxes, while providing few public goods in return. Second, there was a deep-seated antagonism and mistrust between the Mai-Mai Kalehe and their supporters, on the one hand, and the customary Bahavu authorities and their supporters on the other. This was largely because the local customary Bahavu authorities had a history of collaboration with the RCD-G; the customary *chef de localite* (village chief) of Lemera had to be coerced into compliance.[31] Third, its link with Padiri's group and its self-definition as a Mai-Mai group meant that many Bahavu saw it as a Batembo project, which had no right to rule and impose taxes in a Bahavu area.[32] The association of the group with the Batembo was reinforced by its engagement with the *dawa*. These practices were seen as 'something of the Tembo, something of the Rega, but not the Havu'.[33] Other important reasons for its lack of legitimacy were the favouritism[34] that the group displayed towards friends and family members and its corrupt practices of justice. Thus, while the Mai-Mai Kalehe's struggle against RCD-G rule was generally recognized as legitimate, it was not enough to keep people content with its fiscal bargain.[35]

ARMED GROUPS AND TAXATION IN THE POST-SETTLEMENT ERA

The Second Congolese War ended with an inclusive peace agreement, signed in December 2002. A transition process followed, leading to democratic elections in 2006 and the electoral victory of Joseph Kabila. However, the slow return of state authorities to rebel-held areas in Kalehe and Walikale did not

30. Interview, Jacques Nyalakasi, executive secretary of the Mai-Mai Kalehe, Bagira, June 2013.
31. Interview, village chief of Lemera, October 2012.
32. Interview, village chief of Kasheke, Kasheke, 8 November 2012.
33. Interview, sub-village chief of Nyamutwe, 12 November 2012.
34. Interview, village chief of Kasheke, 8 November 2012.
35. Interview, village chief of Kasheke, 8 November 2012; interview, Lieutenant Colonel Cisayura, Mai-Mai Kalehe 21 June 2013.

significantly alter taxation regimes and practices. Severely under-resourced local administrators, customary chiefs and militarized security services continued to rely on (militarized) strategies of resource extraction. By and large, these were considered as harassment by the local population, but in some cases they were seen as taxes which provided a modicum of security in return. This was the case with some of the roadblocks set up in mid-2010, to deter attacks by bandits and rebels who were targeting buses and trucks transporting goods. In the Kahuzi-Biega National Park, which was regularly frequented by bandits targeting vehicles, the roadblock erected by the army was welcomed by the population and was experienced as a public security service providing protection. Similarly, the customary authorities of Buloho chiefdom successfully approached the army to deploy troops to secure the road connecting the main town of the chiefdom, Maibano, to the main market in Bulambika. The road was the economic lifeline of Buloho and even though road users had to pay the troops, this was generally accepted because petty traders were protected against attacks from the mainly Rwandan Hutu rebel group, Forces Démocratiques pour la Libération du Rwanda (Democratic Forces for the Liberation of Rwanda, FDLR).[36] While local citizens expressed a certain amount of sympathy for the plight of local authorities, however, dissatisfaction and disappointment with the government and the overall fiscal burden remained widespread, as people did not see adequate compensation from the taxes paid to the state.

In spite of the formal end to hostilities and the gradual return of state services, armed groups continued to proliferate in more remote areas. These groups were often mobilized by local political-military elites who had failed to secure sought-after positions within the army and other state institutions. In a context of ongoing insecurity and scarcity, ex-combatants and marginalized youth constituted an ever-present reservoir, ready to be recruited (Eriksson Baaz and Verweijen, 2013: 12; Lamb et al., 2012: 24–7).[37] While the main protagonists, the RCD-G and Padiri's Mai-Mai, joined the army reintegration process, in Kalehe and Walikale several groups formerly associated with them remained active, including the Mai-Mai Kifuafua (Walowa-Loanda), the Mai-Mai Kirikicho (Ziralo) and the Coalition des patriotes résistants congolais (Alliance of Resistant Congolese Patriots, PARECO) (Ziralo, Masisi and Rutshuru). Other groups, such as the Raia Mutomboki, have since become part of local military landscapes. Continued insecurity, ethnicized tensions and a lack of faith in the government allowed these groups to emerge as alternative public authorities claiming to provide security for the

---

36. Fieldnotes, July 2010.
37. Paradoxically, policies adopted to address the proliferation of armed groups, such as army reintegration and military operations, have further fragmented public authority to the extent that, in 2015, an estimated 70 armed groups were operating in eastern Congo (Stearns and Vogel, 2015; Verweijen and Wakenge, 2015).

community in return for the payment of contributions, presented as legitimate forms of taxation.

A good example of such a local fiscal bargain based on the notion of community security has developed between the Mai-Mai Kifuafua and local residents in the remote, mostly Batembo *groupement* of Walowa-Loanda situated in southern Walikale. Here, state authorities, including security services, have been absent for a long time. This has fostered a sense of abandonment by the state among local residents and has facilitated their recognition of the Mai-Mai Kifuafua's claims to be a legitimate security force, despite its history of coercive and extractive taxation, and the fact that it provided few tangible public goods and services in return, beyond community defence (Vlassenroot et al., 2016). The group's revenues are mainly derived from the taxation of commerce and palm oil production. For instance, it controls all the markets in the area and anyone entering or leaving a market must pay 500 FC (about US$ 0.6). Similarly, a tax of 2,000–3,000 FC (US$ 2.2–3.3) must be paid for each cow entering the market, and 1,000–1,500 FC (US$ 1.1–1.6) for each goat. Manioc mills and palm oil production are similarly taxed. The strategies that the group uses to generate popular support are set within existing practical and symbolic registers of authority and languages of stateness, to the extent that local residents view the group as a 'state within the state'. The group frames itself as an *armée communautaire* (community army) of Walowa-Loanda and as guarantor of Walowa-Loanda's security. In this context, taxation is justified as an obligation that community members owe to the community for its security.

In contrast to the Mai-Mai Kalehe, the taxation practices of the Mai-Mai Kifuafua are to some extent recognized as legitimate because they are firmly anchored in the local community and because they observe certain values and norms, which underpin the exercise of public authority and taxation. Rather than being enforced solely by coercion, public authority and taxation rights are subject to a high level of negotiation with customary authorities and other local notables, who continue to receive considerable levels of popular support. As one civil society leader put it: 'The Mai-Mai Kifuafua collaborate closely with the customary chiefs because people listen to the customary chiefs; the Kifuafua cannot refuse their counsel'.[38] The collaboration with these customary chiefs has imbued the group's exercise of authority with a modicum of legitimacy. Another factor in its favour is its embeddedness in local society, which reinforces the recognition of the group as an *armée communautaire*. As the chief of Walowa-Loanda explained: 'the collaboration [with] the Mai-Mai Kifuafua is good because they are children from the village. They can protect us; they have houses right next to us. If I see them harassing I summon them'.[39] Their collaboration with local chiefs in the

---

38. Interview with civil society leader, Chambucha, 12 October 2015.
39. Interview with chef de groupement, Busurungi, 16 October 2015.

promotion of development, their participation in community work such as *salongo* and other social activities, and their assistance in vaccination campaigns illustrate both this embeddedness and the recognition they receive from being Kifuafua members.

Yet, this embeddedness does not prevent the taxes imposed by the Kifuafua commanders from being experienced as a considerable burden. This is illustrated by the frequent denunciations of the taxes by members of civil society in Walowa-Loanda, especially those imposed at the entrance to markets. Even if some space for negotiation exists, people are still obliged to pay. In return, they are subjected to less harassment and less random extortion, and gain a sense of heightened community security.

The case of the Kifuafua illustrates how the continuous presence of armed groups in Walikale and Kalehe contributes to fragmented public authority. Decades of scarcity, insecurity, conflict and grievances, and the accumulated fears these have produced, have allowed political-military leaders to mobilize armed self-defence groups anchored in local forms of ethnic citizenship. In some areas of Kalehe and Walikale, such as Walowa-Loanda, these armed groups have become dominant public authorities, which, in return for taxes, try to enforce law and order, promote development and protect the community.

CONCLUSION

In this contribution, we have illustrated how taxation is at the core of the production of public authority of armed groups operating in eastern Congo. The cases presented also show that while the wars in Kalehe and Walikale have produced new forms of taxation, which often revolve around taxes-for-protection arrangements, the taxation practices of contemporary Mai-Mai groups continue, to a considerable extent, to be framed within existing registers of authority and modes of rule, notably by re-activating ethnoterritorial ontologies of local political space, community and citizenship to legitimize extractive taxation practices.

Taxation is one of the main activities of armed groups and one of the most essential links between armed groups and residents. Taxes establish mutual obligations between armed groups and residents. They are constitutive for the establishment of the boundaries of the political community and public authority. In this sense they are constitutive of both citizenship and jurisdiction. When armed groups impose taxes on people in Walikale and Kalehe they often justify them as obligatory contributions to the defence of the Congolese nation state and to a given local customary community. Every member of these imagined communities is enjoined to contribute to the community's defence. Armed groups frame themselves as legitimate public authorities in these political communities because they are the only ones with the capacity to defend them. Such discourses of community security resonate among local populations who have been exposed to insecurity and scarcity for decades. These imagined communities are evoked to impose taxes, often without providing tangible public services and goods in return. Although there is some room for negotiation, people see taxation as a heavy burden which they cannot escape, since it is often underpinned by a more or less open threat of force.

However, as we have argued, neither the coercive, brokered and extractive modalities of taxation that armed groups engage in, nor the territorially bound 'imagined communities' (the nation state and the chiefdom) that they evoke to legitimize these taxes suddenly appeared when war broke out. Rather, they have a long and shared history as part of the colonial language of stateness. This implies that the fragmentation of authority which is currently taking place in eastern Congo should not be seen as an expression of disorder. It is the product of the very constitution of political order itself, based as it is on territorially bound and exclusivist ethnic ontologies of local citizenship and resource extraction.

REFERENCES

Anderson, B. (1983) *Imagined Communities: Reflections on the Origin and Spread of Nationalism*. London and New York: Verso.

Berdal, M.R. and D. Malone (eds) (2000) *Greed and Grievance: Economic Agendas in Civil Wars*. Boulder, CO: Lynne Rienner.

Biebuyck, D. (1957) 'L'organisation politique des Banyanga: La chefferie d'Ihana' ['The Political Organization of the Banyanga: The Chiefdom of Ihana'], *Kongo-Overzee* 23(1–2): 59–98.

Biebuyck, D. (1966) *Rights in Land and its Resources among the Nyanga*. Brussels: ARSOM.

Bishikwabo, C. (1984) 'La politique indigène au congo-belge et son application au Kivu: De la légitimité à l'illégimité (1900–1945)' ['The Native Policy of the Belgian Congo and its Application in the Kivu: From Legitimacy to Illegitimacy (1900–1945)'], *Zamani* 1: 38–88.

Callaghy, T.M. (1984) *The State–Society Struggle: Zaire in Comparative Perspective*. New York: Columbia University Press.

Collier, P. and A. Hoeffler (2004) 'Greed and Grievance in Civil War', *Oxford Economic Papers* 56(4): 563–95.

De Clerck, L. (2004) 'Le régime foncier, le régime minier et le droit des biens' ['The Legal System on Land and Mining and Property Law'], in E. Lamy and L. Declerck (eds) *L'Ordre juridique colonial belge en Afrique Centrale: Éléments d'Histoire* [*The Belgian Colonial Legal System in Central Africa: Historical Elements*], pp. 253–311. Brussels: ARSOM.

Eriksson Baaz, M. and J. Verweijen (2013) 'Between Integration and Disintegration: The Erratic Trajectory of the Congolese Army'. New York: Social Science Research Council.

Fairhead, J. (1992) 'Paths of Authority: Roads, the State and the Market in Eastern Zaire', *European Journal of Development Research* 4(2): 17–35.

Garrett, N., S. Sergiou and K. Vlassenroot (2009) 'Negotiated Peace for Extortion: The Case of Walikale Territory in Eastern DR Congo', *Journal of Eastern African Studies* 3(1): 1–21.

Gille, A. (1951) 'La Politique Indigène du Congo Belge et Ruanda-Urundi' ['The Native Policy of the Belgian Congo and Ruanda-Urundi'], in *Encyclopédie du Congo Belge, Tome III* [*Encyclopaedia of the Belgian Congo, Vol. III*], pp. 709–48. Brussels: Éditions Bielefeld.

Hansen, T.B. and F. Stepputat (2001) 'Introduction: States of Imagination', in T.B. Hansen and F. Stepputat (eds) *States of Imagination: Ethnographic Explorations of the Postcolonial State*, pp. 1–38. Durham, NC: Duke University Press.

Harms, R. (1983) 'The World Abir Made: The Maringa-Lopori Basin, 1885–1903', *African Economic History* 12: 125–39.

Heald, S. (2006) 'State, Law, and Vigilantism in Northern Tanzania', *African Affairs* 105(419): 265–83.

Hoffmann, K. (2014) 'Ethnogovernmentality: The Making of Ethnic Territories and Subjects in Eastern Congo'. PhD dissertation, Roskilde University, Roskilde.

Hoffmann, K. (2015) 'Myths Set in Motion: The Moral Economy of Mai-Mai Governance', in A. Arjona, N. Kasfir and Z. Mampilly (eds) *Rebel Governance*, pp. 158–79. Cambridge: Cambridge University Press.

Hoffmann, K. and K. Vlassenroot (2014) 'Armed Groups and the Exercise of Public Authority. The Cases of the Mayi Mayi and Raya Mutomboki in Kalehe, South Kivu', *Peacebuilding* 2(2): 202–20.

Jackson, S. (2006) 'Sons of Which Soil? The Language and Politics of Autochthony in Eastern DR Congo', *African Studies Review* 49(2): 95–123.

Lamb, G., N. Alusala, G. Mthembu-Salter and J.-M. Gasana (2012) 'Rumours of Peace, Whispers of War: Assessment of the Reintegration of Ex-Combatants into Civilian Life in North Kivu, South Kivu and Ituri Democratic Republic of Congo'. Washington, DC: World Bank. http://www.tdrp.net/PDFs/DRC-Report-2012.pdf

Laudati, A. (2013) 'Beyond Conflict Minerals: Broadening "Economies of Violence" in Eastern Democratic Republic of the Congo', *Review of African Political Economy* 40(135): 32–50.

Louis, W.R. (1963) *Ruanda-Urundi 1884–1919*. Oxford: Clarendon Press.

Lund, C. (2006) 'Twilight Institutions: An Introduction', *Development and Change* 37(4): 673–84.

Mamdani, M. (1996) *Citizen and Subject: Contemporary Africa and the Legacy of Late Colonialism*. Princeton, NJ: Princeton University Press.

Martin, I.W., A.K. Mehrotra and M. Prasad (2009) *The New Fiscal Sociology. Taxation in Comparative and Historical Perspective*. Cambridge: Cambridge University Press.

Mbembe, A. (2001) *On the Postcolony*. Berkeley and Los Angeles, CA and London: University of California Press.

Meagher, K. (2007) 'Hijacking Civil Society: The Inside Story of the Bakassi Boys Vigilante Group of South-eastern Nigeria', *Journal of Modern African Studies* 45(1): 89–115.

Morvan, H. (2005) *Réinventer le quotidien: La cohabitation des populations civiles et des combattants maï-maï au Kivu* [*Reinventing Daily Life: The Cohabitation between Civilian Populations and Mai-Mai Fighters in the Kivu*]. Uppsala and Bukavu: Life & Peace Institute.

Ndaywel è Nziem, I. (1998) *Histoire générale du Congo: De l'héritage ancien à la République Démocratique* [*General History of the Congo: From the Ancient Heritage to the Democratic Republic*]. Louvain-la-Neuve and Paris: Duculot-Agence de la francophonie.

Newbury, C. (1984) 'Ebutumwa Bw'emiogo: The Tyranny of Cassava. A Women's Tax Revolt in Eastern Zaire', *Canadian Journal of African Studies* 18(1): 35–54.

Newbury, D. (1978) 'Bushi and the Historians: Historiographical Themes in Eastern Kivu', *History in Africa* 5: 131–51.

Newbury, D. (1991) *Kings and Clans: Ijwi Island and the Lake Kivu Rift, 1780–1840*. Madison, WI: University of Wisconsin Press.

Newbury, D. (2009) *The Land beyond the Mists: Essays on Identity and Authority in Precolonial Congo and Rwanda*. Athens, OH: Ohio University Press.

Newbury, D. and C. Newbury (1982) 'King and Chief: Colonial Politics on Ijwi Island (Zaire)', *International Journal of African Historical Studies* 15(2): 221–46.

Ngbwapkwa, T.M. (1993) 'L'exploitation du caoutchouc par l'état indépendant du Congo dans le territoire de Banzyville, district de l'Ubangi (1900–1908)' ['Rubber Exploitation by the Congo Free State in Banzyville Territory, Ubangi District (1900–1908)'], *Civilisations* 66(1/2): 291–306.

Njangu, C.-C. (1973) 'La resistance Shi à la penetration europénne (1900-1920)' ['Shi Resistance to European Penetration (1900–1920)']. Mémoire de Licence. Lubumbashi: National University of Zaire.

Northrup, D. (1988) *Beyond the Bend in the River: African Labor in Eastern Zaïre, 1865–1940*. Athens, OH: Ohio University Press.

Pindo, M.B. (1977) 'Essai d'histoire politique des Batembo' ['Essay on the Political History of the Batembo']. Mémoire de Licence, Institut Supérieur Pédagoqiue de Bukavu. Bukavu: National University of Zaire.

Pratten, D. (2008) 'Introduction. The Politics of Protection: Perspectives on Vigilantism in Nigeria', Special issue of *Africa* 78(1): 1–15.

Pratten, D. and A. Sen (2007) *Global Vigilantes: Anthropological Perspectives on Justice and Violence*. London: Hurst.

Raeymaekers, T. (2010) 'Protection for Sale? War and the Transformation of Regulation on the Congo–Ugandan Border', *Development and Change* 41(4): 563–87.

Raeymaekers, T. (2014) *Violent Capitalism and Hybrid Identity in the Eastern Congo: Power to the Margins*. Cambridge: Cambridge University Press.

Roes, A. (2010) 'Towards a History of Mass Violence in the Etat Indépendant du Congo, 1885–1908', *South African Historical Journal* 62(4): 634–70.

Sanchez de la Sierra, R. (2015) 'On the Origins of States: Stationary Bandits and Taxation in Eastern DRC'. Cambridge, MA: Harvard University. https://raulsanchezdelasierra.files.wordpress.com/2013/09/0-paper-1.pdf (accessed 15 January 2016).

Schatzberg, M. (1980) *Politics and Class in Zaire: Bureaucracy, Business, and Beer in Lisala*. New York and London: Africana Publishing Company.

Schatzberg, M.G. (1988) *The Dialectics of Oppression in Zaire*. Bloomington and Indianapolis, IN: Indiana University Press.

Schouten, P. (2013) 'The Materiality of State Failure: Social Contract Theory, Infrastructure and Governmental Power in Congo', *Millennium – Journal of International Studies* 41: 553–74.

Shanyungu, S.A. (1976) 'Les Bahavu: Essai d'histoire politique et sociale' ['The Bahavu: Essay on Political and Social History']. Mémoire de Licence, Institut Supérieur Pédagoqiue de Bukavu. Bukavu: National University of Zaire.

de Soysa, I. (2000) 'The Resource Curse: Are Civil Wars Driven by Rapacity or Paucity?', in M. Berdal and D. Malone (eds) *Greed and Grievance: Economic Agendas and Civil Wars*, pp. 113–36. Boulder, CO: Lynne Rienner.

Stearns, J.K. and C. Vogel (2015) *The Landscape of Armed Groups in the Eastern Congo*. New York: Congo Research Group.

Titeca, K. (2011) 'Access to Resources and Predictability in Armed Rebellion: The FAPC's Short-lived "Monaco" in Eastern Congo', *Africa Spectrum* 46(2): 43–70.

Titeca, K. and T. De Herdt (2011) 'Real Governance beyond the "Failed State": Negotiating Education in the Democratic Republic of the Congo', *African Affairs* 110(439): 213–31.

Tull, D. (2003) 'A Reconfiguration of Political Order? The State of the State in North Kivu (DR Congo)', *African Affairs* 102: 429–46.

Vellut, J.-L. (1984) 'La violence armée dans l'État indépendant du Congo: ténèbres et clartés dans l'histoire d'un État conquérant' ['Armed Violence in the Congo Free State: Darkness and Clarity in the History of a Conquering State'], *Cultures et Développement* 16(3): 671–707.

Verweijen, J. (2013) 'Military Business and the Business of the Military in the Kivus', *Review of African Political Economy* 40(135): 67–82.

Verweijen, J. and C.I. Wakenge (2015) 'Understanding Armed Group Proliferation in the Eastern Congo'. PSRP Briefing Paper No. 7. London: Rift Valley Institute.

Vlassenroot, K. and T. Raeymaekers (eds) (2004) *Conflict and Social Transformation in Eastern DR Congo*. Gent: Academia Press Scientific Publishers.

Vlassenroot, K. and F. Van Acker (2001) 'War as Exit from Exclusion? The Formation of Mayi-Mayi Militias in Eastern Congo', *Afrika Fokus* 17(1–2): 51–77.

Vlassenroot, K., E. Mudinga and K. Hoffmann (2016) *Contesting Authority: Armed Rebellion and Military Fragmentation in the Territories of Walikale and Kalehe (North and South Kivu)*. London: Rift Valley Institute.

Young, C. (1965) *Politics in the Congo: Decolonization and Independence*. Princeton, NJ: Princeton University Press.

Young, C. and T. Turner (1985) *The Rise and Decline of the Zairian State*. Madison, WI: The University of Wisconsin Press.

Index

Rule and Rupture: State Formation through the Production of Property and Citizenship, First Edition.
Edited by Christian Lund and Michael Eilenberg.
Chapters © 2017 by The Institute of Social Studies. Book compilation © 2017 John Wiley & Sons Ltd.